Patrick N. Lynch, 1817–1882

Patrick N. Lynch
1817–1882

Third Catholic Bishop of Charleston

David C. R. Heisser and Stephen J. White, Sr.

The University of South Carolina Press

Published by the University of South Carolina Press
Columbia, South Carolina 29208

www.sc.edu/uscpress

Manufactured in the United States of America

24 23 22 21 20 19 18 17 16 15   10 9 8 7 6 5 4 3 2 1

Library of Congress Cataloging-in-Publication Data

Heisser, David C. R.
Patrick N. Lynch, 1817–1882 : third Catholic bishop of Charleston / David C.R. Heisser and Stephen J. White, Sr.
pages cm
Includes bibliographical references and index.
ISBN 978-1-61117-404-5 (hardbound : alk. paper) — ISBN 978-1-61117-405-2 (ebook)
1. Lynch, Patrick Neison, 1817–1882. 2. Bishops—South Carolina—Charleston—Bishops—Biography. 3. Catholic Church—South Carolina—Charleston—Bishops—Biography. I. Title.
BX4705.L963H45 2014
282.092—dc23
[B]
2014023112

This book was printed on recycled paper with 30 percent postconsumer waste content.

CONTENTS

ILLUSTRATIONS

ACKNOWLEDGMENTS

This biography of Bishop Patrick Neison Lynch is the work of several decades. Dr. David Heisser began his research in the 1980s. A native Charlestonian, he was educated in the Cathedral Grammar School, which was located in the former pro-cathedral building that Lynch commissioned just after the Civil War. He earned his bachelors of arts degree at the College of Charleston, on whose board Lynch sat in the 1870s. Heisser received a doctorate in European intellectual history at the University of North Carolina at Chapel Hill and subsequently earned a master's in library science from Columbia University. He taught history at the University of Miami and at the University of South Carolina-Salkehatchie. And finally he retired from the post of research librarian at the Citadel's Daniel Library. In all of these positions he was a consummate researcher. He traveled all over the United States and to the Vatican Library in Rome in pursuit of information and documentation related to Lynch's life. But alas, illness and death ended his quest to provide a public narrative of his most worthy subject.

One of his dying requests was that I complete his nearly lifelong project. He left behind several essentially complete chapters, along with fifteen boxes of research materials, which included photocopies of primary and secondary sources and unpublished dissertations and theses, as well as complete published works on Lynch's era, Catholic history and theology, and the antebellum and Civil War periods of American history. David's relentless research resulted in a mass of material that will remain for future scholars in the Charleston Diocesan Archives in the "Heisser files."

Along the way he met and incurred debts to many archivists, scholars, and historians, each of whom ultimately became his friend. In Ireland, David joined the Clogher Historical Society and benefited from extensive hunts performed by Theo McMahon and the society's staff. Padrig Clerkin of the Monaghan County Museum filled lengthy e-mails with information gathered about the Lynch legacy in his birthplace in the Emerald Isle. In Cheraw, South Carolina, Sarah Cain Spruill offered hospitality, tours, and much vital historical information on the Lynch family and on the buildings constructed by Conlaw Peter Lynch. In Boston, Dr. William Scott McDougal retrieved records from Massachusetts General Hospital archives relating to Lynch's surgery there in 1877. Dr. William Turner of the Medical University of South Carolina offered expert diagnosis and analysis of the medical condition that led to Lynch's death. David communicated with every Catholic diocese in the eastern United States that might have received correspondence from or sent correspondence to Bishop Lynch. He scoured the Library of Congress and the Special Collections of the University of Notre Dame, Georgetown University, and Catholic University in Washington, D.C., and received tremendous assistance from the staffs of these institutions. He was allowed access to rarely seen documents in the Vatican Library by Monsignor Liam Bergin, Rector of the Irish College, Rome, and by the Secretariat of the Pontifical Gregorian University.

Resources and assistance in Charleston were most vital in supporting David's and my research. Local lawyers and historians Donald Williams and Robert Rosen provided Charleston Irish and Civil War contexts that all historians welcome. Robert Salvo at the Charleston Library Society must be noted, along with many of that institution's staff. Dr. Nicholas Butler at both the South Carolina Historical Society and, later, the Charleston Archives of the Charleston County Library was an indispensable source of help. At the College of Charleston, Addlestone Library Special Collections Department, we must mention Marie Ferrara, Harlan Greene, Gene Waddell, and John White. From the History Department of the College of Charleston, Dr. David Gleason, Dr. Lee Drago, Robert P. Stockton, and Dr. Bernard Powers offered valued input and advice.

The greatest collection of personal and professional papers relating to Lynch's life is contained at the Catholic Diocese of Charleston Archives, housed in the carriage house of the old Pinckney Mansion purchased by Lynch in 1866. Diocesan archivists Sister Anne Francis, Susan King, and Mary Giles all gave unflinching support to both David and me. But by far the largest contribution in both research and advice (serving as a reader on many chapters) came from the current diocesan archivist, Brian Fahey. To these individuals and institutions I offer my heartfelt gratitude in my name and in that of Dr. David Heisser.

Stephen Jennings White Sr.

Prologue

A one-year-old in the arms of his worried and pregnant mother, as the ship rolled across the waves of the northern Atlantic, Patrick Neison Lynch sailed west to his destiny. Alongside, his father held tight the hands of the boy's elder sister, who was but a toddler herself. His parents had braved the dangers of a sea voyage to seek opportunities in the New World. In search of a better life in America, they left behind in Ireland a lineage of ennobled ancestors. Aboard ship, his mother gave birth to his brother, John, who not only became a lifelong friend and companion but also established a distinguished career in medicine. This volume, recounting the life of Patrick Neison Lynch, is a story of journeys across dangerous seas to make a career as a churchman. It encapsulates the stories of thousands who fled Ireland to grasp the opportunities that awaited them in America. For the lure of the United States was that it was a nation of people who risked losing their memories and traditions in a struggle to fulfill or to remake lives in the most open society that humanity had yet created.

The Irish made up a good proportion of the flood of peoples that made America. Four and a half million souls emigrated from the Emerald Isle between 1820 and 1920. The largest number arrived in the era of the Great Famine, between 1846 and 1854, most of them small farmers and farm workers from the hungriest, most impoverished rural counties. Irish immigrants constituted 44 percent of the foreign-born white population in the United States on the eve of the Civil War. Irish labor built the roads, canals and railroads of the United States, performing labors considered too dangerous for enslaved African Americans—actual chattel with retail value—to perform. In the post–Civil War years, millions more came and found doors shut both socially and economically in the northern urban centers. Yet they persevered and clawed their way first to acceptance and then to prominence in every part of their adopted nation.

Charleston and the Carolinas offered more felicitous circumstances than many other landing sites. Irish adventurers were passengers on the first ships that landed on the Ashley River in 1670. Irishmen from the upcountry fought as Whigs and Tories bravely and with distinction in South Carolina during the American Revolution. Four South Carolina descendants of Irishmen signed the Declaration of Independence and the U.S. Constitution, the founding documents of this nation. An Irish-Catholic priest, the Reverend Dr. Simon Felix Gallagher, helped save and taught at the College of Charleston in the early nineteenth century. He also served as the first president of the Hibernian Society.

John England, a Cork native, arrived in 1820 to establish a diocese for Roman Catholics south of Virginia. The Lynches of County Monaghan had landed in Georgetown, South Carolina, just months before the arrival of this Irish cleric. Their paths crossed at the Episcopalian town of Cheraw, and this historic rendezvous fundamentally shaped the story of Catholics in South Carolina. Bishop England was a well-educated cleric. Lynch's father had aristocratic ancestors and had arrived from Erie with both an education and means. Charleston had a well-established and successful class of both Episcopal and Presbyterian Irish American middle- and upper-class businessmen, lawyers, planters, merchants, and clergymen. In spite of the existence of some anti-Catholic sentiment in the city, England and Lynch led Charleston's social, cultural, and intellectual milieu to an astonishing degree. When each man died, the city of Charleston stopped; bells from churches of all denominations tolled; local and national newspapers paid tribute on their front pages; and all of its citizens grieved at the loss of these distinguished Irish-born Americans. They had given their all to their Church, their city, their state, and their nation.

Patrick Lynch became a protégé of his father's friend, England, who took him in as an adolescent and primed him to be his successor. This generous act exposed Lynch to Charleston, provided him with an extraordinary European education, and gave him prestige in the American Roman Catholic hierarchy. Lynch became a successful church leader and much, much more. He was a "Renaissance Man" whose erudition, intellect, and gracious manner were legendary long before his death in 1882.

The *Catholic Mirror* of Baltimore noted, "Bishop Lynch was over six feet tall, well proportioned, and of attractive countenance. His address was patrician and eminently suitable to the episcopal office. His manners were refined, and his knowledge of the ceremonies of the Church singularly full and correct. He was simple in his habits and affable to all. He was beloved by a wide variety of friends, not only among Catholics, but among all other denominations."

Lynch, in 1873, wrote an amusing letter to William Ashmead Courtney, mayor of Charleston, concerning an honor the Washington Light Infantry intended to bestow on John England. The infantry wrote into its minute book a memorial page for the Catholic bishop, who had served as their chaplain for a quarter of a century. Twenty years later Bishop Henry P. Northrop sent this august militia biographical information on Patrick Lynch, who had taken his mentor's post as their chaplain.

> My dear Mr. Courtney,
>
> This is the third time I have been able to procure for you an autograph signature of Bishop England. The two first I put away so carefully that I have never been able to find them. This one I kept only for the few minutes required to pen this note in which I enclose it, and have the pleasure of signing myself.
>
> With great respect and regard,
> Your Ob Servt.
> P. N. Lynch, D.D.
> Bishop of Charleston[1]

All who knew Lynch respected him; many came to revere him. A man of great learning, he was also a humble pastor. While he lived in an age of war and tumult, he was quiet and gracious. He was a man of his age who mirrored that era's great aspirations and disastrous faults. This book recounts his life and times; it brings him not to the bar of historical judgment but to the arena of the man in full.

CHAPTER *1*

Formative Years

Patrick Neison Lynch was arguably one of the most important and accomplished Irish émigrés in the history of Catholicism in South Carolina and perhaps in the entire early history of the city of Charleston, South Carolina. Born in Ireland and carried by his parents to the interior of the Palmetto state at the age of one, he became an exquisitely educated religious, intellectual, scientific, and diplomatic contributor to the development of the Holy City of Charleston during the middle and late decades of the nineteenth century. He vigorously participated in the cultural, scientific, and intellectual societies of antebellum Charleston and rose to become the leader of the Catholic population of the state and region as the third bishop of the Diocese of Charleston. In that role he continued, in the tradition of his predecessor and mentor, John England, to defend his faith from constant public attacks by Protestant ministers. At the request of President Jefferson Davis, he represented the Confederate States of America on a diplomatic mission to the Vatican in particular and to Europe in general. Mayor William Ashmead Courtney of Charleston called on him to lead an inquiry into the geological and chemical factors related to the city's use of artesian wells to enhance the population's water supply. After his cathedral church and ecclesiastical properties suffered severe damage as a result of a citywide conflagration in 1861 and the bombardment during the Civil War, he exhausted himself traveling and begging throughout the northeast United States for two decades to retire most of a nearly $400,000 debt. When he passed away, after prolonged and recurrent illnesses, the residents of Charleston, Protestant and Catholics alike, stopped to pay their respects to a giant of their age. J. Barrett Cohen, a Jewish friend of the recently deceased prelate, published the following in the *News and Courier:*

> In Memoriam. Bishop P. N. Lynch
> When I look on your calm and restful face,
> In which no longer beams the light of light,
> In which no mark remains of that long strife

Through which you passed, and won a well-earned place
Not only in men's hearts, but, through God's grace,
Also in heaven, among the pure and blessed,
The after death find sweet and powerful rest
I can but feel how little is the space
Of time that we can linger on this earth
Ere God shall summon us before His throne
And thinking of the life you have led,
And knowing as I have your priceless worth, I pray that unto me the grace be shown to find such peace as yours when I am dead.[1]

How did such a man arrive in South Carolina? Where did his heralded ancestry originate? Why was he able to achieve such fame and earn such a generous appraisal? This work attempts to answer these and multitudes of other questions to place Patrick Neison Lynch both in his times and above his times.

Ireland

There are many Lynches spread around throughout Ireland, and their descendants dispersed throughout America. Conlaw Peter Lynch, Patrick's father, was a direct descendant of the family that had dominated County Galway in western Ireland for centuries. His great-grandfather, Peter Lynch, was the son of the last of multiple generations who had served as mayor of the city of Galway, having served until expelled by the army of Oliver Cromwell in 1656. This branch of the family then relocated around Clones, a township that straddles the boundaries of County Fermanagh and County Monaghan.[2] There is some mystery as to Peter's exact birthplace, as there exist both a town and a larger parish with the name of Clones. Family references were usually to the town of Clones in County Monaghan. The parish actually spreads across the boundary of Fermanagh and Monaghan. Parts of the Lynch family lived throughout this region. During his visit to the area in 1864–1865, Bishop Lynch met his uncle, Luke Lynch, who was residing in the nearby town of Roslea, in County Fermanagh.[3]

If we go further back into history, we find that the family dates its entry into England and then Ireland from the invasion of William the Conqueror of Normandy, under whose command rode a general, Hugh De Lentz. Hugh's grandson John DeLenche settled in Galway in 1261. In Hardiman's *History of Galway* there is an account of the Lynches of Galway "as one of the most ancient and until the middle of the 17th Century, one of the leading families of Galway." John DeLenche was said to have married the daughter and sole heiress of William De Mareschall. This family possessed the principal power in the city of Galway

Map of Ireland with Counties Fermanagh and Monaghan highlighted. The Parish of Clones straddled the border between these two counties. The town of Clones, where Patrick Lynch was born, fell within the County Monaghan. Map created by Lynne Parker.

throughout much of the fifteenth, sixteenth, and seventeenth centuries. John's son, Thomas, in 1274 was the first to hold the title of mayor of Galway, while a later Thomas Lynch Fitz Ambrose was the last of eighty-four family members to hold that title. He relinquished the title to Cromwell's army in 1656.[4]

Peter Lynch took the family to Clones, from where his great-great-grandson Conlaw Peter Lynch left in 1819 for America. When he and his wife, Eleanor Neison Lynch, departed with a daughter, Anna, and their one-year-old son, Patrick, they were prominent members of this somewhat isolated Irish community. As noted, the family name is said to have originated in the time of the first Norman king of England. Impressed by his army's loyalty and perseverance in an assault campaign on the German city of Lentz, William gave his commander the name De Lentz, from which his descendants eventually arrived at Lynch.[5] The first name Conlaw is a distinctive family name that dates from the fourteenth century. It was found in every generation through at least the early twentieth century.

Robert A. Lynch, grandson of Conlaw Peter, visited the old Lynch Castle in Galway in 1864. He described it as

> old, grim and sturdy. Under one of the windows, on the second floor, is carved a cross and death's head. It was from this window that Fitz Hugh Lynch, who was Mayor and also a judge at the time, condemned his own son to death for murder. On the day appointed for his execution, when he was on the point of being rescued, to avoid disgrace, the father of the young man, rather than see justice defeated, put a rope around the son's neck, and threw him out of the window. The story as told in history would make you weep. It killed the old father, but he died after having performed his duty—semper fidelis.[6]

The Neison family from which Patrick Lynch's mother, Eleanor, descended had as distinguished a pedigree as the Lynches. She was born in County Monaghan, where her relatives were well established. The family history includes an account of her uncle Hugh MacMahon, who was murdered in front of Eleanor when she was but six years old. He was about to give an address at a public rally when an Orangeman stabbed him to death.[7] She was the distant cousin of Marshall MacMahon, the first president of the Third Republic of France.[8]

Conlaw Peter Lynch and his family—coming from a distinguished, prosperous, well-educated middle- to upper-middle tier of Irish society—left their homeland with some means, both education and monetary resources. The question arises, Why then did they remove themselves from a seemingly comfortable setting to expose themselves and their children to the uncertainties of the New World? There are several possible explanations, including the fact that both a famine of some severity in County Monaghan and a bad typhus outbreak occurred in 1817. There also appears to have been some discord in the Neison family with regard to their daughter's marriage.

Conlaw Peter Lynch and Eleanor McMahon Neison were married on the sixth day of May 1816, just days before the birth of their first offspring.[9] Their first child, Anna, was born on May 9, 1816.[10] Their second child and eldest son, Patrick Neison Lynch, was born March 10, 1817. His birthplace has always been given in family documents as Clones, County Monaghan.[11] Apparently Eleanor's father disapproved of the marriage, so he disinherited her. It was said that years later she was informed by one of her brothers that her father had "secured her dowry for her in a local bank," but "she relinquished all claims to it since it was withheld when she had great need of it."[12] This fact, plus "other painful circumstances," gave impetus to the young couple's decision to emigrate. Conditions in Monaghan and adjacent County Fermanagh were dire because of a particularly severe famine, "accompanied by a widespread outbreak of typhus which killed thousands."[13] America at the time doubtless appeared an attractive destination.

Cheraw

Family tradition holds that Conlaw and Eleanor missed the ship that was supposed to take them to North America, so they took passage on the next vessel. The first ship was lost at sea, and Conlaw's mother subsequently died believing that her son and his little family had perished in the Atlantic. Tradition also has it that the young family traveled by way of St. John's, Newfoundland. It is also recorded that the Lynches stopped in Philadelphia, but the young mother suffered from the severe winter, so the family journeyed south by ship to Georgetown, South Carolina. They brought their new son, John—born onboard in the middle of the Atlantic Ocean—to Charleston, where he was christened by the Reverend Dr. Simon Felix Gallagher (1756–1825), pastor of the Church of St. Mary of the Annunciation and at the time one of only two Catholic priests in South Carolina.[14]

In Georgetown, the Lynches came to the attention of John Lyde Wilson (1784–1849), at the time a state senator and later governor of the state from 1822 to 1824. Wilson was connected with prominent people in the new community of Cheraw, the area where he had been born. At the time that he met Conlaw, Wilson had for several years represented the Marlboro District and then the Prince George Winyah District in the state legislature. He was then, as state senator, serving on the claims, military, internal improvements, judiciary, and privileges and elections committees. In December 1822 Wilson was named governor of the state of South Carolina. His personal and professional information regarding the prospects for Cheraw and the Chesterfield region served Conlaw Peter Lynch very well.[15]

Conlaw and Eleanor made this important contact after arriving and initially deciding to settle in Georgetown. But, after being advised by their new friend that land and good prospects were available in the interior, they ventured on. Their destination was a small community at the headwaters of the river, the town of Cheraw, which had served as a marketing site for several centuries for the local Catawba and Cheraw Indian tribes. The town (also known as Chatham) had geographical advantages that had yet to be fully utilized.

Named for the Cheraw Indians, whose main town was nearby, Cheraw began as a small trading post at the heart of navigation on the Great Pee Dee River. This was an advantageous geographical position that had been recognized and utilized by both the Catawba and the Cheraw traders for quite some time before the European incursion into the region. The first significant Caucasian groups that ventured into the area were Scots, English, and Welsh.

Despite its advantageous locale, the town was slow to develop. A visitor in the late eighteenth century remarked that its location on the river and its proximity to a fertile farming region that stretched into neighboring North Carolina should make it a "place of permanent and increasing commercial importance." But until the second decade of the nineteenth century that promise remained unrealized. The community had a meager population and disappointing commerce. An observer as late as 1792 described it as having "contained not more than a dozen houses."[16]

Settlement of Chatham, or Cheraw Hill, began in the mid-eighteenth century in what became Chesterfield District (later County). Joseph and Eli Kershaw had been granted a part of what is now Cheraw in 1768 and shortly thereafter laid out the present wide streets and town green. In the early 1800s commerce began to improve, yet the town was still described as "a small village, [which] contains a few stores." An observer expressed some optimism and "encouragement to the trade of that part of this State, which is partly drawn from North Carolina . . . With the improved navigation of the river."[17] The area became an important center of trade and communications for the South Carolina upcountry. It was reported that in 1818 the community had "a store, three or four dwelling houses, and thirty or forty inhabitants." The bustling settlement quickly grew and was incorporated as the Town of Cheraw in 1820.[18] At that point it boasted

> an elegant Academy, a Printing Establishment from which issues a weekly paper, our houses of Entertainment, thirty Stores, a considerable number of dwelling Houses and at least 1000 inhabitants, two large Steam Boats and a variety of small craft are employed in navigating the river, one Steam Boat plies directly between Georgetown, and the other between Georgetown and Cheraw each boat carries from 600 to 800 bales of cotton a trip, the Steam Boat Pee Dee has performed the entire trip from Cheraw to Georgetown and back in four days. During the last season about 14,000 bales of cotton were sent from this place, and during this season it is computed from the present purchases that 20,000 at least will be sent to market with a variety of other produce.[19]

This view was conveyed to the young Lynches by John Lyde Wilson, who served on the internal improvements committee in the legislature. A project to clear up blockages in the Great Pee Dee would allow the town "to revive and advance until it reached a considerable degree of commercial importance for the Interior."[20] Cheraw was just coming to attention as an important cotton market, as well as an important center of trade and communication for the South Carolina upcountry. The Pee Dee was the vital link to the Atlantic at the port of Georgetown. Enterprising planters and merchants organized to make vital improvements in navigation on the river, culminating in the opening of a steamboat link to Georgetown

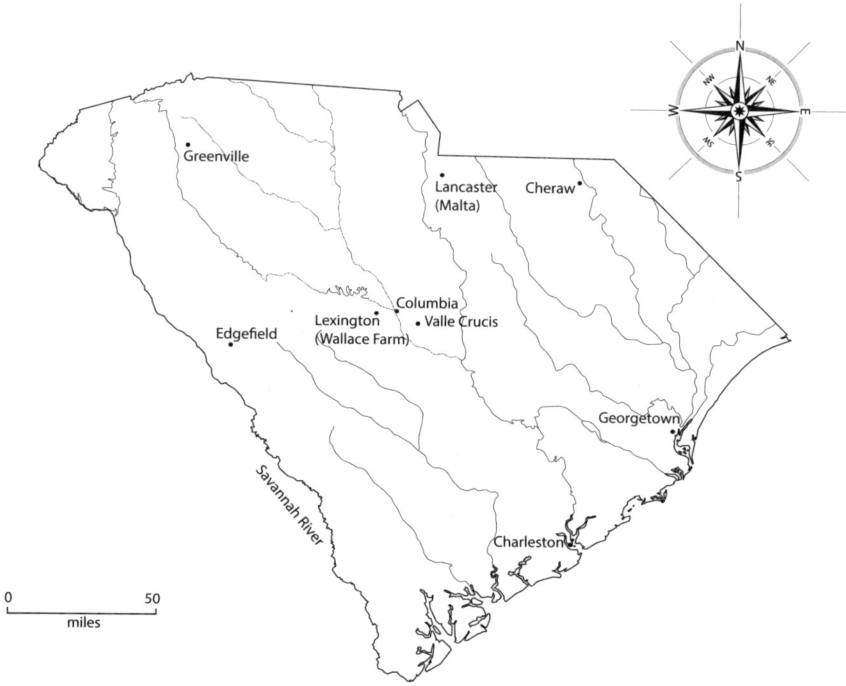

Map of South Carolina. After arriving in Philadelphia, the young Lynch couple, with their three children, landed in Georgetown, where they were persuaded to head inland and settled in Cheraw.

in 1819, the year of the Lynches' arrival in the region. A bustling settlement quickly grew and, as previously noted, the town was incorporated in 1820 as the Town of Cheraw.[21]

By the time the Lynches were convinced to settle there, Cheraw showed signs of becoming a major nexus of trade and expansive agricultural development. This commercial development, in turn, led to some surprising cultural advances as well. Just prior to the American Revolution an Anglican parish had emerged, with the building of St. David's Church signifying some significant growth. The congregation of this parish devoted itself to proper training and preparation for the children of the region. Thus in 1778 a St. David's Society was formed "purposely for the founding of a public school in the said parish for educating youths in the Latin and Greek languages, mathematics, and other useful branches of learning, by those who are not of ability, without assistance, to carry so useful and necessary an effort into effect."[22]

Wilson had given Conlaw letters of introduction to his brother-in-law, General Henry W. Harrington of Marlborough, who was prominent in the Cheraw area and a Revolutionary War hero. In the spring of 1819, it is said, the Lynches took passage on the first steamboat that ascended the Great Pee Dee, but the boat ran aground near Marr's Bluff. Conlaw came down with fever and might have died on the vessel. But a Major and Mrs. James Pouncey rescued them and took them into their own home, where Conlaw was nursed back to health. On his recovery Conlaw presented his letter from Wilson to Harrington, who in turn took them into his home and soon thereafter secured a house for them in Cheraw.[23]

The nineteenth-century diocesan historian Jeremiah O'Connell recounted that Conlaw, who possessed some money and much knowledge and skill in building, employed a carpenter to build a house for himself and his family. According to family tradition he participated in the construction work with his own hands. From then on Conlaw continued to work in pinewood construction and studied building and architecture. He went into business as a builder and acquired a saw mill and a brickyard.[24] He formed a business partnership to build houses and other structures with George H. Dunlap, a Cheraw merchant. The 1850 census recorded Conlaw as a millwright. He constructed the Merchants Bank of South Carolina in 1833, considered one of the two earliest brick structures in Cheraw.[25] Eventually he built several residences and won the competition to design and construct Cheraw's market hall in the 1830s. His crowning achievement would be the completion and opening of St. Peter's Catholic Church on Main Street in 1842.

Conlaw Peter Lynch was a man of strenuous purpose and a faithful Catholic. He had no easy task ahead of him, but, true sort that he was, he made good. His self-reliant bearing and the model character of his household gained the respect and good will of those around him. Conlaw Peter Lynch was a builder and sawmill proprietor, and the Lynches were devout, prosperous, and the leading Catholic family of Cheraw. The family was reliant on monthly visits from Father Simon Felix Gallagher, who would say Masses in their home. In subsequent years Bishop John England was a frequent visitor and similarly served the only Catholic family in the town of Cheraw.[26] Three of the dozen children born to Conlaw and Eleanor entered religious life: Ellen and her sisters Anna and Catherine became nuns (Anna an Ursuline, Catherine a Carmelite), and the eldest son, Patrick Neison Lynch, entered the priesthood, going on to become the third bishop of Charleston in 1858.

Robert A. Lynch wrote about his grandmother, Eleanor Neison Lynch, in his family history (1891). He noted:

> She was a remarkable woman, related to the distinguished French, McMahon family. She raised twelve children, four of whom entered religious life. She outlived not only her husband, but most of her dozen offspring, dying at the ripe age of 83 years old. She had a complexion any girl of 16 might

> have been proud and she could thread a fine needle without glasses never having the occasion to use them. It was a touching sight to see her in her old age meet her son the Bishop, then a man of 60 years and known the world over for his great learning and eloquence. She would first kneel for his blessing, then this great and good old man would kneel for his mother's blessing then they would throw their arms around each other's neck.[27]

According to family lore, as a young boy Patrick exhibited traits that presaged his future role as an ecclesiastical leader. He would position himself on a large chair and deliver mock sermons to his younger siblings. The Lynch children, whose material conditions were more than comfortable, were nevertheless raised with a sense of duty, hard work, responsibility, and faith in the Catholic Church. Both parents were from privileged backgrounds with sound educational and literary training. They exemplified a devotion to their faith that had been tested in their native land by generations of persecution.[28]

Patrick was one of twelve children born to Conlaw Peter and Eleanor Neison Lynch. The eldest, Anna, born May 9, 1816, served the Ursuline nuns for many decades. Patrick, born March 10, 1817, in Clones, County Monaghan, Ireland, came next. Their third child John, born in 1819 aboard the ship carrying the young family to America, became a successful doctor and professor of medicine at

ABOVE AND FACING: Patrick's father, Conlaw Peter Lynch, became a builder and constructed the town's market hall, three residences, and St. Peter's Catholic Church, all of which survive in Cheraw, South Carolina. Photographs courtesy of Sarah Ashley White and the Catholic Diocese of Charleston Archives.

South Carolina College. Francis deSales Lynch, born November 29, 1820, studied law in Charleston and became a successful merchant. Eleanor was born July 28, 1825, in Cheraw, was educated in Ursuline schools, and earned her own fame as Mother Baptista of the Ursuline Convent in Columbia, South Carolina. James Thomas Lynch was born September 4, 1826, and died in 1860, at the age of thirty-four. Catherine, born in 1829, became a Carmelite nun, known as Sister Antonia of the Purification, eventually rising to the position of prioress of the Carmelite Monastery in Baltimore, Maryland, dying in 1873. Conlaw Charles, born March 20, 1830, also died relatively young, in 1856. Hugh Patrick, born April 4, 1833, died in the service of the Confederate Army in 1863. Mary (birth and death dates uncertain) married John Spann, who moved their family to Texas as a very successful plantation owner. Bernard Ignatius was born May 9, 1836, in Cheraw and died there on May 13, 1859. Julia Anne, the last of their offspring, was born July 1, 1838, married into the Pinckney family, and raised a family in Walterboro until her death, on March 23, 1861.[29]

Patrick's formal education began in Cheraw Academy, where, despite the relatively backward and sparsely populated surroundings, he received the rudiments of a classical education. Enterprising and ambitious members of this emerging community had built a two-story structure for the school in 1810. This impressive structure was shared by the local Masonic Order, which occupied the second floor. The Academy used the ground level and remained there until 1836, when the Matheson family purchased the building and turned it into a residence. The site is today a registered national historic site.[30]

Patrick was taught there by Professor I. G. Brown and Dr. Thomas Graham of Drowning Creek, North Carolina. Both of these men were known throughout the Chesterfield District as learned scholars and had benefited from university educations in their native Scotland. Among other renowned students of Cheraw Academy were Alexander Gregg, who became the first Episcopal bishop of Texas, and the Presbyterian theologian Dr. James H. Thornwell, who served on the faculty of the College of South Carolina. The local history of Cheraw also cites "Thomas Gillespie, General W.L. Prince, Benton Prince, Dr. Cornelius Kollock, Thomas Pegues, Reverend Donald McQueen, and his brothers Dr. John and Francis Lynch, all of whom Cheraw is justly proud."[31] For such a relatively small community Cheraw boasted some extraordinary achievements and institutions that made remarkable contributions to the history of the Palmetto State. Patrick Lynch would certainly take a place of honor among the locals who achieved distinction in later life.

Charleston

By the time that he was taken by Bishop England for more advanced studies in the seminary in Charleston, Patrick had already read Caesar's *Gallic Wars* in Latin and was past the early stages of mastering Greek. At the age of twelve, in 1829, he traveled to the coastal city to enter the Classical and Philosophical Institute of the Seminary of St. John the Baptist.

The seminary on Broad Street had been a pet project of Bishop John England from the very beginning of his episcopacy in 1820–1821. He was confronted by a ragtag collection of immigrant priests who squabbled among themselves more than they ministered to the few scattered Roman Catholics to be found in the fledgling diocese. In fact, England's appointment as the first bishop of the newly

John England (1790–1842) from Cork, Ireland, served as the first bishop of the Diocese of Charleston from 1820 until his death in 1842. Courtesy of the Catholic Diocese of Charleston Archive.

created diocese resulted from a prolonged dispute between Irish and French clerics whose behavior had resulted in St. Mary's Church in Charleston being placed under interdiction by the Vatican. In the *U.S. Catholic Miscellany,* also founded by the new Irish bishop, he announced in 1822 the opening of a "Philosophical and Classical Seminary of Charleston." The plan was to offer a private education program as a way of funding the training of local priests to carry out the needed missionary work in the Carolinas and Georgia. This basic education in the classics would thus form the foundation and provide money to support the clerical Seminary of St. John the Baptist. The cost for the English course was five dollars upon entrance and twelve dollars per quarter. For the Belles Lettres, Classics, Mathematics, and Philosophy course the registration fee was five dollars, with tuition set at twenty dollars per quarter.[32]

This was a most ambitious plan to "revive classical learning in South Carolina." It would earn Bishop England much praise for his contributions to higher learning. Monsignor Joseph L. O'Brien, in his biography of Bishop England, explained that the Irishman "planned a classical and philosophical institute in which the boys of the upper classes of society would be encouraged to value mental culture as much as the social graces demanded by their standing in society; also planned was a theological school in which the bishop would train the future apostles of the South. The pupils for the Institute would have to be drawn from the moneyed class of Charleston society—Protestant for the most part." O'Brien said that England knew that his plan to develop his own homebred priests would take years to succeed because of the shallow pool of Catholics in the South. In the meantime he would recruit clergy from afar. Yet he found a remarkable crop from the few members of his Roman Church.[33]

Lynch would benefit enormously from the educational foundation provided by England and his rigorous curriculum. Subsequently he excelled in his university and theological studies in Rome and went on to become one of the most respected minds in the Roman Catholic hierarchy.

In 1836 England was forced to close the Institute temporarily due to persistent attacks from Protestant ministers and lack of financing. When he returned from his European university training, Lynch exerted great energies in an unsuccessful effort to revive the school and to prevent its doors being permanently shuttered. The seminary persisted until 1851 with Lynch as both a teacher and director.

Charleston at the time of the Lynches' arrival in the Carolinas was a society in transition, with some noticeable regression. At its height this seaport served as the cultural, intellectual, economic, and political center of the South. George Rogers, in his *Charleston in the Age of the Pinckneys,* described it as the most beautiful and the most interesting city in America. That would change in the 1820s and 1830s following the Vesey slave insurrection scare. From this point forward Rogers referred to Charleston's future as "bleak, the city in economic decline, and old fears revitalized." This sense of impending doom would shape the mind and environment in which Patrick Lynch developed and lived out his adult life.[34] Slavery and its economic and moral tensions haunted Lynch and his adopted city of Charleston until the violent demise of the practice after the American Civil War.

But, more important for the Lynch family, the cultural and intellectual climate dramatically changed with the arrival of the Irishman John England, and this change made Charleston a much more comfortable environment for the Roman Catholicism they believed in so deeply. England created the Diocese of Charleston out of whole cloth. Upon Patrick Lynch's arrival, in 1829, he saw a relatively new cathedral church, a wooden structure built at Friend and Broad Streets.

It was surrounded by a virtual "Roman empire" that included the seminary and the philosophical academy, as well as a convent for the Sisters of Mercy which the bishop had established. Nearby were schools for boys, girls, and free black children. There was also a library and the first Catholic newspaper ever published in the United States, the aforementioned *U.S. Catholic Miscellany.*[35]

John England, Patrick's father's friend and the young Lynch's mentor, was deeply involved in the cultural and intellectual societies of Charleston. Patrick would have been exposed to the Charleston Library Society and to the Literary and Philosophical Society, in addition to the vigorous program of liberal arts and theological studies designed by Bishop England. The bishop's residence where Patrick lived, at 90 Wentworth Street and, later, at 92 Broad Street, was in the heart of the city, within three blocks of St. Finbar's Cathedral, all of England's educational institutions, and the business and marketing hub of a still very busy port town. He was a stone's throw from what would become the Four Corners of Law with the County Court House, Charleston's City Hall, St. Michael's Episcopal Church, and the city Guard House. From there he could look a few blocks east down Broad Street to the U.S. Customs and Exchange building. And just north of the Catholic hub were the College of Charleston and the sites of many philosophical, cultural and scientific groups. Few of these opportunities for learning were squandered by Patrick Lynch.[36] Upon his return from Europe in 1840, as a still very young priest, Lynch would become a leading member and participant in virtually all of these intellectual societies.

The young Patrick enjoyed living in Charleston, which was the South's most cultured city. At the time of his arrival, in 1829, Charleston had probably seen its best days. One of the most important and wealthiest port cities in the pre-Revolutionary era, the seaport of the old southern colonies was in economic decline. Walter Fraser Jr. described the condition of what he had called "this once flourishing city." He noted that in 1828 Charleston had "shipped its greatest rice crop and the second largest cotton export ever . . . but Chamber of Commerce reported: Charleston has for several years past retrograded . . . landed estate depreciated in value one half. Industry and businesses talent . . . have sought employment elsewhere. Many houses tenantless and the grass grows uninterrupted in some of her chief business streets."[37]

William W. Freehling, in his book *The Nullification Crisis of 1832*, described Charleston as a city in commercial decline whose population had remained stagnant for the previous two decades. The nationalist period of the 1820s, during which John C. Calhoun was a major player in the "war hawks" leadership in Congress and served as secretary of war, was entering its final years. The beginning of the next decade would see Charleston as instigator of the "Nullification Crisis," S.C.'s opposition to the U.S. adoption of the "protectionist tariff," and as a city reeling from the aftermath of the Denmark Vesey maelstrom. Lynch witnessed the turmoil of Charleston's first call for secession from the Union, which took place during his time at the Charleston seminary. When he returned from Rome, in 1840, he was caught up in the more virulent and ultimately violent upheavals of the 1850s and 1860s.[38] Lynch grew to love Charleston and thrived in its intellectual circles and became one of its most ardent defenders in his adult years.

He excelled in his studies at the Charleston Seminary and impressed Bishop England as a perfect candidate for the Holy Orders. He was duly tonsured by the bishop and prepared to study for the priesthood. The most promising of England's seminarians were Lynch and James Andrew Corcoran, a Charleston-born son of Irish parents, who had been raised a short distance from St. Finbar's Cathedral. His parents had run a grocery store near the city market. Corcoran was, in fact, an orphan at the time he and Patrick Lynch set off for Europe. His parents, John and Jane Corcoran, had emigrated from Longford, County Longford, Ireland, to Charleston in 1816 to claim the property of a deceased relative there. In 1817 John became a U.S. citizen and was listed in the *Charleston City Directory* of 1819 as a "grocer at 46 King Street." John, however, died in 1819, just months before their son, James, was born, on March 30, 1820. Young James's mother, Jane, passed away in 1832, while he was studying at Bishop England's Philosophical and Classical Seminary. His exemplary work there led England to choose him and Patrick Lynch to be his first Charleston diocesan candidates for the Urban College in Rome.[39]

Rome

Bishop England wanted his young stars to receive the best European education. He solicited and was granted two places at the Urban College, which was the Roman seminary of the Sacred Congregation for the Propagation of the Faith (Sacra Congregatio de Propaganda Fide). By terms of his agreement with Carlo Maria Pedicini, Cardinal-Prefect of the Propaganda (1821–1834), England sent the two boys to Rome. On December 16, 1833, England wrote to his friend Father (later Cardinal) Paul Cullen (1803–1878) that the boys were coming, asking Cullen to look out for their welfare.[40] Cullen was a learned Irish priest and educator, born in 1803 in County Kildare. He was a graduate of the Urban College, where he received a doctorate in 1828. He had taught there and since 1832 had been rector of the Irish College in Rome.[41] He was later to become the first Irish cardinal. England sent a letter with the boys, which they were to present in person to Cullen. And he later inquired how they were doing.[42] Bishop England was himself in Rome for several months in 1834, for consultations regarding his Apostolic Delegation to the Republic of Haiti. He certainly saw his young seminarians during his stay.[43]

Propaganda Fide, where the Irish College was housed in Rome. Lynch and James Corcoran, sent by Bishop England in 1834, studied for the priesthood here. Photograph courtesy of Stephen J. White Jr.

The Sacred Congregation had been established in 1622 by Pope Gregory XV to organize and supervise Catholic missionary activity throughout the world. In the nineteenth century this was the department of the Roman Curia that administered the Church in countries that were not considered to be Catholic. The bishops of missionary lands reported to the Vatican through the Propaganda, and it was the cardinals of the Sacred Congregation who reviewed nominees for episcopal sees and recommended new appointments to the Holy Father. The entire Church in the United States was under Propaganda jurisdiction until 1908. In 1627 Pope Urban VIII had founded the Urban College, named in his honor, as the seminary of the Propaganda in order to train gifted students from missionary territories.[44] The Urbaniana, as it was also known, was one of a number of seminaries in Rome. The Society of Jesus (Jesuits) ran the Roman College Seminary, which was the largest in Rome. The most advanced degrees were awarded by the Pontifical Gregorian University. There were various national colleges, partly schools and partly residential facilities, for seminarians from different countries—the students included English, Scottish, Irish, and German seminarians. A residential college for students from the United States was not founded until 1858. In Lynch's day the Urbaniana included Americans and some students from the British Isles.[45]

After a long sea voyage and having sailed through the Strait of Gibraltar, Patrick and James arrived in Rome. Patrick Lynch was enrolled in the school on May 16, 1834.[46] On New Year's Day 1835 Lynch signed the oath required of all students, by which he promised to obey the rules and to submit to the authority of the rector and all those placed over him.[47] The seminary and the Sacred Congregation were both housed in a great palace in downtown Rome, on the Piazza di Spagna, a few paces from the Spanish Steps. The building boasted a stately baroque façade designed in the 1640s by Gianlorenzo Bernini. Within the walls of the palace was the exquisite little Church of the Three Magi, the work of Francesco Borromini. The seminarians lived in quarters that were reasonably comfortable, although often chilly in winter, causing the students to catch frequent colds. They lived in the same building where the cardinals of the Propaganda made decisions affecting the universal Church.[48] The Propaganda has been described as a clearinghouse for the affairs of the Church at large; the seminarians could become acquainted with the churchmen who made or influenced great decisions on Church policy, and they heard a great deal of news and gossip about Church affairs. The pope during the student days of Lynch and Corcoran was Gregory XVI, Mauro Cappellari, a Camaldolese monk who had been Cardinal Prefect of the Propaganda (1820–1831), prior to his election. Gregory had special affection for the Urbaniana, which he often visited.[49] Gregory was a conservative pontiff who resisted the democratic impulses that were sweeping through Europe in the nineteenth century. His instincts drove him to emphasize the authority of the papacy, and priests in training became warriors in the campaign to strengthen both the Catholic Church and papal sovereignty. These ultramontane attitudes remained central to Lynch's identity throughout his life.

For Patrick, Rome was an exciting place to live. In May 1834 he wrote to Gregory Duggan, his friend and former schoolmate at the Charleston Seminary, with great enthusiasm, describing his excitement at discovering the sights of the Eternal City and his delight in trying on his new cassock as a Propagandist.[50] Rome was the center of the universal Church and capital of a sovereign country, the Papal States. It was the scene of magnificent ceremonies at St. Peter's and the other great basilicas and the site of ancient and modern classical and ecclesiastical monuments and priceless treasures of art and architecture.

Student living conditions were reasonably comfortable. Food was plentiful, and each student was given a small bottle of wine at dinner (*pranzo*) and again at supper. The Propaganda paid their expenses, except for books and other small items. Each student was assigned to a *camerata,* or dormitory. Daily life followed a routine like that at other Catholic seminaries. There was daily Mass, group prayers morning and evening, the rosary and examinations of conscience. There were two classes in the morning and two in the afternoon, after *pranzo.* Seminarians were required to move to and from classes and spiritual exercises in silence. For all this, the discipline was not strict.[51] Students enjoyed ample opportunity to explore the Eternal City and were encouraged to do so. They often walked up the nearby Spanish Steps to enjoy the famous view of Rome from the Pincian Hill.

The Urbaniana followed a twofold curriculum, totaling eight years. The first four years provided a general education called *studi ginnasiali* (gymnastic or licentiate studies), including two years of philosophy (logic, metaphysics, mathematics) and two of physics and ethics. This course of study was followed by four years of theology. The theology curriculum included courses in theological *loci* (authorities), dogmatics, sacramental and moral theology, Church history, scripture and archaeology, liturgy, canon law, Greek, Hebrew, and other Oriental languages.[52] Scientific learning was a component of the education. The curriculum included courses in mathematics and physics. Several of Lynch's student papers on problems of gravity, written in Italian, survive.[53] From 1830 to 1836 the seminary rector was the young German Monsignor Count Carl von Reisach (1800–1869). In 1836 the school was put under the administration of Jesuit priests.[54]

Patrick took to this life with enthusiasm. He typically devoted as many as seventeen hours a day to study.[55] He was naturally good-natured and friendly, and people liked him. Many years later an elderly Urbaniana porter named Giovanni remembered him with great warmth.[56] The Propaganda owned a country villa at Frascati, in the scenic wine country of the Alban Hills, southeast of Rome. Here the seminarians enjoyed leisure during summer vacations. Lynch recorded a wonderful holiday in company of his fellow students in 1837. The students then lodged for several nights in the ancient abbey of Grottaferrata, on land once owned and occupied by Marcus Tullius Cicero. They explored the surrounding sights and countryside, enjoyed the local wine, sang together after supper, and played a lot of billiards. One afternoon Lynch "climbed up on a tree to study French at my ease" at the Villa Ruffinella in Frascati.[57]

When Lynch came to Rome there were about 88 seminarians, a number that later rose to about 110, from a dozen countries. John Henry Newman said that thirty languages were spoken there, and Lynch's fluency in seven languages indicates that he took full advantage of such a polyglot environment. All lectures were given in Latin. Seminary rules required students always to converse in Italian or Latin; if the rector permitted, they might speak their native language at specified times with their compatriots in the dormitory.[58] It is hard to believe that Lynch and Corcoran (and other Anglophones) did not speak English when they were together.

In fact Lynch became the ringleader of a society of seminarians from English-speaking countries for the express purpose "to perfect ourselves in writing and in speaking English." The plan of the Association for Acquiring a Correct and Elegant English Style was for each participant to write an original composition in good English. This paper would then be circulated among the group to be critiqued and debated in regular meetings held on "Holy Days during the hour of walk." The original members included students from the United States, Canada, and Ireland.[59]

Like all the Roman seminaries, the Urban College aimed to turn out priests loyal to supreme papal authority and uncompromising Catholic orthodoxy. All were intended to be what became known as Ultramontanists. The Propagandists, as the seminarians were known, were regarded as destined to be bishops and to fill the leadership roles in the universal Church. They were taught by a strong faculty. Lynch's principal professors were to constitute the board that examined him for his doctorate, on May 8, 1840.[60]

Paul Cullen, while rector of the Irish College, taught Greek and Oriental languages, as well as courses on scripture based on Hebrew and Greek texts, at the Urban College.[61] The leading professor of Church history was Giovanni Battista Palma, whose lectures spanned the centuries of the Christian era to the beginning of the nineteenth century. Palma was eloquent in his condemnations of non-Catholic interpretations of history, especially those of the Protestant Revolt and its aftermath and the eighteenth-century spirit of agnosticism and secularism.[62] Giuseppe Maria Graziosi (1793–1847) taught philosophy and theology and was a proponent of Thomist studies. He served as theologian of the Vatican office called the Apostolic Datary, which was concerned with benefices, dispensations, and excommunications, as well as the approval of religious communities' constitutions.[63] Filippo Cossa (1803–1868) held the chair of logic and metaphysics for thirty years and also taught dogmatic theology at the Roman Seminary. He was a strong champion of Catholic orthodoxy, and his work was said to have influenced Pope Pius IX in the preparation of the dogma of the Immaculate Conception (1854).[64]

The best-known theologian at the Urban College in those days was Giovanni Perrone (1784–1876). Described as a "formidable Jesuit," Perrone was renowned for his breadth of learning. He was not a theological innovator but rather a pillar of orthodoxy, respected for his ability to relate "his teaching to modern trends in philosophical thinking." Perrone's compendium of theology, first published in 1835, became a standard textbook used in seminaries in Europe and elsewhere, running to thirty editions. His lectures were organized in the form of propositions, counterpropositions, and refutations of opposing positions, with citations to the orthodox authorities. Perrone was a champion of Catholic apologetics and a stalwart opponent of Protestant teachings. His work was to influence Pope Pius IX in his preparation of the schemata for the First Vatican Council.[65]

John Henry Newman was enrolled in the Urbaniana during 1846–1847 as part of his preparation for ordination as a Catholic priest. The future cardinal remarked that neither Aristotle nor Thomas Aquinas, nor in fact any particular school of philosophy or theology, was taught there. A Jesuit professor told him that the faculty adopted "odds and ends—whatever seems to them best. . . . They have no philosophy. Facts are the great things, and nothing else."[66]

In Lynch's day all the seminarians were influenced by the learned Angelo Mai (1782–1854), a friend of Bishop England's, who taught philosophy and paleography. Mai had been prefect of the Vatican Library since 1818 and was a distinguished member of learned societies. He was secretary of the Propaganda from 1832 to 1838 and became a cardinal in the latter year.[67] Influential, too, was Giuseppe Mezzofanti (1774–1849), one of the world's greatest linguists. Fluent in thirty-eight languages ancient and modern, the polyglot scholar and teacher was appointed first keeper (*primo custode*) of the Vatican Library in 1833, succeeding Mai. Mezzofanti taught languages at the Urban College and delighted in spending time there, mingling with the students, whom he engaged in jovial, playful conversation in a variety of languages. Mezzofanti was made a cardinal in 1838 by Gregory XVI, who later put him in charge of all the Roman universities.[68] The kindly Father Vincenzo Pallotti (1798–1850) played a special role. He was charged with the spiritual guidance of the school. He heard seminarians' confessions, introduced the daily schedule of spiritual exercises, and conducted spiritual retreats. Pallotti's influence extended to the City of Rome and beyond, since he founded the worldwide Society of the Catholic Apostolate. Vincenzo Pallotti was later canonized by Pope John XXIII.[69] Patrick was deeply moved by a spiritual retreat led by a Jesuit Father Massa.[70]

The Urban College had a library to support its programs. Rome boasted fairly large academic libraries supporting scientific education, notably that at the University of Rome. The Sapienza, as it was known, was an easy walk from the Propaganda. Patrick's young compatriot James Corcoran proved an extraordinary linguist, attaining fluency in Latin, Greek, Hebrew, and Syriac, in addition to modern languages. Corcoran came to the attention of Giovanni Mezzofanti, who made him a student assistant at the Vatican Library. A seminarian was strictly required always to have a companion when he walked in Rome, and it is possible that Patrick accompanied the younger man on his journeys across the Tiber, some three and one-half miles from the Propaganda. It would be interesting to know how they got there, since the streets of Rome were legendary for their filth, which, especially when wet, ruined many cassocks. In this way, however, Patrick could have had ample access to the Vatican collections.[71]

In the 1840s John Henry Newman wrote a confidential letter in Latin to the Urban College's Jesuit rector Antonio Bresciani, criticizing what he called the intellectual isolation of the seminarians. Newman recommended that the older students be afforded greater opportunity to meet and engage in discussions with others who spoke their own language.[72]

Patrick excelled at his studies. In 1837 he won prizes for achievement in theology, Church history, and Hebrew. In 1839 he won prizes for his work in sacred scripture and canon law. He led his class in Arabic and on one occasion was selected to deliver an address in Hebrew in the presence of Gregory XVI.[73] Patrick Lynch was ordained a priest on Passion Sunday, April 2, 1840, by Giacomo Filippo Fransoni (1775–1852), cardinal prefect of the Propaganda. Following that, he was awarded the degree of doctor of sacred theology (S.T.D.) with honors.[74] Words of praise were recorded in the official register of the College: "a young man of most excellent promise (*optionae spei adolescens*) . . . devoted to study (*studio deditus*) . . . endowed with great affability, eagerness [and] openness of spirit (*multa comitate, animi alacrite condore praeditus*) . . . he advanced exceedingly well in the theological disciplines (*optime proficit in discipliniis theologicis*)."[75] The Propaganda officially informed England that Lynch had graduated magna cum laude, had taken his doctorate, and had been ordained. A later message from Professor Giovanni Battista Palma said that the school was sending his doctoral diploma.[76] He left behind in Rome his confrere James Corcoran, who was to be ordained in 1843.

When they completed their studies in Rome, both Lynch and Corcoran were among the highest achievers in the Urban College. In 1837 Corcoran was awarded prizes for his mastery in the second class of Syriac, Latin oratory, Latin poetry, and Greek rhetoric and humanities, while Lynch received awards for his scholarly accomplishments in dogmatic theology, moral theology, Church history, literary Church history, Hebrew, and Syriac.[77]

For the year 1838–1839, the Children's Catholic Magazine of New York reported continued success in Rome for these Charleston youths: "Patrick Lynch, of Charleston, received the second premium in Church History, the second premium in Moral and Canon Law, and the third premium in Dogmatic Theology. James Corcoran, also of Charleston, received the first premium in elementary Mathematics; the first premium in Greek language; the second class, and the third premium in Logic and Metaphysics."[78] Their performance in the rigorous scholarly program of the Urban College of the Propaganda of the Faith in Rome bears testament to what an outstanding academic preparation Bishop England's

Philosophical and Classical Seminary in Charleston had provided. Further proof of the erudition achieved by Patrick N. Lynch can be found in the Charleston Diocesan Archives, where we find handwritten classroom notes taken by the future bishop in Hebrew, Greek, Latin, French, and German, along with a long list of Latin books he was studying.[79]

On his journey home Patrick stopped in Ireland to visit family before heading to America. He crossed the Atlantic, arriving in New York City sometime around August 13, 1840. He stopped in Philadelphia to visit Bishop Francis Patrick Kenrick and officiated at vespers in St. Patrick's Church, Norristown, Pennsylvania, in Kenrick's presence.[80] He was invited to preach at the Jesuit-run Georgetown College in Washington, D.C., where the future priest and historian Richard H. Clarke was then a student. Clarke later recalled that Lynch delivered "a sermon of marked power, the Roman training, the frequentness of Latin quotes, the strict legal methods, the tall slender figure . . . and brilliant eye, of the young priest, are well remembered."[81] Lynch's parents invited him to Cheraw for a family visit before he took up his duties in Charleston.[82]

Lynch arrived in Charleston as a Catholic priest and a budding scholar. His life had begun in a small village in northern Ireland. But now, in his early twenties, he had become a young man who had seen a good bit of the Western world. His education, begun in the backcountry South Carolina market town of Cheraw, now included a doctorate in theology as well as fluency in multiple languages. Charleston became his base from which he launched a remarkable journey throughout the eastern United States and several more sojourns to Europe and back. His fame would span the north Atlantic basin, and, despite a number of missteps, his illustrious life brought him widespread respect throughout these regions. It was during the 1850s that he realized this potential.

CHAPTER 2

Priest in Charleston

In the early autumn of 1840 Patrick arrived in Charleston, which was to be his home for the rest of his life. On November 8 Bishop England told the assembled delegates to the Second Annual Diocesan Convention that "we also have lately added to our number by the return of one of our students, who for some years has been in the Urban College of the Propaganda at Rome, and who will, I trust, make for many years, to our missions the return which the kindness that he and we received in that quarter so justly demands."[1] Lynch was in attendance at that convocation. The *U.S. Catholic Miscellany* announced on November 21 that he had received his doctorate of divinity degree on September 4, 1840.[2]

Father Lynch lodged at the cathedral clerical residence on Wentworth Street. The bishop assigned him to the cathedral parish, where England named him to teach church history and moral theology in the Seminary of St. John the Baptist. In 1841 England appointed him his secretary and chancellor of the diocese.[3] During England's two decades in Charleston the Church had flourished. England started in 1820 with a team of six priests, not counting the bishop. The church grew under his administration. England's successor was Ignatius Aloysius Reynolds. Reynolds began his ministry with eighteen priests and some seven thousand Catholics in the three states that formed the diocese.

Lynch joined the diocesan clergy at a time when Bishop England was embroiled in the growing national controversy over slavery. In 1835 England had angered the white population of Charleston by opening a school "to educate free colored boys." But public protests and the threat of mob violence directed against Catholic institutions led England to abandon the project.[4] In 1833 Pope Gregory XVI appointed him Apostolic Delegate to the Republic of Haiti, and he duly traveled to the island, which was governed by black men, in an effort to reestablish the Catholic hierarchy and lay the foundation for a concordat, or treaty regulating Haiti's relations with the Holy See. The fact that Bishop England spent time in Haiti between 1833 and 1837 as the guest of President Jean Pierre Boyer offended many white Carolinians and cost him some trust and prestige.[5] Gregory XVI's

Patrick Lynch, in an early painting of Charleston's third Irish Catholic bishop. Courtesy of Catholic Diocese of Charleston Archive.

apostolic constitution *In supremo apostolatus,* in 1839, condemned the taking of slaves, and the international slave trade posed a problem for the American hierarchy. England argued publicly that domestic slavery was licit and that there was no requirement for general emancipation.[6]

Father Lynch served at the Cathedral of St. John and St. Finbar and sometimes at St. Mary's Church in Charleston. In the 1840s he also periodically visited Catholics in the Walterboro area, about fifty miles inland from Charleston.[7] Bishop England was in Europe for much of 1841, on a begging tour in England and Ireland, as the diocese was in parlous financial condition. He had instructed his vicar general, Father Richard Sullivan Baker, to proceed with the Third Diocesan Convention, which duly opened on November 21, in the bishop's absence. England did not return to Charleston until December 9, at which point his health was in serious decline. During the winter he grew weaker. On March 25, 1842, Lynch as the bishop's secretary wrote to Archbishop Whitfield of Baltimore that, in the event of his death, Father Baker was to be vicar capitular "until the nomination of a successor." At the same time he informed the archbishop of England's preferences to succeed him: Richard Baker, first; John Barry, second; and Jeremiah Francis O'Neill, third.[8] Bishop England died on April 11, 1842. The church bells of Charleston tolled, flags were lowered, and much of the city's business came to a halt. There was an outpouring of sympathy from Catholics, Protestants, and Jews in Charleston and around South Carolina and the whole diocese.

Richard Sullivan Baker became diocesan administrator, while Lynch shared duties at the cathedral and took over editorship of the *U.S. Catholic Miscellany*. He took on additional duties over time. Bishop England had established the St. John the Baptist Society, centered in Charleston, to organize support for the diocesan seminary. Lynch chaired its financial affairs committee, which registered an income of $1,335 in 1842. He was guest speaker at Savannah's Catholic Total Abstinence Society. On St. Patrick's Day, March 17, 1843, he gave a rousing sermon before Charleston's Irish Volunteers in St. Patrick's Church.[9]

The matter of England's successor was discussed at the Fifth Provincial Council of Baltimore, which met in May 1843. Baker and Lynch attended. The early provincial councils established legislation and rules by which the American bishops would conduct themselves and manage their dioceses. This Fifth Provincial Council set up restrictions on laymen giving orations in churches, required pastors to reside in their parishes, and prohibited priests from taking out loans without the permission of their bishop.[10]

The Fathers, consisting of one archbishop and sixteen bishops, drew up a terna (a list of three candidates proposed for a higher office in the Roman Catholic Church) headed by Ignatius Aloysius Reynolds, an Irish American native of Kentucky. Both Baker and Lynch were considered. Bishop Francis Patrick Kenrick of Philadelphia wrote his brother Auxiliary Bishop Peter Richard Kenrick (later Archbishop) of St. Louis that Richard Baker appeared "worn out," while Father Lynch, despite "his sincere piety and his command of learning, lacked robust health" and was "rather too young."[11]

Early on the young priest engaged in a press war with one of the South's leading Presbyterian theologians, James Henley Thornwell (1812–1862). In 1841 the Presbyterian divine was professor of sacred literature and the evidence of Christianity at South Carolina College (later the University of South Carolina). He founded the *Southern Presbyterian Review* and also edited the *Southern Quarterly Review*. He published anonymously in a Baltimore journal an essay on what he termed the Apocrypha, that is, books not accepted by Protestants as part of the Old Testament but revered by Catholics. Lynch replied at length in the *Miscellany*, which at the time he edited. Thornwell earned a reputation for his vituperative

The Reverend Dr. James H. Thornwell. He and Lynch attended the Cheraw Academy together in their youth. Thornwell became a Presbyterian minister/theologian, taught at South Carolina College in Columbia, and battled for decades over the differences between Protestant and Catholic beliefs. Reprinted from a memorial commemorating the one-hundredth anniversary of his birth in 1913. Courtesy of Special Collection, Addlestone Library, College of Charleston.

attacks on the Catholic Church, and his essay on the Apocrypha included a broad assault on Catholic teaching and the Church's assertions of infallibility.

There was irony in the mutual antagonism of the two learned clerics, since both men had spent their boyhoods in Chesterfield District and both had attended the Cheraw Academy. Thornwell was four and a half years older than Lynch. Patrick was a pupil at the academy in 1828–1829, and Thornwell left Cheraw in the latter year to study at South Carolina College, so they might have been classmates.[12] At the academy they were taught by John G. Bowen and Dr. Thomas Graham, who was expert in Greek.[13] Lynch and Thornwell both became supporters of slavery and slave owners, and both eventually supported the Confederacy.

James Thornwell gained a reputation for aggressive opposition to those with whom he disagreed on doctrinal grounds, including fellow Presbyterians.

His virulent attacks on Catholicism were extraordinary even at a time when Protestant clerics were typically anti-Catholic.[14] According to Thornwell the Council of Trent had proclaimed the Deuterocanonical books to be divinely inspired scripture.[15] He termed this a "wicked and blasphemous sentence of Rome" and said that the Apocrypha were neither "'sacred nor canonical,' and of course, of no more authority in the Church of God than Seneca's Letters or Tully's Offices." The arguments he raised were not original and followed centuries-old polemics. The books were "not found in the canon of the Jews in the time of Our Saviour and his apostles." He cited statements by Josephus, Philo, and Augustine that they were not part of scripture. He criticized the Fathers of the Council of Trent for lack of scholarly expertise, noting that the leader, Cardinal Cajetan, could not read Hebrew. Since Catholics did not possess the true Bible, he broadened his attack to include the papacy and the Catholic ecclesiastical structure. He wrote, "Despising the authority of Popes and Councils, we bring the matter to the bar of sober reason and sound argument, and we challenge Rome to vindicate herself from the charge of intolerable arrogance and blasphemy in her corrupt additions to the word of God."[16]

Thornwell equated "Popery" with "Mohammedanism" as "successive evolutions of a great and comprehensive plan of darkness, conceived by a master mind for the purpose of destroying the kingdom of light and perpetuating the reign of death."[17] "As left by the Council of Trent, the Papal Church stands completely accoutered in the panoply of darkness—the grand instrument of Satan in the West as Mohammedanism in the East—to oppose the kingdom of God."[18] Rome encouraged "mean and slavish superstition." Veneration of saints was "heathenism."[19]

Patrick Lynch responded in a series of articles in the *Miscellany.* Ever polite, Lynch expressed shock at the tone of Thornwell's anti-Catholic diatribe. "Catholics," he said, "are neither outcasts from Society nor devoid of feeling: they are neither insensitive to, nor think that they deserve such words of opprobrium." He pointed out that lists of the scriptural books had been drawn up by various Protestant denominations, as well as by the Catholic Church. The Catholic canon derived from long tradition of the Church, going back to its earliest days. He asserted, "Your article breathes a spirit, which I will not qualify, but which would exclude the Catholic Church from the right, Protestants boast God has given to all men,—to believe in religious matters according to her own judgment, and to declare what she holds true." Lynch went on to quote various Fathers of the Church in favor of the Deuterocanonicals.[20]

The epistolary conflict dragged on for several years. Thornwell reported: "I have got into a war with the Romanists. . . . A writer in *The United States Catholic Miscellany,* of Charleston, has commenced a series of articles, directed personally to me, which I feel bound to notice. He is a weak scribbler; and . . . he will not be difficult of conquest."[21] Thornwell wrote twenty-nine letters addressed to Patrick Lynch, attacking the Catholics on the matter of the Apocrypha. The letters were published in a book, *Arguments of Romanists from the Infallibility of the Church and the Testimony of the Fathers in Behalf of the Apocrypha, Discussed and Refuted.*[22] This work drew three articles of refutation by Orestes Brownson that were published in *Brownson's Quarterly.*[23]

Thornwell broadened his attack at the General Assembly of the Presbyterian Church meeting in Cincinnati in May 1845. He gave a two-hour-long speech denying the validity of Catholic baptism, which he told his wife "was listened to with breathless attention."[24] The assembly overwhelmingly adopted his position.[25] He published three articles on Catholic baptism in the *Southern Presbyterian Review.* These essays later came out in a book and in Thornwell's *Collected Writings.*[26] He argued that Catholic baptism was invalid on several grounds. Baptism was supposed to be a personal ablution in pure water, but the Catholic Church adulterated the substance with chrism, a mixture of olive oil and balsam. Catholics sought grace in "signs and seals, without any reference to the things represented." Rome was guilty of substituting "mechanical means of salvation" for the true faith. "Pouring water could have no effect on the soul unless the person had previously credited the Word of God." Romish baptism was not valid: therefore, Catholics were not Christians.[27] The *Miscellany*'s reaction was swift and couched in irony:

> It was decided, that Baptism is not validly administered in the Catholic Church, and consequently that we are all unbaptised heathens. The Presbyterian authorities have said many hard things of [Catholics] and yet they seemed to live. They were denounced as idolators . . . their Church was designated in polite language the w—e of Babylon, their chief priest was declared to be nothing less than the antichrist himself, yet they continued to prolong life.

The *Miscellany* pointed out that not only did not all Presbyterians support the Cincinnati decision but that many opposed it. "It is rather strange that Catholics should have been struck with consternation when the late decision at Cincinnati was announced to the world."[28] Controversy continued between Lynch and Thornwell for several years. Thornwell's anti-Catholicism never abated, and he became a supporter of the Know-Nothing movement.[29] These attacks and Lynch's defense of his beloved Roman Catholic Church did nothing to hinder him from becoming one of Charleston's leading intellectual lights. Outside Presbyterian circles, Lynch was viewed most favorably by the community of Protestant clerics in the Holy City.

In fact, Patrick Lynch became a leading man of letters and science in Charleston, the Carolinas, and the American South. His intellectual eminence was one reason he was greatly admired by Charlestonians, especially Catholics, and particularly by the Irish. Lynch had received an extraordinary education. In addition to theology, in which he earned a doctorate, he had acquired impressive knowledge of literature, history, and science. He was fluent in Italian, spoke French and German, and was skilled in Latin, Greek, Hebrew, and even ancient Syriac and Sanskrit. When he arrived in Charleston in 1840 he was one of the best-educated people in Charleston—and he was only twenty-three.

He was a voracious reader who wrote well and spoke eloquently. His brother John Lynch was a prominent physician, and the two corresponded about medical questions.[30] In his spare time Patrick Lynch enjoyed working on mathematical problems and designing chess strategies.[31] He displayed boundless intellectual curiosity. After the Church, his greatest love was modern science. He had studied mathematics and some science in Charleston and, later, in Rome.

It was common for leading American clergymen of the nineteenth century to study and write on learned subjects, including science. For example, Bishop Augustin Verot, of the Diocese of Savannah and St. Augustine, had grown up in Le Puy, in the French province of the Auvergne, noted for its volcanic geological formations. As a boy he enjoyed exploring the local rocks. Verot took delight in mathematics and science. At St. Mary's College, Baltimore, in the 1830s, he was a professor of mineralogy, zoology, geology, and geometry, as well as mathematics.[32] Leading antebellum Southern theologians were well known for their assurance that the physical sciences could only confirm their religious faith. "The clergy," as E. Brooks Holifield has written, "thought that modern science was both the product and protector of Christian tradition."[33] Patrick Lynch fitted well into this tradition.

His first mentor, Bishop John England, had himself received, in eighteenth-century Ireland, a good education in the Age of Enlightenment. Bishop England was interested in the study and promotion of science. He was active in Charleston's Literary and Philosophical Society, which was founded in 1813 and whose membership included the most distinguished men of learning. Their interests included "all areas of knowledge—from mathematics and mechanics to literature and the fine arts."[34]

Frederick Adolphus Porcher (1809–1888), a professor at the College of Charleston, a historian, and a leading intellectual, said of the Literary and Philosophical Society that it "did not require learned men, or eloquent men, but it did require genial men, men who would take an interest in it." David Moltke-Hansen has described antebellum Charleston as "an intimate society, in which everyone among the leaders knew everyone else."[35] Bishop England functioned well in this world. He was an active member of the Society. He laid out his ideas on scientific and other learning in a lecture he gave at St. Finbar's Cathedral in 1832 on the anniversary of the Literary and Philosophical Society's founding. "God has given the lower world, with all its accumulated treasures and productions, as well as the firmament by which it is surrounded, and studded as it is, with so many glorious decorations, as a vast field for man's temporal occupation; to search out their several parts, to discover their relations, their perspectives . . . to turn them to the purposes of his own happiness here."[36]

Scientific discovery, said England, was vitally important and should yield benefits for humanity. England also believed that a good museum was essential to the study of natural science.[37] England was active in the Charleston Library Society, an institution founded in 1748 and still flourishing as America's third-oldest library. The Library Society was South Carolina's outstanding vehicle of the Enlightenment. It actively collected works of science and technology, as well as classical and modern literature. In 1773 the Library Society inaugurated a collection of natural history specimens. This was the genesis of the Charleston Museum, America's oldest.[38] The Library Society's collection of specimens and artifacts grew for decades. In 1813 the physician and respected botanist John L. E. W. Shecut (1770–1836) organized the Literary and Philosophical Society, which had among its principal purposes the organization of a museum. A number of leading Charlestonians were active in both organizations. In 1814 the Library Society donated its museum collection to the new association. Bishop England, who was active in both groups, served as one of the museum's curators.[39]

Antebellum Charleston was an important center of learning and boasted a community of leaders in science, medicine, and letters. These people knew one another and met socially in several learned societies. In the 1840s Dr. Lynch, as he was called, was brought into the circle of Charleston's intellectual and social elite. Like England, he participated in the Charleston Library Society, then located two and one-half blocks from his residence. There he often met his learned friends. He enjoyed the use of the Library for more than four decades, describing it as "an old fogey concern, with old time English books, that one seldom sees elsewhere, and where old fogies like myself sometimes meet to chat and read, or spend a quiet hour." He delighted in "taking out-of-town visitors to the Library Society to show off its collections of books, journals, newspapers, globes, and museum displays."[40]

Father Lynch was inducted into the Elliott Natural History Society, an organization that brought together leading men in medicine and science. Formation of this Society in 1853 was in large part a result of the inspiration of the famous zoologist Louis Agassiz, who lived for several years in Charleston as a professor at the Medical College of South Carolina and who encouraged the growth and improvement of the museum. The first president of the Elliott Society was Dr. John Bachman (1790–1874), pastor of St. John's Lutheran Church, naturalist, and friend and associate of John James Audubon. He collaborated with Audubon on the great illustrated work *The Viviparous Quadrupeds of North America.* The Elliott Society held meetings at which members presented scientific papers, which were published in its annual *Proceedings.* Lynch was elected to membership in 1854. Lynch and Bachman had sparred in the press on religious differences, but they apparently got on well enough in society. In addition to Bachman, Lynch came to know Professor J. F. M. Geddings, with whom he would later work closely on the city of Charleston's artesian wells projects.[41] Lynch played an active role in the Elliott Society, for which he prepared a plan for reorganization of the museum and drafted rules for its use.[42]

He was also invited to join the Conversation Club, a literary discussion group that met once a week at various members' houses for consideration of a particular intellectual topic. Here he got to know people such as College of Charleston professor Frederick Adolphus Porcher. Porcher was a planter and scholar who was considered one of the founders of critical historical scholarship in South Carolina. He was an important leader of the Charleston Library Society and became one of the principal founders of the South Carolina Historical Society, organized in 1855. Other participants were John Bachman, the artist Charles Fraser (1782–1860), and the attorney and civic leader Mitchell King (1783–1862).[43]

Another group that welcomed the priest was an informal but important association of learned men who met in the back room of John Russell's bookstore on King Street, a few blocks from Lynch's residence. John Russell (1812–1871) was a bookseller and publisher of some importance. The conversation club that gathered in his store included the lawyer and important Unionist James Louis Petrigru (1789–1863), Mitchell King (1815-1901), and the poet Henry Timrod (1828–1867). The central figure in their discussions was the Irish-American, William Gilmore Simms (1806–1870), one of the Old South's premier men of letters.[44] One of the participants, the poet, editor, and essayist Paul Hamilton Hayne (1830–1886), described Lynch as "this portly ecclesiastic, in the garb of a Catholic priest, peering benevolently through his spectacles, and offering his enameled snuff-box (the gift of an illustrious Cardinal) in an absent, mechanical way, to all with whom he may converse." This was the group that launched *Russell's Magazine,* the famous literary periodical. *Russell's* became an important venue for many Southern writers. Although he did not publish in the magazine, Father Lynch recruited South Carolina's young state geologist Oscar Montgomery Lieber (1830–1862) to write for it.[45]

Lynch became an associate of Simms, who edited the *Southern Quarterly Review* (*SQR*), published in Charleston from 1842 to 1854, with Simms as editor from 1849 to 1854. *SQR* has been described as the "outstanding non-fiction periodical of the Old South."[46] Simms was Protestant, and the *Southern Quarterly Review* under his editorship was generally hostile to Roman Catholicism, although he admired the Church for its care of the poor, its conversion of the Indians, and its missionary work around the world, and he praised individual Catholics such as Blaise Pascal and Charles Carroll of Maryland.[47] Simms considered Lynch "a very clever priest of the Catholic Church" and invited him "to enter our ranks" by writing for the journal. Knowing Lynch's interest in science, Simms asked him to write a review of Michael Tuomey's report on South Carolina geology. Lynch delayed in writing this, so the review was assigned to another. But Lynch did review Sir Austen Henry Layard's work on his archaeological excavations of ancient Nineveh in Turkish Mesopotamia (Iraq), *Nineveh and Its Remains.* This appeared in the journal in 1849.[48] In the event, Simms was mildly critical of Lynch's review, observing that the priest had not fully grasped the essence of the subject, which he said should have been approached on the moral rather than the merely factual level.[49] Simms said that Lynch had also written a couple of unsigned articles in the journal.[50] Lynch remained a supporter of the periodical, and Simms invited him to be a member of a committee of "friends of the *Southern Quarterly Review*" to attract subscriptions and raise money.[51]

The American Association for the Advancement of Science (AAAS) was founded in 1848, with its first meeting in Philadelphia. In the 1850s its membership included virtually all of America's leading scientists. At the second meeting, in Cambridge, Massachusetts, in 1849, Father Lynch was elected a member. The third AAAS meeting was held in Charleston in 1850. Lynch was probably the first Catholic priest to join the organization. In the view of members, especially geologists, the group's top priority was the promotion of research and discussion; a related goal was the education of the American public about the importance and benefits of science, so membership was relatively open. Members might be affiliated with a local scientific society. Women were invited to attend meetings from the beginning and were admitted to full membership in 1860.[52]

Lynch attended national meetings when he could and was elected to serve on two national committees.[53] At the Baltimore meeting in 1858, Professor G. C. Swallow, state geologist of Missouri, gave a paper on grape culture in that state. In the discussion period that followed, Bishop Lynch gave an extemporaneous discourse on grape growing and wine production in the Carolinas—remarks that drew favorable comment in the press.[54]

Patrick Lynch earned a national reputation for his work on the effort to drill and manage Charleston's artesian wells.[55] As Lynch explained in his writings, the provision of plentiful clean water in Charleston—as in many other cities—posed vexing problems. Along South Carolina's coast it was very easy to dig a well and find abundant ground water—so much so that to this day Charleston houses do not have cellars because of inevitable flooding. A problem was that wells were constantly polluted with human and animal waste. In addition to the human population in an era before adequate sewage disposal, a vast number of animals lived in Charleston: horses, cows, goats, fowl, dogs, and cats.

Gradually Charlestonians came to rely on cisterns to catch rainwater for drinking, but even the cisterns got polluted. In the early nineteenth century some effort were made to provide unpolluted water by digging deeper wells. Reports about the drilling of deep artesian wells in England and France—wells that would flow at the surface without pumping—came to American attention.[56] In 1823 the Charleston City Council authorized a project to drill a deep well, but this effort failed. In 1844 an attempt was made to bore an artesian well within the walls of Fort Sumter, at the mouth of Charleston Harbor. This project was stopped when the drill reached a depth of 347 feet. In 1847 the City Council again started a project to bore a well at the corner of Meeting and Wentworth Streets. This work, which was successful, continued through the 1840s.[57]

Young Father Lynch took great interest in the well projects. He made himself knowledgeable about the emerging science of geology. Like his mentor, Bishop England, he regarded modern science as good and important. Science could uncover truths about God's creation, and Lynch believed that learning should be used to benefit humankind. Deep wells could produce a steady supply of clean water for the people's welfare. In early 1848 he gave a public lecture about the first city well, illustrated with diagrams to explain the geology that made this possible.[58] The Irish-born Michael Tuomey (1808–1857), a native of Cork, was appointed South Carolina's state geologist in 1844. He undertook the extensive second state geological survey. Tuomey produced a detailed study of the stratigraphy of South Carolina. In 1847 he reported to Charleston's mayor and City Council that London and Paris—where artesian wells had been successfully drilled—"are situated upon geological formations of precisely the same age, and in other respects, similar to all upon which Charleston stands."[59] In later years, after he moved to Alabama, Tuomey continued to advise the city government on the boring of deep wells.[60]

The term "artesian well"—from the name of the French province of Artois, where they were first drilled—ordinarily refers to an especially deep well that draws groundwater from an aquifer lying below the Tertiary-Cretaceous boundary. This water has been filtered by the layers through which it has sunk and is free of fecal material. Since the aquifer is under pressure, water flows continuously at the surface, without a pump. At Charleston, drilling had to reach 1,800 feet underground, to what is now called the Middendorf Aquifer.[61]

Lynch was not a scientist in the sense of one who conceives a hypothesis and then uses the scientific method to investigate it. He was rather a man of science: one who studies scientific findings, promotes scientific endeavors, and works to educate the public. In the case of the wells, he was one of the promoters and managers of the projects. In 1848, Lynch recorded the characteristics of the strata through which the well at the intersection of Wentworth and Meeting Streets was drilled and reported these details down to a depth of 913 feet. He believed, correctly, that the boring was all at that point in Tertiary layers and that the Cretaceous layers with their characteristic fossils had not yet been reached. He understood the significance of the Tertiary-Cretaceous boundary, below which it was necessary to drill.[62]

Father Lynch acquired renown for a series of articles about the wells published in *The Charleston Evening News* in 1849. By that time the drilling had been discontinued, and Charleston's city fathers were undecided whether to continue the project. In his articles, undertaken to build public support for the wells, Lynch explained the health hazards caused by polluted water, noting that "our pump water is brackish and our cistern water often only a solution of rats, mosquitoes and filth in rain water . . . the evil will go on until even the negroes will not use pump water."[63] He recounted the history of deep wells through the centuries in Europe and in China. He described the strata laid down in different geological periods, noting that the pure water would be found under the Tertiary-Cretaceous boundary. Equipment needed to bore a deep well was described, as well as the efforts made in Charleston through 1849. And he explained how such a deep well would flow at the surface without a pump. Lynch's articles were successful in spurring public support for continuing the project, and the Wentworth Street well eventually reached a depth of more than 1,300 feet.[64] *DeBow's Review* reported on the first well, praising Lynch as "one of our most distinguished geologists."[65]

In Lynch's time three artesian wells were successfully bored in Charleston. He was one of the principal managers of the overall project. The deepest well "delivered water at the rate of about 250 gallons a minute, or about 360,000 gallons every twenty-four hours."[66] In addition to his goal of securing plentiful pure water, Lynch was greatly interested in contributing to the fossil record of the strata from different geological periods. Fossils that were retrieved from the drilling of the wells were preserved, organized, and described.

He gained a national reputation for his work on the wells and for his contributions to geological science. When he was made bishop of Charleston, the state geologist of Louisiana, the French-born Raymond Thomassy (1810–1863), rejoiced that Bishop England now had a worthy successor, "and moreover one who will contribute to geology."[67]

Later, in the postwar period, Charleston mayor William Ashmead Courtenay (1831–1908) appointed Bishop Lynch to chair a three-person Committee on the Artesian Wells, to direct the project and to conduct a scientific study of the wells. Lynch worked with John Frederic Meckel Geddings (1829–1887), a German American physician, and Charles Upham Shepard Jr., (1804–1886), a Charleston-born physician and analytical chemist at the Medical College of South Carolina.[68] At Mayor Courtenay's request the committee produced a detailed report on the entire project, which was published in the *City of Charleston Year Book*. Lynch recruited the Irish-born Charleston mathematician, engineer, sometime newspaper reporter, and prominent Catholic James Dalton Budds (1828–1887) to keep a detailed record of the strata through which the city drilled in creating the wells. This information appeared in the final report. Detailed chemical analyses of the well water were prepared by Drs. Geddings and Shepard, among others. Lynch wrote the report.[69]

Lynch took great interest in the fossils retrieved from the wells. He sent a collection of specimens to James Hall (1811–1898), a major American geologist and paleontologist who was director of the New York State Museum and who was later named New York state geologist. Hall praised the bishop for his careful collection and preservation of the fossils. Much of Hall's paleontological collection was to form an important component of the collection of the American Museum of Natural History in New York City.[70] The bishop lent his expertise about the wells to the state geologist of New Jersey in 1880, when that mid-Atlantic state was in the process of planning deep wells. George H. Cook, the state geologist, solicited details about the Charleston wells, and Lynch provided information that was published in Cook's annual report.[71]

Bishop Lynch enjoyed a reputation as one of the American Church's outstanding men of learning. Archbishop James Roosevelt Bayley of Baltimore (1814–1877) in the 1870s said he regarded Lynch "as a learned man . . . by far the head of the American hierarchy in this respect." Bayley's successor, Cardinal James Gibbons, called Lynch "distinguished alike for his varied learning & for his genial disposition."[72]

Lynch was a friend of Oscar Montgomery Lieber, a son of the polymath professor and writer Francis Lieber (1800–1872). The father was for a decade professor of history and political economy at South Carolina College (later the University of South Carolina). Oscar received a German education and became an outstanding geologist. In 1855 the South Carolina legislature made him the state's geological, mineralogical, and agricultural surveyor, and he conducted surveys of the state's geological resources from 1856 to1859, mostly in the South Carolina Piedmont. Oscar greatly admired Lynch and knew the Lynch family in Cheraw. He kept Lynch informed of his work writing his first and second annual reports to the legislature. In 1857 he asked whether the priest "will be able to join me in making that Cheraw and Coal Field R. R. examination"—something Lynch lacked the time to do. Nevertheless, Lieber asked Lynch to review the draft of his report and to help him to render "the style more perfect." In 1858 he sent the new bishop some sketches of unusual rock formations for his review and opinion and discussed the writing of his second annual report. He also reported to Lynch some specifics of the language of the Catawba Indians he encountered while conducting his surveys.[73] Oscar looked up to Lynch. He told his parents in 1858 that he found Catholics to be more zealous Christians than Protestants, and he spoke of "having become acquainted with a priest of that Church, who happens to take an interest in my pursuits," and with whom he could discuss "religious or doctrinal subjects." He did not intend to convert to Catholicism, although "Bishop Lynch may think that some day I will become a Catholic."[74] In the event, Lieber remained Protestant.

With his introduction to the city at the age of twelve and again upon his return from Rome as an ordained priest and doctor of divinity, Patrick Lynch blossomed in the intellectual and cultural milieu of Charleston's sophistication and learning. He followed the path of his mentor, John England, in forging a place of respect and civic accomplishment, thus easing the sometimes difficult process of assimilation that confronted Irishmen in other cities in America. Charleston proved to be a welcoming environment for men of such measure as England and Lynch. And they proved themselves worthy of its generosity. The infant born in a small town in Ireland and who spent his youth in precocious Cheraw had become a man of great accomplishment and acclaim in cosmopolitan antebellum Charleston.

CHAPTER 3

Advancement in the 1850s

It was in the decade of the 1850s that Patrick Lynch rose to his position as a prominent member of Charleston's cultural and intellectual aristocracy. All of the hard work he expended in acquiring a good education and applying it to practical areas in serving his Catholic faith, parish, and diocese, as well as his community and his nation, resulted in success and broad recognition. By the end of this decade he had risen to be the religious leader of the Diocese of Charleston and a major player in the collective hierarchy of the American Catholic Church.

During Bishop Reynolds's final years, anti-Catholic feelings were stirred nationwide by writers and public speakers who gained notoriety by purporting to reveal awful secrets of cruelty and sexual misbehavior in Catholic convents and by Catholic priests and nuns. The virulent anti-Catholic tract by one Maria Monk, *Artful Disclosures at the Hotel Dieu Nunnery in Montreal,* published in 1836, was "the best selling work of literature in America prior to publication in 1852 of *Uncle Tom's Cabin.*"[1]

In March 1852 a man named Leahey arrived in Charleston. He was said to be Irish and was described as a Protestant minister and a converted ex-monk of La Trappe. A local newspaper advertised that he would give a public lecture in which he would expose "Popish Confession and Priestcraft." According to the ad in the *Charleston Evening News,* Leahey would speak "on the unchristian treatment of females in the confessional by Popish Priests, according to the standard of Popish Theology."[2] The lecture was to be given in the Masonic Hall, admission would be charged, and, because of the awful revelations to be made, no youths or women would be admitted. It was also announced that Leahey would give sermons at several Protestant churches in Charleston.[3] A storm of Catholic protest erupted, and there were threats of physical violence to the supposed ex-monk, leading to cancellation of the lecture and church appearances.

Leahey appealed to the Charleston City Council to protect his right to free speech. In the Council debate Alderman Dr. John Bellinger (1804–1860), a distinguished Charleston physician, Catholic convert, and friend of Patrick Lynch,

Bishop Ignatius Reynolds (1842–1856), born in Kentucky of Irish parents, succeeded Bishop England in Charleston in 1844. Lynch became an important part of his administration, running the seminary, editing the U.S. Catholic Miscellany, and serving as vicar general. Courtesy of Catholic Diocese of Charleston Archive.

spoke against Leahey. Bellinger was one of the leading Catholic laymen of his time. He had been Bishop England's personal physician. He had vigorously defended Lynch—"our champion"—against anti-Catholic attacks by the Presbyterian divine James H. Thornwell. Bellinger was one of the largest contributors to the cathedral building fund, pledging $4,000 and actually donating more.[4] In the City Council debate he denounced any public attacks on Catholicism. Bishop England, said Bellinger, in his own occasional confrontations with Protestants never did "charge upon the present generations of Protestants, clergy and laity, the immoral practices licensed by their chief Reformer [i.e., Martin Luther] the sanction for which is extant in his on writings."[5] Bellinger's remarks ignited a wider controversy over what Luther had or had not taught regarding marriage—a fight that was played out in the press. Articles appeared in the Baptist organ the *Watchman and Observer* of Richmond, the *Charleston Evening News*—and, of course, the *U.S. Catholic Miscellany.*

Charleston's respected Lutheran pastor John Bachman (1790–1876) got into the fray in a series of stinging articles published in the *Charleston Evening News,* in which he severely criticized *Miscellany* editor James Corcoran, expressing fear that Catholics in political office might seek to restrict the religious freedom of Protestants.[6] The Lutheran pastor had been involved in controversy in 1837–1838 with Bishop England, the result of a sermon by Bachman on the errors of "the Romish Church."[7] There was irony in the fact that England and Bachman publicly respected each other and that both were prominent members of Charleston's learned societies.

In the 1850s the anti-Catholic trend that had been growing for years reached an intensity that affected the diocese and Father Lynch. The trend has been called the "Protestant Crusade" by the historian Ray Allen Billington. Protestant and nativist worries about the growth of Catholicism and the arrival of enormous numbers of immigrants—many of them Irish and other Catholics—were expressed in the press. Catholic periodicals like the *U.S. Catholic Miscellany* were important vehicles for defense and counterattacks. In the 1850s antagonism between members of the different denominations reached a high pitch with the emergence of the American Party, members of which were called the Know-Nothings. The national press reported and commented on the address "The Decline of Protestantism and Its Causes," given by Archbishop Hughes of New York at St. Patrick's Cathedral on November 10, 1850. The archbishop was responding to venomous anti-Catholic criticism with aggressive declarations, and he asserted: "Everybody should know that we have for our mission to convert the world—Including the inhabitants of the United States,—the people of the cities, and the People of the country, the officers of the navy, and the marines, commanders of the navy, the legislators, the senate, the cabinet, the President, and all."[8] Reports of the archbishop's remarks stirred things up.

Then, in 1853, Archbishop Gaetano Bedini, a papal nuncio, visited the United States. The Italian archbishop was accredited to the imperial court of Brazil. He was sent to the United States before taking up his position in South America and commissioned to report to the Vatican on the state of the American Church. The United States had proper, if somewhat limited, diplomatic relations with the Holy See, and the American government received the nuncio cordially enough. But nativists charged that the visit was part of a plot aimed at subjugating America to papal rule, and the archbishop was greeted by protests and even riots almost everywhere he traveled. Bedini's travels in the South were limited. In his eventual report to the Vatican the nuncio said that the only areas in slave states that he saw were Baltimore and Louisville. Warning of widening division among Americans on the slavery question, he said that "it might be better for the

Bishops to show and profess a marked neutrality, although Negroes ought not be deprived of religion because of social or political reasons."[9] The violence, insults, and threats aimed at Bedini and, through him, at Pope Pius IX, were reported by the Catholic press with indignation and protestations of loyalty to the Holy Father. In the *Miscellany*, James Corcoran reported extensively on Bedini's visit, covering his travels and the violence that accompanied him. The newspaper expressed indignation at outrages against the archbishop and the Church and the "brutal inhospitality and ruffianly insult which an innocent, unarmed man, the representative of a foreign friendly power has encountered in this boasted land of freedom and civilization."[10] Corcoran indicted "the whole American people with a few exceptions, by its acquiescence, by its silence."[11] The nuncio did not come to the Diocese of Charleston, and there were no instances of disorder or insult; the *Charleston Mercury* spoke out against the insults to a foreign diplomat.[12]

But interdenominational controversy brewed in Charleston. Late in the summer of 1852 the city experienced a terrible yellow fever outbreak. Bishop Reynolds was in New York at the time, and Father Lynch as vicar general advised him not to return immediately to South Carolina.[13] On August 30, Lynch, "realizing that the disease had reached epidemic proportions and that the city was unprepared to handle it, determined to open a Relief Hospital." A new facility called Roper Hospital had been built near the cathedral across the street from the convent and orphanage of the Sisters of Our Lady of Mercy, but the hospital was not yet in operation. Lynch secured permission for a portion of it to be put in service and staffed by the Sisters, and this was done. Hundreds of patients were treated before the epidemic subsided in November. One of these was the young Conlaw Lynch, Patrick's brother, who recovered his health.[14] Some of those cared for were Protestants and Jews. However, Pastor John Bachman complained that the Sisters had denied permission to Protestant clergymen to visit and console non-Catholics and asserted that this was part of an effort to convert suffering people to the Roman faith. Bachman was joined in this complaint by other Protestant clergy. The Sisters and the vicar general insisted that Protestant ministers had indeed been accorded courteous access to patients.[15] In 1853 Bachman published *Defence of Luther and the Reformation*, which contained a collection of documents and Bachman's narrative and interpretation of both the Bellinger and the hospital controversies. In this he included a stinging essay, "The Roman Catholic Doctrine of Oral Confessions." Here, he claimed indignantly, priests extracted from frightened women their innermost "thoughts at which innocence recoils" and "the secrets (*circa actam conjugalem*) of the nuptial couch."[16]

Lynch did not wish to become embroiled in a direct argument about Luther, but he did publish in the *Evening News* letters countering some of Bachman's assertions about the baleful influence of a Catholic devotional tract called *The Garden of the Soul*, declaring that it was perfectly good and wholesome.[17] The business brought on an exchange of insults in the press between Bachman and Corcoran, leading Bishop Reynolds to try to distance himself from it all. Reynolds wrote a letter to Lynch in April 1853, which was subsequently published in the *Miscellany*. The bishop flatly refused "to enter into any controversy with him [Bachman]" about Luther. As to the Relief Hospital, Reynolds demanded a full explanation from Lynch of what in fact had happened. And he in effect criticized Corcoran, suggesting that his language exacerbated ill feelings. "It is sufficient for me to know, that he [Corcoran] has written nothing contrary to faith, and maintained nothing contrary to the principles of morality.... Dr. Bachman must settle the difficulties with Dr. Corcoran and others concerned, the best way he can; and therefore I dismiss the case, with this only remark, rather consoling, I trust, than offensive, that neither the editor of the *Miscellany*, nor even Dr. Bachman, is too old to learn from experience, or so perfect as to preclude improvement."[18] In the end the Bachman controversies simply faded away. The matter pointed up the interdenominational attitudes in Charleston and Lynch's inclination not to stir things up needlessly.

Another interesting visitor to Charleston in 1853 was an Irish priest, Dr. James Donnelly. He had been sent to America with six other prelates to beg for money for the construction of a cathedral in Dublin. Donnelly hailed from the Diocese of Clogher, which covered the region from which the Lynch family had emigrated. Donnelly traveled all of the United States from his American base in the Archdiocese of New York. In his journal, Donnelly recorded an account of the days spent with Lynch at 80 Broad. He referred to Lynch as "a kind, simple man" who entertained him well. In his household he had some "little slaves ... so funny and frisky." Later, when Bishop Lynch traveled to Rome on his Confederate mission, he attempted to return the favor with a visit on his stopover in Ireland. Dr. Donnelly, however, was not home when the Charleston visitor called.[19]

In 1854, Lynch brought to fruition one of John England's great ambitions. Bishop Reynolds had put him in charge of supervising the construction of a cathedral worthy of the Diocese of Charleston. The architect was Patrick Charles Keely, who became the most reputable designer of Catholic churches throughout the United States. The construction of this cathedral of St. John and St. Finbar was hailed in the *Charleston Daily Courier* as of "the highest reaches of art and grace."[20]

The mid-1850s saw the impressive rise of the nativist American Party, called the Know-Nothings. The party, which harbored anti-immigrant and anti-Catholic sentiments, made little headway in South Carolina, where the Democratic Party ruled with a firm hand. But in North Carolina some three dozen newspapers expressed support for the Americanist cause, and Know-Nothings elected two U.S. congressmen and various local officials.[21] In the *Miscellany*

Cathedral of St. Finbar (1854). Reynolds put Father Lynch in charge of supervising the construction of this new church, which was designed by the architect Patrick Charles Keely. *Harper's Weekly,* December 28, 1861, courtesy of Charleston Library Society, Charleston, S.C.

Father Corcoran voiced concern about the anti-Catholic influence of the North Carolina Know-Nothing leader Kenneth Raynor.

Nativism played a role in the election of the Charleston District (county) sheriff in July 1855. Charles Emile Kanapaux (1827–1870) was a Catholic, a member of St. Mary's Parish, a descendant of French refugees from Saint-Domingue, and a colonel in the militia who had held various public offices through the years. John Edward Carew (1807–1877) was an Episcopalian, a planter, the former proprietor and editor of the *Charleston Mercury* daily newspaper, and a former longtime member of the state House of Representatives. He would later be a colonel in the state militia.[22] Carew won the election on July 9 and evidently benefited from anti-Catholic and anti-foreign suspicions among some of the voters. His supporters charged that there had been a series of rapid and suspicious naturalizations of foreign immigrants, who had allegedly promised to support Kanapaux.

Unfounded rumors spread in Charleston "that the Pope, Archbishop Hughes, etc., had sent in money to support Kanapaux." The event further soured interdenominational relations.[23] Speaking for the Diocese of Charleston, the *Miscellany* assailed Carew's supporters for spreading anti-Catholic slander.[24]

Anti-Catholic attitudes created problems in Columbia. Father Jeremiah J. O'Connell had been pastor in the state capital since 1848. Two years later his brother Laurence Patrick O'Connell (1826–1891) was ordained by Bishop Reynolds and appointed Jeremiah's assistant.[25] The brothers believed the time was ripe for a Catholic school in Columbia, so in 1851 they organized St. Mary's Collegiate Institute for white boys. After some changes in its organizational plan, it was chartered by the South Carolina General Assembly in 1853. The corporation was composed of two priests, M. J. Ryan and Julius Posi (or Posey). There was some opposition to the charter in the legislature, but the act of incorporation was championed by Edmund Bellinger Jr., a Catholic, and other legislators.[26] Jeremiah O'Connell was proud of the college's contribution to the education of Columbia's youth. Qualified boys were admitted "regardless of creed." Protestant lads attended Sunday services at their own churches "under proper guardians," while "the Israelites spent their Sabbaths at the synagogue."[27]

Nonetheless the school was subject to anti-Catholic agitation in 1855, at the height of the Know-Nothing crusade. Jeremiah O'Connell claimed in his colorful prose that bigotry and envy led to threats that escalated to a mob invasion of the school: "An armed band made their way in midday into the hall where the students were assembled for roll-call, and publicly insulted the professors.... The young men, armed with their slates, and other weapons of defense furnished by chance, rose to their feet and prepared to resist the assault at the peril of their lives."[28] The display of resistance led the invaders to leave the school. There were also instances in Columbia of priests and nuns being insulted in public. Only gradually did the anti-Catholic agitation subside.[29]

For all the anti-Protestant teaching of Giovanni Battista Palma and others at the Urban College, Father Lynch was not inclined to be aggressive in any public way toward Protestants in the Carolinas. He had grown up in a land where Catholics were a distinct minority. He had been brought up in a Protestant community by parents who cultivated good relations and friendships with their non-Catholic neighbors. Many of Patrick's friends and associates were non-Catholics. In the South, Catholics were generally a small minority. In 1850, North Carolina, South Carolina, and Georgia had the smallest percentage (0.3 percent each) in the South of Catholics in their populations.[30] But Lynch could indeed rise to defend Catholicism when attacked, if he was convinced that public defense was needed.

Practicing a tradition established by John England, the bishop of Charleston and diocesan leaders did not endorse political candidates or try in any overt way to instruct Catholics on how to vote. In his celebrated address to Congress in 1826, England had declared: "I would not allow to the Pope, or to any bishop of our church, outside the Union, the smallest influence with the humblest vote at our most insignificant balloting box. He has no right to such interference."[31] Lynch's record generally does not contain public statements of support for political candidates. The presidential election of 1856 constitutes an exception, when Lynch was administrator of the diocese following Bishop Reynolds's death.

The election of 1856 came at a time when the Know-Nothing campaign showed remarkable strength in various parts of the country. The newly organized national Republican Party put forward its first candidate for president, John C. Frémont. The Republican platform opposed expansion of slavery to the territories of the West, Ironically, Frémont had spent part of his youth in South Carolina, where he had been a student at the College of Charleston.[32] The Democratic candidate was James Buchanan. The American Party nominated former president Millard Fillmore, who did not campaign on the basis of anti-Catholicism, but the Know-Nothing label hurt him among Catholic voters. The Republican platform worried Southerners with its aim to limit the spread of slavery in the West.[33]

In August 1856 Horace Greeley's *New York Herald* accused the *Miscellany* of publicly supporting Buchanan. Corcoran angrily responded that the paper did not endorse any candidate, but in a long editorial on September 6 he praised Buchanan:

> We have had for years in our possession facts . . . which not only redound to his credit as an honorable man, but also might prove of special edification to our Catholics. . . . Of the three parties that at present seek the mastery, one is evidently unconstitutional [i.e., Republican], and so far immoral in its aims. Another aspires to dominion, in order to have the power to proscribe men objectionable to their petty faction on the score of birth or religion [i.e., the American Party]. A third seeks to frustrate the wicked aims of the two former, to uphold the Constitution, and all rights of person and property by the same solemnly guaranteed.[34]

As diocesan administrator Patrick Lynch was in effect the publisher of the *Miscellany*. Although he did not pen the editorial, it is fair to assume that the sentiments were in line with his own. The Know-Nothing Party and movement substantially collapsed in the months after the 1856 election, and the larger struggle over slavery took center stage.

In the 1850s Bishop Reynolds's health declined. He made Patrick Lynch his vicar general, and Lynch was chosen as administrator of the Diocese of Charleston after Reynolds died. It was clear that Lynch had favorably impressed Metropolitan Archbishop Francis Patrick Kenrick of Baltimore. The latter wrote to his brother Archbishop Peter Richard Kenrick of St. Louis on April 2, 1855, that his recommendations for the See of Charleston were, in order of order of preference, Patrick Lynch, Jesuit Father Hippolyte Deluynes, and the Reverend John McCaffrey. For the See of Savannah he named William Henry Elder, Jesuit Father William J. Clark, and James McGarahan. Kenrick was joined in this recommendation by Bishop John McGill of Richmond.[35] However, following discussions with all the bishops of the province of Baltimore at the Eighth Provincial Council, Archbishop Kenrick wrote to the Propaganda Fide giving a different list of nominees. The provincial prelates recommended, in order of preference, were John McCaffrey, Hippolyte Deluynes, and James Duggan. The terna for Savannah was Lynch, William Henry Elder, and John Barry. Both McCaffrey's and Lynch's names were on the terna for Philadelphia in the event that Bishop (St.) John Nepomuk Neumann should be transferred. McCaffrey was the revered rector of Mount St. Mary's Seminary in Emmitsburg, Maryland, at the time the most prestigious American institution for the training of priests. At the age of forty-eight, McCaffrey was a commanding, even formidable figure. He had been seventeen years a priest. The provincial bishops praised him for sound administration and command of doctrine.

Francis Kenrick observed that Lynch, as an alumnus of the Urban College, was already well known to the cardinals of the Propaganda, to whom his piety, manners, and management of affairs would commend him. Furthermore, Lynch was accustomed to the unhealthy climate of Georgia. It was also noted that Bishop Reynolds had considered Lynch as worthy of becoming his coadjutor in Charleston.[36]

The Propaganda took its time considering the appointments. At the end of November the archbishop of Baltimore had still not heard from Rome about the two sees.[37] As it happened, the cardinals chose McCaffrey for Charleston and Barry for Savannah. John Barry was duly installed in Savannah in 1857. The bulls of election were sent from Rome to Dr. McCaffrey, but he decided to refuse the miter. His appointment had caused some consternation both in Emmitsburg and among alumni of The Mountain, as the seminary was affectionately called. Bishop John McCloskey of Albany (later cardinal archbishop of New York) wrote McCaffrey that "had you accepted the mitre of Charleston I would have grieved for the sake of the Old Mountain."[38] In the meantime, Lynch's name had been sent to Rome as a nominee for the Diocese of Natchez, Mississippi, but William Henry Elder was appointed instead.[39] Archbishop John Hughes of New York wrote McCaffrey: "I confess that for the glory of God and good of the Church, I do prefer to see you at the head of Mount St. Mary's College, rather than see you Bishop of Charleston."[40]

By the spring of 1857 McCaffrey had made up his mind. Kenrick informed Lynch that McCaffrey's refusal was final, while reappointing Lynch administrator of Charleston.[41] Lynch replied that he regretted McCaffrey's refusal and hoped that he would not have to administer the diocese for yet another two years.[42] Kenrick observed that McCaffrey "resists most pertinaciously" and told Lynch that "the bishops of the Province did not suggest to the S.C. [the Sacred Congregation of the Propaganda] to urge his acceptance."[43] The archbishop conferred with his suffragans in Baltimore on the occasion of Bishop Barry's consecration, and they sent a new Charleston terna to Rome. Francis Kenrick, with concurrence of Bishops Whelan of Wheeling, Neumann of Philadelphia, and McGill of Richmond, gave Lynch as their first choice, followed by Martin John Spalding and James Whelan. In Rome the cardinals of the Propaganda agreed with the Baltimore Province recommendation, praising Lynch for his pure doctrine, his probity in conducting diocesan affairs, and his integrity. In their *ponenza* (position paper) they said they were favorably impressed by his seventeen years' service in the diocese and observed that he was fully acclimated to the hostile tropical weather of the Carolinas.[44]

Patrick Lynch was duly appointed bishop of Charleston. The bulls of appointment arrived in February 1858. Upon news of their arrival, the local newspaper responded with the joy that was felt throughout the Charleston community: "So far as we may be permitted to utter our opinion on such an appointment, we are enabled, from our acquaintance with Dr. Lynch, who has been long a resident of this city, and is widely known throughout this his native State and beyond his own communion, to record our decided conviction that the selection has been judicious and well placed."[45] This announcement was followed by a broader, more extensive account of the appointment in Monday's edition, in which the newspaper reported on a special meeting of the Vestry, which sent a request to the archbishop in Baltimore that Lynch be allowed to receive the vestments and powers of his ecclesiastical office in the very cathedral he had help to construct.[46] The next day's newspaper noted in its report on the annual banquet of the Charleston Chamber of Commerce that Bishop-elect Lynch was honored with a welcoming toast and the loudest applause of any of their many guests. "To Bishop-elect Lynch—The scholar, the gentleman, the American Bishop. In this appointment we are all Catholic—none Protestant."[47] This remarkable public reception of a Catholic prelate's appointment to the Diocese of Charleston stands as testimony to degree to which Lynch had built upon the work of his mentor, John England, to secure a place at the community table.

The ceremony of consecration took place in the Cathedral of St. John and St. Finbar on March 14, with Archbishop Kenrick of Baltimore as consecrator, with assistance from Bishop Barry and Bishop McGill. Archbishop Hughes of New York sent Lynch an amethyst episcopal ring.[48] Again the Charleston press covered this event as if every Charlestonian held a keen interest in the minutest details. They spoke of "the imposing ceremonial of yesterday. The gorgeous vestments, the solemn chant of the clergy on the altar, the magnificent swell of the organ, pealing in glorious unison with the bird-like sweetness of female voices, formed a spectacle at once too solemn, imposing, grand and affecting to be noted on paper."[49] The newly consecrated bishop participated in the Ninth Provincial Council of Baltimore in May 1858. Here gathered, under the presidency of Archbishop Francis Patrick Kenrick, seven suffragan bishops, one coadjutor, and a diocesan procurator. It was to be the last antebellum ecclesiastical council in which Charleston was a participant. James Corcoran accompanied Lynch as his theologian and was selected council secretary, responsible for drawing up the decrees, minutes, and report to the Holy See. In addition to resolutions concerning dispensation from abstinence on Saturdays, the fathers asked that the archbishop of Baltimore be granted honorary privileges as the ordinary of the First See of the United States. The bishops discussed the looming controversy over slavery but decided to take no stand for or against the institution. In their pastoral letter to the faithful issued on May 9, the Council Fathers declared:

> The peaceful and conservative character of our principles, which are adapted to Every form of government, and every state of society, has been tested and made manifest in the great political struggles that have agitated the country on the subject of domestic slavery. Although history plainly testifies that the Church has always befriended the poor and laboring classes, and effectually procured the mitigation of the evils attached to servitude, until through her mild influence it passed away from the nations of Europe, yet she has never disturbed established order, or endangered the peace of society, by following theories of philanthropy. Faithful to the teaching and examples of the apostles, she has always taught servants to obey their masters.... Let the dead bury their dead. Leave to worldlings the cares and anxieties of political partisanship, the struggle for ascendancy, and the mortifications of disappointed ambition.[50]

Under the circumstances, the bishops wished to allow the Catholic faithful maximum latitude in making their own political decisions. They recognized that the country was split on slavery and states' rights. The bishops were determined to maintain the bonds that held together the institutional Church. They were themselves of different minds about domestic slavery, and some felt aggrieved by the anti-Catholic sentiments of Northern abolitionists. They sought to preserve peace and in essence believed that maintaining the status quo was the means to accomplish this objective. Bishop Lynch, in remarks he made after the Civil War at a Catholic conference in Belgium, would praise the American hierarchy for having done nothing "to produce that exacerbation of feelings which resulted in the war itself."[51] In essence this conclave opted for the status quo rather than risk the violent upheaval that later proved to be required to end the institution of slavery in the United States.

The Ninth Provincial Council promoted the biblical scholarship of Francis Patrick Kenrick. The scholarly archbishop of Baltimore had been working since 1842 on updating and revising the Douay Bible. His version of the English Bible began to appear in print in 1849, but by 1858 it was still not complete. The bishops of the Council proposed that Kenrick's text "be adopted for common use in the United States." Moreover, since they had heard that John Henry Newman had been asked by the English bishops to prepare a new translation of the Latin Vulgate, they determined to ask that Newman and Kenrick collaborate on "a single version . . . which could be brought into use in both England and these states."[52] The Council assigned to Bishops Lynch, McGill, and Verot the task of communicating the idea to Newman. In fact, Newman had been asked by Nicholas Cardinal Wiseman, archbishop of Westminster, to undertake a translation, but the project had not been funded and had not gotten off the ground. Lynch wrote on behalf of the bishops to Newman and the cardinal. He asked Wiseman to use his influence to see that "the Catholic world will receive a version prepared under such circumstances, as will ensure its ready acceptance by all." Details would be worked out directly between Kenrick and Newman.[53]

The cardinal passed this message on to Newman, and Lynch also wrote him directly, enclosing the Council's printed resolution on the scheme. John Henry Newman was dubious about the project, fearing that it would be very difficult to collaborate with Kenrick. The English bishops had failed to carry through with funding his project. To Lynch, Newman wrote politely that this was a great honor, while describing various problems that made him hesitate to commit himself.[54] As it turned out, Newman never made a complete biblical translation, while Kenrick completed his effort in 1860.[55]

Soon after his consecration, Bishop Lynch announced to his diocesan consulters his intention to open a boys' orphanage in Charleston and to bring the Ursuline Sisters back to the diocese. He proposed to move the Sisters of Our Lady of Mercy from Columbia, where they had charge of the Academy of the Immaculate Conception, back to Charleston to run the orphanage. At the same time he would bring Ursulines to Columbia to operate the Academy.[56] In 1857 Archbishop John Baptist Purcell of Cincinnati had communicated to then-administrator Lynch that Charleston might be able to procure some Ursuline nuns from their convent in Brown County, Ohio.[57] Lynch's plan was for six Ursulines to travel from Ohio to Columbia, after the Sisters of Mercy departed. The Ursuline superior was to be his sister Ellen Lynch, known in religion as Madame Baptista, OSU. Baptista knew of the plans as early as April 1858, although the Sisters of Mercy were not informed until August and were given no choice in the matter. The sudden switch appeared to the Charleston sisters as highhanded on Lynch's part, but they had to go along.[58]

Mother Baptista Lynch (1823–1887) was born in Cheraw, the fifth child and second daughter of Conlaw and Eleanor Lynch. In her youth she attended the Ursuline Academy then located in Charleston, where she decided to join that community. Bishop Reynolds caused the Ursulines to leave South Carolina in 1847, and they moved to Covington, Kentucky, then to Ohio. Eleanor became a novice at the Ursuline Convent of the Assumption, in Cincinnati, in 1848 and was professed as Baptista Aloyisus two years later. In 1854 she joined St. Martin's Ursuline Convent in Fayette, Brown County, Ohio. For the Ursulines and for Baptista, the return to South Carolina in October 1858—escorted personally by Bishop Lynch—was a triumph. For Bishop England's sisterhood, it was hard to accept, but they dedicated themselves to the Charleston orphanage project.[59]

Baptista was Patrick's sibling, friend, and confidante. She wrote frequently to her brother in Charleston for the rest of his life. Her voluminous correspondence reveals her to have played a special role as his eyes and ears in the South Carolina midlands and elsewhere. Mother Baptista was distinguished by her intelligence, learning, strong leadership, and dignified personal bearing.[60] When she took charge of the Ursuline community in Columbia, she wanted to expand the girls' school, for which a larger building was required. So in 1859 Bishop Lynch purchased the former American Hotel in the center of the capital's business district. This action incited opposition among some Columbia businessmen and elicited a surprising degree of anti-Catholicism. The bishop pointed out to critics that the hotel had been vacant for some time and that its new use as a convent and school was in no way a detriment to the community. Nonetheless, a guard was posted to protect the nuns and their charges.[61] Jeremiah O'Connell claimed that "efforts were made to raise a mob either to destroy the convent or disperse its unoffending inmates." Years later, as General Sherman's army approached Columbia, Mother Baptista said, "I fear the rabble of Columbia who stoned us as much as the Yankees."[62]

As bishop, Lynch never had a large contingent of priests, and the support and cooperation of Catholic laypeople were always of vital importance for the life of the diocese. An example was the founding of the Parish of St. Mary of the Immaculate Conception in the early months of his episcopate. The Edgefield District (county) in the upper part of South Carolina was a rich agricultural area. Priests from Columbia visited Edgefield. Beginning in 1849, Father Timothy Bermingham (1797–1872) celebrated Mass there on a monthly basis, and in 1856 he became pastor. Born in County Tipperary, Ireland, Bermingham had studied in Montreal, then at Bishop England's seminary in Charleston, where he was tonsured in 1829 and ordained in 1832. Jeremiah O'Connell recalled him as a tall, slender man, with an ascetic appearance and a long nose: "the impersonation of mortification and ill health."[63]

Edgefield's Catholic community was small, but it included a strong leader in Dr. John Harwood Burt (d. 1861). He was a physician, a highly successful planter, a member of the district's most prominent family, a civic leader and an enthusiastic Catholic convert.[64] He constructed a chapel in his own house, which was the first Catholic church in Edgefield. With the help of Dr. Elbert Bland of Edgefield, Burt opened a subscription list to support the building of a permanent church. In 1856 John Rudolph Niernsee (1823–1885) moved to Columbia from Baltimore,

St. Mary's Church in Edgefield, South Carolina (1856), dedicated by Patrick Lynch while he was serving as diocesan administrator. Courtesy of Catholic Diocese of Charleston Archive.

having been hired by the South Carolina legislature as resident architect of the new state house. A native of Vienna, Niernsee had studied under the German neoclassical architect Karl Friedrich Schinkel and immigrated to America in 1838. He built a successful architectural practice in Baltimore. He was a practicing Catholic who became prominent in Columbia's St. Peter's Parish.[65]

Bermingham approached Niernsee, who contributed gratis a design for a Gothic Revival edifice to be constructed of granite and some marble, reminiscent of European churches. Catholics and non-Catholics—including, notably, Dr. Burt—helped to raise funds as well as the actual stones. Much of the transport of stone was done by slaves, but free white citizens also volunteered to help with the work. Bermingham succeeded in opening a local rock quarry, with a smithy "on the site to keep the wagons and tools in shape." With Lynch's permission, the pastor made a begging tour as far as New Orleans to raise funds. The Church of St. Mary of the Immaculate Conception was dedicated by Bishop Lynch on October 21, 1860.[66]

In the early part of 1861, Lynch also presided over the dedication of two additional Catholic churches within the city of Charleston. On May 5 he opened a new parish of St. Joseph's in the predominantly Irish neighborhood of Ward 5. This modest brick structure on the northern end of Anson Street was "solemnly consecrated to sacred worship . . . filled in every part, the audience composed of members of every denomination."[67] The Reverend Dr. Cummings, pastor of St. Stephen's Church, New York, preached the dedication sermon.

Just a week later, on May 12, Lynch dedicated the first German Catholic church in the Diocese of Charleston. The bishop performed the dedication ceremonies while the Reverend Dr. Cummings delivered the sermon. The reverend pastor of the church, Father Berrschneider was offered "highest credit for the great zeal and untiring energy he has displayed in completing this neat and tasteful edifice for his Catholic fellow-countrymen."[68] While St. Paul's was intended to serve Charleston's ever growing German Catholic population, the dedication was attended by such a crowd that "a large number were compelled to stand during the service and many went away unable to attain admission."[69]

Prior to the war Patrick Lynch did not make any major public statements about the legality of slavery or about states' rights—not in pastoral letters, sermons, or speeches. The *Miscellany* as the official journalistic voice of the diocese rarely mentioned the word "slavery" in the years following Bishop England's letters to Secretary of State John Forsyth. Richard Madden calculated that "all in all there are not five references to abolitionism in the *Miscellany* from 1842 to 1852."[70] During the 1850s James Corcoran wrote editorials, and official diocesan announcements appeared over Lynch's name. Both priests lived on Broad Street in Charleston and were old schoolmates and friends who presumably discussed the issues of the time. It is reasonable to regard the *Miscellany*'s published views as consonant with Lynch's.[71] Corcoran considered that the Church's position on slavery had been expressed clearly by Bishop England. In 1856 Corcoran penned an attack on Henry Ward Beecher, who had been "vilifying the American Catholic Church and its priesthood," and restated England's interpretation of Pope Gregory XVI's *In supremo apostolatus.* "The Letter Apostolic leaves Domestic Servitude just where it was before; it condemns and punishes with spiritual penalties that which by God's own laws is felony, the slave trade." Corcoran assailed "the infamous crusade organized by Northern Protestant ministers, against the constitutional rights and social tranquility of the South."[72] On other occasions the *Miscellany* condemned Free Soilism, socialism, and "'all the other isms' that it saw as the result of European Red Republicanism."[73] Here, until the eve of the war, Charleston's diocesan newspaper was generally in line with the rest of the national Catholic press. The prominent New York Catholic paper *The New York Freeman's Journal and Catholic Register* called abolitionists "a mischievous set of fanatics."[74]

As diocesan administrator and later as bishop, Patrick Lynch did not publicly air his view of secession prior to the event. It is consequently difficult to say exactly when he became convinced that rejection of the federal Union was necessary. It seems likely that, in a general way, he shared the prevailing sentiments of leading whites of his social class and standing in Charleston and throughout South Carolina. James Corcoran's editorial commentary in the *Miscellany* can be taken as expressing sentiments also felt by Lynch. From 1855 on Lynch was in fact the publisher of the newspaper, even though he did not dictate the choice of language employed by the younger priest.

In the 1850s the three leading newspapers were the long-established (since 1803) *Charleston Daily Courier,* the *Charleston Mercury,* and the *Charleston Evening News.* The *Courier* and *Mercury* had the largest circulations, and theirs were South Carolina's most famous journalistic voices. While the more successful *Courier* featured a "mixture of news, business and cultural information and tried to steer a politically neutral course," the *Mercury,* owned by the family of Robert Goodwin Rhett Sr., "preached states' rights, nullification, and eventually secession."[75] While Lynch's activity appeared in all of these local newspapers, he refrained from engaging in their public discourse on these controversial matters.

Patrick Lynch as newly elected bishop of Charleston was a person of purpose and dignity. His views and actions were scrutinized and respected by most people throughout the local community. He had friends and supporters throughout the nation and, very importantly, within the ecclesiastical hierarchy of the American Catholic Church and in the Vatican itself. He was well positioned to play an important role in the most crucial decade in the relatively young life of his adopted city and the nation he had come to love. The decision to sever ties with the United States and to form the Confederate States was not easily made. He saw his role as full of well-intentioned service and yet fraught with much controversy. It would come to define the remainder of his life, that of his city, state, nation, and that of the American Catholic Church.

CHAPTER 4

Slaveholdings

Bishop Lynch did not spell out his views on slavery until late in the Civil War when he published his proslavery pamphlet in Europe. Nonetheless he stood out among the bishops of the South in that he was a slaveholder of some importance. The Archives of the Diocese of Charleston contains a wealth of correspondence and other sources about his slaves and how they lived.[1]

The bishop of Charleston was essentially in line with his fellow Catholic clergy and with the clergy of other Christian denominations in the South. In his actions he proved true to his publicly expressed convictions about how slavery was supposed to function. In Lynch's time the supreme authority of the Catholic Church had declared the forcible enslavement of human beings to be morally wrong. In 1839 Pope Gregory XVI published the apostolic constitution *In supremo apostolatus,* wherein he condemned both the act of enslavement and the international traffic in humanity.[2] Then, as later, Catholic theologians differed as to whether Gregory's teaching implied a call for general emancipation of people already in bondage.[3] At the time, leading American Catholic prelates interpreted the papal ban as applying to the transatlantic slave trade but not to what they termed domestic slavery, that is, the retention in servitude of the descendants of those originally enslaved. In 1840 Bishop John England set forth this distinction in a famous published series of letters to Secretary of State John Forsyth, defending domestic slavery as licit, even if unfortunate.[4] At the time, Bishop Francis Patrick Kenrick, the outstanding American Catholic theologian of his day, wrote in his 1841 manual of moral theology that servitude was permissible, advising that "nothing should be attempted against the laws nor anything be done or said that would make them bear their yoke unwillingly."[5] Antebellum American bishops chose not to publish any collective statement on the legitimacy of domestic slavery. Catholic slave owners in the South neither heard nor read any clear instruction from their hierarchy commanding or recommending general manumission, much less abolition.

Southern bishops, priests, religious communities, and laypersons were slaveholders.[6] Catholic laypersons acquired property in slaves, as did their Protestant and Jewish neighbors. Slaveholding was legal and protected by federal and state constitutions and statutes. Catholic Irish and Irish Americans in the South—who had memories of their mistreatment and depredation at the hands of Protestant landlords in Ireland—enthusiastically acquired slaves as an obvious way to elevate themselves in society. Those who had large numbers of slaves joined the South's social elite.[7]

Slaveholding by Catholic clergy and religious was by no means universal. Clearly many had qualms about black servitude, and some took deliberate steps to cease being slave owners. Slaveholding by Archbishop John Carroll of Baltimore and that by Jesuit Fathers in Maryland are well documented.[8] Two other male religious orders, the Vincentians and the Sulpicians, owned black slaves. Of the dozen communities of women religious in the Old South, all but two owned servants.[9] It is estimated that in 1769 the Catholic Church, taken as a whole, was the largest slaveholder in French Louisiana.[10] The missionary priest Father Stephen Theodore Badin, renowned as "The Apostle of Kentucky," relied on his personal black slaves to support and assist him in his ministry.[11] Archbishop Peter Richard Kenrick of St. Louis owned slaves. Bishop Benedict Joseph Flaget of Bardstown and Louisville purchased slaves for his diocese and bequeathed them to his successor, Martin John Spalding. Spalding also inherited servants from his father. Bishops Louis William DuBourg of New Orleans and Joseph Rosati of St. Louis bought blacks to work for St. Mary's Seminary in Missouri. For nearly thirty years the seminary bought, sold, traded, hired out, and worked African Americans. DuBourg had personal slaves, and Bishop John Mary (Jean Marie) Odin, as vicar apostolic of Texas, used black people from the seminary at his residence in Galveston. Black servants were also owned by Mount St. Mary's Seminary of Emmitsburg, Maryland.[12] The 1860 Census showed Archbishop Antoine (Anthony) Blanc of New Orleans and Bishop Auguste Marie Martin of Natchitoches with two slaves each.[13]

At the time of the Civil War, Bishop Lynch estimated that the Diocese of Charleston had a Catholic population of twenty thousand, of whom two thousand were slaves or free blacks—mostly slaves of Catholic masters.[14] Prominent Carolina Catholics were slave owners, including the first two bishops, John England and Ignatius Reynolds. Bishop England had a manservant named Castalio, a coachman and factotum who accompanied the prelate on his visitation of the diocese in 1831. In those days masters often gave their slaves names drawn from antiquity, and the servant's name was likely derived from Castalia, the mythological fountain of the Muses.[15] In 1835 Bishop England purchased a man named Joseph for the sum of $450 from Antonio della Torre of Charleston. On the bill of sale England declared: "I hold the within named slave Joseph, not as my own private and individual property but in trust for the ladies of the institution of Ursuline Nuns in this city [that is, Charleston]."[16] The 1840 Census did not show England with any slaves, though by law he could have emancipated Castalio only by an act of legislation. He wrote to the Propaganda in 1833 that he considered slavery "the greatest moral evil that can desolate any part of the civilized world."[17]

Bishop Reynolds owned a man named Thornton, described by Jeremiah O'Connell as "a colored [Protestant] preacher . . . quite a clever fellow [who] was the servant in waiting around the premises." Thornton eventually became a Catholic, and when he died he left his life savings to Bishop Reynolds for the cathedral building fund. Reynolds also inherited slaves from Father James Wallace's (d. 1851) estate, but, according to O'Connell, "the most valuable escaped to the Free Sates." Father O'Connell himself owned a slave he called "my man Joe" and reported with pride that Joe remained loyal to him after emancipation.[18]

Patrick Lynch was brought up in a slaveholding family. His close familiarity with the institution convinced him to regard it as workable, fundamental, and essential to Southern society and even as benign. According to Census records, the bishop's father, Conlaw Lynch, had two slaves in 1830 and seven from 1840 to 1860. Dr. John Lynch, the bishop's brother, owned three slaves in 1850 and twenty-eight in 1860. The third son, Francis Lynch, a Cheraw storekeeper and manufacturer of leather footwear, held ten slaves in 1850 and twenty-two in 1860 and purchased at least a dozen more during the war.[19] Two of Bishop Lynch's sisters married slave owners. The Lynches appear to have been benign masters by the lights of their day. The family correspondence included statements of concern for slaves' health, especially the sufferings of black children, and these expressions give evidence of real compassion, not merely economic self-interest.[20] The Lynch family members accepted servitude as part of the established social order. In 1850, when Dr. John Lynch was contemplating moving his family and medical practice from Cheraw to Columbia, he told Patrick that he thought he could manage for a year "by the hire of my negroes." John sold a slave in order to pay off a bond, and, when he did make the move, he evidently sold a young black woman in order to meet the first payment on his house. These matters he reported to his clerical brother with no apparent angst.[21]

The earliest reference found to slaveholding by Patrick Lynch dates from 1857, when, on payment of five dollars, he became the legal owner and trustee of one Catharine and her granddaughter Eliza—both slaves of Césarine Françoise Antoinette Barbot of Charleston (1800–1880), widow of François Barbot. The contract stipulated that the widow would "have the control of the said slaves and the use of their labour and services." In the event of her demise, Bishop Lynch would ensure that the slaves' earnings would go to her heirs. Apparently this arrangement was intended to protect Mrs. Barbot's rights to the slaves' earnings.[22] Shortly before the outbreak of war, Lynch was designated executor of the will of a

Charleston Catholic layman, who bequeathed two slaves to his wife.[23] The 1868 statement in a Munich Catholic journal that Lynch had "on the occasion of his priestly ordination, emancipated all the slaves inherited from his wealthy parents" is erroneous, since Lynch's parents were still living when he was ordained, and no corroborating evidence has been found to support his owning slaves at that time.[24]

Charleston city tax records show Bishop Lynch as the owner of eight slaves in 1858, eleven in 1859, and ten in 1860. The identities and duties of these people are not known, nor can it be said where in Charleston they lived.[25] The bishop was later to express his disapproval of masters allowing slaves they hired out to live at a distance from their owners' dwellings, because he thought such blacks were wont to become "idle and dissipated," a source of trouble for society.[26] Charleston's 1848 local census showed urban slaves typically crowded into quarters behind or adjacent to their masters' residences, but in later years it became

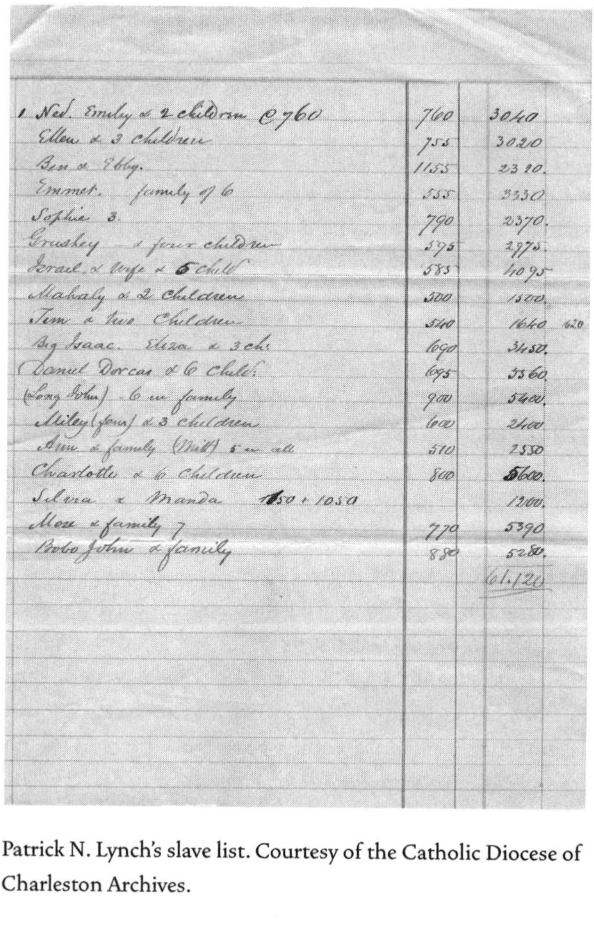

1 Ned. Emily & 2 children @ 760	760	3040	
Ellen & 3 children	755	3020	
Ben & Ebby.	1155	2310.	
Emmet. family of 6	555	3330	
Sophia 3.	790	2370.	
Grushey & four children	595	2975.	
Israel & Wife & 5 Child	585	4095	
Mahaly & 2 Children	500	1500.	
Tim & two Children	540	1640	1620
Big Isaac. Eliza & 3 ch:	690	3450.	
(Daniel Dorcas & 6 Child:	695	5560.	
(Long John) 6 in family	900	5400.	
Miley ([illegible]) & 3 children	600	2400	
Ann & family ([illegible]) 5 in all	510	2550	
Charlotte & 6 Children	800	5600.	
Silvia & Manda 150 + 1050		1200.	
Moze & family 7	770	5390.	
Bobo John & family	880	5280.	
		61.120	

Patrick N. Lynch's slave list. Courtesy of the Catholic Diocese of Charleston Archives.

common for servants to live in rented rooms or houses at a distance from their owners. On the eve of the war, about 15 percent of Charleston slaves lived away from their owners.[27]

Bishop Lynch acquired most of his slaves in 1861, several months before the outbreak of war, from the estate of William McKenna (d. 1859). A native of County Donegal, William McKenna immigrated to the United States around 1800, settled in Lancaster District, South Carolina, in 1803, and became a naturalized citizen in 1809. McKenna was successful in trade as a storeowner. He acquired a large plantation south of the village of Lancaster, along with much real estate in the vicinity. He served in the South Carolina Senate in 1828–1829, in addition to holding other public offices. He became the richest person in Lancaster District and the wealthiest Catholic in the Diocese of Charleston. It is said that he had studied for the priesthood in Ireland, and he was a fervent Catholic.[28] At the 1850 Census he owned 117 blacks, and their number later increased to around 180. Jeremiah O'Connell recorded that McKenna was solicitous of his servants' religion and insisted that all the children be baptized in the Catholic Church. "All were taught the catechism and their prayers on Sundays."[29]

At his death, in 1859, McKenna left an estate worth more than $250,000 and bequeathed most of it to the bishop of Charleston for a boys' orphanage, as a donation to the Sisters of Our Lady of Mercy, and for other purposes of the Church.[30] McKenna was survived by his third wife, Ellen Quigley McKenna, whom he wed in 1852, and by a daughter, Ann, borne by his first wife. Ann was married to John F. G. Mittag. To his family McKenna left comparatively small legacies, so they went to court and succeeded in breaking the will.[31] The family charged that Catholic clergy had exerted undue influence on the dying man, but the bishop and his priests denied this. As practicing Catholics, however, the family members were willing to compromise. By a settlement with the bishop, the family took five-eighths of the estate, the diocese three-eighths.[32] In his will William McKenna also provided for lifelong care of his superannuated slaves and left a few of his blacks to family members, but he directed that most of the slaves be sold, along with the bulk of his land. Much of the estate was put up at auction in Lancaster on January 21, 1861. The sale included the two-thousand-acre Malta Plantation, with its residence, called Rock House, and extensive slave quarters, numerous other properties, and nearly all the slaves. Arrangements were handled by the Charleston firm of Thomas Ryan and Son. Thomas Ryan was an Irish-born broker, auctioneer, slave trader, civic leader, and prominent cathedral parishioner. Ryan's Mart, on Chalmers Street in Charleston, was an important center of the slave trade.[33]

South Carolina law permitted the breaking up of slave families, even the sale of children separately from their parents. Bishop Lynch believed in preserving slave marriages and families, and he conceived a plan with dual purpose. He aimed to secure the financial interests of the Church that the McKenna legacy represented, while at the same time achieving "humane & religious purposes": the protection of black Catholic families. The Archives of the Diocese of Charleston preserves a "List of Negroes," drawn up by Daniel J. Quigley, brother of the Widow McKenna and a future priest of the diocese. This list gives the names and ages of the black parents and children, with indications of those baptized (mostly children) and remarks such as "Practical [that is, practicing Catholic]" or "made first confession." Another list records the Catholic family groups, with prices totaling $61,120—the equivalent of more than $1 million today. Also extant is the auctioneer's printed *Catalogue of Negro Slaves,* listing people in family groups, with ages and occupations. The copy of the *Catalogue* in the Archives of the Diocese of Charleston has the handwritten notation "B" in the margin beside the names of those whom the Bishop acquired—"B" perhaps standing for "baptized" or "bought."[34]

In the antebellum South, purchasers of slaves often made private arrangements with the auctioneer prior to the public sale. Evidently Thomas Ryan accommodated Bishop Lynch, whom he knew well.[35] The prelate acquired Malta Plantation and some eighty-five of the McKenna slaves, bringing the total number of blacks under his control to about ninety-five.[36] Since the will specified that McKenna's slaves be sold, it appears that the bishop accepted people as part of the inheritance. Whose slaves were they? Prewar Provincial and Plenary Councils of Baltimore, where American Catholic prelates met to decide Church policies, had issued decrees to strengthen the practice of vesting ecclesiastical property in the hands of bishops and to provide for its transfer to their successors. In South Carolina much Church property was vested in the bishop's name. Bishops also owned personal property and were responsible for distinguishing between the two, in particular so that ownership would pass on smoothly to their successors.[37] As Jay Dolan observed, "Every major council [from 1829 on] . . . not only discussed this issue, but progressively strengthened the hierarchy's position, so that by the Third Plenary Baltimore Council, in 1884, the bishops' authority in this area was absolute."[38]

The evidence indicates that the slaves Lynch acquired in 1861 were diocesan property. William McKenna had left a great legacy to the bishop of Charleston for the use of the Church, and Patrick Lynch was scrupulous about his obligations. In January 1861 he offered the Sisters of Our Lady of Mercy the option of receiving their portion of the inheritance in the form of slaves. But that Sisters preferred "that the share of the property . . . shall be paid in cash, as there was great need of a building being immediately put up for the convenience and comfort of the invalid Sisters, As well as those in good health."[39]

Even though the slaves were Church property, it was Bishop Lynch who determined their duties and the conditions in which they lived. In the correspondence they were always referred to as his slaves or his people. Bishop Lynch articulated his views about the institution of slavery in the pamphlet he published in Europe in 1864–1865.[40] In this chapter the authors refer to Lynch's pamphlet as a reflection of the principles he thought applied to the institution. For the management of his slaves, the bishop called on members of his family and friends for assistance. Initially he divided the McKenna slaves into groups that he set to work on plantations in different parts of South Carolina, namely the Lancaster, Lexington, and Edgefield Districts. In Lexington the bishop controlled a prosperous 650-acre plantation left to the diocese by Father James Wallace, located in the rich Dutch Fork area, directly across the Broad River from Columbia.[41]

The bishop called on his brother John, now a prominent physician, to serve as his agent to administer the slaves in the Columbia area. The brothers were close and corresponded frequently. John Lynch and his family resided in downtown Columbia. Also in the capital lived their sister Ellen Lynch, known in religion as Mother Baptista, OSU, superior of the Ursuline Convent and Girls' Academy and sibling, friend, confidante, and adviser to her brothers. The bishop assigned one of his slaves—Isaac by name—to work for the Ursuline Sisters, under Mother Baptista's command.[42] John Lynch hired a man named Adam Buff to oversee the Lexington property and took steps to make the Wallace land a working farm. Buff was about forty-eight years old, with a wife and eight children. He had a good reputation and experience in farming.[43]

To manage Malta Plantation the prelate secured the services of his attorney and friend Claudian Bird Northrop, a native Charlestonian of prominent family, who had served in the state legislature, where he impressed colleagues with his oratorical skill. Originally a member of St. Philip's Episcopal Congregation, he was a convert to Catholicism and had been baptized a Catholic by Father Timothy Bermingham in 1844. Claudian Northrop had two sons, Claudian Jr. and Harry P. Northrop, who were to become priests of the diocese, Harry eventually succeeding Lynch as bishop. In June 1861 Claudian's brother Lucius Bellinger Northrop (1811–1894) was appointed by Jefferson Davis to serve as Confederate Commissary General, in which post he remained until1865. The brothers were not close. Both had become involved in a scheme to establish an Irish colony in Georgia. When the operation failed, Lucius blamed Claudian for the fact that his name had been used in promotional materials, even though he had divested himself of the properties. He also claimed that Claudian owed him money. Like Claudian, Lucius was a convert to Catholicism. Both men admired Bishop Lynch. Claudian Northrop moved from Charleston to Lancaster with his second wife, Mary Melissa Pannell Northrop, his younger children, and some twenty-four of his own family slaves. The Northrops took up residence in Rock House. The Lancaster crops of 1860 and 1861 were good, as were the economic prospects for upstate South Carolina.

From correspondence and other sources, both John Lynch and Claudian Northrop appear to have been honest, faithful, courageous, and kindly men, solicitous of the slaves' welfare. Both were devout Catholics. At the outbreak of the Civil War they were optimistic about the Confederacy. Northrop published patriotic verse and essays and was confident of the slaves' loyalty to their owners, predicting that they would become "our pioneers, our scouts, our spies. . . . They depend on their master, and will be as treacherous to his enemies, as they are faithful to him."[44]

In June 1861 the bishop transferred about thirty McKenna slaves to the South Carolina midlands. From then on, Malta had to support nearly ninety souls, counting Northrop's and Lynch's slaves and the Northrop family.[45] Lancaster was about 60 miles from Columbia, 160 from Charleston. It was 40 miles from the nearest railroad, and the mail came only twice a week.[46] Northrop's own servants were urban blacks with no experience in farm work, and William McKenna's nephew, the Irish-born Patrick McKenna—who had managed Malta before the attorney's arrival—complained that this transfer of slaves would result in loss of forty acres of corn and thirty acres of cotton. For his part Northrop thought Patrick had not run the plantation efficiently and believed that he could do much better.[47] Northrop began his Lancaster stewardship by buying horses, mules, corn, and meat and by hiring a carpenter to repair Rock House.[48] He also opened a law office in the town of Lancaster. Lancaster District was described by a contemporary as a beautiful area "stretching away as it does for miles in gentle undulations, and dotted with low pine-trees, which seem like spots of green upon a carpet of rich red and gold. . . . Wheat, corn, oats, cotton, and fruits grow in abundance."[49] On the eve of the war Daniel Quigley told Bishop Lynch that "the seasons here are most delightful—crops never looked better nor promissed [*sic*] a more abundant yield—Farmers are kept busy, but they think such prospects reward them well for their extra labor."[50]

Lynch put seventeen of the McKenna people to work on Clearwater Plantation in Edgefield District, the rest on the Wallace farm in Lexington. Clearwater was the property of Dr. John Harwood Burt, physician, planter, and Catholic convert. When Dr. Burt died, later that year, his estate was broken up and sold, so the bishop's slaves were transferred to Lexington. In 1862 the bishop purchased 130.5 acres of land in Richland District, about three miles from the center of Columbia, from Colonel Ellison Summerfield Keitt, a wealthy Catholic convert and a Confederate military leader. The prelate intended eventually to use the place, called Valle Crucis (the Vale of the Cross), for a new Ursuline convent and school, among other things, but for the present he decided to make it a working farm. Some of the Lexington slaves went there to work in 1862; then, at the beginning of 1864, all the midlands people were transferred there, when the Dutch

Fork overseer quit.[51] For simplicity's sake references in this chapter will be to only two locations: Columbia or the midlands and Lancaster or Malta Plantation.

Throughout the war Lynch paid Charleston city taxes on slaves: eleven in 1862, nine in 1863, eleven in 1864. In February 1863 he purchased one Flora, age forty-two, for $740 from the Charleston firm of Wilbur and Son, Auctioneers. The bishop's motive for buying Flora is unknown, as she was not certified as being of sound health.[52] In his wartime treatise on slavery, the bishop—like many other Southern clergy—described the institution as a system of mutual obligations between master and servant.[53] In keeping with traditional Catholic teaching, he emphasized the inescapable moral obligations of the slave owner toward the slave: "The owner is bound . . . to give to the slaves a reasonable support according to his conditions from infancy to death."[54]

On his instructions the bishop's lands produced no cotton after 1861 but only food crops. As the war dragged on, farm life in much of the South became mainly a matter of growing foodstuffs for the Confederate armies and sustaining those who lived on the land, with little thought of profit, at least for the duration. Lancaster District was cotton country, and many growers there continued to plant cash crops until well into the war, but Claudian Northrop adhered to the bishop's command. Despite the early good prospects, Lancaster's economic conditions soured as the war went on. Northrop organized Malta to make it as self-sufficient as possible. Mrs. Northrop planned and supervised the work of the plantation women to make clothes and perform other chores. The experience of Malta's mistress and female slaves was typical of the lives of many South Carolina women during the war.[55]

In his pamphlet the bishop described the task system as the usual way of organizing slaves' work on plantations. In particular he emphasized that, when slaves had completed their assigned tasks, the rest of the day was theirs to use for cultivating their own patches of land or however else they liked. The task system was typical of the Carolina lowcountry, whereas the gang labor system or a modification of the task system prevailed on upcountry plantations. From available evidence it is not possible to say precisely how work was organized on the bishop's lands, but his emphasis on the task system suggests that some version of it was employed.[56] As the bishop described it, "each slave family lives in a small house of suitable size, and ordinarily has a small plot of ground to serve as a garden. . . . This they cultivate as they please, and its produce is their own. They also raise poultry, and very generally a few hogs. . . . They may either consume [the agricultural products] . . . as luxuries or sell them in order to purchase whatever else they please." Clearly the bishop's people enjoyed a customary measure of free time. They definitely acquired money, and some of it probably came from working their own plots.[57]

Bishop Lynch's methods as slave owner were evident in examples from the areas of religion, medicine, marriage and sexual mores, discipline and impressments. The slaves' religion was of great importance to him. He held that "in the matter of Religion, of morality, and in a measure, his family relations does [the slave] hold himself free." [58] Blacks, he said, were free to join any church they liked or to be unchurched. The prelate disparaged black churches: "The usual characteristics of a religious negro are spiritual pride, and very often, hypocrisy." And yet, he wrote, "although they are very ignorant of the doctrines of Christianity, still they believe in the Divinity of our Saviour, and in the Redemption." "The masters interfere very little with the religion of their slaves, who on Sundays flock to whichever of the country churches they prefer, or stay at home, or visit each other.... Catholic owners, while they can only offer instruction and admonition to grown negroes, deem themselves bound at least in charity, to insist on all the infants being baptized; and take care that they are instructed in the catechism, and if possible, prepared for their first communion."[59]

The bishop's slaves in the Columbia area could easily attend St. Peter's Church. Slaves on Clearwater Plantation were close to St. Mary's Church, Edgefield, and one of the infants was christened there.[60] Isaac received religious instruction from the Ursulines in Columbia and sought the Bishop's permission to bring his children to the Sisters for lessons.[61] Comparatively remote Malta Plantation was visited only every three or four months by a priest from Columbia, yet some of the black slaves were regular communicants. Maintaining the Catholic faith was difficult in the upstate, causing Mother Baptista to lament the danger to slaves' Catholicism posed by their having to work under Protestant overseers.[62] The bishop maintained that the universal plantation practice was to give servants a half-day's leisure on Saturday, "to prepare for Sunday, which was always a day of entire rest. So sacredly is this Holy Day guaranteed to them that I have never known an occasion however pressing the season, in which it was infringed on plantations."[63] Sources give no evidence that the slaves' Sabbath was not strictly respected on the bishop's plantations.

Bishop Lynch taught that a master was obliged to provide lifelong health care to his bondsmen, whose "necessities in sickness and old age are all provided for." Slaves, he said, were given ample food, clothing, and shelter. "There is also a Physician, employed to attend the negroes regularly when ill," and "an actual hospital on the larger plantations."[64] The prelate's concern for his people's health was evident in his agents' reports, which often expressed sadness over the death or suffering of a slave and joy at a medical recovery or a healthy new baby. The Columbia blacks benefited from the frequent personal attentions of Dr. John Lynch, who had become one of South Carolina's foremost physicians.[65] In Lancaster, however, the general rural Southern custom prevailed whereby a doctor was called only after home remedies had failed.[66] Claudian Northrop expressed joy at the apparent cure of Margaret, who suffered from consumption and was treated by a local physician, and sorrow at her death. When Margaret's sister, Ellen, fell ill and had "not had her courses [that is, menstruated] for six months," the doctor was summoned to her sickbed.[67] Northrop complained of the exorbitant fees and ineffectiveness of local medical practitioners, preferring to administer home remedies like castor oil—he once asked the bishop to send up a gallon from Charleston—and the English purgative Morison's pills. But, according to Northrop, Malta slaves preferred to receive the care of a physician.[68] Poor diet and lack of adequate clothing, especially shoes, contributed to slaves' sicknesses. Shortages of wool and shoe leather caused misery all over the South, including on the bishop's lands. Northrop was forced to cut up the carpets for coats and later to sell off family silver in order to pay for "yarn, &c. &c." for winter clothing.[69]

Although Southern state laws did not recognize slave marriages, Bishop Lynch, in keeping with Catholic teaching and in agreement with the beliefs of leading Southern clergy, Catholic and Protestant, asserted that Catholic slaveholders were bound to promote and protect blacks' marital unions and families. Catholic owners, he said, "recognize and are guided by the teaching of the Church, and hold it a sin to separate a man and wife legitimately [that is, in the eyes of the Church] married." When circumstances necessitated the sale of slaves, he said, "the negroes are customarily sold in families, consisting of the father mother and young children. . . . To separate husband and wife, or to separate young children from their mother, would be to outrage humanity, and to outrage the public sense of what is right and proper."[70]

On the plantations, said Lynch, masters "strive as best they can to render the marriage unions of the negroes permanent," often going so far as to purchase spouses belonging to other masters. In fact, slave owners generally respected slave marriages, and many black families were strong.[71] Bishop Lynch's male slaves with wives on other plantations routinely received weekend passes to visit their spouses. Conversely, men belonging to other owners made conjugal visits to his lands. Such was the case of Thompson, husband of the Malta slave Ellen. For a time, however, Northrop forbade Thompson access to the plantation, because of what he termed an "insolent and conceited" attitude; he later relented because of Ellen's poor health and the birth of a new baby girl.[72]

Still, the bishop found the whole question of black servant marriages "very perplexing," because blacks had "very loose ideas on the subject, and very little regard for the sanctity of marriage."[73] American slaveholders were wont to interfere in the personal lives of their bondsmen in the areas of marriage and the family, and Bishop Lynch did so when he deemed it appropriate. A charge of rape made in Lancaster by the teenage fieldworker Mandy against a young man named Aleck was not accepted as proved. Northrop investigated the matter and concluded that, while there may have been "some lewdness," no actual rape had taken place. On the other hand, Northrop and the bishop shared consternation over the scandalous behavior of Milly, an unwed field hand in her twenties—"perhaps the finest woman on the place," said Northrop—who was the "concubine" of Izrael, a married shoemaker and carpenter. In 1861 Milly already had three children by him and was pregnant with her fourth.[74] Still more worrisome to the bishop were the marital problems of the gifted blacksmith Ned and his wife, a field hand named Charlotte. Charlotte complained of beatings and of Ned's attentions to Mahaly, a single twenty-year-old field hand with two babies. When Ned and Charlotte separated, Ned declared that Mahaly was his new wife, and Charlotte took up with Charley, a blind man. Bishop Lynch refused to tolerate these irregularities and, in January 1863, transferred from Malta to the midlands Ned, Charlotte, and their two children, along with Milly and her offspring by Izrael. What the slaves thought of these actions went unrecorded.[75]

Bishop Lynch described plantation discipline as "vigilant and mild." He admitted that some men in all societies used their power to wreak cruelty on those under them. "But that is the fault of human nature, not of the system of Slavery." Visitors to the South, he claimed, "wonder at the patience with which the owners pass over the mistakes and failures of duty committed by negro servants." Cases of real cruelty were "rare, and punishable by law." And yet he defended flogging as "the usual punishment inflicted on the negro." In the case of an insubordinate or especially vicious slave, it was appropriate to sell the person so as not to "demoralize the other negroes. . . . If he has a family, this punishment of exile is not inflicted until other means have been tried in vain, and not unless the evil is insupportable, and the penalty necessary."[76]

As was often the case on Southern plantations in the uncertain wartime environment, the bishop's agents employed a combination of coercion, persuasion, and kindness in order to keep control of the slaves. Northrop said that slave management was a matter of leadership and good example, along with occasional disciplinary action.[77] One applicant for an overseer's position in Columbia—an Irish-born Catholic named Bresnahan—was rejected for fear that the man "might not take a sufficient control over the negroes if it became necessary to use harsh means."[78]

"For grievous offenses against society," said the bishop, "the negro is answerable to, and is judged by the tribunals of the country, but for neglect of work, pilfering from his fellow slaves, or minor offences, his master is his judge."[79] As the war dragged on and economic conditions worsened, slaves were sometimes driven to acts of defiance. On one occasion the dearth of meat in their diet led the Lancaster people to butcher and consume a heifer. The leaders in this episode were the brightest and most talented men: the blacksmith Ned, the wagoner Mose, and Izrael, the carpenter and cobbler. Because these craftsmen were respected and essential for running Malta Plantation, the bishop told Northrop to reprove them but not to punish them.[80]

When the Columbia field hand Emmett ran afoul of the law and was jailed for some transgression, Bishop Lynch showed leniency and took steps to bail him out. But the man escaped, and, when he later turned up on the plantation, the prelate decided to hire him out. When Emmett then refused "to be *hired* quietly," the bishop ordered that he be sold, along with his wife and five young children, for the sake of good order. Even so, the penalty was postponed until the recovery of one of the children, sick with measles and being treated by Dr. John Lynch.[81] Another crisis erupted in the midlands when the overseer Buff strapped the thirteen-year-old son of two field workers, Bobo John and Nelly, for idleness. Nelly sprang to her child's defense, attacking the overseer with a hoe—an act typical of many slave women across the South. The overseer threatened to quit unless the bishop sold Nelly and her entire family, and he apparently did so.[82]

Masters and slaves were as one in their resentment of government impressment of blacks for war work. Slaveholders lamented the loss of labor, complaining that the impressed men were neither properly fed nor cared for. Opposition was particularly strong among slave owners in Lancaster District. African Americans dreaded separation from loved ones and the many hardships impressment imposed on their families.[83] On one occasion Northrop wrote the bishop that Mose's wife Maria "has been pining for her husband; and when you consider that her family consists of two girls and three little children besides you will see how burdened she must be without her husband."[84]

In 1862 and again in 1863, the bishop had to send two of his Lancaster men to work on fortifications, and he was dissatisfied with the poor treatment they received. The Malta teenage plowboy William, while laboring for two months on the breastworks at Bee's Ferry, on the Ashley River above Charleston, came down with "chills & fever" and returned to Lancaster too sick to work. When the authorities requisitioned the Columbia wagoner Daniel for labor on the coastal defenses, the overseer Buff protested that the man was "the only road hand" he had, and John Lynch told his brother that Daniel "should be left at the farm. Otherwise they cannot do much." The prelate decided that Daniel was indeed too valuable, so he sent one of his Charleston slaves as a substitute. On another occasion the bishop paid a $117 commutation fee for not sending men.[85]

When in 1864 Bishop Lynch accepted appointment as Confederate Commissioner to the Holy See, he traveled to Rome and did not see South Carolina again until the end of 1865. Few letters from home reached him during his European sojourn, and information about his slaves is sparse from the spring of 1864 until the end of the war. Jeremiah O'Connell, writing in the late 1870s, stated that the prelate had "sold them to a Catholic family," and this may tell part of the story.[86] But it seems likely that most of the slaves stayed on the bishop's lands until their liberation. The bishop paid municipal taxes on his Charleston slaves in 1864, and by law these were due on the first of June. Many Charleston blacks remained in bondage until the city fell to Union forces.[87]

Columbia and Charleston fell to the Union armies in February 1865. In General Sherman's wake, Columbia burned. (After Sherman departed Columbia, his cavalry under General Hugh Judson Kilpatrick [1836–1881] occupied Lancaster at the close of February.) "Bummers" (foragers) traveling in advance of Kilpatrick seized Malta Plantation, burned Rock House, and demanded money and valuables from Claudian Northrop. When he refused, they hanged him before the eyes of his stricken wife.[88] The bummers earned opprobrium from whites for their abusive behavior.[89] Kilpatrick occupied Lancaster for several days. His men were resented by whites for their rude manners and relentless search for hidden valuables.[90] Sherman's army occupied Cheraw, where the bishop's parents and family lived. Confederate forces evacuated Cheraw on March 4, and Sherman took the town on the seventh. Cheraw offered much plunder in the form of food, small arms, gunpowder, Confederate cannons, and other supplies, but few houses were destroyed, so the town came off relatively unscathed.[91] All of Conlaw and Eleanor Lynch's slaves chose to remain with them, but, as Anna Lynch informed her Carmelite sibling in Baltimore, Sister Antonia of the Purification, "as they are free now we may not keep all in our employment."[92] On the other hand, Francis Lynch's Cheraw tanneries were burned by the Yankees, and "since the freedmen walked off with themselves, Francis will concentrate his labors & work only one yard." Mother Baptista praised her brother's cheerfulness, observing, "If Providence has sent adversity to the South, He has certainly given it a beautiful spirit of cheerful submission to His holy will."[93] From Cheraw the Union army proceeded into North Carolina, occupying Fayetteville on March 1. At Goldsboro troops marching from New Bern and Wilmington joined Sherman. Fayetteville was the site of St. Patrick's Church. The number of North Carolina Catholics was small, estimated at about six hundred at the start of the war.[94]

What happened to the bishop's slaves? In Columbia for nearly a year after emancipation two of the black families stayed on with the Ursulines, before they left to work new lands that they rented.[95] Mary Melissa Northrop tried to run Malta for a time with the freedpersons who stayed on there, but she had little cash, conditions in Lancaster were bad, and there was uncertainty about who was the legal owner of Malta. The land proved to be the bishop's, and Mrs. Northrop eventually moved away.[96] A nagging question involved provisions included by William McKenna in his will to benefit elderly African Americans. To every slave of his estate who reached the age of sixty-five, McKenna promised an annuity of twenty-five dollars. As time passed, an increasing number of aged freedpersons—"very much in need," as Mrs. Northrop put it—claimed the annuities. But Bishop Lynch declined responsibility for them, and in 1879 the Lancaster County Court of Common Pleas decreed that bequests made to slaves were null and void under an 1841 South Carolina statute.[97] Dozens of the former slaves and their families, bearing the surnames McKenna or McKinney, lived on for decades in Lancaster and neighboring York Counties, and some of these were practicing Catholics as late as 1919. The area that had been Malta Plantation became known as Catholic Grove.[98]

Bishop Lynch's slaveholding can be viewed from several angles. The prevailing American Catholic opinion before the Civil War was that slavery was a licit, even if not desirable, practice. During the war all Southern bishops were loyal to the Confederacy. The bishop of Charleston was in line with fellow members of the Catholic hierarchy in his defense of slavery, although he went further than they in his acquisition of a significant number of slaves. He displayed ingenuity in devising a plan that combined practical and humanitarian motifs: protecting the Church's considerable financial interest, while safeguarding the unity of black Catholic families. William McKenna's will dictated that, with few exceptions, all his slaves were to be sold, so the bishop's options were to take the Church's portion of the estate in the form of real and chattel property, to take it in cash, or a combination of the two. He opted to accept a large part of the legacy in the form of slaves. Had he not done so, the families might well have been broken up and sold, and some would most likely have fallen into the hands of owners less benign than the bishop. By the late antebellum period South Carolina laws severely restricted manumission. One may well ask what would have befallen these people had Bishop Lynch not acquired them. Seen in retrospect, the bishop's large investment in slave property was doomed, but in the heady days that followed secession, most white South Carolinians were confident of achieving independence and of ensuring the continuation of servitude.

In the management of his slaves the bishop tried to be true to his publicly expressed principles. Through his agents he tried to care for the black bondsmen in a manner that he regarded as generous and just. During the harsh winter of 1862–1863, Dr. John Lynch and Mother Baptista both advised their clerical brother to sell those slaves who could not practicably be fed and clothed—John even suggesting they might fetch a profit—but the bishop decided to keep and care for all.[99] Leaving aside the Charleston slaves, of whom so little is known, a clear financial motive was evident only in his 1862 acquisition of the field hand Mahaly and her two small children as surety for payment of a debt owed him by Patrick McKenna.[100]

The bishop made strenuous efforts to provide for his slaves' material welfare, and the fact that some of the people stayed on after emancipation and remained in the Catholic faith suggested that their situation had not been altogether intolerable. In his methods of management and discipline he was a benign slave owner, as these things went. These observations are meant not to excuse Lynch but rather to put his actions into perspective. Lynch was fairly typical of a nineteenth-century Irish Catholic slave owner in the South. And, as research shows, he was not atypical among high-ranking religious officials below the Mason-Dixon line with regard to his views on slavery and his practices as a slave owner—be he Catholic, Protestant, or Jewish. There were, of course, exceptions to the rule. Bishop Patrick N. Lynch was not one of them.

CHAPTER 5

The War

Secession

In 1860 the sectional crisis came to a head. Charleston enjoyed one of its last days of peace and joy on March 17, when the Hibernian Society staged a grand banquet and celebration to honor St. Patrick. The guest of honor and speaker was Archbishop John Hughes of New York, the country's preeminent Catholic churchman. Bishop Lynch was his host and accompanied the archbishop on the occasion.[1]

James Corcoran, editor of the *Miscellany,* became an unabashed secessionist, while Lynch chose to maintain a certain distance in his public statements. In April 1860 the national Democratic Party held its disastrous nominating convention in Charleston. Tumultuous sessions took place in the South Carolina Institute Hall on Meeting Street, just three blocks from Lynch's episcopal residence. Hibernian Hall, where Hughes had spoken just weeks before and was a half block closer, was used as "the dormitory of the delegates supporting Senator Stephen A. Douglas of Illinois," while delegates from other factions stayed at the nearby Mills House and the Charleston Hotel.[2]

In the months preceding secession and war, Catholic bishops North and South made public expressions of desire and prayers for peace and distress at the breakup of the Union. Catholic newspapers diverged on the question of which side was right. In the *Miscellany* Corcoran moved to the secessionist position. Commenting on Lincoln's election, he expostulated

> Long years of menace, insult, outrage and unconstitutional aggression have been, at last brought to a close by an event—the election of a Black Republican. . . . There are certain political, as well as social evils, which it is wiser to obviate beforehand than to wait hopelessly in search of their remedy. . . . The evil day has come upon us, sooner than we would have wished, in order that, with free counsel and untrammeled hands, we may deliberate

The Reverend James Corcoran (1820–1889) traveled with Lynch in 1834 to study for the priesthood in Rome. Theologian, editor, and Orientalist, he edited the *Miscellany* for Bishop Lynch and was responsible for its fiery secessionist positions. Courtesy of Catholic Diocese of Charleston Archive.

> upon and work out our future destiny. The calm, determined attitude of our people, the disinterested devotion of these Citizens . . . the sympathy of our Sister commonwealths, the Sovereign States of the South—all are indications that the crisis will leave untouched the honour and happiness of the South.[3]

Following Lincoln's election, pro-Union sentiment in South Carolina collapsed. The prevailing view among the white population was that secession was inevitable and necessary.[4] In Charleston itself, the leading newspapers whipped up the fury of secessionist frenzy.[5] The *Miscellany* kept pace with the Palmetto State's movement toward the breach. In its December 8 issue Corcoran declared: "It needs but little knowledge of our history to discover, whether it was the men, who revere state Sovereignty, or their enemies, that have been pursuing for years an insidious course of aggression upon that constitution, to which these commonwealths have bound themselves as contracting parties."[6] The state's Secession Convention gathered first in Columbia, then moved to Charleston.

On December 20 the delegates assembled in the hall of the St. Andrew's Society on Broad Street, next door to the bishop's residence. There they unanimously adopted the Ordinance of Secession. In the evening they marched through packed streets four blocks to the Institute Hall, where they signed the document, to which South Carolina's historic great seal—dating to the time of the American Revolution—was appended. There ensued an explosion of popular fervor. Church bells pealed, and cannons fired in celebration.[7]

The *Miscellany* welcomed the break with the Union. In its issue of December 22 Corcoran proclaimed: "After years of patient endurance, of energetic yet friendly protest and remonstrance. South Carolina, at last, in solemn convention of her people, Resumed the portion of her sovereignty which she surrendered in 1789; and now stands before the world a free independent Sovereign State. She has taken this noble attitude, in defiance of hostile threats that breathed coercion; in spite of treacherous warnings that, assuming a friendly tone, whispered delay."[8] A week later the newspaper came out as the *Catholic Miscellany*. The editor stated: "All we could do for the present, was to expunge those two obnoxious words, which being henceforth without truth or meaning, would ill become the title of a paper, that, apart from all motives of patriotism, professes to be an advocate of the Truth."[9] Beginning with the issue of January 5, 1861, the paper's nameplate bore the title *Charleston Catholic Miscellany*—which it was called until its demise.

It seems inconceivable that Corcoran would have made these changes without the approval of the bishop, who was the newspaper's publisher.[10] Yet on January 6, 1861 Lynch drafted a letter to Archbishop Hughes in which he asserted, "Dr. Corcoran writes as he pleases. I cannot say that his Editorials are sometimes not to my taste. But he must write without restraint if he would write well." Although Lynch said he disliked some of Corcoran's recent references to political matters—without specifying what these were—"he has said nothing 'contra fidem et mores.'" The bishop went on to observe: "If we are not now in a state of war we are very like it and very near it." In the Secession Convention he said that many who wanted secession nevertheless "wished so to direct things that a conflict could be avoided, and all matters be settled by negotiation." Perhaps peace could be secured by an agreement to let the South's institutions alone. If the rupture should be permanent, however, "Let the Union be broken,—we at the South will suffer to some extent. But the North will have to drain the cup, of which they have but taken a sip as yet." "I do not claim to be a Union man myself," he added, "yet I would regret to see the Government, after a glorious, though brief ascent, burst like a rocket, and leave only burnt & noise some [i.e., noisome] fragments. I fear, too, future civil war strifes, and miseries,"[11] As to his differences with Corcoran, it is more likely that Lynch was dissembling. Lynch was to argue, after the war, that he had not been a promoter of secession. "I took no part whatever in that movement. Standing aloof from politics, and not even having voted for years, I did not feel called on to judge the political questions involved."[12]

The Lynch family shared in the excitement of the time. From Columbia Dr. John Lynch wrote the bishop on November 16: "Political excitement is at its highest, if *they* can keep it at what is till after the Convention, then the Union will be dissolved.... We have large meetings every night and speeches."[13] In the wake of secession, Francis Lynch, tanner and boot maker, wrote the governor of South Carolina in hopes of winning a contract to supply footgear to the state. As it happened, the state did not take up Francis Lynch's offer right away, causing criticism of the governor, since Lynch's shoes and boots were highly regarded.[14]

Events followed a different course in the northern part of the diocese. In North Carolina the sentiment for immediate secession was not as strong as in South Carolina, and there were in fact many Unionists and others who preferred caution.[15] In early 1861 Lynch informed Archbishop Kenrick of Baltimore that he favored splitting off North Carolina as a separate Diocese of Wilmington.[16] North Carolina public opinion did not turn decisively in favor of secession until April with the firing on Fort Sumter. North Carolina seceded in May 1861, making the entire Diocese of Charleston part of the Confederacy.

Patrick Lynch, a Southern aristocrat and member of a slave-owning family, shared feelings of loyalty to his class and his native state. Lynch's learned Charleston friends were nearly all proponents of secession at the end.

The Roman Question

For American bishops as far as the Catholic Church worldwide, the year 1860 was a time of crisis. In Italy the Kingdom of Piedmont-Sardinia and the revolutionary army led by Giuseppe Garibaldi combined force to unite the great part of the territory of Italy, which was proclaimed a kingdom that year under King Victor Emmanuel II of the House of Savoy. Because of Pope Pius IX's firm opposition to unification and the geographic location of the Papal States across the Italian peninsula, most of the papal territory was occupied. The lands except for Rome and its surrounding region of Lazio (Latium) were incorporated into the newly proclaimed kingdom. To most American Catholics this was a disaster, and the event won great sympathy for the beleaguered pope. The Roman-trained Lynch felt especially aggrieved, and he launched a campaign to raise money for the pope's support. The equivalent of 11,000 francs (more than $2,000) was raised in the Carolinas, and Father Timothy Bermingham carried the donation to Pius. While some Southern secessionists identified with Italian patriots and the Risorgimento, Lynch rejected the comparison. Corcoran, writing in the *Miscellany,* denied that the Southern cause was anything like that of the Garibaldian and Sardinian "brigands" who invaded and despoiled the sovereignty of the Holy Father.[17] Bermingham reported that when he had his audience with Pius, the pontiff held up the money high "with an exclamation of joy, gave special blessings to Bishop Lynch, the clergy, religious and faithful of Charleston," and invited Bermingham to join him in saying the *Angelus.*[18]

Outbreak of War

Following South Carolina's secession, Major Robert Anderson, commander of the federal troops around Charleston, moved to garrison Castle Pinckney, a fortified island in the harbor less than a mile from downtown Charleston. On December 26 he moved his main forces from Fort Moultrie on Sullivan's Island to Fort Sumter, at the mouth of the harbor. These actions infuriated the secessionists. The first federal military post to be captured and occupied by secessionists was Castle Pinckney, which, along with Fort Moultrie and the federal arsenal in the city, was guarded by only a dozen troops. These points were seized by South Carolina troops on December 30. The brand-new South Carolina national flag, a white palmetto tree and crescent on a blue field, flew over these facilities. The Reverend Anthony Toomer Porter (1828–1902), an Episcopal priest and pastor of the Church of the Holy Communion, preached to the troops on Castle Pinckney shortly after its seizure. Some of the occupying force were Catholics of the Meagher Guards, part of the Charleston Rifle Battalion. On January 1, 1861, the Feast of the Circumcision and a holy day of obligation, Bishop Lynch visited Castle Pinckney, celebrated Mass for the Guards, and "preached a sermon suitable to the occasion."[19]

Archbishop Kenrick of Baltimore was greatly upset by the act of secession, which risked splitting his ecclesiastical province. He was on record as having supported the licitness of domestic slavery. In January 1861 he wrote to Lynch, asking if the Charleston suffragan would favor a meeting of all the bishops of the Baltimore Province and suggesting that they issue "a joint statement on the subject of slavery, which would distinguish between the lawful and illegal aspects."[20] Lynch replied in favor of a provincial council, since "the Church should be seen to stand firm and in no wise disturbed." However, he added,

> As to the making any declarations on the Subject of Slavery, touching its lawfulness, I do not think it necessary, or expedient, for the question has

> never been put in doubt here,—At Rome they are unwilling, or formerly were, to say any thing on the Subject. . . . As to the duties of Catholic owners to the slaves, especially Catholic ones, that is a very important part, and one really coming home to us here, where the difficulties are so great as to make many feel meliores homini foret if he never owned one. On that point I may try to draw some questions.[21]

As it happened, events prevented any council until after the war. To Kenrick, Lynch held back from overt championing of secession. In his letter of February 9 he remarked that "Dr. Corcoran is indeed very belligerent,—much more so than any of us."[22] Later that month Father Timothy Bermingham visited Kenrick on his way to Rome. He told the archbishop "that the Bishop [Lynch] does not favor secession, which the editor of the paper [Corcoran] does."[23] Bermingham himself was hopeful that war could be avoided and the Union preserved.[24] Lynch heard from Bishop James Wood of Philadelphia and other bishops about their desire for peace.[25]

But events moved steadily toward armed conflict. On January 9 cadets of The Citadel, the South Carolina Military Academy, fired cannon on the Union ship *The Star of the West,* sent to resupply the federal garrison on Fort Sumter. In the view of many, then and now, this was the first act of war.[26] The following day, January 10, Bishop Lynch dispatched Father Patrick Ryan under flag of truce to Fort Sumter "in order that the Catholics at F. Sumter may be able to perform the Religious duties which some will feel consoling in fulfilling." The bishop promised Major Anderson that the priest's "Mission is purely religious and in no wise civil or military." In fact the majority of the enlisted men and workmen at Sumter were Catholics, and Ryan celebrated Mass at the fort occasionally thereafter.[27]

Other Southern states followed South Carolina into secession, and on February 22 the Confederate States of America was proclaimed at Montgomery, Alabama. The war broke out on April 12, when Confederate batteries around Charleston Harbor launched a bombardment of Fort Sumter. In a hopeless situation, Major Anderson surrendered and was able to evacuate the fort honorably. In celebration, Bishop Lynch ordered a solemn *Te Deum* sung in the Cathedral of St. John and St. Finbar. When criticized about this years later, he explained that this was an act of thanksgiving that the fort had fallen without bloodshed.[28] The *Miscellany* hailed the bloodless triumph: "It is surely the merciful finger of God."[29] The bishop, his family, and most of South Carolina's white Catholics rejoiced in the South's easy first victory and the rosy prospect of Southern independence. Dr. John Lynch wrote him from Columbia on April 12 that "we hear all kinds of reports here about the Bombardment, since Eleven Oclock, the telegraph has been working and we get the news oftener than you do perhaps." John looked forward to victory.[30]

On that day Mother Baptista Lynch and the Columbia Ursulines finished a magnificent flag for the Emmet Guards, an Irish unit organized and commanded by Captain Ellison Summerfield Keitt, a planter and a Catholic convert, who was a friend of the bishop's. The flag was "the common infantry size, on one side Blue, with Palmetto tree, with an Irish harp (entwined with shamrock,) leaning against the trunk, worked in Silver, and brilliants, and a crescent in the corner also of Silver, the other side is white, with large Cross, capped with seven stars above and mottow [*sic*] below, ... in Gold & Brilliants, mottow Pro Deo et pro patria.... It is a splendid affair.[31] Anther flag made by the girl pupils at the Ursuline Academy was presented to the Irish Volunteers in a great ceremony at the cathedral in Charleston. This one featured "the Irish Harp wrought most exquisitely in raised gold work adorned with brilliants. Encircling the harp is a wreath of needlework representing the oak, the olive and the native shamrock of Ireland ... over the wreath ... eleven stars—the number [of] states in the Confederacy, and above in gold letters are the words 'Erin go Bragh.'"[32] In Charleston the Sisters of Our Lady of Mercy and their young female pupils in the Academy of Our Lady of Mercy embroidered flags during the summer. One was for the Irish Volunteers in South Carolina, a second one for Irish Volunteers who were sent to fight in Virginia. On September 11 James Corcoran blessed the flag that was to go to Virginia. This was a green and white banner with a palmetto tree on one side, the Irish harp on the other. The banner made for the Irish Volunteers in South Carolina was solemnly blessed by Bishop Lynch in a grand ceremony in a packed St. Finbar's on September 16. Addressing the Corps, the bishop said that "Religion knows that the soldier is not the less a citizen, nor the less a Christian, because he is a soldier. ... [Religion] stands by to instruct and guide him how to be faithful to God and faithful to his country without becoming the slave of his passions of revenge—how to vindicate his own rights, without treading on those of others."[33] Across the South, women were making battle flags for Confederate units. In elaborate ceremonies in cathedrals and parish churches, Southern bishops and priests solemnly blessed banners for the use of Catholic military units.[34]

Although the Catholic Church did not split along the new national lines, it experienced difficulties due to secession and war. The Province of Baltimore in particular was divided. Archbishop Kenrick of Baltimore was able to get his preferred candidate for the See of New Orleans, John Mary Odin, selected over two other nominees—one of them James Corcoran (whom Kenrick considered too rashly pro-secession).[35] When the See of Savannah was to be filled in 1861, Lynch joined with Bishops Quinlan of Mobile and McGill of Richmond in recommending as their first choice Father Anthony D. Pellicier of Montgomery, Alabama. Quinlan told Lynch it was time to "cut adrift from the North in many things ... we of the South have been too long in 'leading strings.'"[36] In the event Archbishop Kenrick preferred Augustin Verot, the vicar apostolic of Florida, and

Archbishop John Joseph Hughes (1797–1864), was born in County Tyrone, Ireland. He immigrated to the United States and was ordained a priest in Philadelphia. He was the fourth bishop and first archbishop of the Archdiocese of New York, serving between 1842 and his death in 1864. He and Lynch were friends and yet conducted a controversial public debate over the institution of slavery and the South's right of secession. Courtesy of Library of Congress.

he succeeded in having the pope transfer him to Savannah, while still retaining responsibility for Florida. Verot and Lynch were friends at the time, and he visited Lynch in Charleston on his way from Baltimore to take possession of his Georgia diocese.[37]

Hughes-Lynch Exchange

In the summer of 1861 Lynch engaged in what became a famous public exchange of views with Archbishop John Hughes of New York over the South's justification for secession. Lynch wrote to Hughes on August 4 giving his take on the situation. Hughes published Lynch's letter in his own newspaper, the *Metropolitan Record,* on September 7, along with his lengthy reply. The archbishop explained that he took this step because of the uncertainty of the mails and his wish that both prelates' words be communicated. The news did reach Charleston, and Lynch then published the text of his August 4 letter in the *Miscellany* on September 14. In his remarks Lynch gave an eloquent defense of the South's position. Prior to the rupture, he maintained, the American Union had been a model of prosperity: "where each was free to develop to the fullest extent those branches of industry In which it could excel, and could draw from the other those products which it needed, but could not produce as well or as cheaply as they could. Even a child could see vast benefits to all from the mutual cooperation." But it was the Yankees, he said, who "taking up anti-slavery, making it a religious dogma, and carrying it into politics, . . . have broken up the Union." He was confident that the North would suffer more economically as a result of the split, deprived of markets for its manufactures and of agricultural products of the South. Even the naval blockade imposed by the North was benefiting the South, "forcing us to be active, and to do for ourselves much that we preferred formerly to pay others to do for us." But he admitted that a prolonged blockade would hurt if it prevented the South getting its cotton to markets abroad.

"The separation of the Southern States is *un fait accompli*. . . . Sooner or later it must be recognized. Why preface the recognition by a war equally needless and bloody?" Fault lay with the Black Republicans. They themselves should take up arms in the war and "not send Irishmen to fight in their stead." "When they carried it into politics, gaining no State Government after another, and defining their especial policy by unconstitutional laws and every mode of annoying and hostile action, and finally, with increased enthusiasm and increased bitterness, carrying the Presidential election in triumph, and grasping the power of the Federal Government, what could the South do but consult its own safety by withdrawing from the Union?"[38]

In his reply dated August 23, Hughes was at pains to express esteem for his brother bishop. He complimented Lynch on his explanations of the causes of the war from a Southern perspective, which he said were "mildly, and even plausibly stated." He granted that the South in fact "has had much reason to complain" of "Northern assaults, made upon her civil and domestic institutions and Sovereignty." He thought that North and South might have continued to follow different paths on the slavery question under the U.S. Constitution and the Union.[39] But Hughes did not accept that Lincoln's election justified secession. Southerners were mistaken in believing that "the Federal Government and the people of the North are determined to conquer and subjugate them." The goal of the North was only to "bring back the seceded states to their organic condition—*ante bellum*." And he persisted in hoping that conversations might yet be held by representatives of South and North where lists of grievances might be drawn up as a preparation for a larger settlement involving perhaps a revision of the U.S.

Constitution, so that all views could be accommodated. In their exchange the two prelates did not debate the morality of servitude. Their ideas on the legitimacy of slavery are discussed later in this work. The *Miscellany* did not publish the text of the archbishop's response, claiming that its length made it unwieldy, but Corcoran also opined that Hughes's letter had been "a great failure, as far as it was meant to be a reply to argument and facts."[40] The epistolary debate drew a lot of press comment both North and South, with parts or all of the letters being published in numerous Catholic and secular newspapers. Coverage was sometimes uneven. The New Orleans *Catholic Standard,* for example, printed Lynch's letter in full but not the archbishop's, "which however, would not add to his honors."[41] After the war Lynch would assert that his 1861 letter had been written to Hughes privately and that the New York prelate had published it without his knowledge or approval.[42] The validity of Lynch's postwar disclaimer is by no means certain.

Lynch and the Diocese in the Early War Years

Lynch supported the Confederacy, as did all the Southern bishops. All earned respect and praise for their work and that of their clergy, religious and laypeople, for aid to soldiers, seamen, prisoners of war, and the afflicted and destitute people of their dioceses. He stood out among them in three areas. First, he was a slave owner of significance. Second, he accepted high office in the Confederate government, for which he undertook a mission to the Holy See in its behalf. Third, he penned and published the South's last great proslavery treatise.

In the first year of the war Lynch's practice was to visit in person and to send his priests to visit sick and wounded Confederates, as well as Northern prisoners. All the Southern bishops did likewise. Bishop Lynch pointed out later that he always showed kindness to federal prisoners, starting with those brought into Charleston in 1861. In his own words, he became "accustomed to visit the Military Prisons, especially in Charleston and Columbia."[43] In 1861 the South Carolina General Assembly named him to an important board for coordinating relief to destitute families of servicemen.[44] U.S. forces launched amphibious assaults on the Carolinas in the first year of war. In November 1861 such an operation captured Port Royal, on the coast between Charleston and Savannah. Hilton Head Island was also taken. Union troops occupied the town of Beaufort on November 9 and held it until the end of the war.[45] St. Peter's Parish, Beaufort, which was served from the cathedral, was effectively cut off from the diocese.[46]

The Great Charleston Fire

Even greater misfortune came on December 11. The most destructive fire in Charleston's history broke out that evening near the Cooper River waterfront.

Ruins of Catholic Cathedral of St. Finbar, burned in the great Charleston fire of December 1861. With all of the other diocesan property destroyed in the fire of 1861 and the destruction from the siege of Charleston, the Catholic Diocese amassed a debt of close to $400,000. Lynch spent his entire postwar life dedicated to retiring that debt. Courtesy of Library of Congress.

Whipped by strong winds, the conflagration swept across the Charleston peninsula. As the fire spread Bishop Lynch walked to the Convent of the Sisters of Our Lady of Mercy to warn its residents that the fire was coming. Shortly before midnight soldiers and others came and worked in the night to save the convent and orphanage. They moved furniture and other belongings to a nearby normal school, which was not threatened. No efforts were made to save the cathedral, since the nuns and children were deemed to have first priority.[47] Catholic homes and institutions were consumed. The convent and orphan house on Queen Street caught fire but were saved, although damage made them uninhabitable for several months. Charleston's commissioner of public works provided temporary space in the undamaged normal school.[48] Sparks from these buildings reached the Cathedral of St. John and St. Finbar, and the beautiful church was lost. Many local residents had put their silver, furniture, and other valuables in the church, thinking it to be fireproof. The bishop's residence, along with his miter, crozier, and vestments, were lost. Gone, too, were the hall of the Catholic Institute and much of its library. Many of the library's books were rescued, thanks to efforts by local inhabitants. These were then stored in a temporary location in disorder, rendering them practically unusable.[49] The entire library of the former seminary was destroyed. Lost too was St. Mary's Free School, taught by the Sisters of Mercy, as were the Sisters' kitchen and the orphans' refectory. Another casualty was the *Catholic Miscellany*. The issue dated December 12, describing the blaze, was its last.[50]

The loss of the cathedral was particularly painful, because the insurance policy on the building had lapsed, it was said, due to nonpayment of the premium. Jeremiah O'Connell wrote that this resulted from "an oversight on the part of the clergyman in charge of this department of the domestic economy."[51] At the time, many Charlestonians believed that the fire had been set deliberately by black slaves or free arsonists to damage the war effort, since the buildings where the Ordinance of Secession was adopted and signed were destroyed, but the view later prevailed that the disaster had been a terrible accident.[52] The conflagration burned more than 540 acres and 575 private homes, numerous business and public buildings, and fine churches. Miraculously, no one died. Charleston mayor Charles Macbeth appointed a special committee of thirteen prominent citizens to solicit and administer contributions to aid and "promptly redress . . . with shelter, food and clothing, those whose misfortunes have deprived them of their necessities." Lynch and the Reverend A. Toomer Porter were clergymen who served. For a period they met daily, and people could apply to them for aid. It was specified that free colored persons had to "make applications through their Guardians." The committee established a free market for distributing food to victims.[53] On behalf of the committee Lynch wrote to Mayor Macbeth and the City Council to urge that the indigent fire victims be given "remunerative employment" working on cleanup and repairs such as "filling up the cellars an other excavations and low places of the burnt District," "removing noxious rubbish," and restoring the ruined drains. Unemployed women could be employed by sewing for the army. The committee expressed its concern about the bad effects of idleness as well as poverty.[54] Overall Lynch's committee estimated that the city's net losses totaled $2 million. Funds raised for relief were estimated at $300,000, of which $260,000 would be paid to victims.[55]

In 1862 Bishop Lynch played a leading role in continuing the free market in Charleston "to supply provisions, free of charge, to the needy families of soldiers and seamen who are fighting the battles of our country." This effort depended on public donations. Under the bishop's direction, Father Timothy Bermingham sought and was granted some funding from the French Society for the Propagation of the Faith.[56]

North Carolina Invaded; Charleston Threatened and Besieged

In February 1862 a federal assault on Roanoke Island began the occupation of the coastal areas of North Carolina. Lost to the diocese was the town of New Bern, an important Catholic center with the beautiful Gothic-style St. Paul's Church, the oldest house of Catholic worship in the state.[57]

In 1862 Charleston was directly threatened for the first time. Union forces landed on James Island, a sea island across the Ashley River from the Charleston peninsula. Their immediate goal was occupation of the riverbank opposite the city, from which they could control the inner harbor and bombard the town at will. On June 9 the *New York Tribune* declared that "'Doom' hangs over wicked Charleston."[58] Fearing disaster, many citizens evacuated the city, among them a lot of Catholics.[59] Sister Mary Agatha McNamara of the Sisters of Our Lady of Mercy—she was Dr. John Lynch's sister-in-law—wrote to Sister DeSales on May 29: "The enemy's gun boats draw near us daily; our ears are sometimes dunned by the reports of the big guns."[60] Father John Moore told the bishop that the doctors "all left town." "The city is being deserted every day more and more. It would appear that they are resolved to defend it; they are digging rat-holes along Meeting Str. for sharpshooters."[61] The Confederates did indeed defend Charleston. Southern troops, outnumbered eight to one, held off the Union attack on June 16 in the fierce Battle of Secessionville. The five hundred defenders included Irish volunteers, many of them Charleston Catholics. The Northern troops withdrew, and Charleston was safe for another year.[62]

On April 7, 1863, began a Union naval operation aimed a retaking Fort Sumter. U.S. Navy monitors attacked. Sumter held, although the fort was reduced to rubble over the next few months, and was not taken until 1865.[63] In July, Lynch told Bishop McGill that "things really look dark.... If the Yankees try long enough and hard enough, and spend lives enough, of course they can take Charleston. But we will fight hard."[64] In that month began the federal assault on Confederates holding Morris Island, the barrier island south of the harbor entrance. In fighting marked by great carnage, Confederate defenders held Battery Wagner (or Fort Wagner). It was here that the Massachusetts Fifty-fourth Infantry Regiment, composed of African American soldiers under the command of Colonel

Robert Gould Shaw (1837–1863), attacked Wagner on July 18 but was repulsed by Southern troops. Battery Wagner withstood the siege until General P. G. T. Beauregard ordered its evacuation on September 7, 1863. Federal forces then occupied Morris Island, and heavy artillery placed there, in cooperation with the Union Navy, effectively closed Charleston Harbor. Charleston ceased to be a blockade-running port. With Charleston effectively sealed off and other harbors of the coast of the Carolinas either occupied or blocked, the remaining port for blockade running was Wilmington, North Carolina, where James Corcoran became pastor, from October 1863 until the end of the war.[65]

From Cummings Point at the northern tip of Morris Island, Union guns could bombard the old city of Charleston, at distances of from 4.7 to 5.2 miles. The shelling began on August 22. Exploding shells spread terror among Charlestonians. Many had already evacuated the city, and the bombs caused more people to leave for the interior, as the lower part of the peninsula became quite dangerous, so many families and businesses relocated to the northern parts of town.[66] Gunners took aim at the lofty white steeple of St. Michael's Episcopal Church, two blocks from the ruin of St. Finbar's. After the fire Bishop Lynch and his priests had moved to a house on Archdale Street, a few blocks north of the cathedral site.[67] The bishop recorded that two temporary chapels for the cathedral congregation's use were imperiled by bombs and had to be abandoned. St. Mary's Church was repeatedly struck. Its organ was wrecked, as were many tombstones in the churchyard. The church was not used for many months, so its congregation worshipped in the private homes of parishioners. Few members of the parish remained, as many had left town.[68]

The Sisters of Our Lady of Mercy decided to remove their girl boarders from Charleston. A contingent of Sisters left their motherhouse and the orphanage, which had survived the fire, and moved to Sumter, South Carolina, about one hundred miles from Charleston. There they established a convent and academy in a house donated by a Charleston Catholic layman, Edward Lafitte. The Sisters who remained in town took up residence in the northern part of the city.[69] With the bombardment of Archdale Street, the episcopal residence soon became uninhabitable. Lynch observed that the entire lower half of Charleston was affected by bombing. "The continued bombardment," he said, "has no military purpose, for it leaves our fortifications and defensive works intact; it can only have as it purpose to destroy houses needlessly, to harass and exterminate women, children and non-combattants [*sic*]." "When I heard bombs all around my house up to 150 meters away, when one of these projectiles even landed in my yard, I and my clergy moved to a house further away from the danger."[70] Lynch and his secretary, Dr. John Moore, took up residence in the rectory of St. Joseph's Parish Church, a half mile to the northeast. The priests did not move back to the neighborhood of St. Finbar's until after the war.[71] St. Joseph's Church itself was damaged by shells, one of which destroyed the organ, another of which took out a wall. In January 1864 the Reverend James R. Sheeran, a Redemptorist priest and Confederate army chaplain, visited Charleston. He recorded that Bishop Lynch "gave me a cheerful welcome. He lamented the fact that he could not invite me to stay with him during my sojourn, as he was compelled to abandon his home on account of the proximity of the shells. Whilst conversing, a large shell burst about two hundred yards from the house."[72] While preaching at Mass to a packed congregation at St. Joseph's on January 17, he and the congregation heard "a hundred pound Parrott shell whizzing directly over the roof of the church . . . [which] ploughed right into the earth some fifty yards distant." Many of the flock panicked, but Sheeran said "What are you afraid of? Do you think God is not able to protect you from Yankee shells?" He was able to restore order and continued preaching for another half hour.[73]

Aid to Prisoners of War

In addition to nursing sick and wounded Confederates, the priests and religious of the diocese also provided assistance to Northern prisoners of war. Sisters of Our Lady of Mercy "each day made the rounds of the Confederate prisons and hospitals" in Charleston.[74] Prisoners of war were incarcerated in the yard of the jail (which still stands), the workhouse, Roper Marine Hospital, or the racecourse. Sisters visited prisons daily, bringing food and clothing to the men. They offered to get prisoners' messages to loved ones or to friends in the other prisons in Charleston. These duties continued throughout the bombardment. The situation of prisoners of war became more complicated in the summer of 1863, when two dozen black soldiers of the Massachusetts Fifty-fourth Infantry Regiment were first incarcerated at Castle Pinckney in the harbor, then transferred to the Charleston jail—where there were also free black Union sailors. The African American servicemen posed special problems, since under Confederate and state laws they might be executed or sold into slavery. The matter was delicate, since there was the possibility, even the likelihood, that the United States would inflict corresponding punishments on Confederate prisoners held in the North. South Carolina governor Milledge L. Bonham appointed a distinguished Charleston Irish Catholic attorney, Nelson Mitchell (1812–1864), to serve as legal counsel to the African Americans. Edward McCrady Jr. (1833–1903), an attorney and later historian of colonial South Carolina, assisted Mitchell.[75] Bishop Lynch intervened and worked with Mitchell to secure fair treatment for the black men. They were not subject to extreme, atrocious punishments. Lynch was proud that he helped secure what he deemed a just resolution of the matter. All the time the black soldiers and sailors were imprisoned in Charleston, Sisters of Mercy regularly visited and tried to help them. Most of the blacks were later transferred to the terrible prison stockade at Florence, South Carolina, where some died of disease. Most are believed to have survived the war and returned to their homes.[76]

The Sisters of Mercy remained in Charleston to continue their nursing and other charitable work. But after a shell exploded in the convent yard on November 24, 1863, they were compelled to move to a house "in the upper part of the city in an area entirely out of the reach of the enemy's fire."[77] Through the war years Bishop Lynch, his priests, and the Sisters distinguished themselves by their kindness to prisoners of war regardless of creed or color. Kindness and care were offered to civilians made destitute by the war.

Lynch's intervention to spare the lives of two Union captives is recorded in a manuscript written by Captain Henry Washington Sawyer (1829–1893), First Regiment, New Jersey Volunteer Cavalry. The source was discovered by Clark T. Donlin, who is preparing a biography of Sawyer. On July 6, 1863, Sawyer and Captain John M. Flinn (1833–1872) of Company F, Fifty-first Indiana Volunteer Infantry, were chosen by lot to be executed at Libby Prison, Richmond. The action was taken in retaliation for General Ambrose Burnside's execution of two Confederate Army chaplains for spying behind Union lines. As Sawyer and Flinn were being marched to the place of execution, a carriage containing Bishop Lynch appeared and stopped. He inquired of the Confederate officer what was taking place and asked that the action be halted so that the men might have time to prepare for their deaths. The bishop was concerned that the men were charged with no crime—making their execution something he deemed unjust. He sought a stay of execution from President Jefferson Davis, who admired Lynch, and in the event the men did not die. Months later they were exchanged for two Confederate prisoners.[78]

On more than one occasion Bishop Lynch played a role in the exchange of prisoners. On July 24, 1863, in Charleston Harbor, there occurred an exchange of wounded prisoners. Lynch was responsible for the 104 Union men, whom he escorted on a "flag of truce boat" to a point less than fifty feet from the U.S. Navy hospital ship *Cosmopolitan,* which bore forty Confederates. The bishop and the Union chief surgeon, Brevet Lieutenant Colonel John J. Craven, M.D., later praised each other for their politeness and propriety. But Lynch said that Southerners were "somewhat mortified" that the Yankees "had taken so much better care" of the Confederates "than we had of theirs."[79]

Jefferson Davis admired Lynch for his work with sick and wounded servicemen and prisoners of war, and the bishop was a member of the president's entourage when he visited Charleston in 1863 to inspect the city's defenses.[80]

Lynch at Fort Sumter in 1861. Lynch and the Sisters of Charity of Our Lady of Mercy gained much credit with both sides in the conflict for the care they gave to the wounded. Lynch also became acquainted with President Davis on a later visit to harbor defense sites in November 1863. Courtesy of the New-York Historical Society.

Bishops' Views of Slavery

In the early days of war Bishop Lynch did not publish his views on the institution of slavery. He nonetheless became in law a slaveholder of significance and would later publish a detailed analysis and defense of African American bondage. During 1861 two bishops did disseminate their ideas about slavery. In January, Augustin Verot, then vicar apostolic of Florida, preached a sermon on the national crisis in his cathedral at St. Augustine. This later was published as what was in effect a Confederate pamphlet, *A Tract for the Times*, and it gained much attention.

Verot had it printed in Baltimore, and Lynch assisted in getting the printed copies to its author.[81] Verot quoted scripture to show that "both the New and Old Testaments admit, sanction, and authorize Slavery from which we conclude that this state of life is not against the Divine and positive law."[82] As Bishop England had done two decades earlier, Verot drew a sharp distinction between the slave trade condemned by Pope Gregory XVI and licit domestic servitude.[83] Verot's sermon was translated into French and received some distribution in the South and elsewhere. Although the pamphlet was published in Baltimore, Archbishop Kenrick would not allow its distribution there, fearing it would create "an excitement."[84]

In the summer of 1861 Auguste Marie Martin, bishop of Natchitoches, Louisiana, issued a pastoral letter in French "on the occasion of the South's war for its independence." Martin asserted the South's right to secede and urged loyalty to the Confederacy. The people of Africa were, he said, the race of Ham, still bearing the curse of outraged Father Noah. Blacks were entrusted by God to the care of the privileged members of the human family, that is, whites, whose duty it was to care for their unfortunate brethren. How widely known this letter became in America, which was not published in English, it would be difficult to say. But it came to the attention of the Holy Office in Rome, which was concerned about scriptural references and later secretly scrutinized the pamphlet.[85]

Archbishop Kenrick's Death

Francis Patrick Kenrick died at his Baltimore residence during the night of July 6–7, 1863. The archbishop was a gentle, scholarly man, appalled by the carnage of war. In his last weeks, in response to an indirect request from U.S. Secretary of War Edwin M. Stanton, he communicated his private view on a possible way to restore peace. He proposed that the Confederate States be recognized so that some but not all of the states that had seceded could form the new country.[86] Nothing came of this proposal, but it was an indication that the metropolitan of Baltimore was willing to work for a peaceful resolution. In May Lee was victorious at Chancellorsville, but he was beaten in July at Gettysburg. On the fourth of July Vicksburg fell to the Union forces, splitting the Confederacy in two. Kenrick's passing left a vacancy in the most divided ecclesiastical province and posed special problems for the Southern suffragans who wanted to play a role in choosing his successor. Bishop McGill wrote Lynch that, on account of the war and uncertainty about its outcome, he thought it best "to leave his successor unappointed till after the termination of the war." McGill wrote to Cardinal Barnabò in this vein.[87] Lynch doubted that the see would remain vacant for long. He favored a new man in the job, not a transfer of a current prelate. He proposed "somewhat jocosely" that Secretary of State William Henry Seward be asked for permission for "the three suffragans from the Confederacy to go on to Baltimore to see to the election of a Successor." If Seward refused, as he probably would, that refusal "might bring him such odium as would help to disgust still more the Catholic and Irish element at the North." Lynch doubted that Maryland would "ever belong to the Southern Confederacy—and we cannot look for a Southern man to succeed Abp Kenrick." He thought that Bishop Bayley of Newark "would do admirably."[88] As it happened, the Southern bishops found it impossible to go to Baltimore for the funeral. They discussed obtaining permission to cross the lines, but McGill recalled that he had earlier been denied such authorization, and he did not want to be rebuffed.[89]

Archbishop Kenrick had made a list of three Baltimore priests as his nominees for successor. The suffragans who attended his funeral, after consulting with Archbishops Hughes of New York and Purcell of Cincinnati, added Bishop Martin John Spalding of Louisville and Richard Whelan of Wheeling.[90] The bishop of Wheeling was supposed to send the list to the Propaganda and to inform the Southern suffragans when the names of Bishops John McCloskey of Albany and John Timon of Buffalo were added to the list. Other recommended men included Bishop William Henry Elder of Natchez and Patrick Lynch of Charleston. This was the first of two instances where Lynch was nominated for the See of Baltimore. Bishop Whelan did not notify the Confederate bishops of the province of the actions taken until December 1863, and the Southerners did not appreciate being excluded. McGill commented in September: "It does seem to me, that while it is so easy for them [the Northern bishops] to obtain permission to send letters to us by flag of truce, they should inform us, and take our views on this."[91]

The cardinals of the Propaganda decided to transfer Bishop Spalding from Louisville to Baltimore. The bulls of appointment were sent from Rome on May 18, 1864. Spalding was, like Lynch, a graduate of the Urban College. He was installed in Baltimore on July 31, 1864, at a time when Bishop Lynch was in Rome on his diplomatic mission for the Confederacy.[92] Lynch's correspondence with Spalding was cordial and respectful, and he seems to have genuinely liked the metropolitan.

The year 1863 was a difficult one for the diocese. The winter of 1862–1863 was harsh, causing increasing privations for the people both black and white. Casualties and shortages resulting from the blockade mounted, adding to the woes. Mother Baptista wrote the bishop in March from Columbia asking him to seek permission from their friend and fellow Catholic, Lucius B. Northrop, the Confederacy's commissary general, so they could purchase flour in Richmond. Baptista said it was selling at twenty-two dollars a barrel there, while she had to pay sixty dollars in Columbia.[93]

As the carnage increased, the South had to come to grips with its inadequate medical capabilities.[94] A Confederate congressional investigating committee reported in January 1862 "that it was 'deeply impressed with the inadequacy of the preparations and provisions for . . . sick soldiers.'" After Port Royal was captured, Bishop Lynch informed the Council of the Sisters of Our Lady of Mercy that it was now "more probable that a hospital for the sick and wounded would be established in some part of the state" and that they should "hold themselves in readiness and be prepared to go wherever their services were needed."[95] As it turned out, the Sisters were needed elsewhere. Lynch's best friend in the Southern hierarchy was John McGill of Richmond. During the war Lynch traveled often to Virginia by train, as long he could safely go. In December 1863 he told the Sisters that McGill had asked him to send some of their community to run a Confederate military hospital at White Sulphur Springs. He assigned five of the Sisters to go as nurses to Virginia. These were Sister M. Ignatius Clark, Sister M. DeSales Brennan, Sister M. Bernard Frank, Sister M. Helena Marlowe, and Sister Stanislas Coventry.[96] Father Lawrence P. O'Connell accompanied them as their chaplain. O'Connell's appointment as chaplain was later confirmed by the Confederate Senate.[97] Shortly after the Charleston fire, the nuns and the chaplain traveled by rail to Virginia. They were able to go by train to Staunton and then traveled by stagecoach to White Sulphur Springs and the hospital, which was housed in the famous Old White Hotel at Greenbrier White Sulphur Springs. The Sisters faced hardship and disappointments but performed admirably, earning lasting praise for their hard work and kind service to the sick and wounded. Seven sisters cared for seven hundred patients. Father O'Connell was crippled by rheumatism and had to return to South Carolina for rest. At the end of April 1862 Bishop Lynch was traveling in Virginia and paid a visit to the hospital, where he took Father O'Connell's place for a time. He arrived just before a Union army advance in the area, which placed the Greenbrier in imminent danger of capture by federal troops. The Sisters and Father O'Connell were told to evacuate to a safer location sixty miles to the south, a location called Montgomery White Sulphur Springs (now in the State of Virginia). In fact, Union troops occupied the Greenbrier, and the Sisters set up their hospital at Montgomery Springs. For a time people in the Carolinas feared (incorrectly) that the bishop and the others had been taken prisoner.[98] The Charleston Sisters ran and staffed the hospital at Montgomery Springs until the end of the war. In 1863, after the Confederate Army retook Greenbrier White Sulphur Springs, they returned for a time to the Old White Hotel. Bishop Lynch later visited the hospital at Montgomery Springs.[99]

Tragedy befell the Lynch family in 1863. The bishop's younger brother Hugh Patrick Lynch (b. 1833) had been trained as a bookkeeper and had worked as a merchant in Cheraw. He volunteered for Confederate service in the first year of the war and was commissioned a first lieutenant in the Twenty-first Regiment, South Carolina Volunteers. In the winter of 1861–1862 he did duty in operations on the South Carolina coast, where he developed a lung disease, perhaps tuberculosis. Bishop Lynch, convinced that army conditions had caused it, asked the army's Board of Surgeons to declare him exempt from military duty. After a summer of rest, Hugh was partially recovered and eager to return to the army. The bishop appealed to General Beauregard, who offered Hugh a clerical post in his office. The young man tried to perform this assignment, but his health was not up to it, and he returned to Cheraw, where he died on March 20, 1863, and was buried in St. David's Episcopal churchyard. His family considered Hugh to be a casualty of war.[100]

Throughout the American Civil War, Lynch attempted to continue his duties as leader of the Catholic Diocese of Charleston. He faced personal danger, privation, and much distress and persisted in spite of all that confronted him and his beloved city, state, and region. His efforts, though ultimately in vain, were premised on his devotion to his people and his faith. He ministered to all to whom he could offer assistance regardless of their race, creed, nationality, or political persuasion. His actions won him admiration and perhaps sympathy after the end of the conflict, when pardons became necessary.

CHAPTER 6

Rome Mission

President Jefferson Davis in 1864 appointed Bishop Lynch to be commissioner of the Confederate States of America to the States of the Church. In this position, Lynch undertook a mission to Europe to win recognition of the Confederacy by the Holy See. As part of his contribution to the Southern cause, he wrote a tract on slavery that was published in Europe in Italian, German, and French. David Heisser brought out an edited and annotated complete English-language text in 2000–2001.[1] Lynch accepted appointment on March 3, 1864; on April 4 Secretary of State Judah Philip Benjamin (1811–1884) handed him his instructions and other documents. The wartime mission to Rome was the central drama of Lynch's career and remains the most memorable event in his life.

The basic premise of the Confederacy's diplomatic efforts was summed up in the words "King Cotton." In the years leading up to the war, Southern leaders developed the theory that Europe's need for cotton must inevitably bring recognition and support for the South's independence.[2] As the war dragged on, the governments of both North and South directed attention to the Vatican. Both tried to influence the foreign policy of Pope Pius IX and to obtain his favor or at least his continued neutrality.[3] Since 1797 the United States had had a consul in the Papal States. In 1848 the U.S. Senate approved President James K. Polk's proposal to have a chargé d'affaires at the papal court. The American representative's title was minister to the States of the Church, and he was treated with great respect by the Holy See. In the 1820s the Vatican appointed a consul at New York, with twenty-one vice consuls in various cities, including Charleston.[4] Since 1848 the United States had maintained correct, even cordial relations with the papal government. Washington had stayed neutral in the tumultuous and sometimes violent affairs of the Italian peninsula, as nationalists of the Risorgimento fought to unify the country—a goal that could be attained only through a reduction or elimination of the Papal States.

By the time of the American Civil War the new Kingdom of Italy had been proclaimed, and Pope Pius had lost all his territories except the city of Rome and

Jefferson Davis (1808–1889), President of the Confederate States of America (1861–64). He visited Charleston in November of 1863, and Lynch accompanied his party to several sites in the inspection of the city's defenses. In the Spring of 1864 he commissioned Lynch as a special emissary to the Vatican in the hope of attaining diplomatic recognition for the CSA. This mission failed. Courtesy of Library of Congress.

its immediate surroundings. The great aim of Vatican diplomacy was to retain its temporal power, that is, at least part of its territorial domain. There was very little trade between the United States and the Papal States, but Secretary of State Seward wanted stable relations with Rome because of the great and growing number of Catholics in the country. However, Seward's attention focused mainly on London and Paris. In November 1861 Archbishop Hughes of New York traveled to Europe at the behest of Lincoln's government and met with high officials in Rome. Ostensibly his purpose was to foster better relations between America and the great powers, but he strove to influence public opinion in favor of the North and sent confidential reports on what he heard to Secretary Seward.[5] Hughes obtained an audience with Emperor Napoleon III and Empress Eugenie at the

Tuileries. He sought to dissuade the French from recognizing the Confederacy and to encourage Algerian cotton production as a way to free France from dependence on the Southern states' staple. In Rome he promoted goodwill toward the North in meetings with high Vatican officials and visiting prelates from various countries. On his way home he stopped in Ireland, where he made speeches celebrating the attractions and achievements of the United States. Upon his return to America, the archbishop met with harsh criticism from some of the Catholic press that favored the South for having served a political cause.[6] While Hughes supported Lincoln and the Union, his views on slavery and the question of emancipation were complex and are discussed later.

Vatican attitudes toward the American conflict varied over time. At Rome, two important periodicals, the official daily newspaper of the Holy See, *L'Osservatore romano* (Roman Observer), and *La Civiltà Cattolica* (Catholic Civilization), a biweekly edited by Jesuits—both reflecting the opinions of high Vatican officials—were skeptical about the aims of Lincoln's government and were often sympathetic toward the South.[7] Although *La Civiltà Cattolica* was not an official voice of the Holy See, the journal had a close relationship with the highest Vatican officials. Prior to publication, the text of every issue was reviewed and approved by the office of the Secretary of State. Pius IX met with the editor-in-chief every two weeks on plans for the next issue.[8] While writers in the two periodicals favored the continuation of the American Union, they expressed doubt about Lincoln's motives, questioning whether the federal government really cared about the welfare of the slaves and expressing horror at the violence and ruin that would likely result from sudden mass emancipation of blacks. Lincoln's provisional and final Emancipation Proclamations elicited statements of sympathy for the Confederacy.[9]

Giacomo Cardinal Antonelli (1806–1876) was Pius IX's secretary of state, effectively the foreign minister of the Holy See and the pope's principal international policy adviser. With casualties mounting horribly, the Vatican expressed hope that the conflict might somehow end by having the warring parties reach a settlement. Cardinal Antonelli mentioned this to William J. Silliman, the U.S. consul, in September 1862. Silliman replied that the North must not abdicate national sovereignty and that the war would be carried "with vigor to final triumph." Antonelli observed that "there is but one course for the [U.S.] government to pursue and that is to carry on the war to its utmost ability. But it is a pity that you entered into it."[10]

Pius decided to make a public appeal to the belligerents to try to restore peace. In late summer 1863, papal letters containing identical language were delivered to two leading American archbishops, Hughes of New York and Odin of New Orleans. The pontiff assured them of his sincere wishes and prayers for peace and urged reconciliation between the warring sides. He also entertained the idea that he might be able to play some role as a mediator between the belligerents. The papal letters were dated October 18, 1862, but for reasons that are unclear they were apparently not delivered until the following summer. They were published in the press in both the North and the South.[11] Confederate bishops composed pastoral letters calling on their faithful to say special prayers for peace in response to the pope's urging. Lynch's "Pastoral Prayers for Peace," published in November 1863, recalled the horrible suffering caused by the war: "Who shall count the thousands and tens of thousands already slain on the battlefield, or who died of disease in the camp or the hospital, or who returned home maimed and decrepit for life?"

Lynch expressed sadness for the loved ones of the lost men, while lamenting also the "pernicious influence of camp life on habits, morals, and character." He praised "our rulers and our armies . . . [who] are making every effort, and shrinking from no sacrifice, to bring this struggle to a happy determination," urging his people to make novenas "and other special devotions" to ask for peace.[12] There is no doubt that Lynch was appalled by the carnage and suffering brought on by war. Davis later recalled that at one particularly difficult moment he exclaimed: "This war, Mr. Davis, this war. I am heart-sick, heart-sick, heart-sick!"[13] Bishop Verot of Savannah likewise composed public prayers and wrote to Archbishop Hughes asking him to join the effort, but Hughes would not, thinking that such action would harm the Union cause.[14]

The Confederate government saw the pope's endeavor as an opening to approach the Vatican, ostensibly in response to the papal letters. It was hoped that some favorable gesture on the Vatican's part could put the South in a good light. A more specific, practical objective was to seek the Catholic Church's influence in dissuading European Catholic men from immigrating to the United States in large number and joining the Union army. The greatest numbers of these came from Ireland. *The Economist* estimated in 1864 that since 1861 100,000 Irishmen had enlisted in the U.S. Army.[15] After Ireland, the greatest number of immigrant federal recruits came from the South German Catholic states. In an effort to discourage such immigration, the Confederacy dispatched agents to Ireland, beginning in 1863. These included Robert Dowling, James L. Capston, and, most important, John B. Bannon (1829–1913). Father Bannon, an Irish-born priest who was loyal to the South, had served as an army chaplain.[16] Bannon accepted a commission to be a secret Confederate agent. He was an intelligent and charming man and spoke with many Irish clergy and other prominent Catholics. He reported to Richmond that he was convinced he had made a difference, although it is difficult to ascertain whether his efforts significantly reduced the stream of Irish emigrants to the U.S. military.[17]

In conversations with President Davis and Secretary of State Benjamin at Richmond in September 1863 before he undertook his secret mission, Bannon suggested that the Confederate government make a diplomatic approach to the pope in an effort to obtain formal recognition. Benjamin prepared a letter from the president to the pope, which was consigned to Bannon to take through the blockade to Europe. Bannon accordingly gave the document to the Confederate propaganda agent in London, Henry Hotze. Hotze in turn sent it to Ambrose Dudley Mann (1801–1889), the Confederate commissioner stationed in Brussels. Davis thanked Pius for his letters to the two archbishops. Benjamin commissioned Mann "to convey to His Holiness by letter his own thanks and those of our people for the Christian charity and sympathy displayed in the letter of His Holiness." Mann was to travel to Rome and personally deliver the president's letter to the pope.[18]

In his letter to the pope President Davis asserted:

> That we desire no evil to our enemies, nor do we covet any of their possessions, but we are only struggling to the end that they shall cease to devastate our land and inflict useless and cruel slaughter upon our people, and that we be permitted to live at peace with all mankind, under our own laws and institutions, which protect every man in the enjoyment not only of his temporal rights, but of the freedom of worshipping God according to his own faith.[19]

On November 14 Dudley Mann was received by the pope in an audience lasting forty minutes. Pius opened the envelope containing Davis's letter with scissors. Since he did not know English, Mann's secretary translated. Pius stated that the Lincoln government "had endeavored to create an impression abroad that they were fighting for the abolition of slavery, and that it might perhaps be judicious in us to consent to gradual emancipation." Mann responded that the disposition of slavery as a matter for the states to decide, not the U.S. federal government, and that, "if indeed, African slavery were an evil, there was a power which in its own good time would doubtless remove that evil in a more gentle manner than that of causing the earth to be deluged with blood for its sudden overthrow." Mann also protested against the Union's practice of "decoying innocent Irishmen from their homes to be murdered in cold blood." Pius promised to write a letter to Davis, which could be published.[20]

The pontiff addressed a letter to Jefferson Davis, dated December 3. The letter was written in Latin and the salutation can be translated to "Illustrious and Honorable Sir, Jefferson Davis, President of the Confederate Sates of America." The pope expressed gratitude "that you and your people are animated by the same desire for peace and tranquility" that the pope had expressed in his letters to Hughes and Odin, and he promised continued prayers for peace.[21] Mann sent the papal letter to Benjamin along with his enthusiastic conviction that "We are acknowledged by as high authority as this . . . to be an independent power of the earth."[22] The pope's letter and Mann's appraisal were received in Richmond on January 18, 1864. Mann communicated the document to Confederate agents James Murray Mason (1798–1871) in London and John Slidell (1793–1871) in Paris, and they distributed it to diplomats and to the press. Henry Hotze made it available to Bannon, who had the English text printed as a poster for wide distribution in Ireland.[23] Benjamin had the pope's letter published in American newspapers and thought it "had a good effect" on public opinion and Southern morale. Judah Benjamin thought that the salutation "'President of the Confederate States' is a formula of politeness to his correspondent, not a political recognition of a fact."[24] Cardinal Antonelli assured the American minister, Rufus King (1814–1876), that the pope's letter "was a simple act of courtesy and devoid of any political design, or significance."[25] On the other hand, Dudley Mann told Davis that "the Pope is well pleased with that which he has done in emphatically recognizing you as Executive of a nation. The good man is willing to do more, and is disregardful of consequences."[26] In fact, Mann always resented Benjamin's refusal to treat the pope's letter as conferring true diplomatic recognition, attacking the latter's "criticisms of lawyer like special pleading, and illogical animadversions."[27] A suspicion among American politicians that the pope had recognized the rebel government was one reason that Congress terminated funding for the American diplomatic mission in 1867.[28]

The pope's letter spurred a decision by Richmond to send a commissioner to reside in Rome. Bishop Lynch recorded that on February 1, 1864, "I received at Charleston S.C. a letter from a Confederate friend of the President . . . informing me that the Government wished to send a Commissioner to Rome and was deliberating whether to send a Bishop or a Layman of liberal views. If the former, then I was the person they wished to send. It touched on the several reasons for and against each course; the letter was marked 'confidential' and was to be destroyed on perusal. I did so destroy it."[29] Evidence has not been found as to whether Lynch had been consulted on the decision to send Dudley Mann to Rome the previous fall. Lynch did travel to Richmond by train periodically and was highly regarded by Confederate officials. He stayed with Bishop McGill when he visited Richmond and was a friend of Commissary General Lucius Northrop. Lynch assured his unnamed correspondent that it would be difficult for a bishop to leave his diocese "for any considerable length of time." He would soon be going to Richmond and would call upon the writer in person. In fact, he got to Richmond on February 23. He and his interlocutor met with Secretary Benjamin, with whom he discussed the matter at length. Benjamin told him that the president preferred to send a bishop. The secretary of state and Charleston's ordinary agreed that a mission lasting no more than six months would be sufficient. Lynch conferred with Bishop McGill, who said "he did not see how, if I was asked to go, I could refuse, but he would give no decided advice." He then went to Montgomery White Sulphur Springs to visit the Sisters of Mercy, and he sought the advice of Father Croghan, who "expressed himself strongly in favour."

In Patrick Lynch the Confederate government chose an acknowledged leader of the Catholic Church in America. He was Rome educated, fluent in Italian, and skilled in other European languages. He was acquainted with Alessandro Cardinal Barnabò (1801–1874), prefect of the Propaganda Fide and an influential adviser to Pius IX.[30] From Montgomery Springs on March 3 Lynch penned his letter of acceptance to Benjamin. "After mature reflection I conceive it my duty to accede to the desire of the Government" for a period not longer than six months. If "urgent reasons should require it, the Government will consent to my return at an earlier period." He was conscious of the fact that he had "no previous training" for a diplomatic mission. He needed time "to arrange my ecclesiastical and personal affairs" but hoped to be able to start by the end of March.[31]

Again conferring with Benjamin in Richmond, Lynch agreed that he must try to run the blockade from the port of Wilmington, as Charleston was blocked. The plan was for the bishop "to interrupt the British mail steamer from St. Thomas for Halifax at Bermuda, which would require me to leave Wilmington about the 8th or 10th of April; and that I should previously visit Richmond on the 5th of April, to receive my commission, and the Instructions which would there be drawn up, on the strength of the latest accounts which then have been received."[32] He returned to Charleston around March 20. He wrote to Benjamin to say that he "wished to be at liberty to employ such Secretaries as I might choose, when I would arrive at my post. For most of my correspondence would be in Italian and French and I desired to employ persons who could write these languages well."[33]

The lives of Patrick Lynch and Judah Benjamin present interesting parallels. Both were born in the British Empire—Lynch in Ireland, Benjamin on the Island of St. Thomas in the West Indies. Both were born to large families in minority communities, Catholic and Jewish. Both spent part of their boyhoods in Charleston, where they were schooled, residing only a few blocks apart. The boys were not exact contemporaries, and the difference in their ages rendered it unlikely for them to have been friends in Charleston. Nevertheless, they were to collaborate in a great endeavor to save their adopted country in its hour of greatest peril.[34]

Bishop Lynch's impending mission was no secret, and it elicited much favorable comment as he made preparations. From Savannah Bishop Verot wrote "that things have come to such a pass" that there was "good & urgent cause for the clergy to do what they can to stop the awful bloodshed." Verot inquired about sending a French priest of his diocese—a Father Renouf—to accompany Lynch as a companion so that he might for health reasons return to his home in Normandy.[35] Lynch explained to Benjamin that Renouf would accompany him as his chaplain. In the event, however, Renouf refused to travel and stayed in Georgia.[36] Verot urged Lynch to seek an audience with Emperor Napoleon III and to

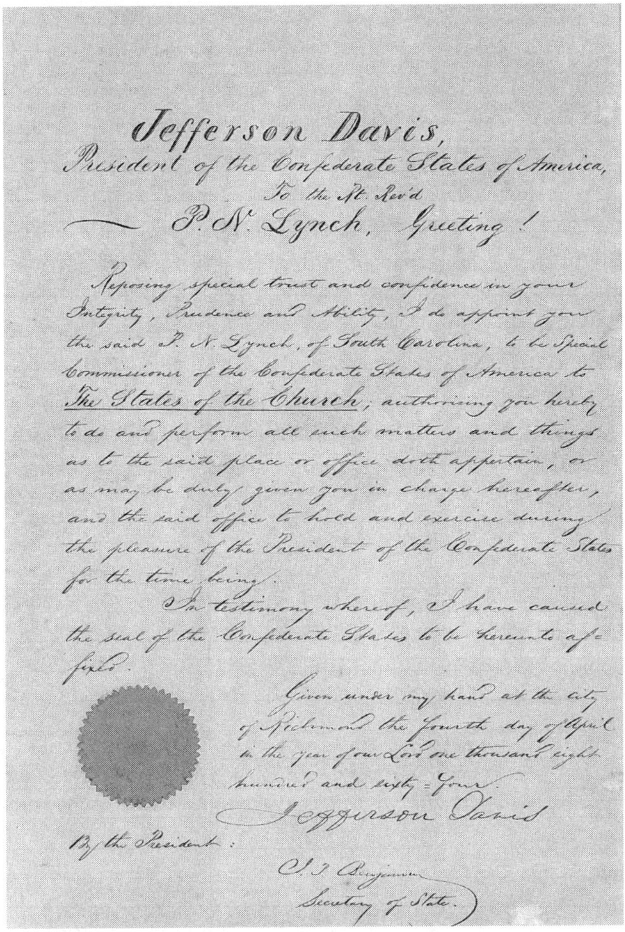

Jefferson Davis,
President of the Confederate States of America,
To the Rt. Rev'd
P. N. Lynch, Greeting!

Reposing special trust and confidence in your Integrity, Prudence and Ability, I do appoint you the said P. N. Lynch, of South Carolina, to be Special Commissioner of the Confederate States of America to The States of the Church; authorising you hereby to do and perform all such matters and things as to the said place or office doth appertain, or as may be duly given you in charge hereafter, and the said office to hold and exercise during the pleasure of the President of the Confederate States for the time being.

In testimony whereof, I have caused the seal of the Confederate States to be hereunto affixed.

Given under my hand at the city of Richmond the fourth day of April in the year of our Lord one thousand eight hundred and sixty-four.

Jefferson Davis

By the President:

J. P. Benjamin
Secretary of State.

Commission from Jefferson Davis, April 4, 1864. "Jefferson Davis President of the Confederate States of America, to the Rt. Rev. P.N. Lynch, Greeting! Reposing special trust and confidence in your Integrity, Prudence and Ability, I do appoint you the said P.N. Lynch, of South Carolina, to be Special Commissioner of the Confederate States of America to The States of the Church; authorizing you hereby to do and perform all such matters and things as to the said place or office doth appertain, or as may be duly given you in charge hereafter, and the said office to hold and exercise during the pleasure of the President of the Confederate States for the time being. In testimony whereof, I have caused the seal of the Confederate States to be herewith affixed. Given under my hand at the city of Richmond the fourth day of April in the year of our Lord one thousand eight hundred and sixty four. Jefferson Davis. By the President. Judah P. Benjamin, Secretary of State." Courtesy of Catholic Diocese of Charleston Archive.

"beseech him to have pity on this poor distracted country once so prosperous & now plunged in unspeakable sufferings."[37]

To undertake such a mission in the midst of war posed serious risks and problems. Not only were there potential physical dangers associated with running the blockade, but the bishop would be leaving his sprawling diocese at a time when it was suffering greatly. Significant coastal areas were under enemy occupation, and the war had occasioned a grievous loss of life and treasure. Life in the Carolinas had become hard and full of uncertainty. The planter system was experiencing strains both agricultural and social. Why did Patrick Lynch accept the Roman commission? His motives were twofold. For one thing he felt strong loyalty to the Confederate cause. If he could win any measure of European support for the South, he wanted to do so. Another, more subtle reason supported the decision. After the South's defeat, he was to explain his motives in these words:

> In the early months of 1864, it seemed to me, as it seemed to many others, North and South, that three years of war had intensified the passions of both Sides, that neither was willing to take any step acceptable to the other by which hostilities might cease, and that each had the means of continuing the war for years to come. In common too with many I could not help entertaining the hope that a friendly disinterested voice from abroad [that is, the pope], spoken on some fitting occasion during the war, might be listened to by both parties, as it counseled peace and reconciliation. Entertaining this opinion of the future & this hope, and earnestly desirous of peace, I acquired in an official proposal unexpectedly made to me, and I came to Rome.[38]

His decision to go to Rome was generally respected by Catholics of the diocese. James Corcoran, now pastor in Wilmington, encouraged him. From Sumter, South Carolina, Father Timothy Sullivan wrote on March 22 of the pleasure with which news of the mission had been received there, adding: "All here would be delighted if you could favor us with a short visit before your departure. I am sure it would do much good."[39] To his clergy and faithful the bishop explained: "Diocesan and other reasons require me to visit Europe." To run the diocese he appointed two vicars general. Father Leon Fillion was put in charge of the city of Charleston "and the missions immediately dependent on the clergy of the city. Should Charleston fall under the power of the Federals, then all other portions of the Diocese, also in their hands, and with which there may be early communications will be considered as annexed to this portion." He noted that Fillion's "French citizenship will exempt him from many annoyances to which a citizen of S. Carolina might be subjected at the hands of Federal military and civil authorities." The rest of the diocese, comprising "the interior," in effect most of North Carolina, was assigned to James Corcoran. Both deputies were given full faculties for the duration.[40] Father Sullivan voiced approval of these arrangements. But the appointment frightened Fillion, who told the bishop that, while he accepted reluctantly, he felt he could not possibly manage both his parish and the Savings Bank and begged Lynch to put the finances into the hands of young Father John Moore. He also asked that the vicar generalship be assigned to Father Sullivan until such time as the Yankees took Charleston—at which point he would resume the title.[41] But the bishop was displeased by what he took to be Fillion's desire to avoid responsibilities, saying "I am loth [*sic*] just as I am starting to upset arrangements deliberately made." He insisted that Fillion perform both duties but asked Father Moore to help the older priest with financial matters and "in every way in your power . . . doing what in you lies, to keep things straight until I return."[42]

Lynch's commission was signed at Richmond by Jefferson Davis and Judah Benjamin on March 4, 1864. The bishop was vested with full power "to agree, treat, consult and negotiate concerning all matters and subjects interesting to both governments, and to conclude and sign Treaties, Convention or Conventions."[43] The commission was accompanied by detailed instructions. The European powers, said Benjamin, had so far unjustly withheld formal diplomatic recognition of the South. It was unlikely that the Vatican would "assume the responsibility of being the first to recognize our independence and to cast a seeming censure on the great powers." He said it would "seem to be ungracious and inconsistent" to ask Lynch to try to "compel His Holiness to go against the powers in granting recognition." In the event a suitable occasion arose for Lynch formally to present his credentials as Confederate Commissioner, he should do so.

> If, on the contrary, you become satisfied that the result would be unfavorable, you will content yourself with the maintenance of those informal relations which are usual in the case of a Government not yet formally recognized. It is rather to the indirect mission that we are disposed to look for fruitful results. Combining, if you will, the advantages of eminent ecclesiastical and political position; located, as you will be, in the center from which radiates the influence of the Holy See; brought, as you must necessarily be, into immediate contact with not only those who control the policy of the States of the Church, but with the trusted representatives of all the Catholic powers of Europe—opportunities will be afforded for enlightening opinions and molding impressions. . . . If you should think it proper during your absence, either before or after proceeding to Rome, to visit the capitals of the principal Catholic powers, where you would assuredly be welcomed, the President would approve of such action.[44]

Along with the commission and instructions, Benjamin made a suggestion that Lynch confer with John Slidell in Paris about visits to the Catholic powers. Lynch was given a document containing his grant of full powers, as well as a letter of introduction to the cardinal secretary of state, two Confederate passports, letters of introduction to Henry Hotze in London and John Slidell in Paris, and copies of the letters exchanged by Davis and the pope.[45]

Lynch was to receive a monthly salary of $1,000 while abroad and was authorized to draw an additional $500 per month for contingent expenses. He might also hire a secretary for up to $300 a month, plus other staff.[46] Salary and expenses were paid by the Liverpool branch of the trading firm of Fraser, Trenholm and Company. The import-export company handled the sale of Confederate cotton to Europe and was the principal depository of Confederate Treasury money—in effect, the Richmond government's bank in Europe. A principal owner of the firm was the Charlestonian George Alfred Trenholm (1807–1876), who served as Confederate secretary of the Treasury in 1864–1865.[47] Bishop Lynch also established a private bank account with the firm, unconnected with the Confederate government.[48] Benjamin directed Hotze and Slidell to offer Lynch information and assistance.[49] The bishop also carried a letter from General P. G. T. Beauregard, along with the general's autographed Photograph, containing a request to be remembered to John Slidell, his brother-in-law.[50]

The bishop took with him two young men, the soldier-artist Conrad Wise Chapman (1842–1910) and the seminarian Daniel J. Quigley (1831–1903). Chapman was the son of the Virginia artist John Gadsby Chapman. The Chapman family had lived in Rome since 1850. When war broke out, Conrad had returned to America and enlisted in the Confederate Army. He was wounded at Shiloh. Since he was a gifted artist, General Beauregard commissioned him to paint pictures of Confederate fortifications around Charleston, including Fort Sumter. On learning that his parents were in difficult straits and that his mother was seriously ill, Conrad requested and received a furlough and permission to travel to Rome. As he spoke Italian, Bishop Lynch agreed to take him on as an assistant.[51] Quigley, the brother-in-law of William McKenna, had shown a desire to become a priest and had studied at Mount St. Mary's Seminary. The bishop decided that he should complete his studies at the recently established American College (later called North American College) in Rome.[52]

Before departing, Patrick Lynch paid a visit to his family in Cheraw. Then he went on to Richmond to receive his commission and other documents. He asked permission from Stephen R. Mallory (1812 or 1813–1873), the Confederate secretary of the navy, to take with him "five bales of cotton in the same vessel, with a view to covering some personal expenses or to meet any emergency that may arise."[53] Mallory replied that he might travel from Wilmington on a navy vessel or one belonging to the War Department.[54] The bishop left Richmond on April 6, arriving in Wilmington on the eighth. There he met Quigley and Chapman and visited James Corcoran. Major General William Henry Chase Whiting

(1824–1865) assisted him in arranging passage on the commercial steamship *Minnie.* The *Minnie* crossed the bar during the dark night of April 10. Chapman later recalled that the *Minnie* passed the U.S. fleet "so close that we could hear the tread of the sentinel on the deck. [We h]ad bundles of dispatches ready to throw over board if captured."[55] The *Minnie* reached Bermuda safely on April 14. From St. George's Lynch sent a short message to Benjamin and a detailed account to his sister, Mother Baptista.

The *Minnie* was a small ship crammed with seven hundred cotton bales. The bishop and a half dozen passengers and crew had lots of tea in the small pantry, and he also shared wine with the British captain. Lynch spent much of his time on deck sitting on a cotton bale "holding a little hand valise with all the papers I wished to destroy in the event of capture,—and well laden with oyster shells to ensure its sinking when thrown overboard."[56] On the ship over to Europe Chapman whiled away the hours making pencil sketchers of passengers and crewmen.[57] The bishop described blockade running as a "game of naval bo-peep . . . seeing your opponent before he sees you."[58] He was surprised and delighted to encounter on Bermuda his nephew Robert A. Lynch (1843–1928), the eldest son of Dr. John Lynch. The young man having expressed an early interest in the priesthood, Bishop Lynch had sent him to the seminary at Combrée, France. Deprived of all news from home since the war's outbreak, Robert had become disillusioned with seminary studies and run away from college. He took refuge with Commissioner John Slidell in Paris. Slidell, he later recalled, "took a great interest in the runaway boy, furnishing him with letters of introduction to people in London, and keeping him hidden away from the French police, who were searching for him, to return him to the college authorities." Robert got to England and traveled from there by ship to Bermuda. Two days after he reached St. George's, his uncle arrived. The bishop learned that Robert planned to catch a blockade runner to Wilmington, with the intention of joining the Confederate Army. He persuaded his nephew to accompany him back to Europe, saying that "if he really has no vocation, he can return with me or some other arrangement can be made."[59]

The party sailed to Nova Scotia on the British mail packet *Alpha,* arriving on April 21. In Halifax the bishop was the guest of the Irish-born archbishop Thomas Louis Connolly. Connolly took him to call on the acting governor, and the Charleston bishop was fêted at a banquet given by some of the leading men of Halifax, including the chief justice and the attorney general. [60] He preached at Sunday high Mass in the cathedral.

On April 29 the party sailed in the R.M.S. *Asia* bound for Liverpool, and the bishop disembarked at Queenstown (Cobh), Ireland, on May 8. On the way over the bishop drafted an appeal to the Council of the Society for the Propagation of the Faith, the French charitable organization that contributed funds to help dioceses in mission territories. He promised to speak in person with the Council when he visited Paris. He noted a communication from the society promising aid that had been sent from Paris in November 1863 but received in Charleston only in February 1864, after having been captured by the federals.[61] On board the *Asia* Chapman made a pencil portrait of Daniel Quigley.[62] Patrick and Robert paid a visit to the bishop's uncle Luke Lynch, his cousin James Kiernan, and others in Rosslea and Clones.[63] Bishop Lynch was the honored guest of Paul Cullen, archbishop of Dublin since 1852, and preached in Cullen's cathedral on Trinity Sunday. He met John Bannon in Dublin and James L. Capston in Cork; the work of both of these men had impressed him. In conversations with leading bishops and other clergy he added his voice to urge them to dissuade Irishmen from fighting for the North. The bishop reported to Benjamin that the Irish clergy were mostly united in opposition to U.S. recruitment of their nationals. Bannon said he considered his work in Ireland to have been a success. He asked to accompany Bishop Lynch to Rome as his chaplain, and Lynch agreed.[64]

Lynch and his party crossed the Irish Sea to Liverpool, where the bishop made financial arrangements with Fraser, Trenholm, then traveled by rail to London. He conferred with the Confederate agents, dined with Nicholas Cardinal Wiseman, and met several bishops and members of Parliament, although with no cabinet members.[65] The party then traveled to Paris. There the bishop met with John Slidell and with Archbishop Georges Darboy (1813–1871). He secured the assistance of the apostolic nuncio, Archbishop (later Cardinal) Flavio Chigi (1810–1885), who accompanied him to a meeting with Foreign Minister Edouard Drouyn de Lhuys (1805–1881). That meeting took place at the minister's offices at the Quai d'Orsay on June 13. Drouyn told Lynch he thought the Confederacy was having some military success. By Lynch's account, Drouyn said "that long ago, the French Government was disposed to intervene, and propose terms of peace, [but,]unwilling to act alone, it had proposed a concert of action in the matter to the English Government. But the proposal was not accepted."[66] Although he was polite to Bishop Lynch, Drouyn de Lhuys favored a path of neutrality for France.[67] Lynch asserted the Southerners' fierce determination to resist conquest and confiscation of their property by the Northern government. "The war," he said, "was continued in a spirit of hatred and caused loss of life and destruction of property." The Frenchman pointed to slavery as a great obstacle, "and on that account the French nation felt opposed to us." Slavery was generally unpopular in France, which had abolished the institution in its colonies in 1848. Chigi and Lynch requested an audience with the emperor, and Drouyn promised his support. On the next morning, June 14, Lynch was received in private audience at the Tuileries by Napoleon III. The emperor was cordial and spoke in great detail about the war. When he inquired about "the demeanour of the negroes," Lynch told him they "had never been more quiet and submissive; that the tumult of the war seemed to have oppressed them with awe." The emperor wished for "some decisive battle so that England and France might at once recognize the South." The bishop had a second, farewell meeting with Drouyn de Lhuys. He also pleaded the Southern cause with a number of French bishops and other important clergy and laymen. He remarked to Benjamin that "if we could smooth down their prejudices on the subject of Slavery, our task would be easy." Lynch could not know that, during his days in Ireland, London, and Paris, General Sherman's army was bearing down on Atlanta and the Battle of the Wilderness was fought by Grant and Lee. While in Paris he conferred with Confederate agents Slidell, Hotze, and Edwin De Leon. De Leon (1818–1891) was a member of a prominent Sephardic Jewish family of Columbia, South Carolina. He had been a newspaper editor and a political activist and had served as U.S. consul general in Egypt. During the war he was appointed a Confederate agent to serve in Europe, working especially as a propagandist.[68]

Father Timothy Bermingham joined Bishop Lynch in Paris. Bermingham had been traveling in Europe and the Holy Land on a personal pilgrimage and to raise money for the diocese. He had made a successful European begging tour, aided by a letter of introduction to various bishops from Cardinal Barnabò. He had evidently made a good impression on European churchmen.[69] He and Bishop Lynch dined as guests of Archbishop Darboy. Lynch paid a visit to the council of the French Society for the Propagation of the Faith to plead his case for financial aid. While Quigley stayed on for a time in Paris, the bishop, accompanied by Bermingham, Bannon, Chapman, and his nephew Robert, journeyed on to Rome, arriving on June 26.[70]

William McCloskey (1823–1909), rector of the American College, offered Bishop Lynch a place to stay at the college, located on the Via dell'Umiltà in downtown Rome. But the bishop declined the invitation, not wishing to be the cause of dissension between Northern and Southern seminarians. He told Claudian Northrop, a Charleston seminarian then in residence, that he thought "it is better for the college that he does not stay here." Rector McCloskey had made it a policy to discourage discussions of the war among the students. McCloskey also thought that, as the bishop's party was numerous, "he probably feared that he would incommode us."[71] The situation of the Southern seminarians was not easy during the war. The blockade made it difficult for them to return home. They were forbidden access to secular newspapers but might read the Catholic press from the North and from England. The Charleston seminarian William G. Meriwether had written Bishop Lynch in 1863 from the college that "we avoid as much as possible the discussion of politics as regards the Civil War that is laying waste our land."[72]

Shortly after arriving in the Eternal City, Bishop Lynch took an apartment on the Via Condotti, a short walk from the Palace of the Propaganda. Then, as now, Via Condotti was a fashionable street, and Lynch would entertain prominent people at his lodgings, acquiring a reputation for gracious hospitality.[73] Soon after his arrival the bishop called on Cardinal Barnabò, "with whom I had already some acquaintance," and explained the purpose of his journey. As Lynch reported, Barnabò "entered at once into my views, and offered to see Cardinal Antonelli" and to arrange for Lynch to have a special audience with the pope "in my character as Bishop."[74] The last words meant that Lynch would be received by the pope as a bishop making his regular *ad limina* visit to Rome, rather than as the South's diplomatic envoy.

On the morning of June 28 Lynch had his first interview with Cardinal Antonelli, the papal secretary of state. The cardinal displayed what to Lynch seemed

Giacomo Cardinal Antonelli (1806–1876). He was the Cardinal Secretary of State from 1848 until his death; he played a key role in Italian politics, resisting the unification of Italy and affecting Roman Catholic interests in European affairs. He was often called the "Italian Richelieu." Most of Lynch's meetings at the Vatican in 1864–1865 were with Cardinal Antonelli, rather than the pope. Courtesy of Catholic Diocese of Charleston Archive.

a wide knowledge of events and conditions in America. "I have not, thus far," he remarked, "found any European on the Continent who seemed to be so well informed on the merits of the American question as Cardinal Antonelli." Antonelli told Lynch that when Pope Pius had written to Archbishops Odin and Hughes urging peaceful reconciliation, the Holy Father had not realized how deep was the animosity between the two sides. Now it was evident "that in the ruling condition of popular feeling such a settlement [as the pope had proposed] was then impossible. Sooner or later he [the pope] deems an arrangement must conclude the contest." The cardinal also told Lynch that, after Pius IX's letter to Jefferson Davis had been published, the U.S. minister general, Rufus King, had asked for an explanation of the form of address he had employed. Antonelli explained "that the matter was simple enough." To the Holy See "the Confederate Government had an existence, and exercised the functions of a Government," so it was only proper to address Davis "by the title which his country gave him."[75] The bishop explained "informally" to Antonelli "the purpose and character of my visit to Rome, and the purpose of the Confederate Government in sending me as Commissioner to the States of the Church." The cardinal seemed to Lynch to be "pleased, and did not make any direct reply."[76] Lynch recounted his conversation with Napoleon III, and Antonelli expressed his appreciation of the attitudes of Britain and France. The English, he thought, "had become jealous and rather fearful of the growing power of the United States" and looked on the current troubles "with satisfaction as reducing for a time, the only power which could compete with her in commerce." The British might in fact step in and recognize the South as "the means of preventing... the Unite States from reasserting its former maritime pretensions."[77] The bishop described this interview as "very cordial" and noted that "I have since learned that the impression I made was not unfavourable."[78] Lynch did not comment on the fact that the French army garrisoned Rome, preventing its occupation by Italian forces. Antonelli was not going to advise the pope to do anything contrary to Napoleon while the Vatican remained dependent on France for protection of the Papal States.[79]

On the morning of Monday, July 4, Lynch and his party traveled across Rome to the Vatican in two open carriages. Pius IX received the bishop in private audience, in a simply furnished room. Lynch was received in his "quality as Bishop"—not as a Confederate emissary. The pope inquired about the condition of Charleston and the damage caused by bombardment. The bishop conveyed President Davis's "respect veneration and good will." The pope deplored the destruction of life caused by the war, and Lynch told him that the toll of the dead had reached 120,000 from battle wounds and disease. Pius also expressed his appreciation for an offer of $1,000 from Bishop Timon of Buffalo to help him in his present difficulties; but he had ordered the money be donated in equal portions to Northern and Southern military hospitals.[80] The pontiff took pleasure

Pope Pius IX's papacy began in 1846 and ended with his death, in 1878. Lynch had at least three audiences with Pius during his time as Special Commissioner for the Confederate States. Yet he stated that he never broached the topic of Vatican official recognition of the CSA. This pope and Charleston's bishop became friends, and the latter served an important role in the First Vatican Council in 1871 as he defended Pope Pius's proposed proclamation of papal infallibility. Courtesy of Library of Congress

in recounting a recent occurrence when he was asked by the U.S. minister, Rufus King, to autograph some photographs of himself that were to be sold at a church fair to be held in New York City. He signed the pictures and wrote above his name verses from scripture: *"Mitte gladium tuum in vaginam, et Deus pacis erit vobiscum"* [Put up thy sword into the scabbard (John 18:11). And the God of peace will be with you (Philippians 4:9)]. The pope "finished his narration of this incident by observing playfully, '*Valeat quantum valeat*'" [may the admonition have its weight].[81] At the pope's request Lynch recounted his conversation with Emperor Napoleon III, the import of which he figured Antonelli had already communicated to Pius.

Lynch explained the official character of his Roman visit and why the Richmond government had decided to send a bishop. The pope replied that he appreciated the courtesy shown him by the Confederacy. He spoke of a future when, he believed, peace terms would have to be agreed on between the belligerents.

> It is most clear that you are two nations.... When some foreign power will have to be called in as umpire, then, perhaps, by a miracle, for it would be a miracle if the North should consent, that I might be called in as umpire, I wish it to be understood before hand that I could not say any thing directed to confirm and strengthen slavery. I hold that Christianity has benefited society as to the position of women and as to the position of the slaves. The first has been elevated and made equal to men, and has her appropriate sphere of action. I am happy to believe that [nuns on] both sides have done and are doing immense good in the hospitals. The condition of the Slave was likewise improved, until in the course of time it ceased to exist. As to your slaves, I see clearly that it would be absurd to attempt, as it were to cut the Gordian Knott [*sic*], by an act of Emancipation. But still something might be done looking to an improvement in their position or state, and to a gradual preparation for their freedom at a future opportune time. I have already said this much to several Americans from the South and they seemed to agree with me.[82]

Lynch said he chose not to reply to this. After his conversation with the pope, Bishop Lynch presented to the pontiff Fathers Bannon and Bermingham, his nephew Robert, and Dr. Elisha Gregory, a physician from St. Louis, Missouri. The pope recognized Bermingham, whom he had met before. Bannon, a tall man with a full black beard, made an impression, and the pope called him "*cet homme magnifique.*" Pius asked him who had given him permission to grow a beard. Bannon, bowing low, replied he was "only a poor Confederate chaplain" who had grown the beard when living in army camps. The pope then said, "My son, you may wear your beard."[83]

Although he had made clear the reason for his Roman visit to Cardinals Barnabò and Antonelli and to the Holy Father himself, Bishop Lynch did not at this time seek to present his letters of credence. Indeed, at no time did he do so. As he put it later to Father Isaac Hecker, "that Commissioner could use his own discretion as to where he would present, or withhold his Credentials.... On his arrival in Rome and considering the State of things he judged it best to withhold them. They were never presented.... The Commissioner may have been received very kindly, but it was on his personal character and because Pius IX was always kind and cordial."[84] Lynch asserted to Archbishop John McCloskey in 1865 that "although I accepted an appointment,—yet de facto, I have never been received nor have I sought to present myself here [at Rome] in an official position. I have done no more than I would and could have done, were I here simply as an individual."[85] Lynch was to hold further conversations with Antonellli and Barnabò. He appears to have made a favorable impression on the Holy Father. At the end of July the British minister to the Holy See, Lord Odo Russell (1829–1884), was received in private audience by Pius at the papal summer residence, Castel Gandolfo. Russell reported: "Turning to America the Pope expressed his deep regret that he could do nothing towards the re-establishment of peace between the Federals and the Confederates. He had written to both Presidents Lincoln and Davis, but without success. At the same time he would not conceal from me that all his sympathies were with the Southern Confederacy and he wished them all success. There were, His Holiness added, far more conversions to Catholicism in the South than in the North."[86] Paul Schmidt has suggested that more letters and written reports were reaching Rome from Southern bishops and alumni of the Urban College, and perhaps from this correspondence Pius formed the impression that there were more conversions.[87]

Seward let it be known that the United States was prepared to sever diplomatic relations with the Vatican if Rome made any move toward recognition of the Confederacy. Rufus King paid close attention to Lynch's activities in Rome and reported to Seward that the bishop "has not met with any official recognition from the Papal authorities, nor from what I can learn, is he likely to do so."[88] In his work on the history of the Diocese of Charleston, Father Scott Buchanan has pointed out that, although the Vatican was unenthusiastic about the Union cause and there was considerable sympathy for the Confederacy, there was no desire to appear to approve of the continuation of slavery. The Holy See had cordial relations with the United States, and Antonelli did not wish to alienate any of the powers in a time when the States of the Church were in danger of being occupied and overthrown by the new Kingdom of Italy.

The end result of Bishop Lynch's diplomatic mission for the Confederate States of America can be judged as nothing more that inconclusive. He never presented himself in any official capacity to Pope Pius IX. He had friendly meetings with various Vatican officials, and he impressed them with his intelligence and sincerity, yet no official responses to his conversations were ever pronounced. He became subject to suspicion and condemnation from officials of the soon-to-be triumphant government of the United States and thus was forced to remain in Rome as a wanted belligerent-fugitive until a presidential pardon ended his exile. In this mission he risked much and lost much. The Confederate States gained little and soon were forced to surrender.

The toll on his ecclesiastical career was likewise difficult to discern. He was immediately welcomed back into the upper tier of the American Catholic bishops. His renown as a captivating preacher and public speaker allowed him to relentlessly plead for assistance in rebuilding his diocese throughout the eastern regions of the United States. His American colleagues continued to promote him for and expected his appointment to higher positions. And yet, he never moved out from the burdens that had befallen the Diocese of Charleston. No documentation exists, but much suspicion persists that Lynch's relationship to the Confederate government and his published defense of slavery condemned him to clerical limbo in the eyes of the inner powers of the Vatican—especially after the death of his friend Pope Pius IX.

CHAPTER 7

Slavery Treatise

Bishop Lynch concluded that he would not be able to secure formal recognition of the Confederacy, so he turned to the other charge in his instructions—to influence European opinion in favor of the South. Just after his first audience with Pius IX he wrote in his third and final report to Benjamin: "I am now engaged in drawing up a paper on the actual condition and treatment of slaves at the South, at the request of Msgr. Nardi, one of the judges of the Rota, or supreme court of the papal states." Francesco Nardi was an English-speaking Vatican official who was already acquainted with Timothy Bermingham.[1]

Confederate Propaganda in Europe

All Confederate agents had to contend with the poor reputation that slavery gave their country. They had organized a propaganda effort in Europe. Henry Hotze was probably the most effective. He edited and published the *Index,* a London newspaper that presented the Southern point of view. Across the Channel the French emperor and his supporters generally favored the South, and pro-government newspapers reflected this, but Napoleon III was compelled to pay close attention to French public opinion. Edwin De Leon regarded slavery as an insurmountable public relations problem for the Confederacy among the French. De Leon had published in 1862 a tract that described the slaves of the South as contented and faithful to their masters.[2] In Germany Eduard Maco Hudson, former acting first secretary of the United States legation in Berlin, wrote *The Second War of Independence in America,* in which he described slavery as humane and paternalistic.[3] James Williams, former U.S. minister at Constantinople, brought out *The South Vindicated* in London in 1862, and this was published the following year in Germany, with a foreword by Hudson. Here Williams stressed the property rights of slaveholders, estimating the slaves' value at $2 billion. Berlin's big conservative daily, *Die Kreuz-Zeitung,* reviewed Williams's book with high praise.[4]

In Italy a Confederate sympathizer named Manetta planted articles in the Turin newspapers and wrote for the *Index*. The Roman periodicals *L'Osservatore romano* and *La Civiltà Cattolica*—although they were not vehicles for Confederate propaganda—expressed skepticism about the aims of Lincoln's administration and sympathy toward the South.[5] While it cannot be said with certainty that slavery was decisive in the South's failure to win diplomatic recognition[6], Southern officials and agents believed it was an important factor.

Although Bishop Lynch was fluent in Italian, he drafted his slavery treatise in English and received help from Monsignor Mansi, a member of the College of Consultors in the Sacred Congregation of the Index, in preparing an Italian translation and in making arrangements with a Roman publisher. The bishop evidently worked on the project in July and early August. During this time, Atlanta was taken and burned, and Sherman's army began its march to the sea, while Grant was pushing Lee to the outskirts of Richmond. In Richmond government leaders recognized that desperate measures were required to save the Confederacy.[7] Bishop Lynch did not have regular, prompt communications with his State Department. Few letters from America reached him in Rome, and it is uncertain whether his report of July 5 reached Richmond. He was dependent on reports in Europe and out-of-date Northern U.S. newspapers.

Lynch's Draft of the Pamphlet

He must have completed his work on the pamphlet by mid-August, for the Italian edition, in the form of a letter to a "Dear Friend," bears the date of the Feast of the Assumption, August 15.[8] The Italian version was published anonymously in late 1864 under the title *Lettera di un missionario sulla schiavitù domestica degli Stati Confederati di America.* The copy in the Vatican Library is finely bound in red leather with gilt-stamped decorations and bears a dedication in Lynch's hand to Flavio Chigi "in token of highest respect and homage" by "the author."[9]

He sent a draft to Paris for review by Edwin De Leon, who offered to translate it into French. In vain De Leon recommended that Lynch publish under his own name, arguing that the bishop's sterling reputation would lend credibility to the treatise.[10]

De Leon had run afoul of John Slidell by opening a confidential dispatch from Benjamin to the commissioner. Around the first of February 1864 he received a letter from the secretary of state dismissing him from Confederate government service. Although some historians have stated that De Leon's career as a Confederate propagandist was over, it is clear that Bishop Lynch relied on him for assistance and advice until the end of the war.[11]

For help with a German edition the bishop turned to Francis J. Shadler, a young man born in Germany (1834) and raised in America, who was studying for the Diocese of Charleston at the episcopal seminary (Bischöfliches Seminar) of Mainz. Shadler was devoted to the bishop and was friendly with Robert Lynch.[12] In the autumn Bishop Lynch passed French and German drafts for review to Princess Wittgenstein, an acquaintance in Rome. Françoise zu Sayn-Wittgenstein-Berleburg (née Schweitzer) was a Catholic member of the highest German nobility. Her husband, Prince August, was sometime minister-president of the Duchy of Nassau. The princess had befriended Lynch and introduced him to influential people in Rome. She approved of the German text but declared that the French was execrable, even ludicrous. She strongly recommended having a real Parisian writer retranslate the work into French.[13] Lynch followed her advice and had a really professional translation prepared. The translator's identity is unknown.

In September he made a short trip to Naples so that he could witness at close range the phenomenon known as the liquefaction of the blood of St. Januarius (San Gennaro), a subject on which he later published. He invited to accompany him as his guest young Robert Seton (1839–1923), then a student at Rome's Accademia. Seton, later an archbishop, was a grandson of Elizabeth Ann Bayley Seton (1774–1821), who founded the American community of the Daughters of Charity of St. Vincent de Paul and who was canonized in 1975. Seton thought Lynch "a well set up man and a scholar" who possesses "an exaggerated idea of Good Blood & Family." He declined Lynch's invitation, because "as a loyal American, I would not travel on money furnished by the disloyal Government of Richmond."[14]

In late October word got around Rome that Lynch was preparing to leave the city.[15] He traveled north to important Catholic centers in order to meet with leaders of church and society to promote the Confederate cause and to make arrangements for publishing his treatise. In Florence, then capital of the Kingdom of Italy, he met and charmed Archbishop Giovacchino Limberti.[16] His visit to Turin, capital of Piedmont-Sardinia, was noted and praised in *L'Unità Cattolica,* Northern Italy's most important Catholic newspaper.[17] Antonio Saverio Cardinal DeLuca gave him letters of introduction to Archbishop Gregor Scherr of Munich and to Josef Othmar Cardinal von Rauscher, Prince-Archbishop of Vienna and Primate of Austria. Princess Wittgenstein helped him to gain entrée to important people at the Habsburg court.[18]

In Mainz Lynch conferred with Shadler about the German edition and discussed his mission with Bishop Wilhelm Emmanuel von Ketteler (1811–1877), a leading German hierarch and social reformer. He so impressed the seminary rector, Dr. Christoph Moufang (1817–1890), that the latter gave a lecture to the local Catholic institute in which he praised Lynch and his ideas. Ketteler and Moufang were important in German Catholic and political history. They were proponents of social reforms and founders of a movement that eventually led to the establishment of the Center Party in the united German Empire after 1870. The seminary at Mainz was an important center for the revival of Thomistic theology in the Church.[19] The German edition came out around January 10, 1865, as *Die Sclaverei in den Südstaaten Nord-Amerika's, dargestellt von einem katholischen Missionär.*[20]

The French version appeared in February as *L'Esclavage dans les Etats Confédérés, par un missionnaire.* There were two Paris editions, identical except for paper quality, the first being deluxe.[21] Edwin De Leon handled arrangements with the publisher, including advertising. To the French translation was added a seven-page appendix giving statistics on American blacks, intended to show that they were a people declining in numbers.[22]

Lynch's Treatise

In reading Lynch's essay, it is important to understand that he was raised in South Carolina in a slave-owning family. His parents had about seven slaves, who did not work on the land. The evidence indicates that the elder Lynches were comparatively benign masters, by the lights of their time. The bishop grew up seeing slavery at close range and did not regard it as cruel or inhuman. Also he was himself a slaveholder of some importance, with about ninety-five slaves. (Lynch's slave ownership is discussed in detail in chapter 4).

The Archives of the Diocese of Charleston preserves four handwritten drafts of the pamphlet in English. One of these, in Lynch's hand, with many emendations, appears to be the earliest version and has been designated by this author as "Draft 1." A somewhat more polished text, evidently written by an amanuensis, is labeled "Draft A" by an unknown hand. Another text—also by an amanuensis—has chapter headings added in, and this author has designated it "Draft B." A fourth manuscript, in Bishop Lynch's hand, is very polished and includes chapter headings. This author has designated this as "Draft C." He has published an edited, annotated English-language version of Draft C, with text supplied from other drafts where necessary. The four English drafts have been compared with the three published European versions. As noted herein, there were three European published translations, in Italian, German, and French. Of the English texts, quotations in the current work are taken from the annotated English-language text.[23]

Bishop Lynch's pamphlet was an ambitious Confederate propaganda salvo aimed at the single most difficult public relations problem faced by the South. It was part of a war effort, and its publication came at a time of desperation. This was one of the last proslavery treatises and the longest published discussion of the institution by a Confederate prelate. Slavery was a fundament of Southern civilization. To Lynch and to the leading members of his flock, the question of slavery was no abstract problem but something central to their way of life. Slave ownership was typical of leading Protestant and Catholic churchmen, who were

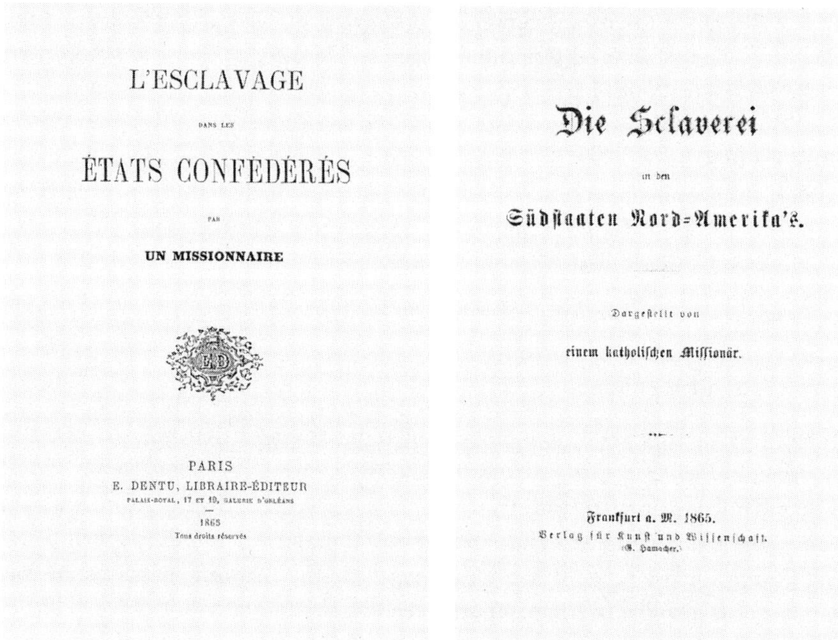
L'ESCLAVAGE

DANS LES

ÉTATS CONFÉDÉRÉS

PAR

UN MISSIONNAIRE

PARIS

E. DENTU, LIBRAIRE-ÉDITEUR

PALAIS-ROYAL, 17 ET 19, GALERIE D'ORLÉANS

1865

Tous droits réservés

Die Sclaverei

in den

Südstaaten Nord-Amerika's.

Dargestellt von

einem katholischen Missionär.

Frankfurt a. M. 1865.

Verlag für Kunst und Wissenschaft.

(G. Hamacher.)

Cover of Lynch's slavery treatise as published in French and German. Written by Bishop Lynch in Rome while on his diplomatic mission. This treatise was also published in Italian. No records remain regarding the manner or quantity of its circulation. Courtesy of Catholic Diocese of Charleston Archive.

among its most articulate apologists. Well-to-do Southern Catholics often owned slaves, and prominent laypeople of his diocese aided Bishop Lynch in the acquisition and management of his slaves.[24]

Southern white clergy—Lynch among them—typically defined slavery as a system of mutual obligations between master and servant and taught that slave owners had clear Christian obligations toward their bondsmen.[25] Like other Catholic prelates, Lynch opposed the abolitionists, associating them with Know-Nothingism and virulent anti-Catholicism.[26] He followed his predecessor, Bishop John England, and his erstwhile metropolitan, Archbishop Francis Patrick Kenrick of Baltimore, in distinguishing between the slave trade, condemned by Roman pontiffs from Pius II to Gregory XVI, and domestic slavery, teaching that the latter was licit.[27]

A master had an inescapable duty to provide slaves with adequate food, shelter, clothing, and health care, plus secure retirement in old age. Lynch had applauded Bishop Augustin Verot's *A Tract for the Times* (1861) and had assisted in its distribution. Like Verot, Lynch stressed whites' obligation to promote and protect slaves' marriages and their families' integrity. He shared Verot's view that "the laws of morality are not different for the different races of men."[28] Like Martin John Spalding, he contrasted the slaves' happy state with the degraded condition of free blacks and feared that emancipation would unleash a race war leading to black Americans' extermination.[29] Lynch's opinions largely mirrored those of his personal friend and political adversary, Archbishop Hughes of New York, arguably the most influential American Catholic figure of his time. Hughes thought slavery was sanctioned, if not ordained, by God, acceptable because it afforded blacks physical and economic security, and preferable to "Africa's barbarism." Hughes opposed the abolitionists' solution, because it failed to provide for freed slaves' welfare once they were free, and because abolition, if precipitate, would bring about "disruption" leading to a replay of the horrors of Haiti, which he described in the most lurid terms. The New York prelate saw gradual emancipation as "the only alternative to a reign of lawlessness and economic chaos."[30]

In his wartime essay Bishop Lynch disclaimed any intention to write "philosophy," seeking instead to give a scientific description and analysis of the actual institution.[31] He prefaced the German edition: "To say that *freedom is better than slavery*, is to my mind very much like saying that *health is better than sickness*. . . . In these pages I have given . . . a diagnosis of slavery."[32] American slavery had often been described by travelers, novelists, "philanthropists and fanatics," all of whom had distorted the facts.

The ill-informed thought the American South a "slumbering volcano," ready to erupt in a massive slave revolt. But the course of the war belied this, since, even following the Emancipation Proclamation, slaves continued to work contentedly for their masters: "I do not believe that five out of a thousand have voluntarily gone to the Yankee Armies."[33] Domestic slavery, said Lynch, was "simply the continued retention in slavery of those who were originally brought in by the slave trade"—which he condemned.[34] Nevertheless, the slaves had left behind in Africa horrible conditions and an "almost normal state . . . of *bellum omnium in omnes*. . . . Only three years ago, the present King of Dahomey celebrated the obsequies of his Father by slaughtering, it is said, five thousand captives, letting their blood flow into the grave as a last tribute to the deceased King."[35] Slaves enjoyed peace and security in the New World, where they could "at least obtain a knowledge of the true God, and might save their soul." Southern proslavery apologists frequently depicted Africa as "the scene of unmitigated savagery."[36]

There were three main classes of slaves: house servants, "those who hire their own time," and agricultural workers. "The house servants do not differ in their treatment and work from the house servants in every civilized country, except that unfortunately three of them will not do as much work as one European or Northern White servant." These received no wages, but "they receive abundant gratuities, and love to give full evidence of it in the natty hats the broadcloth coats and the polished boots of the men the silks and ribbons and flashy jewelry of the women, as they parade the streets or assemble in church on Sundays." [37]

Slaves "who hire their own time," said Lynch, were numerous in cities and towns and "may be said to enjoy, at least to some extent, the privileges of freedom. . . . It is generally found that they become idle and dissipated, and plunge into drunkenness and other vices. . . . They are generally a bad population for themselves and for the other negroes with whom they mingle."[38]

Agricultural laborers, or field hands, constituted nine-tenths of the slave population. In a climate injurious to whites, "the African constitution claims its privilege and the negro exults in the fullness of health in a tropical heat." "Negroes receive in strong solid food, fully as much as they can consume, and have something over to satisfy a negro's natural inclination to waste. . . . The work of the [Negro] . . . is light; his food is abundant; his condition is one of comfort, his necessities in sickness and old age are all provided for."[39]

Responding to charges of inhumane punishments and cruel treatment of slaves, the bishop admitted that cruelty sometimes occurred in all societies: "But that is the fault of human nature, not the system of Slavery."[40] He defended flogging as the main punishment inflicted on slaves for wrongdoing. "Imprisonment for days or weeks would not answer. If the imprisonment be light and merely nominal, it ceases to be a punishment and becomes a reward, allowing the negro to indulge in that greatest of all his luxuries,—idleness. . . . Flagellation is used for slaves as for children, because it pains without inflicting injury, and punishes without incapacitating for work." "Where a negro is insubordinate, or vicious to an extent to demoralize the other negroes, and cannot reclaimed by ordinary punishments, he is sold away from the scene of his offences."[41]

Southern states forbade teaching slaves to read and write. Lynch said that legal proscription of black literacy resulted from fear that abolitionists would incite slaves to revolt, thereby bringing on "a renewal in their midst of the horrible atrocities of St. Domingo."[42] Dread of the "horrors of San Domingo" was particularly strong in Charleston and the South Carolina lowcountry, where some five hundred whites from Saint-Domingue had taken refuge in the 1790s following the great slave uprising. Their descendents were prominent in the Catholic community, and their atrocity stories profoundly influenced the attitudes of white Carolinians, who saw in Northern abolitionism a new French Revolution that would bring on another Haiti in their homeland. Yet, like most Southern white clergy, the Charleston prelate favored "oral religious instruction of the negroes, old or young in the doctrines of Christianity."[43]

Lynch stated that slave owners' claims were limited to labor service. "In the matter of Religion, of morality, and, a measure, of his family relations, does [the slave] hold himself free." Blacks might join any church they chose. "Essentially a sensuous race, loving the excitement of an hour, and having generally good voices, and a natural sense of Music, the negroes love to join in prayer meetings or assemblies of their own, where much of the service consists of all singing hymns together; where the discourses are generally rude and impassioned." "With strong passions and prone to give them license, the negroes run readily into Antinomianism."[44] One black, "a prominent member of the Church, being called to account by his minister for licentiousness, and warned of the consequences of his sin before the judgment seat of God, is said to have replied: 'What does the Scripture say we must do to be saved? *Believe,* and *be baptized.* Well, I believe, and I have been baptized. I have got to be saved. That is all about it.'"[45] Yet "Negroes believe firmly in the Divinity of our Saviour, and in the Redemption." Catholicism "has a wonderful power over the negroes, when they yield to God's grace. They love exercises of piety, and are enchanted by the pomp of the Ceremonial. They are naturally kind, are willing to make sacrifices for charity; and among our Catholic negroes we sometimes find exemplary instances of that to them most difficult virtue,—purity." Except in Maryland and Louisiana, with their large Catholic populations, little progress had been made in elevating the moral state of blacks. This was due to the scarcity of Catholic clergy. Yet only through Roman Catholicism could they "be raised from their present state of moral turpitude."[46]

"The negroes are, as a race, very prone to excesses, and unless restrained, plunge madly into the lowest depths of licentiousness." This was not caused by slavery; in fact, the free blacks were "far more immoral than the slaves," and plantation discipline worked to restrain immorality.[47] The bishop labeled "grossly false" the charge "that masters, abusing their authority over female slaves, riot in debauchery."[48] Nonetheless, "the passions of men exist and will seek their gratification whether Slavery exists or not." Some young unmarried white men engaged in sexual intercourse with black females, "and . . . the partners of their guilt are generally free coloured women. It should be further noted as a fact, that just as such females abound, and debauchery is thrown into that channel, the white females are exempted from its influence. Nowhere save in Ireland are they so pure as in the South. . . . There is unfortunately too much libertinism between the white race and the negroes, whether free or slaves, in the South. But it replaces libertinism which would otherwise exist in greater extent than it does in the white race itself."[49]

Southern state laws did not recognize the validity of slave marriages, but slave owners strove "to render the . . . unions of the negroes permanent." It was customary for a master to permit weekend conjugal visitations when husband and wife lived on different plantations, and often an owner would purchase a spouse from another so that the couple might live together. "So far as Catholic owners are concerned, they recognize and are guided by the teaching of the Church, and hold it to be a sin to separate a man and wife legitimately married."[50]

Lynch flatly and correctly denied the charge that many plantation owners bred slaves for profit.[51]

Considering the future of slavery, Lynch reviewed in turn different scenarios. Examples of manumission of individuals and families were, he said, "not rare." He lauded the unofficial practice of trusteeship, whereby a slave became nominally the property of a white who in fact left the person to live "in freedom, . . . at liberty to work and earn for himself."[52] He opposed sudden, general emancipation: "Its first and immediate consequence would be to put two races face to face, in the most deadly antagonism and to inaugurate at once an inhuman war unparalleled in the history of the world." "We may lament, but we cannot deny facts." He pointed to the deadly fighting in New Zealand, where the Maoris were facing extinction—a development deplored in debate in the House of Lords.[53] Uncompensated seizure of slaveholders' property—which he estimated at 9 billion francs—would exacerbate this conflict.[54] Freed slaves would be ill equipped to fend for themselves in the modern world, and "a very large portion would soon be found in such want as to become a burden on the charity of the rest of the community."[55]

He claimed that during the war at least a quarter-million Southern slaves had come under the jurisdiction of Union forces and had been declared free. But the Northern army had failed to take good care of the freedmen, so that "not one half are now living." Each published edition of the pamphlet included a translation of an article from the London *Index* about the lamentable fate of freedmen under U. S Army care on Louisiana plantations. The account was one of great pathos: blacks dying of hunger, disease, and despair—summed up, said the bishop, in the cry of an expiring man to an army officer: "There is nobody to care for us." The quoted article was in fact based—with some embellishments—on genuine federal reports.[56] The bishop asserted that the blacks would have been far better off in the care of "some kind and careful owner, like an esteemed friend of mine, the richest proprietor of South Carolina, who would provide for their necessities." He was serving in the U.S. Congress when he learned of a cholera outbreak among his slaves. He left Washington and hurried home, not to return to Congress until the cholera had disappeared.[57]

Mass transportation of blacks slaves to Africa could not succeed, for this would require an unparalleled and costly concerted effort by all the leading Christian countries. The societies the freedmen might establish in Africa would be dreadful. "Of self government the negroes are incapable. Left to themselves they would fall under a tyranny like San Domingo, equally cruel as ludicrous,—the ferocity of Africa clothed in a travesty of imperial Europe."[58]

In his conclusion, the bishop held out a glimmer of hope, a Catholic solution, as he saw it, and one of special interest, since it foreshadowed some of his own postwar actions. "One feature of the African mind might guide us,—their innate, though vague reverence for Religion." Communities of freedmen "might be put under the entire charge of some religious body, like that of the Society of Jesus. The negroes would yield readily to this religious, almost theocratical rule. . . . It is only in such a way, that these communities can be successfully and prosperously governed. It is only doing on a larger scale what was done so well in the Indian missions of California and of Paraguay in the last century." Unless something of the sort could be achieved, "at least, then, the Slaves of the Confederate States may ask to be left in their present state of quiet and content, waiting the future which God only knows; and not be doomed at once to ruin, if not speedy extermination, for the sake of a mere theory."[59]

Lynch wrote for an audience of sophisticated, influential Europeans. He did not present slavery as superior to European free labor systems, which were often characterized as inhumane by Southern apologists. He did not cite scripture in defense of servitude or cast his arguments in theological language. Lynch was respected as a man of science, and he chose to present his view of slavery as that of an impartial observer of nature. He did not follow the example of Bishop Auguste Martin of Natchitoches, Louisiana, whose 1861 pastoral letter cited the "curse of Ham" and other scripture in support of slavery. During 1864 the Holy Office was secretly scrutinizing Martin's epistle, and possibly some Vatican official warned Lynch against using such an approach. Ironically, just when the German and French editions were in press, the Confederate government dispatched Duncan F. Kenner to Britain and France with a promise of general emancipation in return for diplomatic recognition. No available evidence indicates that Lynch was aware of Kenner's secret mission, which proved a failure.[60]

On June 14, 1864, the Confederate Congress passed a manifesto reasserting the rectitude of the Southern cause, the sovereign rights of the member states, their peaceful aspirations, and the guilt of the North for having committed aggression against them.

The eight millions of Southerners "animated with one spirit . . . can never be conquered." The manifesto promised that the war would cease if the Union stopped its "aggressions against us."[61] The document was aimed at obtaining diplomatic recognition, and Benjamin dispatched copies to Mason, Slidell, and Mann. Meeting in Paris, the three commissioners planned to submit it to the European governments. Slidell asked James T. Soutter, a prominent physician from Norfolk, Virginia, who was traveling to Rome, to deliver to Bishop Lynch the manifesto, the commissioners' letter to Cardinal Antonelli, and a written instruction to Lynch. When Soutter arrived in Rome, the bishop had already departed on his northern travels. So the physician sought a meeting with Antonelli, presented the manifesto to him, and even obtained an audience with the pope. Pius IX assured Soutter "that he had done all that he could" and would continue to pray and work for peace, and the doctor came away "convinced that the Pope was our earnest friend, not only in the interest of humanity, but because he thought we had justice and right on our side."[62] As it turned out, the manifesto did not change European attitudes. Foreign ministers Russell of Britain and Drouyn de Lhys of France responded with restatements of their governments' neutrality. In like manner, Cardinal Antonelli wrote of the pope's "continuing benignant disposition." The only other government that responded was Sweden's.[63]

While Bishop Lynch was away from Rome, John Bannon decided to return to Ireland. He wrote Lynch that he felt useless as an aide and unable to get along with Timothy Bermingham. He was to spend the rest of his life in Ireland as a member of the Society of Jesus.[64] Lynch liked Bannon, and there seems to have been no ill feelings between them. The bishop lent him money, which he dutifully repaid as soon as he was able. Bermingham, for his part, later expressed cordial feelings toward Bannon.[65] While staying in Rome, Conrad Wise Chapmen, still an ordinance sergeant in the Confederate Army, experienced health problems that forbade his prompt return to active duty. At the request of his father, Bishop Lynch, in his official capacity as Confederate commissioner, authorized an extension of the young man's furlough. This allowed Chapman to spend time in Paris until he could obtain passage home. As it happened, Conrad left Rome in December 1864 and did not return to America until after the fall of the Confederacy.[66]

Impact of the Pamphlet

Lynch's pamphlet caused a stir, though not as great as he had hoped. In Rome *La Civiltà Cattolica* welcomed a statement of the "true condition of slavery in the American South . . . set forth in this letter written by an impartial person, superbly well-informed and of broad and just views." The Paris edition was hailed by Hotze's *Index:* "No one has had better opportunities than Dr. Lynch for forming a just estimate of the condition of the slaves in the Confederate States, since he has passed his whole life in the South and exercised his holy calling there for the last twenty-four years." The British *Army and Navy Gazette* called the French edition of the pamphlet "by far the best which has appeared on the subject of slavery." *L'Unità Cattolica* of Turin described the work as "*preziosissima* [most valuable]." Favorable comments appeared in the London *Standard* and other European periodicals.[67] But severe criticism came from Catholic liberals in France. Count Charles de Montalembert (1810–1870) declared in *Le Correspondant:* "I refuse to acknowledge the priestly character of the author. If the writer of this shameful book really were a priest, and if it had sufficed for him to live, as he says, among American planters for 24 years, to proclaim the utility and legitimacy of black slavery, to see in their very servitude the only possible barrier to their licentiousness, the sole fact of such perversion of moral feeling and priestly conscience would constitute the severest argument against the social and religious regime of the slave countries."[68] Montalembert's friend and antislavery author Augustin Cochin wrote Lynch: "May I bless God with all my heart that He has permitted the death of this stubborn plague which weighed upon your country and the Christian conscience."[69]

Lynch wrote from what he considered a Catholic perspective. He published in Italy, France, and the German Rhineland—all Catholic countries. He asserted that Catholicism must play an essential role in the education and salvation of African Americans, especially as they won their freedom. He foresaw a need for Church guidance, in particular by courageous religious communities. The pamphlet documents a transition from defense of slavery to an apostolate to blacks. The real long-term impact of the pamphlet was in fact a negative one on Bishop Lynch's career. His proslavery essay was to prove his albatross when he was nominated for the See of Baltimore in 1872 and as coadjutor of New York in 1880.

While the bishop was traveling in Europe, Sherman's army marched through Georgia. Confederate forces evacuated Savannah on December 21, and the Union army took possession of the city on the twenty-second. When they marched in, Bishop Verot was saying Mass. "I heard their yells and hurrahs," he recorded.[70] At that moment Lynch was in Paris, unaware of this turn of events. Having met with leading Europeans and arranged for publication of his pamphlet, he felt that he had done all he could for his country. Writing from Paris on Christmas Eve, he informed Cardinal Barnabò that he had sent his resignation to Richmond effective February 1865. He hoped to leave for America around January 20.[71] The bishop was shocked by the speed of the Confederate collapse. Many copies of the German and French editions of his treatise went unsold.[72] As things turned out, almost another year passed before he could return to Charleston. Again, in the final analysis, the publication of his defense of slavery as practiced in the American South, would have to be considered a failure. He failed to bring about a change in the general European perception that the end of slavery was rightfully inevitable.

CHAPTER 8

War's End and Return Home

While the bishop was out of the country, the war dragged on to its horrible end. While the number of Catholics in the two Carolinas who became casualties of war is not known with certainty, it is estimated that one in every fourteen or fifteen white South Carolinians died and that between 31 and 35 percent of the state's young white male population was killed.[1] Both black and white Carolinians were affected by shortages of food and other commodities. By the end of 1864 most people were aware that the end of the Confederacy was near.

Columbia

General William Tecumseh Sherman's army entered Savannah on December 22. It crossed the Savannah River into South Carolina on February 1, 1865, and began a rapid march north toward Columbia. The capital city had been considered a place of safety, and many people from the coast had taken refuge there, bringing with them much of their property. Father Jeremiah O'Connell later recalled that he was "the innocent cause of detaining in Columbia many families who were fleeing before the Federal army since it first touched South Carolina and were disposed to retire still farther into the interior." But Sherman, "that man of iron will, a gentleman of first class military education," would not allow things to get out of hand.[2] Thousands did flee Columbia, and Confederate troops commanded by General Beauregard evacuated the city early on February 17. Public order broke down as the Union soldiers marched in. Great quantities of whiskey were available, and the troops became drunk and disorderly. There were wild scenes of looting, and many fires, some accidental, some deliberately set, broke out, the flames fanned by high winds.[3]

In the disaster that befell Columbia during the terrible night of February 17–18, Catholic institutions and people suffered spectacular losses. As the first Union troops entered the city, Mayor T. J. Goodwyn and a group of citizens met them to surrender the city. Jeremiah O'Connell was a member of the group, and he asked for protection of the Ursuline Convent and school. Mother Baptista Lynch, superior of the convent and girls' academy, sent a letter to Sherman. As Sherman recalled, Baptista informed him that she had been a teacher at the Ursuline Academy in Brown County, Ohio, when his daughter Mary ("Minnie") was enrolled. Sherman had Colonel Charles Ewing, who was also his brother-in-law, assure Baptista "that we contemplated no destruction of any property in Columbia at all."[4]

Around midnight, drunken soldiers broke into the convent, and some looting took place. With fires breaking out all around, Baptista and Father O'Connell concluded that the Sisters and their young charges must evacuate the convent and school. The convent was located in the center of downtown Columbia, at the corner of Richardson (Main) and Blanding Streets. It would have been difficult to save the building in a general conflagration, and that is what broke out during the night.[5] The Sisters wanted to remain in the convent with their pupils, although in the evening Father O'Connell removed the Eucharist from the chapel to St. Peter's Church, a few blocks away. Conditions in the capital descended into chaos. High winds spread the flames of the many fires, and the U.S. Army did little to fight the flames. It was to become the lasting conviction of many white South Carolinians that Sherman ordered the burning of the city. Of the many horrors of that night, the burning of the Ursuline Convent would be seen as emblematic of Sherman's disregard—even contempt—for human decency and for religion itself. At the time, many Southerners such as Mary Chesnut believed that Sherman was a Catholic and condemned him for sacrilege.[6] In fact, Sherman was not Catholic, but his wife, Ellen, was devoutly so, and his son Thomas would later be ordained a priest.[7]

Under the firm, cool direction of Mother Baptista, the nuns and their girl pupils prepared to evacuate. Carrying only a few essential belongings, two groups walked in procession through the burning streets to the nearby St. Peter's Church. Eyewitnesses were impressed by the discipline and good order of the evacuation. The Urusulines recorded in their "Annals" that "each young lady had given to her a small bundle containing a change of clothing & all were desired to take their rank as usual [that is, walk in their usual disciplined order]" to prevent straggling or panic. According to the Sisters, the convent was plundered by soldiers. Almost all the property of the convent and school and the pupils' personal belongings were burned or looted. The nineteen nuns and more than seventy pupils spent the night in the churchyard, assisted by Father J. J. O'Connell and by Dr. John Lynch (the brother of Mother Baptista and the bishop), whose house in the neighborhood was spared. Around 3:00 A.M., the cross atop the cupola of the convent fell, after which the building was lost. The "Annals" of the convent record that on the next day Sherman rode by the churchyard, and Mother Baptista went to him. He was sitting on horseback, smoking a cigar and "apparently in high spirits." Dismounting, he approached her with his hand extended, saying "in a bright and cheerful manner, 'Ah! Sister these are times in which to practice Christian fortitude and patience.' 'You have made them thus to us, General,' she replied, extending her hand in an equally cordial and cheerful manner. 'I am sorry, truly sorry, that your Convent was burned,' said he, and a short interview followed in which it was beautiful to witness such an absence of passion and resentment between the injured by the injurer." The general, raising his voice, exclaimed, "This is the fault of your Negroes who gave whiskey to my men! It is the fault of your Mayor, who ought to have destroyed all the liquor before the Army entered your town."[8] Sherman always maintained that he had not ordered the burning of the city. "It was accidental," he said, "and in my judgment began with the cotton which General Hampton's men had set fire." At night the high winds fanned the flames, and the conflagration got out of control.[9]

Mother Baptista recorded that General Sherman "made us a visit, expressed his regret at the burning of our convent, disclaimed the act, attributing it to the intoxication of his soldiers, and told me to choose any house in town for a convent and it would be ours."[10] In a kind of form letter she sent to various bishops after the fire asking for assistance, she referred to the convent's "accidental" destruction.[11] The U.S. Army assigned the home of General John Smith Preston (1809–1881) to the nuns and their pupils and allocated food and other provisions. Shortly afterward the nuns and their students moved to Bishop Lynch's property at Valle Crucis, some three miles from downtown Columbia.[12] After the war Mother Baptista blamed the conflagration on drunken soldiery and praised Sherman for having been "a splendid General and . . . a magnanimous enemy who cheerfully and promptly raises a fallen foe."[13] Mother Baptista herself earned renown for her courage and leadership. Contemporaries described her as "a person of high mental attainments. . . . Indeed no one ever came into her presence without admiring her. She was majestic in her carriage and demeanor."[14]

The Ursuline Sisters' losses amounted to some $150,000. Through the years they made claims to the U.S. government seeking an indemnity for the destruction of their property, but nothing came of this, since the government never accepted that the fire had been deliberately set. The Sisters and Catholics of the diocese—indeed, Columbia generally—always put the blame for the fire and destruction of one-third of the city on the Union army. Controversy over "who burned Columbia" persists to this day. The Southern view was that such wanton destruction went beyond the accepted practices of war and resulted from barbarism. The U.S. Army's view was that what happened was unfortunate but simply the result of a war that had become progressively more destructive.[15]

After Sherman departed Columbia, his cavalry wing under General Hugh Judson Kilpatrick (1836–1881) occupied Lancaster at the close of February. Kilpatrick occupied Lancaster for several days. His men were resented by whites for their rude manners and relentless search for hidden valuables.[16] Sherman's army occupied Cheraw, where the bishop's parents and other family lived. Confederate forces evacuated Cheraw on March 4, and Sherman occupied the town on the seventh. Cheraw offered much plunder in the form of food, small arms, gunpowder, Confederate cannons, and other supplies, but few houses were destroyed, and the town came through relatively unscathed.[17] From Cheraw the Union army then proceeded into North Carolina, occupying Fayetteville on March 11. Troops marching from New Bern and Wilmington joined Sherman at Goldsboro. Fayetteville was the site of St. Patrick's Church. It was estimated that there had been only six hundred Catholics in North Carolina at the start of the war.[18]

Charleston

On February 17, 1865, Charleston fell to the enemy. The long siege ended amid scenes of disorder, fires, and looting. Soldiers of the Twenty-first U.S. Colored Regiment occupied the city, to the happy cheers of black Charlestonians and the horror of the remaining whites—Confederate soldiers and most of the wealthier whites having abandoned the town. Union officers did work to stop looting and to restore public order. Regular city government was suspended for some eight months.[19]

The weight of responsibility for administering the Church in Charleston fell squarely on the shoulders of Father John Moore, who had just become pastor of St. Patrick's Church. John Moore was a young man, born in 1834 in Castletown, County Westmeath, Ireland. His family were Famine Irish who had emigrated to the United States in 1848 and settled in Charleston. He studied for the priesthood in the Charleston Diocesan Seminary, then at the Seminary of Combrée in France, and finally at the Urban College, where he was awarded a doctorate in theology in 1860.[20] After the deaths of Fathers O'Neill and Fillion, Charleston and its outlying missions were served by two priests: John Moore and Father Richard Sullivan Baker, pastor of St. Mary's. Baker was elderly and often in poor health and had a somewhat difficult personality. Conditions in the conquered city were terrible—as they were throughout the state. Moore recorded that Fillion died on February 21 "of a malignant typhoid fever contracted attending the Federal prisoners at the stockade near Florence in this state."[21]

Moore did not know the whereabouts of Father Croghan, thought to be with the Sisters of Mercy at their hospital in Virginia. He had no means of communicating with James Corcoran and no contact with Jeremiah O'Connell in Columbia. There was great confusion and misery among the Catholic people of the Carolinas. On the day after Fillion's funeral Moore wrote to the Metropolitan Archbishop to apprise him of the situation. He described his duties at St. Patrick's and in Charleston and its surrounding areas as "very onerous." He feared that "unless we get prompt assistance from your Grace we cannot long endure the fatigue.... Bishop Lynch's presence was never more needed than now, in Charleston." Spalding had already intervened in the northern part of the diocese. Moore reiterated his concerns in a second letter, on March 30.[22]

In October 1864 a Catholic layman wrote to Spalding from New Bern, North Carolina, on the need for a priest in that area. John Prime had for many years been a lay reader and leader of the Catholic congregation of Washington, North Carolina. When Union troops arrived, the Catholic parish church was destroyed, along with much of the town. Prime had relocated to New Bern, where there was no priest but where Catholics assembled at the church every Sabbath. They feared the building might be seized as abandoned property. They also collected books for a small library. Prime asked the archbishop to send a priest to serve the numerous Catholic soldiers, sailors, and laypeople. Spalding thereupon asked the Redemptorists for priests, and they sent two to North Carolina. The archbishop judged that he must take responsibility for the Charleston diocese.[23]

In response to Moore's appeal, Spalding appointed him to act as vicar general until Lynch could be heard from. It was Spalding's intention to put the young Moore in place of the deceased Fillion for Charleston and its dependent missions. James Corcoran would continue to be vicar general for the rest of the huge diocese, provided he could be contacted. Otherwise Moore was to have full authority, and he was empowered to judge the situation for himself.[24] Corcoran learned in a roundabout way of Moore's appointment, and he inquired of the archbishop whether he still had faculties given him by Lynch. Spalding assured him that he was still vicar outside Charleston.[25] Moore and Corcoran had no direct contact with each other for months, and this caused confusion and made it difficult for the few clergy to minister effectively to the faithful.

From Moore's perspective, conditions were appalling. In the spring, Charlestonians who had evacuated the doomed city were returning to their homes in great numbers—in part because food was scarce in the interior of the state—and calling increasingly on priests for assistance. "Our people are without money; I never saw such distress in this City." Workers were being paid a pittance, "and for their work, and the very life's blood is ground out of them for taxes." Moore was grateful for monetary help from a Northern Irish Protestant, John King, who came with the Union army.[26] The young priest said he was in good health and felt that he could "stand at my post" with two additional priests, for St. Joseph and the cathedral. Father Hippolyte Gaché, a Jesuit recruited by Spalding, came to lend a hand. Gaché and Moore were kept constantly busy with "sick calls from the country" and other demands for aid. Father Baker was not in good health and was willing to do only what he could not avoid. Moore and other priests carried out their duties in spite of South Carolina's steamy summer heat and the menace of smallpox. In June the Sisters of Our Lady of Mercy and their chaplain,

Father Charles Croghan, made their way home from Montgomery White Sulphur Springs, returning by way of New York and Baltimore, but Croghan delayed reporting for work in South Carolina, in part because he resented being made subordinate to a younger priest.[27]

The Sisters and Father Croghan arrived in Charleston on July 9, and Moore appointed Croghan pastor of St. Joseph's Parish—"at present the very best in the diocese."[28] Father Patrick Ryan had left the Charleston area in the winter of 1864–1865 to visit missions between there and Augusta, Georgia. But Ryan traveled where he chose, and for six months did not report his whereabouts to anyone in the see city. John Moore felt that he was abandoned in trying circumstances, not least the sweltering Charleston summer. His growing frustration with the distant bishop erupted. Priests such as Croghan, Ryan, and even Baker had been too much indulged by Lynch. "My heart is nearly broken with him for the last four or five years. He is everything except a Bishop."[29] Moore, citing several cases, complained that some of the priests of the diocese "will never be satisfied unless they have the choosing of their own position. Bishop Lynch is a great deal to blame for the spirit of insubordination which has grown up among his clergy." "To all appearances he does not feel for their wants on the poor missions of the diocese, makes no exertion to encourage them, appears never to think of meeting them;—he has never visited his diocese: the children are growing up without confirmation—If he never comes to us a changed man we had better no Bishop at all."[30]

In fact, Charleston's capture did not crush the spirit of all its Irish Catholics. St. Patrick's Benevolent Society had been founded in 1817 to assist poor Irish immigrants. Traditionally the Society put on a grand parade and celebration on St. Patrick's Day. Festivities had been suspended during the war, but just a month after the federal occupation, on March 17, 1865, the Society organized a parade and attended Mass at St. Mary's Church. A traditional celebration took place at the Masonic Hall with "tumblers" and "trays of cake and cheese." A joyful participant in the festivities was Colonel Stewart L. Woodford of the U.S. Army, post commander of the occupying force, who was made an honorary member, along with his adjutant general.[31]

In Lynch's absence John Moore was left holding the bag in Charleston and its dependencies; he did not like it. Catholic faithful were hurting, many were destitute, and conditions were deplorable. Things got worse in the heat of the Charleston summer. In September Moore expressed his exasperation to the archbishop:

> It is my earnest prayer that Bishop Lynch come back to us a changed man; but if not, we, his priests and people, are to be pitied indeed. Lest I should appear to give expression to fears that have no foundation, I will endeavour

> to make it a statement of his debts: I feel pretty sure that I can ascertain that he owes one hundred thousand dollars. Considering the impoverished state of the diocese it is not easy to see how he will meet the calls that will press upon him on his arrival. Still I would hope and sacrifice my life for Almighty God in his diocese, if he would only cease to be: a digger of artesian wells, a Railroad engineer, an architect giving his knowledge in that department even to ornament the Unitarian Church, a diplomatist, a politician, a banker, &c. and be—a Bishop. He will be more popular among the Protestants of the South on his return than ever before, and this will be an evil, because he fails to turn his influence to account for the Church and he does not appear to reflect that his popularity will not avail him in the day of judgment. He is not popular with Catholics, because they have some knowledge of what a Bishop should be.[32]

Spalding tried to reassure Moore that things would get better. He was "sorry to hear financial condition of Diocese so unpromising & that the Rev. Clergy seem to me so little organized & well regulated. I trust however, that in the return of yr Bishop things will march better than you anticipate."[33]

In July Moore complained that a letter Lynch had written in Rome on May 10 to former Governor Aiken had passed through his (Moore's) hands; yet Lynch's own clergy had not yet heard from him.[34] That month Moore read a news item in the *Charleston Daily Courier* that stated that the bishop was already in New York—although this proved to be erroneous. By mid-August Moore did receive a letter from Lynch. Difficulties of communication puzzled Lynch's correspondents. Eventually even Mother Baptista complained in a letter to her brother that their father, Conlaw Lynch, "thinks it very strange that he has never received a line from you & that now when the posts are open you do not write."[35] No one was more annoyed by the bishop's apparent silence than John Moore. But Lynch did in fact write to Moore from Rome on August 21—a letter that Moore received:

> I cannot understand how it is I receive no letter from you. This is the fifth I have written, and I yearn for some reply. Please let me know how things are getting on ecclesiastically. . . . Have you received the draft on Paris I sent you for fr. 10.000? Please let me know, if you can find out, what became of the four drafts for fr. 5.000 each I left in hands of Rev Mr. Fillion, and another draft for 240—the former at least never came to Paris for payment and I presume they were still in his hands at the time of his death. R.I.P. . . . Give me a full account if you can of how things stand. For if I cannot get back at once I may have to make important arrangements—which indeed I would

> have made ere this, but that I wished or hoped to receive such details as would guide me.[36]

Lynch presumed that Father Croghan had returned to Charleston and that the newly ordained William Meriwether and Harry Northrop had arrived, so that Moore would have the needed assistance. Both Daniel Quigley and John Schachte were completing studies at the American College (where Lynch was staying) and would come to the diocese. Lynch described to Harry Northrop his frustration in trying to communicate with Charleston.[37] Clearly Lynch was trying to make contact and resume his administration of the diocese. But Moore was put off by Lynch's absence and what he took to be his lack of interest in Charleston. This was to prove a permanent disillusionment with Lynch as a worthy shepherd of the Catholic community and was to have consequences for Lynch's career later on. Spalding asked Moore to inform Baptista that Lynch had been granted a pardon (discussed in the next section) and that would be coming home soon. On October 12 Spalding wrote that he was expecting Lynch's arrival any day. Moore had asked about appointing priests to various parishes and missions, but Spalding counseled patience so that the bishop could make those decisions.[38]

Before Lynch's return, Spalding took steps to alleviate the desperate humanitarian situation in the South. In addition to appeals from Moore, he had received a plaintive letter from Jeremiah J. O'Connell about the losses suffered in Columbia.[39] He made a special collection in the Archdiocese of Baltimore for "the suffering poor of the South." In October he sent $1,600 to John Moore and $300 to J. J. O'Connell for distribution to destitute people without regard to creed in Charleston and Columbia. In addition, $1,300 was sent to North Carolina, most of it to James Corcoran in Wilmington. Corcoran reported that he shared the money with Wilmington's Episcopalian, Methodist, Baptist, and Presbyterian ministers, giving only to white congregations, because the "colored churches have the Freedmen's Bureau or Northern charitable associations at their beck."[40] Corcoran had written to Spalding to inform him that Lynch had named him vicar general for all parts of the diocese outside the city and surroundings of Charleston. In the event of Wilmington's capture by the federals, he could choose whether to "retire within the Confederate lines" or to remain with the Catholics of Wilmington. Wilmington fell to Union forces on Washington's birthday, February 22, 1865. This portended a rapid end to the Confederacy, for Wilmington was the port through which vital supplies reached the South.[41] Corcoran sent the bishop's faculties to Father Timothy Sullivan in Sumter, South Carolina, but Sullivan would not accept them.[42] In the event, Corcoran remained for some time in Wilmington to help the people there. Although he had to accommodate to the situation of Union occupation, it was always a point of pride with him that he never took an oath of allegiance to the United States government, and federal authorities never molested him.[43]

Return from Rome

The collapse of the Confederacy meant ruin for many white Catholics of the Carolinas and a new life for black Catholics. It also brought personal and professional crises for Patrick Lynch and a great problem for the Church. News of the fall of Charleston reached Rome on March 4, 1865, which coincidentally was the first day of Abraham Lincoln's second term as president.[44] The American minister, Rufus King, informed Secretary of State Seward that Cardinal Antonelli had told him that he anticipated the "speedy cessation of hostilities and the submission of the insurgents to the constituted authorities of the country."[45] Bishop Lynch, noted King, was still in Rome, "tho' in no accredited official position," and King was hearing stories that Lynch was telling his associates that he expected that the European powers would yet make some effort in the South's behalf.[46]

The month of April brought news of the capture of Richmond, the flight of the Confederate government, Lee's surrender at Appomattox Court House, and the bombshell of Lincoln's assassination. Father William McCloskey observed that supporters of the North in Rome went into mourning, "the ladies wearing black, the gentlemen crape on the left arm." "Dr. Lynch's position," he added, "is becoming daily more unpleasant. . . . The news has saddened him a good deal." A newspaper account Lynch saw led him to believe—mistakenly—that his father had died.[47]

Lynch wrote to his metropolitan, Archbishop Martin John Spalding, about May 20 to explain his situation and to ask for help. This was his first communication with the archbishop, who had not taken office when Lynch left for Europe in 1864. "The recent events in the United States have left me stranded, in a position of some embarrassment, and at this distance, I scarcely know how to steer my way. . . . I now wish to return home to the peaceful and exclusive discharge of my duties." He asked Spalding to intercede with President Andrew Johnson and Secretary of State William H. Seward to obtain permission for him to come home "without molestation." Here Lynch outlined what was to be for the rest of his days his explanation of his motives and behavior in the wartime mission to Rome. He claimed that the only reason that he accepted his commission from the Confederacy was that he wished to help bring about peace and to end "so many years of destructive and internecine warfare." He could not have foreseen that the South would be conquered in a single year, and he had expected that European influence would be needed to bring about peace.

"I really do not think," he asserted, "they ought to class me among the 'heads of secession' for I was personally disinclined, to say the very least, to such action on the part of the South, and deprecated it, and used such little influence as I had, against it.... I very much doubted its prudence." He had always shown concern and kindness to federal prisoners, including the sick and wounded. Of his famous letter of 1861 to Archbishop Hughes, he claimed that it had been a private message that Hughes had decided to publish "without my knowledge."[48] As David T. Gleeson has pointed out in his seminal work on the Catholic Church and Reconstruction, Lynch's explanations were less than honest, and he was in effect trapped by his own actions.[49]

He wrote in the same vein to Archbishop John McCloskey of New York and to Bishop James Frederick Wood (1813–1883) of Philadelphia. He told McCloskey that he feared being incarcerated at Fortress Monroe or some other prison, and he asked the archbishop to intercede with Secretary Seward, whom he knew was an acquaintance.[50] Father William McCloskey commented to the New York archbishop that Lynch's was "a very sad case" and that the Charleston prelate "no doubt wishes heartily that he had never gotten into it."[51] Lynch received the bad news that his Confederate government salary was cut off, although he still had £1,000 invested with Fraser, Trenholm and Company of Liverpool that was available to him. He was forced to give up his fine apartment on the fashionable Via Condotti, where he had been accustomed to entertain prominent people, and to accept the hospitality of the American College in the Via dell'Umiltà. Now that the war was over, his presence there was not considered an irritant to relations between Northern and Southern seminarians. Rufus King thought that Lynch was compelled to accept financial support from the Propaganda.[52]

Lynch's letter of May 1865 to Archbishop Spalding was his first direct communication to his metropolitan since before undertaking his mission to Rome. This is difficult to understand, since he could have sent easily messages from Rome to Baltimore. The critical situation in the Diocese of Charleston, coupled with the problem of getting Lynch home, meant a great headache for Spalding. Father John Moore wrote his bishop on April 28, informing him of Charleston's distress, and Lynch received this missive. Spalding wrote on June 27 to report what actions had been taken in his behalf. "Meantime your Diocese is suffering greatly, & while I will do all that I can for its Relief, I can do but little.... I would be glad [if] you would yourself appoint a Vicar General for the Diocese—either Dr. Corcoran or someone else; also give instructions for the management of the Diocese during yr absence. Any thing of the kind you may choose to do, if sent under cover to me, will be attended to. It would be well for you to lay the state of affairs before the Cardinal Prefect [Barnabò] . . . that he may advise what is best."[53] Spalding considered it his responsibility to organize a campaign to enable Lynch's return.[54]

On April 28 Father Moore wrote to his bishop about the terrible situation in the diocese. He reported Archbishop Spalding's appointment of James Corcoran as "first V. general for the whole Diocese and myself the second until your pleasure can be known." Moore said that there had been numerous rumors about Lynch's whereabouts: he had been rumored to be in Cuba, Nassau, Bermuda, and even Texas. No letter had been received since he wrote to the Columbia Ursulines from Halifax on his way to Europe.[55] "Poor Father Fillion took it greatly to heart that you should have, seemingly, forgotten your V.G. and the thought helped to kill him. Can you come to our assistance in any way? There is here now only Mr. Baker and myself, and what is to become of us two in the heat of the summer? . . . What will become of us all? . . . Write soon and often and come here yourself as soon as possible. I am almost discouraged and I fear I may not long be able to hold out."

The lamentable state of the diocese was reinforced by Archbishop Spalding in a letter to Bishop Lynch in June. Lynch's long absence and silence were clearly subject to criticism. Archbishop McCloskey reported that New York had no priests to spare for Charleston, adding: "I hope it will occur to the Bishop of Charleston that Rev. Birmingham [*sic*] could be better employed at home than wandering about over Europe as he has been for the last three or four years."[56]

Spalding received assurances of support from Bishop Wood of Philadelphia and Archbishop McCloskey of New York for the effort to secure Lynch's return.[57] The Baltimore prelate wrote on Lynch's behalf to his old friend, U.S. Attorney General James Speed (1812–1887), a Kentuckian and a product of St. Joseph's College, Bardstown. He told Speed that Lynch's return "would have a beneficial influence towards tranquilizing the minds of the fiery Carolinians" and that he could be counted on not to cause any trouble. Spalding chose to describe the bishop's Roman mission as having "a sort of semi official character . . . somewhat like that which the late Archbishop Hughes was [given] by the Secretary of State." He noted that Lynch "was not the only one that was greatly moved by what is, I believe, for I am no politician—called State Rights." He charged the Reverend Jacob A. Walter, pastor of St. Patrick's Church on Capitol Hill, with delivering his letter by hand to the attorney general.[58] At the same time Spalding asked Major General Quincy Adams Gilmore (1825–1888), who commanded the Department of the South, to ensure that the Catholic churches and schools of Charleston would not be commandeered for other than Catholic purposes.[59] Bishop John Timon (1797–1867) of Buffalo wrote at Spalding's request in the same vein to Secretary of State Seward, an old friend of his. Spalding followed with his own appeal to the secretary, which was accompanied by a letter of introduction from Timon. Several days passed before Spalding received any reply, which puzzled him.[60]

The Baltimore archbishop also asked Archbishop John Baptist Purcell of Cincinnati for support. Purcell promised to sign any petition that Spalding might circulate for Lynch. Spalding was a rarity among American bishops in that he had come out openly against slavery and had favored emancipation. His archdiocesan newspaper, the *Catholic Telegraph,* dropped a bombshell on June 28 by commenting on Lynch's application for a pardon: "He *may* get it for his political offences from President Johnson; but for his higher crime of prostituting his sacred office and dignity, and attempting to drag down the church to the infamous purposes of the Southern slave breeders, he will have to appeal to a higher Judge, incorruptible, who tempers justice with mercy." The editorial comments are thought to have come from the pen of the editor, Father Edward Purcell (1808–1881), the archbishop's brother. The *Catholic Telegraph* had been the first Catholic newspaper to call explicitly for emancipation.[61] This distressed Spalding, who called the Cincinnati paper "little better than a Jacobinical sheet" and suggested that McCloskey and Timon advise Archbishop Purcell to set a less severe tone "towards a conquered & humiliated people."[62]

Seward informed Spalding that he had forwarded the latter's letter to the attorney general. Jacob Walter reported that Attorney General Speed had told him "that Bp Lynch would not be allowed to return to this country at present. After affairs are settled South he might be permitted to return. This was determined at a Cabinet meeting." William McCloskey feared that the administration might give Lynch the same harsh treatment that was likely for the other three Confederate commissioners, Slidell, Mason, and Mann. President Johnson had on May 29 issued his proclamation granting amnesty to all who had participated in the rebellion, provided that they swore an oath of loyalty to the Union and the Constitution. But there were exceptions, including "all who are or shall have been pretended civil or diplomatic officers." These must obtain a presidential pardon.

When the proclamation became known in Rome, Southern sympathizers resented being compelled to swear an oath in order to obtain papers to travel, and Lynch feared that he would be barred from returning home without a pardon.[63] He contacted Rufus King through a mutual friend to express his wish to return to America and inquired what he must do. Cardinal Antonelli in his contacts with King urged that Jefferson Davis's life be spared, and he reiterated that Lynch had never been received as a diplomatic representative. Lynch met personally with King and offered to take the oath of allegiance. The bishop spoke of traveling to Havana "and there make his appeal to the Federal authorities," and King observed that he thought Lynch "effectively cured of his Secession folly."[64]

On June 24 Lynch penned his own direct appeal to Seward and sent this to Spalding for transmission to the State Department. The bishop said that he had privately "deprecated" the secessionist movement but did not do so in print and always avoided "all political questions" in the pulpit. This statement is impossible to prove and is disingenuous at best. He recalled his service and that of his priests and nuns to Union prisoners of war, both black and white. He explained his 1861 letter to Archbishop Hughes as a private message, published without his prior knowledge or approval. He asserted that he had never written about politics in the *Miscellany* "except against the Know Nothings." The historian David T. Gleeson has pointed out that Lynch was less than honest here, since the diocesan newspaper contained "Confederate stances." Lynch's appeal to Seward was misleading, but he was in a tight situation and dissembled in order to be allowed to return home.[65]

The delay in securing Lynch's pardon was in part to the result of a burst of anti-Catholic sentiment in the United States in response to news that Mary Surratt and others arrested on the charge of conspiracy to assassinate Lincoln were Catholics. Mrs. Surratt was in fact the object of some Catholic sympathy, and Father Jacob Walter had publicly expressed his belief in her innocence. He had accompanied her to the scaffold on July 7. Spalding heard talk of a plan by some Catholic clergy to publish proof of her innocence. Fearing a resurgence of anti-Catholic nativism, Spalding refused to intervene on her behalf but counseled quiet and restraint until public agitation died down.[66] In the climate prevailing after the conspirators were hanged, Bishop Wood believed that the U.S. government would in fact arrest, try, and imprison Lynch, and he thought the Charleston prelate should remain in Rome until tempers cooled. Spalding also learned that Mother Baptista had been told by Charleston district commander General John Porter Hatch (1822–1901) that the absence of her brother was "for the present a *public necessity.*"[67]

Bishop Lynch asked Archbishop McCloskey to forward letters from him seeking support for Lynch to two Carolinians: Provisional Governor Benjamin F. Perry and a former U.S. congressman and friend of the governor, William W. Boyce. Andrew Johnson's appointment of Perry, a Greenville native, was popular with white South Carolinians, and the bishop was optimistic that Perry would support his pardon application. He asked Boyce to use his influence with Perry and in Washington. He also wrote to his friend, former South Carolina governor William Aiken.[68]

Lynch also sought to get in contact with General George Meade's family, to let them know that he had done his best to help his nephew Lieutenant Robert Meade when he was a prisoner of war in Columbia.[69] Archbishop McCloskey approached a powerful acquaintance of his, the New York politician Thurlow Weed (1797–1882). Always an opponent of slavery, Weed now supported Andrew Johnson's plans for Reconstruction and worked against the Radical Republicans in Congress. Weed had influence with his fellow New Yorker William H. Seward, and he met with Seward in Washington to speak on Lynch's behalf.[70] Spalding himself appealed directly to the president—the only letter he wrote to the president, even though Washington, D.C., was in his archdiocese—asserting that Lynch "would strongly tend to conciliate and tend to facilitate your plans for reconstruction."[71]

Bishop Verot journeyed to Europe, arriving in Rome on July 8. He spent more than a week in Lynch's company, visiting the monuments and filling in his Charleston colleague on events at home. Verot suggested that Lynch write to Augustin Cochin, who, he said, was acquainted with the American minister to France, John Bigelow.[72] Augustin Cochin (1823–1872) was a writer and politician and a member of a distinguished family of lawyers, professionals, and civil servants. He was a friend of Count Charles de Montalembert and a leader of the liberal Catholic movement in France. He had published works advocating the alleviation of the condition of the poor in France and, in 1861, published a famous book calling for abolition of slavery. This had been honored by the French Academy and was published in English translation in Boston.[73] Cochin had written Lynch in May 1865 expressing his joy that God had "finally allowed the demise of this stubborn plague which weighed upon your country and the Christian conscience." He reported that a society was being organized in Paris to raise funds for assistance to American freedpersons.[74]

On Verot's advice, Lynch wrote to Cochin, who, in the names of Montalembert and himself, asked Bigelow to help Lynch: "The return of the Bishop of Charleston to that city so justly, but so severely tried, seems very desirable. If Irish immigrants were called into that region to reorganize labor, collisions may take place with the blacks which would render the presence of the prelate especially useful." Bigelow had always firmly opposed slavery. He told Cochin that Lynch needed to take the oath of allegiance and to write to the president "setting forth his claims to a pardon." Referring to the New York draft riots, he added: "It is precisely such prelates as Bishop Lynch, partisans at once of slavery and treason, that have planted in the breasts of many of our Irish adopted citizens, prejudices against the blacks which have proved one of our most serious obstacles to the suppression of the late rebellion, and which on quite recent occasion resulted in a massacre which deluged the streets of our commercial metropolis with African blood. . . . Bishop Lynch's place in the church can be readily supplied by men whose influence with their flock has never been weakened by Treason." In reporting to Seward, Bigelow said of Cochin that "there is no other man probably in or out of France, in whose estimation every thing is more completely subordinated to the interests of the Church." The American minister called it "effrontery" for Cochin to represent Lynch as "'a loyal intelligent and charitable man.'" Bigelow was among those U.S. officials whose dispatches to Washington "prejudiced" Lynch's case.[75]

The No. 22 Presidential Pardon was signed by Johnson on August 4 and was communicated to Spalding for transmission to Lynch. Spalding wrote immediately to Barnabò and to the American archbishops.[76] Lynch received notification of his pardon from Spalding shortly thereafter. As word spread in the United States about the pardon, there was speculation about the conditions Lynch

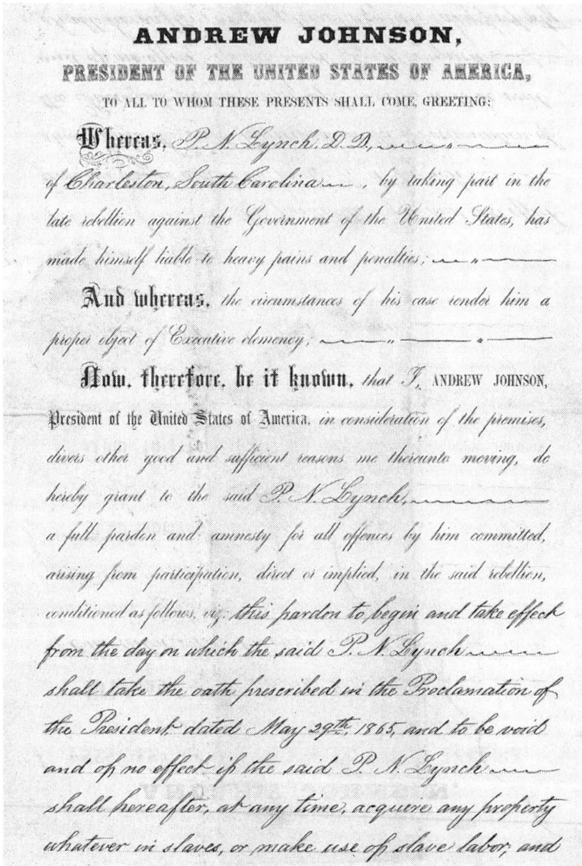

ANDREW JOHNSON,
PRESIDENT OF THE UNITED STATES OF AMERICA,
TO ALL TO WHOM THESE PRESENTS SHALL COME, GREETING:

Whereas, P. N. Lynch, D. D., of Charleston, South Carolina, by taking part in the late rebellion against the Government of the United States, has made himself liable to heavy pains and penalties;

And whereas, the circumstances of his case render him a proper object of Executive clemency;

Now, therefore, be it known, that I, ANDREW JOHNSON, President of the United States of America, in consideration of the premises, divers other good and sufficient reasons me thereunto moving, do hereby grant to the said P. N. Lynch, a full pardon and amnesty for all offences by him committed, arising from participation, direct or implied, in the said rebellion, conditioned as follows, viz: this pardon to begin and take effect from the day on which the said P. N. Lynch shall take the oath prescribed in the Proclamation of the President dated May 29th 1865, and to be void and of no effect if the said P. N. Lynch shall hereafter, at any time, acquire any property whatever in slaves, or make use of slave labor; and

Presidential Pardon. Issued by President Andrew Johnson on August 14, 1865. Conditions required for a full and complete pardon were swearing oath of loyalty to the United States, never owning slaves ever again, and notifying the Secretary of State that he has received notice and accepted conditions of the pardon. Courtesy of Catholic Diocese of Charleston Archive.

would have to observe. A Philadelphia correspondent wrote to Monsignor (later Archbishop) Tobias Kirby, rector of the Irish College in Rome, that Americans expected that Lynch "will have to leave politics and attend solely to his Episcopal functions. And never since there was a church, did a diocese more need an efficient head than does that of Charleston, and I suppose all concede to the Bishop piety . . . and full efficiency and hence every good Catholic must anxiously desire his return to his home where as everywhere he is loved and respected."[77]

Upon receipt of the good news on September 9 and after making a previously planned spiritual retreat, Bishop Lynch proceeded to plan his departure from Rome. Cardinal Barnabò encouraged him to make haste, although the pope and some cardinals thought he should wait until the situation in America became calmer.[78] Before leaving Rome, Lynch petitioned the Propaganda to award a doctorate of sacred theology to Timothy Bermingham. He made a strong case for Bermingham's learning, mastery of languages, and sermons, speeches, and writings in defense of Catholic teachings and against Protestant critics. The Propaganda awarded the diploma in August.[79] Cardinal Antonelli issued a Vatican passport to both Lynch and Bermingham for their travel to Paris. They went first to Lyon, where Lynch met with officers of the French Society for the Propagation of the Faith, in order to make his case for funds to be used in rebuilding the Diocese of Charleston. Then they proceeded to Paris, where the bishop took the oath of allegiance on October 14 before John Bigelow, received a U.S. passport, and met with the Paris Council of the French Society. He also purchased new episcopal garments, explaining that his wardrobe in South Carolina had been "reduced to ashes" by General Sherman. To the French Society Lynch gave as many details as he knew about the destruction of Catholic institutions in the Carolinas.[80]

Whether Lynch fully appreciated the efforts Spalding had made in his behalf is unclear. He told John Bannon that "I wrote to Seward, asking 'pardon &c—' The letter left Rome about July 5, reached Washington August 5—Seward was away. But Mrs. Patterson, the President's Daughter took it up, and in half an hour the affair was decided."[81] He arranged passage on the steamer *Europa* from Brest to New York. After a "very stormy" crossing, followed by several days' quarantine, the two clerics arrived in New York City on November 7. Lynch was received with honor by Archbishop McCloskey. Nothing was made publicly of the reason for his wartime Roman sojourn. McCloskey invited him to preach at the dedication of the new Church of St. Gabriel on October 2, and his sermon made no allusion to the war or to things political. He stopped briefly in Philadelphia, then in Baltimore, where he met with Spalding. The archbishop advised him to avoid Washington, D.C., and he went to Richmond to see Bishop McGill. According to Monsignor Richard Madden, he then stopped at Fortress Monroe, Virginia, to pay his respects to the imprisoned Jefferson Davis. He arrived home in Charleston on December 1. On the third, he celebrated Sunday Mass before a large congregation.[82]

Did Patrick Lynch accomplish anything by his Roman adventure? From the evidence, the endeavor must be judge a great failure. He did not succeed in obtaining Vatican recognition of the Confederacy, even though this was not the sole reason for his trip. His pamphlet on slavery did indeed elicit some favorable comment among upper-class Europeans, but it came far too late in the war to affect the outcome. There was confusion at the time and later over whether the Holy See did in fact grant recognition. Many both North and South believed it had done so. In 1866 Horace Greeley's newspaper asserted that the pope had been induced by Lynch "to recognize Jeff Davis as a potentate; which no other monarch openly did." Lynch was at pains to respond that "the Pope was not induced by me or any one [*sic*] else to recognize the Confederate Government. It is incorrect to say that such recognition was ever given." He later emphasized that "no such recognition was ever asked." Yet the story had a long life. The Southern poet-priest Father Abram Ryan in 1868 praised Pius IX as "the only European sovereign who recognized the Confederacy as a nation."[83]

The Roman sojourn meant that Lynch was absent from his diocese and faithful in their time of greatest trial and destruction. His protracted absence and long silence merited severe criticism. His published defense of slavery would come back to haunt him. Before the war, Patrick Lynch had been one of the rising stars of the American Church, destined in the eyes of many to be an archbishop, perhaps a cardinal. But the South's disaster and his involvement in it cast a shadow over his career from which it never fully recovered. It is difficult to comprehend what he thought he was doing and why he undertook the mission when he did. Had he gone to Europe before Antietam/Sharpesville or even before Gettysburg and Vicksburg, it is possible to suppose that he might have had some success. But to go so late in the war, when the Confederate cause was rapidly sinking, appears now to have been senseless. Perhaps Lynch shared in the widespread self-deception that characterized so many Southern whites. Certainly he expected the Confederacy could hold out longer than it did, and he was profoundly shocked by the speed of its collapse.

When Lynch returned home, he found Charleston and the diocese in terrible condition. "I got to Charleston to sit like Marius amid ruins architectural and ecclesiastical and nerve myself for the work of 'Reconstruction.' But the sinews of war are as wanting to me, as ever they were to Lee and to Johnston. But I do not surrender yet."[84] To Bishop Elder of Natchez he commented: "I am like Marius amid the ruins of Carthage. There are ruins on every side of me, architectural, ecclesiastical, industrial, religious, & Social. But I trust in God things will come straight."[85] He asked Archbishop McCloskey, "Was your Grace ever at Pompeii? Columbia is more like that than any place in America."[86]

The situation of many, black and white, was desperate. Letters asking for help came from people humble and proud. A Charleston man had a debilitating illness that made him destitute. War had made a family "quite poor" and needy. A woman wrote of need because her husband had been unable to find work. A Charleston man, son of a physician, could not find work and asked the Bishop for "even 2 or 3 dollars." The old plantation society had been swept away, and many of the old aristocracy faced ruin. People of proud family backgrounds were forced to work as bank tellers or even as common laborers, to take in sewing, or to convert their mansions to boarding houses. A Charleston lady of high social standing recounted to the bishop the story of her family's destitution and asked for a loan and help in finding employment. A Charleston matron wrote: "I do not come to beg—I am above be[g]ging—but I am asking for a loan."[87] Because of the failure of Confederate bonds and currency, savings that Catholics had deposited in the St. John's Savings Association—a kind of savings bank operated by the diocese—was lost, hurting especially the immigrant poor. The Archives of the Diocese of Charleston contain letters requesting or demanding the refund of deposits. Father Corcoran was badgered and vilified for months by his Irish-born former housekeeper about money she had invested in the savings association.[88] Another woman pursued the bishop for the great sum of $2,700, claiming that she had entrusted her money to the late Father Patrick O'Neill, whom she called a "swindler."[89]

People wrote to the bishop to say that they had not received the sacraments for a long time, asking him to send a priest to them. A group of Greenville, South Carolina, Catholics hoped the bishop would establish a parish church there and promised $800 to help, believing that immigration to the area would be encouraged.[90] Another group in the Charlotte, North Carolina, area collected $500 to help support a priest to serve them.[91] The Sisters of Our Lady of Mercy in Sumter, South Carolina, could not attend Mass or receive the Eucharist at Christmas 1865 because there was no priest to attend them.[92] Before Lynch's return, a North Carolina laywoman had written Archbishop Spalding asking that a priest be sent to "the little abandoned flock of Edenton [North Carolina]." Spalding asked Lynch to send a priest from New Bern to serve this congregation.[93]

All Southern bishops were compelled to seek money to rebuild and to help their faithful after the war.[94] All American bishops wrote begging letters to European Catholic charities that supported missions. Even before he left Europe for home, Bishop Lynch had marshaled the information he could glean about his diocese to make an appeal the French Society for the Propagation of the Faith, which was run by councils located in Lyon and Paris, and in October 1865 he submitted to them a statement of the needs of the Charleston Diocese. In September he had sent an appeal to the Leopoldinen-Stiftung (Leopoldine Foundation) of Vienna. He listed church buildings and institutions destroyed or damaged by military actions and the Charleston fire. The cathedral loss he estimated at $106,000. Lost also was the bishop's residence ($7,000), the seminary ($10,000), the diocesan library of seventeen thousand volumes ($20,000), the boys' orphanage ($15,000), and the girls' school ($2,500). Damage sustained by the Convent of the Sisters of Our Lady of Mercy in the fire and, later, in the bombardment amounted to $12,500. Shells had damaged St. Mary's, St. Paul's, and St. Joseph's churches, as well as St. Joseph's rectory ($9,500). Outside Charleston, two churches had been damaged or destroyed ($4,000). In Columbia, the Ursuline Convent and school had been destroyed by fire when Sherman took the city ($33,000). Father J. J. O'Connell's residence and school were also burned ($15,000). He included an estimate of his debt on the Ursuline Convent ($10,000), money lost in bank stocks, railway shares, and other securities ($43,000), and loss of cotton bought as security but destroyed by fire ($21,000). In all, he calculated the total losses to the diocese at $316,500. He did not include the great losses to the diocese and to the Catholic laity of property in slaves resulting from emancipation. This was never publicly discussed, but it constituted a great part of the financial loss to Southern society.[95]

Over the years Lynch sent reports to the European societies, especially the French, on what was done with the generous sums they contributed. Charleston came out well in donations from the French, ahead of other dioceses.[96] The Austrian Leopoldine Foundation had given the diocese more than $30,000 between 1846 and 1860, but Commander George (Georg) Schwarz informed Lynch in October 1865 that only some £275 could be given at that time, and it was unlikely that anything would be forthcoming the following year.[97] Lynch obtained a grant of several thousand dollars for repair of the German-congregation St. Paul's Church in Charleston from the Bavarian Ludwig Mission Society.[98] Private individuals and groups in America also came to his aid. A group of former U.S. prisoners of war in New York raised $1,700 for the diocese.[99] Mary Mildred Hammond Sullivan (1836–1933), wife of New York attorney and judge, Algernon Sydney Sullivan (1826–1887), a Southern sympathizer imprisoned by Lincoln for pro-Confederate activities, organized the New York Ladies' Southern Relief Society, whose members raised some $20,000 to aid suffering Southern people, money that was distributed through select Southern clergy; Lynch received more than $1,800 along with donated clothing for the needy of the diocese.[100] A charity called the Missouri Southern Institution of St. Louis raised more than $16,000 to be distributed to the needy in South Carolina.[101]

Much more detailed accounts of the exhaustive labor Lynch executed on behalf of the reconstruction of the Diocese of Charleston will be given in subsequent chapters. Suffice it to say that he surrendered all ambitions and personal desires to this herculean task. For the seventeen years remaining in his temporal existence, Lynch spent every waking moment begging, borrowing, and exhorting others to aid him in his responsibilities to remake the Diocese of Charleston. He often expressed that he felt personally responsible for the disorder that had come into his see, and he would not let himself rest until recompense had been fully achieved. He literally died in the midst of that effort.

CHAPTER 9

Baltimore Second Plenary

After his disastrous wartime trip to Rome, Bishop Lynch was no pariah among the American hierarchy. He was one of Archbishop Spalding's confidants and was welcomed by his fellow bishops when he visited their dioceses on begging trips. He and Father James Corcoran both played significant roles at the Second Plenary Council of Baltimore, held in October 1866.

Unlike some of the Protestant denominations, the American Catholic Church had not broken apart because of the war. Northern and Southern bishops gave allegiance to the adversarial governments and advised their people to do likewise, but they did not waver in their loyalty to Rome or to the Church itself. When peace returned they were promptly able to resume regular contacts and patterns of cooperation. From the time Bishop England called for councils to set policies and establish discipline, the American hierarchy had developed a strong conciliar tradition.[1]

In June 1865, Archbishop Martin John Spalding proposed to Rome that a plenary council of all American bishops be held. It was important to show the unity of the Church. New dioceses needed to be established to serve the rapidly growing Catholic population. Spalding wanted "to establish greater uniformity among the various provinces." One of his important aims was to consider how to address the problems and opportunities posed by the emancipated blacks.[2] He worked on gathering information about councils here and abroad during 1865. The Vatican was slow to respond, and the archbishop complained about this to Lynch in January 1866.[3]

Cardinal Barnabò sent approval of the Council to Spalding in a letter of January 31.[4] The archbishop solicited input and support from his brother metropolitans and bishops. He tapped a group of theologians to help him draft the schema or proposed texts of decrees to be discussed. He especially wanted James Corcoran to come to Baltimore for this work. Corcoran was regarded as a preeminent theologian and gifted Latinist. Corcoran departed Wilmington for Baltimore on

April 28, leaving Father Harry Northrop to fill in for him. Corcoran told Lynch that the archbishop "has me under positive arrest till October next."[5]

Pope Pius IX had issued in 1864 the *Syllabus of Errors* listing beliefs that Pius judged not acceptable to the Church. The *Syllabus* raised in some American bishops' minds questions whether American beliefs about church-state relations and freedom of religion were in any way in conflict with the teachings of the Holy See. Bishop Lynch, like Archbishop Spalding, was a Roman-trained alumnus of the Urban College. All the Propaganda alumni believed in papal primacy and infallibility. At the same time he had been Bishop England's student and protégé and was committed to American principles of freedom of religion, separation of church and state, and the collegial tradition going back to England's call for plenary councils to legislate for the American church.

The Second Plenary Council opened on October 7, 1866. It was the grandest Catholic event in American history to that date. Great crowds gathered to see the spectacle of the procession of forty-five archbishops and bishops and two mitered abbots from the archiepiscopal residence to the doors of the cathedral, while a full orchestra played the grand march from *Tannhäuser.* Every evening there was a prayer service at which one of the prelates preached. Patrick Lynch was chosen to give the first sermon on the evening of opening day. He extolled the unity of the Church and called on bishops to pray for the unity of the Council.

Lynch and Corcoran played important roles in the two-week-long Council. Spalding chose Lynch to be the first of two promoters: the officials responsible for directing the work of the body. Theirs was a difficult task, because of the great volume of texts to be discussed. Corcoran served as first secretary, whose duties included recording minutes of the confidential sessions and preparing texts of the final decrees and the eventual report to Rome. Lynch also brought with him his vicar general, Father Timothy Bermingham.[6]

The schemata or texts of decrees discussed were divided into sections or titles (*tituli*) that were given to congregations or commissions for initial debate and discussion. An important section concerned new dioceses. By the time of the Baltimore Council the Catholic population of the United States was almost four million among thirty million American citizens. The Church grew by some 1.3 million Catholics in the decade of the 1860s, including about 700,000 immigrants.[7] To accommodate this growth, the Council discussed the establishment of new dioceses and vicariates apostolic. Lynch wanted North Carolina to be separated from his diocese. He had found it impossible to visit all the scattered Catholic communities of the Old North State in anything like a timely manner. As the Catholic population was concentrated in South Carolina, the northern part was in effect a stepchild.[8] The Council agreed and prepared for Rome a *terna* for a new vicariate. The first choice was young Father James Gibbons, born in America and raised in Ireland. He was, at the time, Spalding's secretary. In second place was Father

Matthew O'Keefe, pastor of St. Mary's Church of Norfolk, Virginia. Third was the Charleston diocesan priest Jeremiah J. O'Connell. In his comments, which were eventually sent to Rome, Spalding described Gibbons as a man well suited to administer missions in both urban and rural settings, a good preacher, a dutiful priest, and a man liked by everyone. In the Council Lynch strongly promoted O'Connell's candidacy. Reflecting Lynch's arguments, Spalding noted in his report to Rome O'Connell's excellent education, his knowledge of Latin and Greek, and his years of experience running a college in Columbia. He was "wise, physically fit, long-suffering, resolute, of sterling reputation as a priest."[9] The cardinals of the Propaganda eventually confirmed the Council's first choice, and James Gibbons was to be installed as vicar apostolic of North Carolina in 1868.

Most of the Council's decrees were disciplinary, concerned with the Church's institutional structure, educational work, and publishing efforts. The Fathers recommended establishment of new dioceses and vicariates.[10] Special problems and opportunities were posed by the emancipation of the slaves. In the new age of black freedom the bishops witnessed the mighty effort by some Protestant churches to proselytize Southern blacks. It has been estimated that there were at the time of emancipation about 200,000 black Catholics in the United States. But this number has been questioned as being too high. Bishop Lynch, in 1867, estimated that there had been about four million slaves before the end of the war. Their number had been reduced somewhat by war, famine, and other disasters to about three and a half million; of these he estimated that there were 150,000 Catholics.[11] The freedmen were mostly poor and in need of education. Many, if not most, Southern whites regarded Negroes as inferior and effectively treated black Catholics as second-class members of the Church.[12]

In the opening days of the Baltimore Plenary Council, the Charleston *Daily Courier* reported on its concerns. It particularly addressed the issue of the mandate issued to the American Catholic hierarchy by Cardinal Barnabò, quoting directly from his text: "It is the wish of the Sacred Congregation that the Bishops of the United States, in fulfillment of the charge which has been entrusted to them of feeding the Lord's flock, should consult together respecting some uniform method of providing for the salvation and Christian education of the emancipated blacks."[13] The Council discussions proceeded at such a slow pace that it became clear the bishops could not complete their work in two weeks. Bishop Lynch, as first promoter, therefore proposed that Spalding, as apostolic delegate appointed by the Holy See, and two assistants select the most important decrees to be discussed.[14] Lynch's intervention helped the Council get through most of the material. The question of Negroes was included in Title X, "On the Care of Souls" (*De salute animarum efficacius promovenda*). The text—which was mainly an expression of Spalding's thought—urged bishops, in the words of Thomas Spalding, Martin John Spalding's biographer, "to make positive efforts in their behalf, urged that churches, schools and orphanages be built for them, and exhorted priests 'through the bowels of the Mercy of God' 'to devote their lives to the work.'"[15] As the question of whether to designate an apostolate to blacks was thorny, it was decided to schedule a special session after the formal closure of the regular Council. The closing ceremonies were fittingly grand and were attended by President Andrew Johnson.

Spalding had wanted prelates to approve the appointment of a special ecclesiastical coordinator (*vir ecclesiasticus*) or prefect apostolic to plan and lead the effort to proselytize African Americans. Prior to the Council, the Vatican had approved the text of Title X for discussion. Spalding suggested that the coordinator be a consecrated bishop, to strengthen his role—although he would not govern a diocese. It was further suggested that he might reside in Baltimore, although his duties would range widely, leading an effort to recruit priests for special missionary work among blacks.[16] The extra meeting held on October 22 proved long and acrimonious. Many hierarchs questioned whether blacks in fact posed a significant problem; if they did, the participants considered this to be the case in only a few dioceses. Most would not support the idea of a special national coordinator for black Americans.

Title X called for religious education of black youth in order to counter the "work of the Protestant schools which were propagating errors."[17] The Title had originally been assigned for discussion to a commission of theologians, bishops, and priests, headed by Bishop William Henry Elder of Natchez. Among the topics the commission considered was whether separate churches should be organized for Negroes. Timothy Bermingham served on the commission, along with Napoleon Perché, vicar general of New Orleans. Perché said that in New Orleans no separate churches were needed because of the frequent intermarriage of blacks and whites. But Bermingham took up the position already expressed by Lynch in Europe, that separation was needed to keep blacks in the Catholic Church because in cases where they worshipped with whites, they were forced to sit at the back or side, so they stopped attending Mass.[18] Bishop Lynch said in the debate of October 22 that in general he did not favor racially separate congregations. However, in Charleston he thought separation necessary, "because of the danger of serious troubles if the Irish workers were together with the Negroes in one church. For the Negroes would assert their rights, and Lynch thought that fights and even bloodshed might result."[19]

The theologians of Bishop Elder's commission recommended that the Holy Father be asked to canonize Blessed Peter Claver and name him "special patron of Negroes." Claver had been beatified on July 16, 1850, by Pope Pius IX and would finally be canonized on January 15, 1888, by Pope Leo XIII. They also suggested as patrons St. Benedict the Moor and Blessed Martin de Porres of Lima. They further recommended distributing English-language lives of the three patrons for edification of American blacks. In fact, the Council Fathers signed and sent to Rome a petition calling for Peter Claver's canonization. Thirty-four of the forty-five archbishops and bishops attending signed this. All the Southern bishops signed except Odin of New Orleans, Martin of Natchitoches, and Lynch. The reason for this is unknown.[20]

The special extra session was attended only by archbishops and bishops. Spalding reminded them that Propaganda Fide had specifically instructed the Council to consider developing a plan for blacks. Archbishop Odin of New Orleans objected that he saw no discrimination in New Orleans between colored and white Catholics, so he thought no new actions were called for—although he would welcome additional missionary priests to work with freed slaves. Bishop McGill of Richmond said there were too few black Catholics in his diocese to merit special action. A number of bishops raised objections to the idea of a special priest or bishop administrator (*vir ecclesiasticus*). Archbishop Peter Richard Kenrick of St. Louis protested against any special bishop who might come into his archdiocese. If such a man were imposed on him he would, he asserted, resign his see. Bishop John Quinlan of Mobile did not think it necessary to do anything special for Catholic or non-Catholic blacks. Bishop Elder worried lest an effort to raise contributions in Europe for American blacks would make it harder for bishops to obtain money from abroad. He was already on record as having doubts about blacks' willingness to follow the teachings of the Catholic Church regarding the sanctity of marriage and avoidance of sexual sins.[21] Practically the only bishops who supported a special program were Bishop Augustin Verot of Savannah and Bishop Richard Whelan of Wheeling.[22]

It was proposed that religious orders be invited to work among blacks. Bishop Lynch had already approached communities to work in South Carolina. The Council Fathers hoped that some diocesan priests would be willing to share this work, "and if there be any priests of the large numbers of priests who are in Europe, who, moved by the spirit of God, wish to be of assistance in this work, the bishops remind them that 'here the harvest is great but the laborers are few.'"[23] The original text called for bishops as a group to seek donations for special work with blacks from the European missionary societies. But Archbishop McCloskey of New York expressed the belief of many prelates that the Southern dioceses should bear the responsibility for raising funds, as the problem of freed slaves did not greatly concern the Church in the North.[24] On motion of Archbishop J. B. Alemany of San Francisco, seconded by Archbishop Odin, it was decided to leave the development of plans for black Americans to diocesan synods and provincial councils.[25]

There were 534 decrees, grouped in fourteen titles or sections. Only one of these specifically concerned the apostolate to American blacks. The Fathers affirmed their devotion to and reverence for the Holy See. They supported continuation of the temporal power of the pope, while making it clear that this was not essential to the papacy.[26]

The bishops decided that letters should be sent in the name of all to the European missionary societies, asking for aid for blacks. Bishop Verot was assigned the task of writing to Europe. He sent a strong appeal to the French Society for the Propagation of the Faith: "It is our duty to attract them [Negroes] by founding for them churches, schools and orphan asylums. . . . We therefore propose to you these works for the poor blacks, who are so much abandoned, so much despised."[27]

On October 21 the Council issued a national pastoral letter. On the matter of blacks, the tone has been characterized by David Gleeson as "dripping with a condescending paternalism." But the lettert did say that some aid was "imperative."[28]

> We must all feel, beloved Brethren, that in some manner a new and most extensive field of charity and devotedness has been opened to us, by the emancipation of the immense slave population of the South. We could have wished, that in accordance with the action of the Catholic Church in past ages, in regard to the serfs of Europe, a more gradual system of emancipation could have been adopted, so that they might have been in some measure prepared to make a better use of their freedom, than they are likely to do now. Still the evils which must necessarily attend upon the sudden liberation of so large a multitude, with their peculiar dispositions and habits, only make the appeal to our Christian charity and zeal, presented by their forlorn condition the more forcible and imperative.[29]

The language is reminiscent of Lynch's wartime slavery pamphlet. The pastoral letter was the only document published by the Council at the time. The decrees could not be released until approved by Rome. Texts of the minutes (*Acta*) and decrees (*Decreta*) in English and Latin were prepared by Corcoran for submission to Propaganda Fide and eventual publication. Corcoran earned kudos for his hard work before and after the close of the Council.[30] On October 24 Bishop Lynch, as first promoter, wrote to Cardinal Barnabò to inform him of the successful completion of the Council. Spalding entrusted the documents to Bishop John Baptist Lamy of Santa Fe, who departed New York for Europe on November 17, for an *ad limina* visit. The Vatican proved slow in giving its approval to the acts and decrees, and approval was not given until 1868. Only then were the decrees published, along with the names of new dioceses and vicariates. [31] Nevertheless, enough information had been released that the American Catholic and secular press praised the bishops for their achievement. Newspaper accounts were based on the national pastoral letter and on rumor. Northern papers lauded the hierarchs for their intention to help blacks, although some suspected a "Catholic plot to take over the Negroes."[32]

Lynch and Corcoran could both take satisfaction from their work in Baltimore. After more than five months of Council labor, Corcoran returned to Wilmington on November 16. He told his North Carolina parishioners they would soon have their own bishop, but he did not name the man.[33] Immediately after the Council, Bishop Lynch paid a visit to Jefferson Davis at Fortress Monroe. Davis and his family were charmed by the bishop, who left behind some Catholic publications, in hopes that the president might be led to convert to Catholicism. Davis had been brought up in a Baptist family but had as a boy been educated in a Catholic school and had once expressed an interest in converting. He always showed great respect for the Catholic Church and clergy, and he did not support the Know-Nothings in their anti-Catholic campaigns of the 1850s. He praised the sacrifice of Catholic priests and nuns who cared for soldiers and all who suffered from the war. He admired the Sisters of Our Lady of Mercy, "not one of whom he could ever pass without raising his hat." In prison he was profoundly touched by the words of Pope Pius IX, who sent him an autographed portrait photograph. Jefferson Davis had become an Episcopalian and at his death was buried with Episcopal ceremonies.[34]

After his return to Charleston, Lynch wrote of his satisfaction with the work of the Council. In his 1867 Lenten pastoral he praised the unity of the Church and the gradual emergence of the diocese from the ruins of war. He spoke of the condition of freed slaves and Americans blacks in general.

> The altered condition of the freedmen likewise calls for special action. Here, a vast field is opened for the energetic working of Catholic charity. Their freedom has brought them new rights and new privileges; and has entailed on them new duties and new wants. It is equally necessary that rights and privileges should be acted upon, and not abused; that duties should be fulfilled and wants supplied; and in doing this—so as to produce order and not chaos, kindness and not enmity, charity and not bitterness of spirit, ready submission to law and not violent outbursts of passion. A spirit of religion, and not the spirit of fanaticism, the action of the Catholic Church will be most potent.... And what shall stay her? Want of means? God will provide them, if we bring willing hearts and Christian feelings to the work.[35]

The Second Plenary Council has come to be regarded as a triumph for Catholic unity and a landmark for ordering the Church administration. On the matter of policy and action for African Americans, however, it is judged to have been a great missed opportunity and a failure. Spalding's urgings that decisive measures be taken for outreach to blacks were not followed. Some bishops did not consider that the number of blacks in their dioceses merited special measures. Immigration from Europe and the natural population growth meant huge increases in the number of white Catholics, and bishops judged that these most needed the attention of clergy and religious. A number of bishops—Lynch among them—thought that special religious orders were needed to work among blacks. When Archbishop Spalding was in Rome in 1867, he presented a petition in the name of the entire American hierarchy asking the Holy Father to request or even command the heads of several religious congregations to aid the bishops in their work for blacks. To this he received no reply.[36] One may ask why American bishops did not determine to commit their own secular clergy to more intensive work for black Catholics and potential converts. Certainly there was a lot of resentment among whites, North and South—Catholics among them—of the freedmen; this no doubt contributed to the prelates' reluctance. In the 1860s there was no serious consideration given to ordaining black Catholic priests. Many white clergy regarded "Negroes" as innately inferior.[37] Jeremiah O'Connell articulated the view of many priests in 1879, saying of blacks: "The moral sentiment of the race has been so utterly corrupted, that even now after fifteen years of emancipation they cannot realize the requirements of the sixth commandment, and the efforts of our foreign missionary priests, as well as our own endeavors, fail in making them Catholics."[38]

Once again, Lynch proved himself to be a man of his times. His Christian instincts told him that the problem of the emancipated slaves needed a far-reaching solution. Yet he was unable to convince his ecclesiastical colleagues to do what was necessary. He surrendered to the prevailing attitudes of the overwhelming majority of the white Catholics in his diocese and refused to force them into fully integrating black Catholics into their parishes. He first proposed separate colonies on sea islands and then constructed separate churches (St. Peter's and Immaculate Conception) because of the persistence of whites' belief in the inferiority of their darker brethren.

While the second Baltimore Plenary Council demonstrated that Patrick Lynch had not lost his prominent place among the American Catholic hierarchy, it showed that his rank did not allow him to successfully execute his plans for accommodating and proselytizing the newly freed slaves. The rest of Lynch's career was emblematic of the esteem with which his American Catholic colleagues regarded him. Yet his fate was to never rise above the rank of bishop. While they passed on his name several times to Rome for promotions, some elements within the Vatican passed on him in favor of those with less controversial pasts.

CHAPTER 10

Reconstruction

The efforts to restore his diocese would occupy the rest of Bishop Lynch's life. He devoted all of his energies to this task, sacrificing all previous ambitions. He was subjected to bitter and harsh criticisms, particularly as it related to his role in the Confederate war and diplomatic attempts to broker peace. While his ecclesiastical and pastoral duties were at the forefront, he nevertheless also assumed social responsibilities to help remake Charleston's social and economic life. Three areas in particular help to illustrate both his sense of duty and the breadth of his vision. While, by many counts, he was not entirely successful, the energy and determination he displayed manifest his character and his sense of his place in God's plans.

Reconstruction of Church Property

When Bishop Lynch returned to the ruined Charleston and South Carolina scene, he got to work promptly to repair and rebuild. A priority was to provide a temporary pro-cathedral. There was no money to repair the burned church or to build a new one. Lynch's commitment to rebuilding the physical infrastructure of his stricken diocese was unfailing, and he was aided by the friendship of a fellow Irish-born architect and builder of genius, John Henry Devereux (1840–1920). Devereux was hired to construct a temporary building on Queen Street at the northern edge of the cathedral property. The structure Devereux erected was a plain brick building of undistinguished outward appearance. But the interior was lavishly decorated with a great marble altar, statues, and other accoutrements. Lynch saw to it that the tabernacle of the burned cathedral, which had come through the fire unscathed, was enshrined in the pro-cathedral. Lynch had in mind that the edifice might later be used for a boys' asylum. It was, in fact, to serve until the present brownstone cathedral was completed in 1907. It was usually referred to as the Cathedral Chapel or St. Finbar's Chapel. In the twentieth century the building housed the parish school and was the site of the first Catholic high school in the diocese.

Devereux, born in Wexford, Ireland, in 1840, came to Charleston with his parents around the age of three. He attended the Seminary founded by Bishop England and there he was taught by newly ordained Father Patrick Lynch. Identified in his teens as an artistic prodigy, he excelled in sculpture but yearned to design and build beautiful structures. In the late 1850s he founded a building company named Devereux Brothers. In the Civil War he rose to the rank of captain in the Confederate Cavalry and was an inspector of depots for the Confederate War Department.

It was in the postwar period that he made his mark designing houses, commercial buildings, theaters, and many churches throughout Lynch's diocese. He started with the pro-cathedral (1866) on Queen Street, on which he had advised Lynch as early as 1862. Also included were St. Peter's on Wentworth Street (1868), St. Mary's in Aiken (1869–70), St. Mary's in Greenville (1872), Stella Maris on Sullivan's Island (1873), Immaculate Conception at Coming and Shepherd Streets (1880), and St. Anthony's in Florence (1884). One of Charleston's most distinguished architects, Devereux later designed the U.S. Post Office and court house and St. Matthew's Lutheran Church—his masterpiece.[1]

Devereux was not merely a church architect. He was a personal friend and generous benefactor of the bishop and his diocese. The Diocesan Archives are full of letters from Devereux to Lynch on matters architectural, financial, and very personal, as well. Years after the death of his mentor and friend, Devereux directed the reconstruction and beautification of St. Mary's on Hasell Street in Charleston (1896) and refused to take any payment for his labors. His friendship with Lynch and his devotion to his faith made Devereux a perfect partner in their reconstruction of the Charleston Catholic diocese.

The bishop also needed a residence to replace the one that burned down in 1861. A grand mansion became available at 114 Broad Street, a few doors from the ruined cathedral. This was one of Charleston's finest classical revival structures, built around 1829 and called the Colonel Thomas Pinckney House. Since 1866 the elegant building has served as the Bishop's House and is one of the architectural gems of Charleston. At the time, however, the purchase was strongly opposed by Fathers Bermingham and Moore. Bermingham thought Lynch had paid too much and urged him "honorably [to] get out of the purchase, in God's name." Moore complained that the bishop had "bought a house on speculation instead of a church [the cathedral] for his people."[1] This wonderful structure, nevertheless, remains to this day as the residence of the bishop of Charleston.

The Sisters of Mercy convent had been badly damaged and was in great need of repairs. Much of this was accomplished with the assistance of a grant from the U.S. government. They were given $12,000 in compensation for the medical care they provided soldiers on both sides of the conflict throughout the Civil War.[2] In his *Catholics in South Carolina,* Monsignor Richard Madden wrote that this

Pro-cathedral (exterior) at 105 Queen Street. Lynch hired the Irish-born architect John Henry Devereux to build a temporary church to serve as the cathedral. It would perform this mission until a new Gothic structure replaced the edifice destroyed by the fire of 1861. At that time the pro-cathedral was converted into the Cathedral Grammar School. Courtesy of Catholic Diocese of Charleston Archive.

Pro-cathedral (interior) contained the altar and tabernacle from the original St. Finbar's Cathedral. Courtesy of Catholic Diocese of Charleston Archive.

Pinckney House. Lynch purchased this house at 114 Broad Street upon his return from Rome in the spring of 1866. It has served as the official residence of all Catholic bishops of Charleston from then to this day. Courtesy of Catholic Diocese of Charleston Archive.

was taken care of "in the "Efficiency Appropriation" for 1871 and that "Congress included $12,000 for the Sisters of Our Lady of Mercy for their orphanage in consideration of the care they had given the sick and wounded soldiers."[3] With this financial assistance the Sisters purchased a stately mansion at 51 Meeting Street, which is today known as the Nathaniel Russell House. This wonderful house served as the main convent and site of the school for young girls for decades.

In June 1867 the St. Patrick's Male Orphan Society established a home for boys on Cannon Street on property Bishop Lynch had purchased in 1866; the home moved to 173 Calhoun Street in 1870. The *Charleston City Directory* of 1882 defined its objective as "the support of orphan male children of Catholic parentage. Conducted under the auspices of Queen Street Church; Sister Vincent, directress; number of inmates, 45."[4]

St. Patrick's parochial school was started by the parish vestry in 1869. This educational institution was the initiative of Father Moore but was done with the approval of the bishop, who advised them on how to finance the building with the debt to be paid off in a matter of a few years.

A Free School for Boys near the cathedral was established in the summer of 1869. The Reverend Daniel Quigley built a small school of wood, which opened in October of that year. There were about two hundred pupils led by their principal, Mr. Gannon. Two women, including a teacher, Margaret Sweegan, assisted Mr. Gannon. St. Paul's, the former German Catholic church on Society street, was converted into a Free School for Girls in 1873. It was run by five nuns from the Sisters of Mercy order.[5] These schools proved so successful that Monsignor Quigley in 1875 purchased a building on George Street between St. Philip and King Streets that became the Central High School. The Brothers of the Sacred Heart came to Charleston to run this high school and remained there for nine years. Upon their departure in 1886, the Central High School, which had been damaged in the August earthquake, closed its doors.[6]

Black Catholics—Postwar

Before his return to America Lynch began to form his plans for accommodating the newly freed slaves and all other black Catholics. In his wartime pamphlet on slavery he laid out an idea for special missions or colonies for blacks under clerical rule, on the order of the eighteenth-century missions of California and Paraguay.[7] After the Confederate debacle he explained his view of what was needed to the French Society for the Propagation of the Faith at Lyons, France, in September 1865, suggesting that a high priority should be "establishing a special church in Charleston for the emancipated Negroes, and of providing Catholic schools for them." Prior to the war, he noted, blacks and whites typically worshipped in the same churches, although sitting in separate parts of the church. But emancipated slaves "will claim as a mark of their equality the right of occupying seats intermixed with the whites." This would be resisted by whites and would cause "much trouble." He was asking for donations to make it possible to provide a separate church, and he knew there were enough blacks to form a "good congregation." A separate church would "give us further scope to adapt the preaching and instruction to their capacity, far more limited than that of the whites." And he reiterated his view that Catholic rituals "would satisfy the cravings of their still tropical nature for pomp and ceremony more attractive than the "cold services of Protestant worship."[8]

Upon his return to America, before going to Charleston, Lynch visited Archbishop Spalding in Baltimore. There he expressed the ideas then being developed. He wrote in more detail after his return to Charleston. "I think the Negroes will be driven fast as possible from Virginia, N. Carolina and the upper parts of S. Carolina & Georgia, and will be pushed down to the coast & the Sea Islands which they now hold almost exclusively." Lynch was looking for an island on the coast near Charleston that could become a black community of five thousand souls. Lynch's interest focused on Folly Island, a barrier island six miles long, a half mile wide, with an area of 12.3 square miles, located some ten miles from downtown Charleston.[9] Spalding told him, "I like your project of procuring that Island for the Negroes, & making a Colony ala [*sic*] Paraguay—i.e., if you can succeed in doing so." Lynch had written to the Benedictines of St. Vincent's Abbey in Latrobe, Pennsylvania, asking for priests to run such a colony and to Father Edward Sorin (1814–1893) of the Congregation of the Holy Cross (and founder of Notre Dame College). Spalding doubted that either would give help, suggesting that Lynch might have better luck with the French Marists.[10]

Benedictine Abbot (later Archabbot) Boniface Wimmer (1809–1887) turned him down, saying that he could not spare men and was focused more on the American Midwest, where the German-speaking Catholic population was growing. Moreover, wrote Wimmer, "It would not be an easy matter to organize such a colony of lazy, filthy, degraded Negroes."[11] Father Sorin replied that, while he admired Lynch's plan, he needed more information about the island. He was writing to Cardinal Barnabò to ask his direction. Sorin did in fact write to Rome, indicating that he lacked the manpower to assist Lynch, hoping that he would not be told to do so. He enlisted the help of Bishop John H. Luers of Fort Wayne in telling the Propaganda that he could not help unless he received additional priests and religious from France. The Propaganda asked him to reconsider and to try to support the project, but in fact Sorin did not help Lynch.[12]

Once in Charleston, Lynch promptly made the acquaintance of the military commander Major General Daniel Edgar Sickles (1819–1914). General Ulysses S. Grant, commander in chief of the U.S. Army of Occupation, appointed Sickles military commander of the Department of South Carolina. Sickles arrived in Charleston in September 1865 and took up residence in a grand mansion on Charlotte Street, the J. Thomas Hamlin White House, while his command headquarters were in the fortress-like building of The Citadel Military College.[13] The military governor exercised a wide range of executive, legislative, and judicial functions. He supervised elections and was supposed to ensure the voting rights of freedmen and the registration of all citizens entitled to vote. He tried to run the state according to the new laws, though he often incurred the wrath of the white planter and business classes. Sickles tried to reassure the leading whites that he would work to help them rebuild and regain prosperity. Bishop Lynch strove to cultivate good relations with the general, whose responsibilities were expanded in June 1866 to include North Carolina—thus the whole Diocese of Charleston. By his order the army distributed rations to thousands, black and white. Recipients included the Ursulines of Valle Crucis and their young charges, who drew rations for many months. The Sisters of Our Lady of Mercy received some $1,800 worth of bread, meat, and other groceries for their reestablished girls' orphanage.[14]

The bishop cultivated cordial relations with Sickles, whose wife, Teresa Baglioli Sickles (d. 1867), was Catholic.[15] On occasion he dined with the general, along with General George Meade and his sister Margaret Meade, and used their influence to obtain help from the federal government for the Sisters of Mercy for repair of their fire-damaged convent and in reopening their girls' orphanage. Sickles supplied wood to build the convent's porches and "furnished horses for the Sisters' ambulance." He ordered the army quartermaster to provide the diocese a horse and bridle. He was respectful of the Church. Mother Baptista recorded that he paid a call on the Ursulines when in Columbia for a session of the state legislature, and she was charmed by his "conversational power" and his "style of a perfect gentleman." Sickles had two large "cloister-like" chairs crafted in Charleston, which he offered to the bishop for the cathedral chapel.[16]

The bishop outlined his island plan to Sickles, who indicated that he was favorable. Lynch reported this in a letter he drafted for General O. O. Howard, head of the Freedmen's Bureau. In explaining his idea, he noted, "It is necessary to choose . . . [an island] where the Religious would not die out speedily of fever—where secondly they [the blacks] could have around them their families or individuals that would be under their [the priests'] instruction and guidance, and where their labours would not be thwarted by too frequent intercourse with other negroes of perhaps very different habits—and finally where the products of their industry could be easily & regularly sent to a Market." He emphasized his belief that if white labor could be obtained to work the land of the [South Carolina] upstate, "the Negro can be dispensed with," and "they will be forced down on the Seaboard,—the unhealthiness of which will prevent whites from settling there." If Folly Island could not be obtained, Lynch would ask for another island on the South Carolina coast now under Howard's control. The draft of the letter to Howard is marked "not sent"—apparently in Lynch's hand.[17] There was no response to this letter, and a search in records at the National Archives and other institutions has not found evidence that the letter was ever sent.[18]

Lynch knew of U.S. government efforts to help African American farm workers on the South Carolina Sea Islands south of Charleston. When Union forces invaded, beginning in 1861, white planters fled, abandoning their lands. During the course of the war the federal government allowed blacks—who became freedpersons with the Emancipation Proclamation—effectively to take possession of the lands. Northern Protestant missionaries came to the area to teach and proselytize the blacks. The Freedmen's Bureau initially gave blacks title to much of the land, especially on Edisto Island and around the towns of Beaufort and Port Royal. In some places the African Americans organized institutions of

Immaculate Conception Church. This was the second church opened by Lynch for African American Catholics. John Henry Devereux designed and built this church for his friend and mentor. It was located on Shepherd Street near the intersection with Coming Street. Bishop Lynch dedicated it in 1880. Courtesy of Catholic Diocese of Charleston Archive.

local self-government. In a sense Bishop Lynch was proposing to go in a different direction, believing that blacks needed firm guidance to prepare them to function well in the modern world.[19]

The bishop continued to solicit help from Sickles, and in the spring of 1867 the general promised that he would try to obtain government support for the plan.[20] That fall, in addressing a congress of European clergy in Belgium, Lynch still expressed hope that the island project would succeed.[21] In the Carolinas white opposition to Sickles grew increasingly strident, and President Andrew Johnson removed him from his post in August 1867. Lacking cooperation from the U.S. government or a religious order and without needed funds, the bishop abandoned the project, turning his attention to other work on behalf of African Americans. He was philosophical about the failed dream: "I spoke of it to officials of the government. The reply was that everybody was trying his plan. We were, of course, perfectly free to try ours."[22]

Shortly after his return to Charleston, he informed Archbishop Spalding that he also desired "to have a Negro church—I have the ground for it."[23] Some months passed before a black church became a reality. He spoke to Spalding about his idea for a colony for black Catholics on an island on the South Carolina coast.

Consistent with his concerns about potential tensions between white and black Catholics in church services, Lynch proceeded with plans to establish separate congregations. Lynch purchased a suitable property toward this end in November 1866. St. Peter's Catholic Church was fashioned out of an old Jewish synagogue on Wentworth Street. The Irish architect John Henry Devereux was again engaged to carry out the transformation. Bishop Lynch consecrated the refurbished facility in early January 1868. In April 1880 further growth in the numbers of black Catholics in Charleston brought about the dedication of a second building, the Church of the Immaculate Conception, consecrated by Bishop Lynch at Shepherd Street near Coming Streets. This modest wood-frame building was again designed and built under Devereux's direction. In both instances the opening ceremonies were attended by biracial standing-room-only crowds of worshipers.

Attempt to Reconstruct a Diocesan Press

Lynch understood that a vibrant Catholic press had allowed his predecessor and mentor, Bishop John England, to create a diocese out of whole cloth. He himself had edited and written regularly in the *U.S. Catholic Miscellany.* He had fully availed himself of the national press in his role of "defender of the Faith" as well as in his attempts to convince the world of the righteousness of the cause of Southern liberty. Thus he sought a way to reestablish a written organ to assist the broader efforts of reconstructing his diocese. This effort was played out in the person of James Dalton Budds, who edited a secular Irish Catholic paper called the *Gazette.*

The *Gazette* had been established in February 1867 by the Caulfield and Ford printing establishment. The proprietors sent Bishop Lynch a prospectus as well as a plea for approval, if not outright endorsement of their objective to defend the Catholic faith in "these troubled times. We find it a source of regret that Catholics should feel it expedient, at any time, or in any country, to define their position as to their relation to the Church after a negative manner . . . we feel confident that the drift of the circular, as it runs, will carry with it no compromise of principle."[24]

This new newspaper was dedicated to the presentation primarily of news of Ireland but also to the publication of some other international and regional reports. In addition the editors promised local news, poetry, prose, and "apologetics." It was the newspaper's intent to promote all things Irish first but to be "reviewed by the proper ecclesiastical authority." Its readership was to include people in the Carolinas, Virginia, Georgia, Tennessee, Kentucky, Alabama, and New Orleans, as part of an effort to "reach every Irishman in the South."[25]

Caulfield and Ford were quite ambitious in sending out a first printing of thirty thousand copies across the southern states. But they were unable to make it a success, and in June 1868, Bishop Lynch purchased their entire operation for $5,000. James Dalton Budds signed the bill of sale as a witness and was given editorship of a newspaper dedicated to the defense of the Catholic Church in the Diocese of Charleston.[26]

Budds had arrived in Charleston in 1856 from Kilkenny, Ireland, by way of New York City. As early as 1859 he was described in the *Charleston City Directory* as a reporter for the *Evening Standard* of that city. The January 1860 edition of the *Charleston Mercury* announced that Budds was to be the agent and collector for that storied newspaper. Budds took his family to Sumter for the duration of the Civil War, but upon his return to Charleston he once again took up employment at the *Charleston Mercury.* It was from this capacity that Lynch hired him to edit the *Gazette,* as well as to pose as its proprietor.

Interestingly, one of the local competing newspapers paid tribute to the reputation that James Budds had already achieved throughout the Charleston community. A notice in the *Charleston Courier Tri-weekly* announced his promotion to the editorship of its new competitor in the local press. It said:

> The Charleston Gazette, the organ in this State of the Catholic Church, has passed to the proprietorship of Mr. James D. Budds, and will hereafter be conducted under his editorial management. Mr. Budds has enjoyed a long experience in journalism, principally as a valued member of the corps of the Mercury. Indeed much of the success which has attended our contemporary in late years is due, we believe, to his indefatigable exertions, and the loss of his services cannot therefore be unfelt. We cordially greet him to his new sphere of usefulness, and hope that his enterprise will be accomplished with abundant reward.[27]

The founders of the newspaper announced the impending transfer in the following advertisement:

> THE GAZETTE
> Saturday July 4, 1868
> "Office of the Gazette"
> Charleston July 1, 1868
> Having sold to James Budds All my right, title, and interest in The Gazette, those indebted to the paper will please make payment to Mr. Budds, or his authorized Agent. M. Caulfield

> The Gazette Establishment having been purchased by the Undersigned, the paper will continue to be conducted as a first class Catholic Journal. No pains will be spared to render its columns a vehicle for useful and attractive information. The new Proprietor trusts that his long identification with newspaper interests in Charleston will ensure him a liberal measure of public support. J.D. Budds[28]

They further alerted their readers about the new ownership by declaring victory and success. They also went out of their way to assure their clients that the principles of the paper and the quality of the editorship would not be compromised. They wrote of the new editor in the most glowing terms:

> THE GAZETTE
> July 4, 1868
> "Valedictory"
> Twelve months and more have elapsed since the first issue of The Gazette. ... Through all these [ups and downs], The Gazette has happily passed in safety. Obstacles, at first sight appalling, were met and overcome. Our object had been, in defiance of croakers, "To pluck from the nettle danger, the flower Safely," and we succeeded. Thus The Gazette stands confessedly today, the equal of any weekly paper in the United States. We endeavored from the first to make it a "number one Irish Catholic paper."
>
> With this issue, *The Gazette* passes into the hands of an able and worthy gentleman J.D. Budds, Esq. To those of our city, he is too well known to need mention. The long, life long, I may say—association of this gentleman with the press, has familiarized him to us all. Universally recognized by the newspaper world of the State, as one of its most efficient and enterprising men—his presence alone is sufficient to warrant the future success of any paper, with whom he may happen to be connected. To him is entrusted the future guidance of this paper. If prompt attention, ready skill, an experienced head, and willing hands can give satisfaction, the readers of *The Gazette* will find no cause to complain.... The paper may have, as is the future of all papers, given offence to some one party or the other, on some occasion, or the other, but never in the whole course of its career has there appeared upon its face, language than that calculated to reflect credit upon Ireland and Irishmen. With the above crude remarks, we bid you goodbye.[29]

The new regime, however, ushered in a shift of emphasis from particularly Irish content with attention to theological correctness to a Catholic and literary journal that would include a section of "Irish News." Perhaps because its ownership was actually in the hands of Bishop Lynch, Budds felt obligated to state this intention up front. He would argue unsuccessfully throughout his tenure for Bishop Lynch to allow him to designate this paper as the official organ of the Diocese of Charleston. This is James Budds's statement of objectives, published in his first official issue, in July 1868:

> With this present issue, *The Gazette* takes a fresh start under new auspices. Established originally to supply what was felt to be a pressing want—for there was at that time no Catholic Journal in all the region of the country between Baltimore and New Orleans. Its success up to this time, has been so marked and rapid, as to give it a circulation and influence second to that of no weekly paper published anywhere in the South.
>
> Our aim, in the future, will be to impart greater variety and attractiveness to its columns, so as to make it at once a useful chronicle and a welcome visitor to every Catholic household. While the department of Irish News will receive the same attention as heretofore, it will be our earnest endeavor to present each week, a full and carefully digested abstract of everything of interest to Catholics, transpiring in every quarter of the globe.
>
> The Sketches or Stories which will appear, will be given complete in a single issue—experience having shown, this to be the more satisfactory plan to regular, as well as transient readers.
>
> With this brief statement of the general plan upon which *The Gazette* will hereafter be conducted, we leave the paper, in other particulars, to speak for itself.[30]

In spite of Budds's vast experience and his determination to make this venture a success, he met with chronic financial and administrative difficulties. Correspondence between Budds and Bishop Lynch reveals a series of problems and crises that ended in near bankruptcy and the demise of the *Gazette*. In a letter of July 11, 1868, Budds wrote about the beginnings of the problems. He thanked the bishop for having left money with Thomas O'Keefe, a machinist, before he left for Columbia. He noted that one of his printers, Mr. Roberts, was missing, even as he himself was having to continue to spend time helping out with the *Mercury*. He claimed fifty new subscribers and new potential revenue from additional advertisers. T. Tupper and Sons' bill for paper amounted to $148, and the dentist W.H. Shaffer, whose office space they rented at 307 King Street, was owed $118. He asked Bishop Lynch to "place the missing funds to square them off." He closed this first of many pleas with some additional requests: "I know, Dr. Bishop, its hard in this dull times to Call on you for too much, but as the outside world believes that I am now Started on my own b/c I would like if possible to get the old indebtedness settled—even a portion of it. When fully under way in a few months I can paddle the canoe. Any spare time to write an article or two for the Gazette? Truly yours J.D. Budds."[31] Less than three weeks later he again wrote to Bishop Lynch to discuss management and financial matters related to the *Gazette.* In addition, he asked for some editorial advice as well as some literary contributions from his ecclesiastical superior. He thanked him for the $300 and said that he could again pay Tupper for paper and supplies. There was, however, only enough to pay half the overdue rent. Budds asked Lynch if he had received and read the latest issue. Promising to report on his "current congress," he asked the bishop himself to send in reports with some "facts and information," assuring him that "no one need know who is the contributor." He was hoping for payments from at least forty subscribers to ease the paper's financial stress.[32]

At the end of August Budds again wrote to Bishop Lynch thanking him for the article he had sent. But quickly the embattled editor returned to the dreadful subject of finances. He assured the bishop that measures that he had taken would eventually fix most of the problems. But his predecessor had left him with such a mess that an immediate infusion of revenue was necessary. Merchants clamored for payment for past shipments of supplies. Budds claimed that the previous owners had left the enterprise in such confusion and with such bad accounts that the only revenue that came in was from new accounts that he had procured. It was necessary for him to take out a loan from a Mr. O'Keefe to cover back rent. The newspaper could be made profitable, but he needed more funds from the bishop in the meantime. W.C. Dolan (printer at 75 Broad) and Walker, Evans and Cogswell (printers, 3 Broad) were constantly clamoring for payments. He also indicated that in desperation he would be traveling south to attempt to collect on subscriptions and to expand the readership in Savannah, Georgia.[33]

The financial distress of the newspaper continued such that by October, Budds agreed to travel across the Southeastern states on a fund-raising tour. In the absence of Bishop Lynch, he sought authorization of the vicar general, the Reverend Timothy Bermingham, who wrote a note as a letter of recommendation. He described Budds as "a gentleman who is very favorably known in Charleston, and particularly to me, whose avocation is literary." Bermingham recounted the bearer's history as a reporter for the *Charleston Mercury* and the current editor of the *Gazette,* "which paper is now under the patronage of Rt. Rev. Dr. Lynch." The letter described Budds's intention to collect debts and to obtain new subscribers in Atlanta, Mobile, New Orleans, and various cities in between. In closing, he described Budds as "a highly respectable Citizen, an exemplary Catholic and worthy of confidence and Success." Addressing the letter to "all on whom he may have pleasure and honor of calling," Bermingham recommended him in "the absence of Rt. Rev. Bishop Lynch."[34]

Unfortunately, there is no follow-up correspondence, and no accounts of this trip can be found. But we know that distribution of the newspaper to far-off points as well as the collection of subscription fees continued to be problematic. His successor would later complain that while there were close to nine hundred subscriptions on the books, only a little more than sixty were paid up. So, Mr. Budds was left with constant travels in his attempts to survive in this far-flung one-man operation.

At the start of 1869 Budds was still sending pleas for more money as creditors zeroed in on him. He planned a trip to New York, again, for fund-raising purposes one would presume. Another printer, Mr. Dohlen [*sic*], was owed forty-one dollars and was "becoming quite troublesome." Budds asked Lynch either to send a list of supplies to the office of the *Gazette* or to contact potential suppliers to ensure that Budds could get a line of credit extended on the bishop's name. Printing paper was most urgently needed. And, as pressure mounted at the *Gazette,* Budd's personal finances grew more and more precarious. He asserted that both city and county sheriffs were about to put his house up for sale for nonpayment of back taxes.[35]

In a letter sent in mid-February 1869, James Budds appeared quite desperate and announced that he was relinquishing the role of editor to Father Quigley, a prominent parish priest. There is no indication, however, that this transfer of editorship ever took place. He thanked the bishop for sending a shipment of paper and, more important, the means with which to make payment on the necessary supplies. He again tried to make the case for naming the *Gazette* the official organ of the Diocese of Charleston. He pointed out that Bishop Gibbons had declared the *Mirror* of Baltimore that diocese's official newspaper. He speculated that "I do not think he would have done that were *The Gazette* known as your official organ and now with Fr. Quigley as Editor, I think you may authorize us to place at the head of the paper 'official organ of the Diocese of Charleston' or something similar to show that we are official." Budds finished the letter with a desperate flourish, describing one creditor, Dohlen, as "getting insolent." The sheriff had placed ads in the newspaper for the sale of Budds's house. Budds asserted that he had personal bills out for the baker, butcher, and grocer. As the last straw on the camel's back, he asked Bishop Lynch for a personal loan of "a couple hundred dollars that would relieve me, and I don't think there will be another straw."[36]

The end was clearly near. Budds had worked very hard to cover all of the bases. His background up to this point had been as a reporter and then as a collector of accounts for the *Charleston Mercury.* At the *Gazette* he was required to act as the editor, managing editor, subscriptions solicitor, procurer of news and literary items, collector of fees, traveling agent, and everyday office manager. Caulfield and Ford had given this enterprise its start, but they relinquished control over it after just a little more than one year. And after Bishop Lynch's ownership and Budds's editorship, the next owners would find their tasks so difficult that they would relocate to another region of the state and change the name as well as the editorial focus once again. Monsignor Richard Madden, the chronicler of the history of the Diocese of Charleston, had little to say about the many paths followed by the owners of this ill-fated journalistic effort. He presented Father Quigley's role as nothing more than a desperate idea of Budds's concoction. Six months after Lucius C. Northrop purchased the paper, he was demanding that Lynch buy it back from him. Not long after that, he moved the enterprise to Columbia and changed the name to *The Southern Celt.* [37]

In June 1869 Bishop Lynch had had enough and resolved to sell the newspaper to the brother of a future bishop of the Diocese of Charleston. This ended James Budds's short career as proprietor and editor of the *Gazette.* Northrop paid $2,140 to purchase the newspaper.[38] Its office continued to be located at its initial site at 307 King Street and was now recorded as under the proprietorship of Northrop, who resided at 156 Queen Street.[39] Yet Mr. Budds was not finished as a newspaperman, nor had he heard the last of the discussion about his tenure at the *Gazette.* By August 1869 Northrop wrote to Bishop Lynch concerning his inability to pay bills and collect debts owed to the paper. And on October 30, 1869, an even more ominous note arrived in the bishop's office from Northrop, who detailed the paper's mounting debts and suggested that he had been deceived about the actual value and condition of the *Gazette.* He went into great detail about the contract and financial condition of the *Gazette,* suggesting that Budds had misrepresented the assets and perhaps minimized the liabilities. Northrop had been told there were 964 subscribers, yet far fewer than that ever paid their bills. The physical assets had also been grossly exaggerated, according to Northrop. The number of subscribers had melted to fewer than five hundred, and yet the postmasters delivered the papers throughout the South, ignoring the fact that hundreds never left the post offices in city after city. Finally, he referred to "false books," all but accusing Budds of fraud and theft.[40]

Northrop proposed the purchase of better presses and a merger with another paper, the *Banner of the South.* Finally, he begged Bishop Lynch to void the contract or at least to put him on a regular salary. "If you can make neither of these arrangements, will you cancel our contract on the ground of my being entirely deceived where I most trusted or will you allow me any fixed salary for running the paper. If I have worked well for nothing, I would do better if possible, when paid. The clergy have everywhere relished and assisted the paper and notwithstanding my deep interest I shall be pleased to resign the control, whenever you appoint another."[41]

Bishop Lynch was in no financial position to comply with Northrop's requests. He had hoped that the newspaper would aid in his attempts to rebuild and reunite the Diocese of Charleston. He had actually hoped that the reestablishment of a diocesan newspaper might be a source of revenue. But as soon as he determined that it was a drain on church funds, he dumped both this business venture and Mr. Budds.

In each of the three areas of reconstruction Bishop Lynch met with some success but just as many failures. He nevertheless endured throughout the ups and downs of each experiment. In his effort to rebuild the physical infrastructure of the diocese while also reducing the massive financial debt, he made steady progress at the cost of his own physical health. In his attempts to provide "a solution" to the problem of accommodating and proselytizing the newly freed slaves, he failed, as did the rest of the South and the nation in general. Two new African American Catholic churches were provided in Charleston, and there was recognizable growth in the number of black Catholics in the diocese. The project to establish a new Catholic journal to replace the *U.S. Catholic Miscellany* was an abject failure and resulted in a personal financial debacle for his deputy, James Dalton Budds. The rest of Lynch's life would be a constant struggle to beg and borrow as he traveled thousands of miles trying to recoup the losses his extremely poor diocese had incurred through the ravages of war and the destructive fire of 1861. He literally died trying.

1870s to His Death

The last decade and a half of Patrick Lynch's life was spent traveling all over the United States, mostly in the Northeast, as he pursued an endless quest to reestablish the Diocese of Charleston on a firm financial footing. He was mortified that his tenure was marked by the accumulation of nearly $400,000 in debts. Clearly, most of this sum was not of his making, as the great Charleston fire of 1861 and the destruction of the American Civil War hardly fell into his responsibilities. He, nevertheless, felt it his moral obligation to repay all of the negative accounts that his diocese had accrued in those tragic events.

The records and letters are full of much criticism directed toward Lynch for his extensive absences from Charleston. Those complaints began to be voiced by Father Moore during the Civil War, particularly when Lynch was gone for eight months on his Rome mission and subsequent exile.

When he arrived back in the United States after his mission to Rome for the Confederacy, on the seventh of November 1865, he was welcomed by Archbishop McCloskey in New York City and within a few short days he delivered a sermon to a standing-room-only audience in St. Patrick's Cathedral. He would remain one of the American church's most appreciated speakers for the rest of his life. Giving guest lectures and sermons became the "modus operandi" that allowed him to repair his broken diocese and restore fiscal health throughout its jurisdiction.

Lynch spent some time in New York City and then traveled south toward Charleston. He made stops at Philadelphia, Baltimore, Richmond, and Fortress Monroe (in Virginia), before arriving back in Charleston by the first of December. *The Charleston Daily Courier* posted this announcement of his return: "Rt. Rev. Bishop P.N. Lynch—We are happy to welcome once more among us this distinguished divine. We hear that he officiated in the Catholic Church last Sunday and met with a joyful reception from his congregation. We are also glad to learn that the Bishop has been promised assistance to rebuild St. Finbar's Cathedral."[1] Within a few months he was back in New York City. In May 1866 Lynch was invited by Cooper Union to deliver a public address during the intermission of a concert given to raise money for the Charleston orphans. The *New York Times* reported that he made "an eloquent address to the assembly." Beginning with a description of the ancient civilizations of Greece and Rome, then proceeding into the connections to early Christianity, he declared that the most vital link was the "grander virtue of the love of little children." Children were easy to love because of their innocence. Jesus, of course, emphasized this love as exemplified by Mary and Joseph's observance of Him as a child with the Temple priests. Lynch then described his efforts just prior to the war to construct an orphan house in Charleston, of which "not one brick has been left upon another." In conclusion he called upon the "fraternal relations of Union, now growing stronger," which he hoped would lead to assistance for the growing number of orphans in his war-torn homeland.[2] The newspaper account made reference to the audience's generous response.

It has been previously chronicled that Bishop Lynch and his longtime friend Monsignor James Corcoran played major roles in the Second Plenary Council of Baltimore in October 1866. Observers of the period remark about how felicitous was the reunification of the Roman Catholic Church within the United States, which had just recently been torn asunder by four years of warfare. This process of almost instant cooperation among the Northern and Southern hierarchies can be largely attributed to Patrick Lynch and the friendships he had engendered before the outbreak of war.

Lynch left for Rome, once again, in June 1867 to attend the ceremonies surrounding the 1,800th anniversary of the death of St. Peter. At this gathering the pope made use of the presence at Rome of nearly five hundred bishops, who had come to attend the celebration to make the first public announcement of the proposed council at a consistory, to be held on June 26, 1867. Lynch was also listed in an article published in the *Chicago Tribune* on July 23 as among the American bishops at a congregation celebrating the temporal rights of the papacy. This was in response to the recent confiscation of the Papal States by the revolutionary armies of Garibaldi.[3]

While Lynch was there, he met Father Aloysius Louis Folchi, S.J., who wanted to move to a warmer climate to improve his health. Lynch talked him into coming to the Diocese of Charleston to assist in tending to its growing number of Italians. Folchi became a tireless worker in the name of Catholicism throughout the diocese, given charge of the mission for black Catholics when Lynch dedicated St. Peter's Church in January 1868. After serving all of the missions of the state in one capacity or another, he left the diocese to rejoin the Jesuit Order in 1877.

When Lynch returned to Charleston from this great assemblage in Rome he once again set about performing his duties to the diocese. The Charleston local newspaper announced a series of lectures to be delivered by Bishop Lynch at the Catholic Institute. The first talk in this program, to which the general public was invited, came on January 12, 1868, at seven o'clock in the evening in the pro-cathedral chapel. The Charleston press described an overflow audience in which hundreds of people were turned away for lack of space in the relatively small edifice on Queen Street.[4]

By late February, the bishop was again out of town though. The *Charleston Daily Courier* reported that the Charleston prelate was up in Boston and had preached at St. Mary's Church there. The appreciative audience demonstrated its generosity with donations totaling $650 for the benefit of the reconstruction needs within the Diocese of Charleston. The *Courier* quoted an article in the *Boston Pilot* about the "great success of the worthy object of the learned bishop is now appealing to his brethren of the North."[5]

In March 1868 the Vatican announced the separation of the state of North Carolina from the Diocese of Charleston. Lynch had advocated this move for several years, having first proposed it at the Second Baltimore Plenary in 1866, and had made a persuasive argument for the division during his visit to Rome the previous year.

The actual announcement by the Vatican of the elevation of a new church official for North Carolina appeared in the *Charleston Daily Courier* in August. Lynch served as one of the co-consecrators of James Gibbons, the new vicar apostolic of what would later become the Diocese of Raleigh.[6] According to an account in the *New York Times,* "The ceremonies were most imposing and solemn. The cathedral was densely crowded and thousands were unable to gain admittance.[7]

Lynch's return to Charleston appeared in the local press with this announcement: "PERSONAL—Right Rev. Bishop Lynch returned to this city yesterday, after a protracted Northern tour."[8] On June 24, St. John's Day, the bishop celebrated a Pontifical High Mass at the cathedral chapel. He preached a sermon on St. John the Baptist, whose feast day is often referred to as Midsummer Day because it occurs so close to the summer solstice. His theme covered the fact that the Knights of St. John, of Jerusalem, the Hospitalers, were rivals of the Knights Templars during medieval times. The newspaper account reported that while only Masons generally recognized its importance, both Catholic and Episcopal churches in Charleston marked this day with religious services. The Cathedral church that eventually replaced the edifice that Lynch had built and fire destroyed would eventually bear the name of this patron saint.[9]

A *New York Times* article of September 1869 reported that "Right Rev. Dr, Lynch, Bishop of Charleston, will ordain Rev. Henry S. Lake, now a deacon, to the priesthood, tomorrow (Thursday) at 8 o'clock A.M., in the Church of the Paulist Fathers, corner of Fifty-ninth-street and Ninth-avenue." Several other Paulist postulants received the orders of Tonsure and Minor as well.[10] As in all of these distant activities, Lynch used the occasion to make pleas for help meeting the needs of his ravaged Diocese of Charleston.

In October 1869 Lynch was again off to Rome to attend the ecumenical council announced the previous year by Pope Pius IX. The First Vatican Council convened in the midst of political turmoil and military conflicts surrounding the unification of Italian city-states and principalities into the modern nation of Italy. In this nation-building process, the papacy lost nearly the entirety of its temporal empire and was reduced to the physical confines of the one-square-mile parcel that today is known as Vatican City.

The purpose of this worldwide council, to some degree, was to respond to these impending losses by asserting the place of the Roman Catholic Church and its pontiff as the "true spiritual heir" to leadership in Christendom. The Council unanimously adopted the principle of *Dei Filius,* signifying "The Holy Apostolic Roman Catholic Church" as preeminent. The most famous pronouncement of the First Vatican Council is the doctrine of papal infallibility when "he speaks ex cathedra." Lynch's distinction at this gathering was to be the first American prelate to endorse publicly this principle.[11] Lynch also provided an American audience with reports from this auspicious Church conclave that were published in the *Catholic World,* as well as in the local Charleston press.[12] He spent, by his own accounts, five months in Rome attending council meetings. The Council was suspended when Rome was disrupted by invading armies and by ongoing conflicts.

At this international conclave the English-speaking bishops constituted the second largest group, with only the Italian clergy attending in greater numbers. The American bishops met weekly with Archbishop Spalding presiding. The minutes of the meetings indicate that Bishop Lynch acted as the secretary for the group.[13] Lynch had actually asked for permission to stay in Charleston as his financial situation made it difficult to travel to Europe at the time. After receiving approval, he went to Rome anyway and played a significant role, at the very least in the American delegation. As previously mentioned, the *Catholic World* published a series of eight lengthy letters in which Lynch reported on the events and discussions of the First Vatican Council.[14] In his final missive he reflected on the sometimes heated debates on the most controversial issue the Council tackled—that of the doctrine of infallibility. "In a word, that the Council of the Vatican did not break up months ago in disorder and irreconcilable enmity is because it was God's work, and not man's; it was because charity ruled in it, in spite of defects, and not the passions that govern the political debates of men."[15]

Upon his return to Charleston from the First Vatican Council, Bishop Lynch gave an address in the pro-cathedral on Queen Street, detailing his experience at this momentous event. Of all the coverage given to the Ecumenical Council he observed that not 1 percent of what was to be found in newspapers throughout America was accurate. He continued his staunch defense of Pius IX and the important role of the pope and the Church as the protector of true Christianity.[16] He provided a lengthy and logical explanation of the meaning and consequences of the doctrine of papal infallibility. As was reported in newspapers throughout the nation, he said, "I felt more than ever the unity, the Catholicity of the Church. From China to California, from Lapland to the Cape of Good Hope, from Hudson's Bay to Chile, from every quarter, there was heard one faith, one baptism, one Church of Christ there assembled in her majesty, and there about to declare the faith of Christ to this world."[17] Once again at New York City's Cooper Union Institute on October 21, 1870, Lynch delivered a lecture on the subject "Charity." The beneficiary was the Catholic Home for Boys at 53 Warren Street, operated by the newly formed Society of St. Vincent de Paul, and its success was demonstrated by the overflow crowd. The *New York Times* reported, "The lecture, which occupied an hour and a half in delivery, was listened to with marked attention by the large audience present, and at its close the reverend Bishop was heartily applauded."[18] Lynch's responsibilities as bishop of Charleston took him on regular jaunts across the state of South Carolina. On July 4, 1870, he spoke at an overflow crowded assemblage at St. Joseph's Academy in Sumter, South Carolina. Dressed in his episcopal robes, he addressed the audience on the subject of the "demoralizing influence of extravagance in female dress, its effect elsewhere in multiplying divorces, and raising up in the minds of many a discouragement and barrier to marriage."[19] This appearance was occasioned by the presentation of "premiums" at this popular school and drew people of all creeds from throughout the community.

The *Charleston Daily Courier* announced on the day after Christmas 1870 that "Bishop Lynch was in Greenville last week, "the first time a Roman Catholic divine [meaning a bishop] had ever visited that city." He preached "a sermon of decided ability, free of denominationalism" in a large room in the Mansion House. The *Courier* went on to say that a planned lecture on his time spent at Vatican I Council had to be canceled due to inclement weather. Plans to build a Catholic church in Greenville had also been discussed.[20]

Bishop Lynch, in the seventeen years after the war, traveled to every major city along the entire Atlantic coastal region of the United States. He attended every major liturgical event in every diocese that welcomed him. He gave guest sermons and lectures at the slightest invitation. In all of these travels and labors his primary objective was to beg funds for the reconstruction of churches, schools, and orphanages throughout his war-torn diocese. In April 1875 he attended the solemn ceremonies in which his longtime friend John McCloskey was conferred with the scarlet berretta, making him a cardinal with jurisdiction over the Roman Catholic Church in the United States. Lynch was among sixteen bishops and five archbishops who attended, along with an official papal legation representing the Vatican, U.S. president Ulysses S. Grant, New York governor Samuel J. Tilden, New York City mayor William H. Wickham, and hundreds of additional clergy.[21]

Cardinal John McCloskey (1810–1892), archbishop of New York from 1865 to 1885. In 1875 he became the first American cardinal. A personal friend of Bishop Lynch, the Charleston prelate stayed with him on his many post–Civil War visits to New York City. Lynch was often mentioned as the most likely candidate to become McCloskey's coadjutor. Courtesy of Library of Congress.

Later that same year, on December 12, 1875, Lynch was in Boston for the dedication and consecration of the Cathedral of the Holy Cross. The ceremonies were celebrated by the first archbishop of Boston, John J. Williams, and the honored guest speaker was Bishop Lynch. Interestingly, the cathedral was designed by Patrick C. Keely, with whom Lynch had worked on the construction of his cathedral in Charleston in the early 1850s. The Boston cathedral is in the same Gothic Revival style, and its steeple, like that of the second great Charleston cathedral designed by Keely, was never completed.[22] In 2009 the southern edifice finally received its crown.

In the fall of 1876, Lynch was again in the upper regions of South Carolina dedicating the new Catholic church for Greenville, South Carolina. The parish of

Our Lady of the Sacred Heart of Jesus resulted from the efforts of Father Folchi, whom Lynch had recruited while attending the 1867 anniversary celebration of the death of St. Peter in Rome. Again the Charleston papers covered this event with a fairly lengthy description of the ceremonies. Lynch preached a sermon on the evening of the dedication on the subject of "Purgatory, explaining fully the teachings of the Church on this point." The bishop, along with a group of altar boys from the cathedral and St. Mary's church choir, traveled from Charleston for the dedication, which took place on October 15, 1876.[23]

In late 1877, upon the death of Archbishop James Roosevelt Bailey, the Most Reverend James Gibbons was named as successor to the See of Baltimore. This most solemn ceremony of "investing the Pallium" was attended by hundreds of clergy from throughout the entire United States. Bishop Lynch, of Charleston, was assisted by the Right Reverends Foley, of Chicago, and Decker, of Wilmington, Delaware. The *Washington Post* reported that "Bishop Lynch delivered an address upon the lessons taught by the occasion, and the Archbishop responded in a fitting manner."[24]

On the very next day the *Washington Post* announced that a Pontifical High Mass would be held at St. Patrick's Cathedral in New York City as a memorial to the late Pope Pius IX. The writer of the article reported that most of the priests from the Diocese of Washington and from throughout the northeastern United States would be in attendance, Bishop Lynch, a personal friend of the recently deceased pontiff, was scheduled to deliver the sermon. On February 13, the same newspaper included a report that a "grand and impressive ceremonial of the solemn Mass of Requiem for Pope Pius IX was observed in its entirety to-day in the Cardinal's church, St. Patrick's Cathedral. Bishop Lynch, of Charleston, preached the sermon, which was an elegant tribute to the late Pope, and his church."[25]

A week later Lynch was in Philadelphia to again honor his friend, the deceased Pope Pius IX. The *New York Times* reported that on February 21 "a solemn mass was celebrated at the Cathedral for the repose of the soul of Pope Pius IX." The church was filled to capacity, and a great number were left outside, unable to attend. In a setting heavily colored in mourning were representatives of many local Catholic organizations, including two hundred diocesan priests, students from the seminary of St. Charles, and members of the Catholic Club and the St. Vincent de Paul conference. Archbishop Frederick Bryan Wood presided over a form of a mock funeral, with a coffin bearing a pall with the papal tiara and crossed keys on a catafalque encircled by several candelabra. "The panegyric was delivered by Right Rev. P.N. Lynch, Bishop of Charleston. It was followed by five absolutions, given by Archbishop Wood, Bishop Lynch, the Right Reverend Bishop O'Hara, the Very Reverend Dr. Corcoran, and the Very Reverend Father Walsh.[26]

Lynch was back in New York City in the spring of 1878 for the laying of the cornerstone for the new church of St. Francis Xavier parish in the Chelsea district on 16th Street between Fifth and Sixth Avenues. This was to be another glorious Gothic Revival structure designed by the famous church architect Patrick C. Keely. The *New York Times* reporter described Lynch's address as being delivered in a loud clear voice, "audible to nearly the whole mass of spectators." He spoke on the history of the parish and of the two previous structures that had occupied the site. Recalling conversations he had had with the late Archbishop John Hughes concerning the great growth of the Catholic Church in America, he drew parallels to the expansion of the parish of St. Francis Xavier. He closed his sermon with "a eulogy of the mission of the Church and an appeal for earnest and constant endeavor in its behalf."[27] He seemed to have an innate ability to tailor his remarks to every occasion and audience. His public lectures and sermons always attracted a large and welcoming audience.

Still in New York a week later, Lynch was part of a welcoming ceremony at St. Patrick's Cathedral upon the return of John Cardinal McCloskey from the official funeral of Pope Pius IX and the selection of a new leader of the Roman Catholic Church by the College of Cardinals. The *New York Times* announced that plans were being made for a grand reception at St. Patrick's in the cardinal's honor. Lynch, as a colleague and dear friend of Cardinal McCloskey, was asked to deliver the main address on behalf of all of the American clergy.[28] Richmond, Virginia, was the scene of Bishop Lynch's next appearance at an important regional liturgical occasion. Father Keane was consecrated in St. Peter's Cathedral as bishop of the Diocese of Richmond on August 23, 1878. Archbishop Gibbons of Baltimore performed the ceremony at a High Pontifical Mass He was assisted by Bishops Foley of Chicago and Kain of Wheeling, West Virginia. Bishop Lynch of Charleston delivered the sermon. The *Washington Post* reported that the event was an "occasion of great interest, and will be made one of great beauty and enjoyment." It further commented that this Catholic ceremony would likely attract the largest number of people to the old Confederate capital since the end of the Civil War.[29]

On March 3, 1879, Bishop Lynch was back in New York City visiting his friend, Cardinal McCloskey. The *New York Times* reported that the cardinal officiated at a mass in St. Patrick's Cathedral, and once more Bishop Lynch delivered the guest sermon. Since he was speaking during the Lenten season, he preached on the virtues of fasting. After the Mass the two prelates processed out when the opening ceremonies of the "Forty Hours of Devotion" had begun.[30]

Still in New York City in late May 1879, Bishop Lynch joined three dozen bishops, six archbishops, and Cardinal McCloskey for the "imposing ceremony" of dedication and blessing of the new Roman Catholic Cathedral of St. John the Evangelist at 50th Street and Madison Avenue. In addition to the distinguished Church officials in attendance, there were representatives of the national, state, and municipal governments as well as of newspapers from around the region.[31]

The Charleston newspaper announced on Saturday April 10, 1880, that a new Catholic church at the corner of Shepherd and Coming Streets was to be dedicated by the Right Reverend Bishop Lynch. This Church of the Immaculate Conception was to be the second Charleston parish for the growing African American Catholic membership. A fair at Byrnes Hall on King Street had been held for the purpose of paying for the building, which according to the paper was "a substantial frame edifice 30 by 60 feet, and is enclosed by a white picket fence." The edition of April 12 carried a complete account of the event. The ceremony "was attended by a large crowd of persons, white and colored, who not only filled all the standing room in the church but all the available room in the enclosure." Bishop Lynch performed the elaborate services, assisted by six priests. They marched around the exterior and interior of the church sprinkling the walls with holy water while reciting a multitude of Latin prayers. At 11 A.M. a solemn Mass was held when "Bishop Lynch preached an eloquent sermon appropriate to the occasion, and the large congregation was dismissed with the Pontifical Benediction."[32] Thus Lynch continued his efforts to build his diocese and accommodate the needs of growing numbers of Catholics from the freed slave population.

Bishop Lynch's fame and influence reached far and wide. In spite of the controversial role that he played with his defense of slavery and his support of the Confederacy, the respect he received from his colleagues in the American Catholic hierarchy remained strong. When Archbishop Spalding died, in February 1872, Lynch was listed as one of the most likely candidates to be his successor. Amid reports of his imminent appointment, the Charleston bishop in an extraordinary letter begged off, alluding to his massive responsibilities and his commitment to return the Charleston Diocese to financial solvency. In the message to Cardinal Barnabò he wrote, "The Diocese of Charleston is in a very difficult and embarrassed pecuniary condition . . . [and] it would pain me exceedingly to tear asunder all the ties of relationships and friendship, that have grown up from my boyhood."[33]

A similar, somewhat awkward, circumstance arose in 1877 when his longtime friend Cardinal McCloskey decided to appoint a coadjutor bishop, a post that necessitated a move to the Archdiocese of New York. Because of his high qualifications and his close relationship to the cardinal, the entire collection of American prelates assumed that the only choice would be Patrick N. Lynch. Cardinal Gibbons wrote to Lynch saying that he expected congratulations would soon be in order. Rumors concerning the impending appointment appeared in many newspapers throughout the United States. Lynch felt compelled to publicly deny he had indeed been appointed. The *New York Times* published this denial, which had originally appeared in the *News and Courier:* "The good Bishop says that he has himself reached an age at which it would be more fitting that he should seek a coadjutor than a coadjutorship. Moreover, the American Cardinal is now in excellent health, and it is by no means certain that he requires any assistance in the administration of the Archdiocese. However this may be, Bishop Lynch has no thought or expectation of ever leaving the See of Charleston, the restoration and welfare of which he has made his life-work."[34] Lynch's name was at the top of the list of three candidates presented by the American bishops to the Vatican for approval. In this instance Rome went outside the known candidates and rendered Lynch's reluctance a moot point.

In 1880 the *New York Times* was full of additional rumors concerning the possibility that Bishop Lynch would be elevated to high liturgical offices within the American Catholic hierarchy. On September 19 it reported from an anonymous "high authority that the Right Rev. Dr. Lynch, of Charleston, S.C., is to be appointed Cardinal McCloskey's coadjutor."[35] And later in October, when the Vatican's decision had been announced, the same newspaper offered this explanation: "Three candidates were chosen by the Cardinal and his suffragan bishops. ... The three whose names were finally forwarded to Rome were Lynch, Loughlin, and Corrigan. Bishop Lynch is an old and close personal friend of the Cardinal and was understood to be his choice for the coadjutorship. Instead of falling to him it was given to Corrigan."[36]

The fact that Lynch's name repeatedly appeared on short lists for higher positions within the American Catholic hierarchy is a tribute to the respect that he had earned throughout his distinguished career. The question arises as to why he never did receive such an elevated station within the Church. His display of expected humility is not an entirely sufficient explanation. Some ecclesiastical scholars have posited the theory that in spite of his welcome back into the community of American prelates after his role in Confederate diplomacy, the officials within the Vatican would never have allowed him to become a member of the College of Cardinals. They feared embarrassment and potential controversy in a nation that already displayed a predisposition toward anti-Catholicism. There is no documentary evidence supporting this historical interpretation, even though there is a certain logic in its favor.

Personal Losses and Death

In the final phase of his life, Lynch faced not only hardship and public struggles but also increasing personal loss and suffering. Amid the unending financial obstacles, debilitating travels, and unceasing demands of his diocese, he suffered declining personal health, deaths within his family, and the realization that his mission would not be completed within his lifetime.

On May 27, 1870, Bishop Lynch lost his father, Conlaw Peter Lynch. He had been an outstanding builder and civic and religious leader in the town of Cheraw.

He won contracts to design and build the town market hall and had personally granted the land and constructed St. Peter's Catholic Church with his own hands. His standing in the community was so high that neighbors of varying Protestant faiths assisted in the building of this Catholic edifice. There remain today in the town of Cheraw at least three private residences built by Conlaw Peter Lynch, including the boyhood home of his son, Bishop Patrick Lynch.

Letters from Mother Baptista, Patrick's sister Ellen, to the bishop, who was attending the Vatican I Council in Rome, kept him apprised of his father's declining health. The messages indicate that Conlaw was very ill during the Lenten season, and he was described as "feeble" on Good Friday. He received the sacrament of Extreme Unction on that day.[37] On May 27 she wrote, "A telegram calls brother John to Cheraw. Anna says our dear venerable father was released from his sufferings this morning about 8 o'clock. May our dear Lord establish him in eternal peace and blessedness. So good a life merits eternal happiness."[38]

Conlaw had purchased a family plot in the church graveyard attached to St. David's, which, although an Episcopal parish, allowed townspeople of all faiths to be interred there. In addition to those of Conlaw and his wife, Eleanor, the graves of several of Lynch's siblings are also located in St. David's. An obituary in the *Banner of the South* gave this tribute: "In our mourning we lament the loss of one who , as a master, was kind; as a husband, true and affectionate; as a father, gentle, yet firm; governing his household in the fear of the Lord; as a friend, staunch; as a citizen, honest and honored; and, as a Christian, an ornament to the holy Faith."[39] Later in 1870 Lynch, after returning home from abroad, also had to deal with nearly losing his mother and with the tragic death of his young sister Anna. Baptista reported to her brother that their mother and sister had "been very much exhausted nursing father, but neither they nor he could be satisfied to have it otherwise."[40]

Lynch's mother, Eleanor Neison Lynch, died June 27, 1877. She was eighty-three years old and had outlived her husband and five of her dozen children. The last years of her life had been spent with her son, John, in Columbia, and her eldest daughter, Ellen, who ruled over the Ursuline convent at Valle Crucis, outside Columbia, South Carolina, as their Mother Superior Baptista. She wrote to her brother the bishop:

> I am with you in spirit all the time & near our precious mother. Let us bless the Almighty that we are the children of such a mother. What a true Catholic Christian she has always been. The truly valiant woman. How faithful. Almighty God would not be outdone in generosity. His goodness to her fills my soul with deep gratitude. He preserved her from the imbecility of old age & from ordinary helplessness. She possessed her every faculty to the last.

> Always cheerful, strong and sweet. She was the support, counselor & model of all who approached her—whether the mature in years or the playful school girl. All found in her a true Mother.[41]

The *Columbia Register* notice of her death indicated that "out of respect for Mrs. Lynch the Academic Institute would not hold its annual commencement" scheduled for that date. Initially she was buried in the Valle Crucis cemetery. Later, she was moved, and, like her husband and several of her children, she is now buried in the family plot in St. David's in the quaint old town of Cheraw, South Carolina.[42] It is interesting that while at his mother's funeral Bishop Lynch began to develop and publicly exhibit some of the symptoms of the physical affliction that would bring on his own demise.

Bishop Lynch also had to endure the loss of five of his eleven siblings before his own demise. His younger brother Conlaw Charles died on May 3, 1856. Bernard Ignatius died before his time, on May 13, 1859. Julia Anne passed away March 23, 1861. Hugh Patrick, who served in the Confederate Army on James Island, took sick and was allowed to return home to Cheraw, where he died on March 20, 1863. The family considered him a casualty of the war. And finally, Lynch's elder sister Anna became seriously ill during her father's fatal illness and went on to her heavenly reward seven months later, on December 30, 1870. They are all interred in the family plot next to their parents in St. David's Church Cemetery in Cheraw.

Bishop Lynch suffered from urinary infections throughout much of his adult life. He was continually seeking advice and remedies. In 1877 Lynch's health reached a crisis point that led him to seek treatment in Boston. In August 1877, while visiting Brockton, Massachusetts, Bishop Lynch was "seized with a terrible and angry inflammation of the bladder, blood, pus, and thick matter coming with the urine, with painful spasms and burning." The doctors initially treated the pain with opium to give him an occasional brief sleep. He was treated by a Dr. Porter, whom he described as a doctor and surgeon.[43]

After extensive and very probing examinations he submitted himself to surgeons at Massachusetts General Hospital. He was diagnosed as having a "vesical calculus," which consists of concreted deposits in the bladder. Lynch most likely eventually died from a "sepsis" or virulent infectious poisoning.[44] In Boston, which had more modern facilities and procedures than were available in Charleston, he subjected himself to some painful treatments. He underwent a crushing of bladder stones through a lithotrite,[45] a rather primitive stone crusher. As the doctors located the stone with a metal rod-like instrument, he experienced unimaginable pain. He would have been put under a general anesthesia induced by ether. There were a series of three operations over several days that lasted "one and three quarter hours, two and a quarter hours, and finally another of the same or greater length."[46] In his correspondence with Father Quigley he advised his assistant to find his last will and testament and to set his things in order. Lynch survived this medical ordeal, but the "cure" was not permanent by any means. He recuperated from the operations with a longtime friend, the Reverend James McGlew, in Chelsea, Massachusetts.[47]

The effects of this medical ordeal seemed to alleviate the most extreme conditions for about two years. Then the symptoms began to recur on an increasingly frequent basis. While in the upper part of his home state, in December 1881, he suffered another severe attack, and upon his return to Charleston he was laid up in great pain. He planned at trip to St. Augustine, Florida, hoping the warmer climate might relieve some of the agony, but at the last moment had to abandon the plans. As he grew weaker and weaker, his brother John, a practicing physician, traveled from Columbia to be with him. Another brother, Francis Lynch, traveled from Cheraw to Charleston around the twentieth of February to be by his bedside. Many family members, friends, priests, and nuns surrounded his bedside in the final days and hours.

His deteriorating health in late 1881 prevented him from attending the consecration of Henry Northrop, as bishop of North Carolina in Baltimore on January 8, 1882.[48] On Saturday, February 25, he fell into a coma, and his local doctors, Chaval and Geddings, attempted to revive him and also performed a desperate operation. An all-night vigil, which included his vicar general, Monsignor Daniel J. Quigley; his personal confessor, the Reverend Patrick L. Duffy; and another cathedral priest, Father Chapus, was maintained. The last rites were administered as he made a profession of his faith: "I have lived a member of the Holy Catholic Church, I believe all its doctrines and have tried to the best of my abilities to obey its precepts. I die a Bishop of the Holy Roman Catholic Church, and, in dying, profess my faith in all its truths taught by the Church. I ask the forgiveness of God for all my shortcomings and trusting in God's mercy, I resign my soul to His hands."[49] At 6:30 Sunday morning, as the end was imminent, prayers for the dead were said by all present. Bishop Lynch raised his hand to give a final blessing "to the clergymen who knelt at his bedside." Personal friends, members of the Vestry, and Sisters of Mercy were ushered into his room for a final blessing from their beloved bishop, and "at half past 10 o'clock . . . the soul of a good man had departed to rest."[50] His official death card in Charleston county records attributes his death to "chronic supperrated cystitis," as pronounced by his physician, Dr. J. P. Chazal.[51]

The death of Bishop Lynch was greeted in Charleston with great sorrow, if not shock. His declining health was well known throughout the city. Yet the loss of such a prominent figure who managed to be seen as a friend across all levels of the social order was received as a universal tragedy. News of his passing was announced at the late Masses on Sunday afternoon, and people were seen to be weeping publicly. The *News and Courier* editorialized about the life and accomplishments of this humble Irishman:

> Bishop Lynch was, in many ways, one of the most remarkable men of the day. Breadth of view was one of his marked characteristics. Endowed with a mind highly analytical in its nature, he was, nevertheless, comprehensive and far-reaching in his conception and treatment of every subject. There is oftentimes, in scholars, a profundity that tends to obscurity. The ample stream of Bishop Lynch's knowledge was equally clear and deep. None better than he could illuminate an intricate and complex subject and make it plain and simple, but in popularizing a question he never became shallow or superficial. The ardent flame of his ripe intellect revealed, in its complete truth, what in the shadows of partial knowledge might be felt but was not seen. Those who knew him most intimately failed to find a subject to which he was a stranger. At the Vatican Council in 1869, and at the two Plenary Councils of Baltimore, his erudition was generally recognized. In the natural sciences he was as completely at home as in theology. He was an accomplished classical scholar, and to Greek and Latin, he added a thorough understanding of Sanscrit [*sic*]. When a student at Rome he was selected to deliver before the Pope, the annual collegiate address in Hebrew. French, German, Spanish and Italian he spoke fluently. There were no bounds to his thirst for information. Whatever was of human interest had an unfailing charm for him. It can be truly said that he touched nothing that he did not master. Long before his consecration as Bishop, his papers in the Charleston Catholic Miscellany bore evidence of his research, his skill in dialectics, and his command of "English undefiled." The articles on "the Councils of the Vatican," published in the *Catholic World,* were admitted to be models in manner and in matter, the most learned and vivid description in English of that memorable gathering. Passing to a widely different theme, his essay on the Transit of Venus, a few years ago, caught at once the attention and commanded the admiration of men of science. In his lectures on the Early Discoverers of America he blazed out the path for future students to follow. His lecture on Tunneling the Alps exemplified further the versatility of his intellect. The pamphlet on the Liquefaction of the blood of St. Januarius is a conspicuous example of his perspicuity and closeness of reasoning, as well as of the fairness with which he invariably stated the objections made by those having different opinions from his own. Coming nearer home, we find that, for more than forty years, Bishop Lynch interested himself actively in the construction of the different Artesian wells in the city. His report on the new well, as chairman of the scientific committee appointed by the City Council, was completed and submitted last week.

With the ocean currents, with the law of storms, with physical phenomena of every kind, he had an intimate acquaintance. Of the progress of the Charleston Jetties he was a close observer. Upon the revival of the Isthmian canal project by M. de Lesseps, Bishop Lynch, in his spare moments, undertook to read up the whole subject of Interoceanic canals and railways. At the time of his death he was, also, engaged upon a work intended to demonstrate, in the light of the latest archeological and ethnological discoveries, the absolute agreement of science and the Mosaic revelation. In the pulpit his delivery was, at times, monotonous, but his sermons were logical, heartfelt, rich in illustration and comparison and marked by what has been aptly called "grand simplicity." Nothing, indeed, came amiss to him. Much reading, much writing and much speaking made him full, exact, and ready. His mind absorbed and assimilated the most diverse facts and all that he knew was always at command in the pulpit, in the lecture room, or in casual conversation. Throughout his life no quality was more conspicuous in Bishop Lynch than his exquisite and unfailing charity. Surely he, indeed, loved God with his whole heart and his neighbor as himself. A sprit of kindliness permeated his whole being, and he sought always to extenuate even the faults he could not choose but see. None has heard him speak harshly of a living soul. Pity for the offender went side by side with reprobation for the offence. Another shining quality was his modesty. It was difficult in the extreme to extort from him any mention of his own achievements. How devoted he was, as Priest and Bishop, the people of this city know full well. During the epidemic of 1848, he had charge of one of the hospitals, and himself contracted the fever. To the very last Charleston, in his heart, came next to the Church and his immediate family. In whatever concerned Charleston he took the liveliest interest. Feeble and worn as he was, when the fever made its appearance here in 1871, he came instantly back to Charleston to be at the post of duty in the midst of his people. Well might he be universally respected in South Carolina. Bishop Lynch, we are confident, has not an enemy in the city or the State. Stately in appearance, dignified in manner, unassuming, courteous, self-possessed, learned and pious, Bishop Lynch was honored wherever he went, and was not without honor in his own country. Others will take up the burden which has slipped from his shoulders, and begin where he left off. But none has gone before, or will come hereafter, more loyal to his Church, more loveable in the estimation of all conditions of men, more earnest, more self-sacrificing, and more true than the good Bishop who, has passed away. For him God's truce with worldly cares, the sacred rest of Sunday, is now without end![52]

Preparations for a fitting farewell to this beloved figure had been in the works for days, if not weeks. The daily morning and evening newspapers carried and described the plans in minute details. Arrangements were made to house visiting dignitaries, of whom there would be many from all along the eastern United States. Telegrams were sent out to all prelates in the province. Cardinal McCloskey, a warm and personal friend of Bishop Lynch, was of course invited and expected to attend. National newspapers received wires containing the specifics of Lynch's death and the timing of the ceremonies.[53]

Responses of sadness and regrets came in from afar in large numbers. Bishop Hendriken of Providence, Rhode Island, wrote, "Many men have died eminent, but few as universally loved. The Church will miss him as a great defender and the South as a self-sacrificing patriot and true son."[54] From the vicar general of the Diocese of New York, Monsignor William Quinn, came this message: "Accept my sincere regrets and sorrow. The death of your Bishop and our dear friend is deeply lamented here."[55] In the end the procession and requiem service included two archbishops, six bishops, three vicars general, and dozens of priests taking part in the final tribute to the deceased Charleston bishop.

At the request of dozens of members of the Bar in Charleston, the presiding judge in the Court of Common Pleas suspended business for the entire day of the funeral. The mayor and City Council members of Charleston offered their salute at their meeting the night before the funeral, and many attended the services the next day as honored guests. The local newspaper listed among those present:

> Mayor Courtney, Judge Bryan, Judge Fraser, Hon. Wm. Porcher Miles, George W. Williams, Esq., Hon. N.N. Middleton, Prof. F.H. Holmes, Prof. Bruns, Major E. Willis, Hon. S.Y. Tupper, Geo. E. Seigling, Hon. Patrick Walsh of Augusta, ex-Mayor Cunningham, Postmaster Taft, Dr. J.S. Buist, Chief of Police Rhett, and a number of the leading merchants and members of the bar. The vestrymen of the Catholic congregations of the city occupied seats near the bier, and Mr. Francis Lynch, the brother of the deceased prelate, and other relatives were also seated near the Sanctuary.[56]

Churches of all faiths tolled their bells throughout the day. Many businesses closed their doors during the services. The church was so filled with guests that thousands thronged in the streets outside. The city of Charleston came to a virtual standstill in honor of the Right Reverend Bishop Patrick Neison Lynch. At the conclusion of the Requiem Mass a procession took his remains to their final resting place alongside those of his mentor, Bishop John England, and his immediate predecessor, Bishop Ignatius Reynolds. They were incased in a vault created at the back of the ruins of the Cathedral of St. Finbar, which had been destroyed in the Great Charleston Fire of 1861. The next day the *New York Times* reported,

"Prominent citizens, without distinction of creed, attended the funeral. The city bells tolled all day, and the bell of St. Michaels at intervals. The mourning for the dead prelate is as sincere as it is general."[57]

Just over two weeks later the *News and Courier* published this stark announcement:

> The observance of St. Patrick's Day in Charleston this year, on account of the recent death of Bishop Lynch, will not be marked by the usual public demonstration. The Montgomery Guards, Irish Volunteers and Irish Rifles will meet in full uniform at their respective armories, and without music will march to Hibernian Hall where they will met by members of the St. Patrick's Benevolent Society. The column will then march to the Cathedral Chapel where the usual St. Patrick's Day Mass will be celebrated. There will be no oration.[58]

The Hibernian Society did put on its annual banquet that evening with the noted addition to its normal tributes of a memorial toast to the departed Catholic prelate, "and the memory of the late Bishop Lynch was honored standing and in silence."[59]

During the year between the death of Bishop Lynch and the arrival of the new bishop, Henry P. Northrop, the Diocese of Charleston was administered by Monsignor Daniel J. Quigley. Patrick Lynch's replacement had a tough act to follow, just as Lynch had experienced in filling the shoes of his mentor, John England. In many respects, an objective viewer of history would have to conclude that the man from Clones, Ireland, and Cheraw, South Carolina, more than lived up to the task.

Later Accomplishments and Recognition

Patrick Lynch gained acceptance in the innermost circles of Charleston's intellectual and social elite. This fact was a source of pride for the Irish of South Carolina and Catholics generally—that one of theirs, an immigrant, could rise so high to become a respected leader of the community. And Lynch used his access and influence to help and benefit his people. He never forgot that he was an Irish immigrant. He could speak for his people and for all Catholics. For this, he was loved. His scientific efforts were to cause some resentment on the part of Father John Moore, but Lynch appears generally to have been respected by Catholics and others of the Carolinas.

It is also the case that the members of Charleston's elite tended to reinforce one another's views on Southern identity, states' rights, and defense of Southern institutions, including slavery. After the war their common concerns included resentment of the Reconstruction governments and support for the Redeemers,

Daniel J. Quigley (1829–1889), of Scottish origin, ordained a priest in 1866. He spent much of the Civil War in Europe trying to raise funds for the diocese. He became an important part of Lynch's postwar administration. He served as the administrator of the Diocese of Charleston after Lynch's death until the consecration of Lynch's successor, the Right Reverend Henry P. Northrop, on January 27, 1883. Courtesy of Catholic Diocese of Charleston Archive.

who overthrew Reconstruction and restored white rule. Lynch in large part shared the convictions of his peers.

Lynch was a natural teacher. He was headmaster of Charleston's Catholic boys' academy and the clerical seminary. He was gifted as a popularizer of science and other areas of knowledge, and he did this through public lectures and in articles published in newspapers and magazines. In the 1870s the Charleston City Council elected him a member of the board of trustees of the College of Charleston, where he served on the Museum Committee. What later became the Charleston Museum was housed at the College in those years. In the late 1870s and early 1880s the College was struggling to recover from the war. In Lynch's time on the board a plan was launched to expand the museum in a new building.[60]

After the war especially, he raised money for his ruined diocese through public lectures and magazine articles. He could get as much as $200 for an article. With a doctorate in theology, Lynch sometimes wrote and spoke on theological topics. James Corcoran recruited him to write an article for *American Catholic Quarterly Review* titled "The Divinity of Christ." This drew some praise from reviewers. But Lynch was not considered an original theologian, and he apparently preferred writing on more worldly subjects.[61] He preached countless sermons. These tended to be long, and even his admirers considered that "in the pulpit his delivery was, at times, monotonous."[62]

In the 1850s the dredging of Charleston Harbor began. Father Lynch wrote an article explaining to the public the technology and benefits of the first dredging, with a detailed description of the dredge equipment.[63] After the war, in many cities, Lynch gave a lecture called "America before Columbus," for which he charged admission. In it he laid out various theories about visitors to the Western Hemisphere from overseas before 1492. He promoted the idea that Vikings had made it to Labrador and eastern Canada. Further afield were theories, popular since the 1830s, that America had been discovered and settled by ancient Phoenicians. He himself admitted that this lecture was meant to be entertaining rather than strictly scientific and was given mainly to make money for his diocese.[64]

He wrote pieces for the national magazine the *Catholic World,* which had been founded by Father Isaac Hecker (1819–1888). Hecker was a convert from Protestantism who organized the community of priests called the Paulist Fathers. Their special mission was to make Catholicism appeal to Americans, not to seem something strange and foreign. Lynch was a great friend and supporter of Hecker. In 1874 Lynch wrote an article for the magazine on an important astronomical event called the Transit of Venus. About once a century the planet Venus appears to cross the sun twice, eight years apart. This occurred in 1874 and 1882. Astronomers figured that if they could get precise times for the transits from a lot of different points on the globe at exactly the same instant, they could use parallax formulas to calculate the distance from Earth to Venus, Earth to sun, and Earth to the other planets. Many countries of the world cooperated to enable astronomers to make the observations at the same time. Lynch was fascinated by the event and wrote of its significance. He cautioned that human scientific knowledge can give only an approximation of truth. From the Transit of Venus, he said, humans will "see more clearly than before how the heavens declare the glory of God."[65]

He gave a public lecture in 1873 titled "What to Read & How to Read" to raise money for a New York City charity. In this talk he advised his audience that one should not try to read omnivorously but instead to follow a plan. There were after all encyclopedias—he recommended *Appleton's American Cyclopedia.* Unsurprisingly, he said that "a man should possess a fuller and more accurate knowledge, a more scientific knowledge . . . of the doctrines of our holy Religion and the arguments which prove their truth." One should read about one's own business or profession. More broadly, he recommended history and science, with special emphasis on astronomy and geology. He suggested that readers should be on guard against anti-Christian contradictions in some scientific writing, even as he asserted that the "Catholic fears not Science," while "Protestants do." By taking the words and stories of the Old Testament as absolute truth, not allegorical moral lessons, he meant biblical literal fundamentalism. As to literature, it was important to read the great poets: Homer, Virgil, Dante, Milton, and Shakespeare. When it came to novels Lynch praised those of Sir Walter Scott and James Fenimore Cooper, but he disparaged the cheap popular novels of the day. "Novel reading [is] very like gambling: one must ever be on guard against it."[66]

He gave a lecture he called "Tunneling the Alps," about the Mont Cenis tunnel connecting the railroads of Switzerland and Italy. He had visited and observed the site while it was under construction in 1864. His lecture drew much praise.[67] He was respected for his knowledge of the building of jetties in Charleston Harbor.[68]

He wrote about the emerging deciphering by archaeologists and linguists of the cuneiform writings of ancient Mesopotamia and the early stories that paralleled and, he maintained, confirmed biblical stories such as the Creation, the Garden of Eden, the Fall of Man, and the Flood. That such similar accounts of the ancient events should have been recorded in places as geographically distant as Mesopotamia and Egypt (Moses's place of origin) was, he said, in itself proof of the veracity of the recorded events.[69] Bishop Lynch always wanted to make a real contribution to reconciling the knowledge gained from modern science with the teachings of Christian faith. He published a series of articles on the event, said to occur in Naples, called the liquefaction of the blood of St. Januarius. Januarius (San Gennaro), said to have been bishop of Benevento and to have been martyred at Pozzuoli, near Naples, in the early fourth century, is the principal patron of Naples. A vial of his dried blood is said to liquefy several times a year—an event that takes place in the Neapolitan Cathedral of San Gennaro. During his wartime mission in 1864 Bishop Lynch traveled to Naples and was allowed to stand next to the priests who retrieved the vial from its locked cabinet and to look closely at the event. He then used what he called scientific techniques to study whether there was a natural explanation for the liquefaction. He used tables showing temperature and humidity readings on days when the liquefaction was said to take place. He concluded that there was neither fraud nor natural causes behind the event; therefore, a miracle had taken place. "But if any one . . . will examine it seriously and candidly . . . he will come to the sure inevitable conclusion to which such an examination has heretofore led so many other candid and intelligent inquirers: *Digitus Dei est hic:* The Finger of God is here." Lynch's articles and their subsequent publication in pamphlet form generated a lot of comment.[70]

The bishop took up the case of Galileo. Galileo Galilei (1564–1642) was compelled by the Inquisition in 1633 to declare that he had been wrong to assert that the Earth revolved around the sun and that in fact it was the sun that revolved around the Earth. Lynch wrote to defend the Church against the charge that it was opposed to science, while of course acknowledging that Galileo's understanding of astronomy was correct. Lynch called the affair a great misfortune. He asserted that Galileo had been advised by Cardinal (Saint) Robert Bellarmine, who ran the Holy Office investigation, that the astronomer would not get into trouble if he presented his defense of the Copernican theory only as a theory and did not make any statements about the accuracy of scripture. Galileo had not shown good sense, contributing to the unfortunate event. The whole matter of Galileo and the Copernican system, he observed, might be summed up in the words of an Italian scholar: "At a time when the majority of the theologians firmly believed the system of Copernicus to be contrary to the Holy Scriptures, God did not permit His Church to pronounce a solemn judgment against it."[71]

From the time of his youth Patrick Lynch aimed to reconcile the knowledge revealed by geological science with the teachings of Christian faith. He lectured in Charleston in the 1840s on the "connection of the modern geological discoveries with the scriptural account of the Creation."[72] He returned to the topic in lectures through the years. One of his aims was to publish a definitive statement on the subject. Monsignor Corcoran had asked him to prepare an article on the subject for the *American Catholic Quarterly Review.* However, he was working on such a piece for the *Catholic World* in the last days of his life.[73] This was not completed and was never published. The Lynch Papers in the Charleston Diocesan Archives contain a draft in Lynch's hand for a work on the question, titled "On an Objection against the Truth of the Scripture and Its Divine Inspiration, Based on the Discoveries of Geology."[74] It is uncertain when this manuscript was written, but it does express his ideas in maturity and gives insight into his thought on the religious implications of geological research. Here Lynch provided an exposition of the development of the wonderful learning he believed had come from modern geology. He described the layers of rock and sediment deposited in past periods over what he termed "myriads" of years and described the way past ages were characterized by different species of plants and animals. In the rocks, he asserted, was the natural history of the planet.

"Coal," said Lynch, "is evidently a vegetable product, and the immense quantity of coal that has already been discovered in various portions of the globe calls for a most abundant vegetation." He noted the more than three hundred specimens of plants, of which two hundred are ferns, that have been fossilized as coal. He spoke of the "shell fish" abounding in the Cambrian and Silurian strata,

Photograph of Patrick N. Lynch. Courtesy of Library of Congress.

especially ammonites and trilobites. He explained the Mosaic story of the Creation in six days as a literary way of expressing the truth that God created all things. The days told in Genesis did not mean periods of twenty-four hours. Lynch accepted the discoveries of modern geologists that the Earth was formed over many time periods, each of immense duration. He suggested that the different species represented in the fossil record might be seen as corresponding to the successive Mosaic days of the Creation.

Lynch described the dominant animals whose fossils were found in different layers of rock. In the Cretaceous and earlier layers were the great reptiles or dinosaurs—he called them "saurians"—which he found fascinating. The ichthyosaurus he called a "fish-lizard reaching thirty feet in length. His head was that of a crocodile. His long jaws were garnished with 150 to 180 teeth. His eyes were more than a foot in diameter. A long broad tail served as a propeller and its power was aided by four paddles." The plesiosaurus was a reptile with a small head and a long neck. "He floated on the water but might also crawl on land." "Overhead flew the Pterodactyl, the greatest wonder of this age. It had the head of a crocodile, the long neck of a bird, and the wings of a bat."

The bishop recognized that the fossils of simpler animals were found in the deeper layers of rock, those of more complex ones above. The nearer the surface, the closer the animals were to those of the present day. Humans came to the scene very late, and this he thought fitted well with the story in Genesis. For all this, the bishop did not speak of metamorphoses or evolution of later from earlier species. And he railed against those who, in the name of science, would deny the truth of religion. He declared: "Nothing that the Geologist can bring to light can in any way be urged against the truth of revelation." No reference to Charles Darwin has been found in any of Lynch's papers or publications. Darwin published *The Origin of Species* in 1859 and *The Descent of Man* in 1871. Given his interest in geology, it is inconceivable that Lynch had not read Darwin or at least read what others were writing about him. Lynch clearly subscribed to a form of intelligent—or rather divine—design. But he was part of a movement away from biblical literal fundamentalism.

Michael Tuomey, a geologist whom Lynch admired, asserted that the fossil record gave no evidence of a "series of metamorphoses" from earlier, simpler organisms to later, more complex ones.[75] In the United States, controversy over Darwin was retarded somewhat by the Civil War, but some leading Catholic thinkers such as Orestes Brownson condemned the idea of evolution as "repugnant to the whole of Christian doctrine and order of thought."[76] Although the Holy See did not issue any formal condemnation of Darwin's theory, the Office of the Index of Forbidden Books worked quietly in Lynch's last years to encourage retractions by priests who had written in favor of Darwin. Whether Lynch was aware of these actions is not known, although he was often well informed of currents of opinion within the Vatican.[77]

Patrick Lynch earned great respect for his learning and his gifts as an educator. He was in his time one of the most admired men of learning in South Carolina and in the American Church. Thus, his passing was not merely an event in the theological world, the ecclesiastical world, the political world, or the world of the Roman Catholic hierarchy. His passing was a sad and significant event in the cultural, intellectual, and scientific world of his city and his nation. He was a man of accomplishment. He was not a man without flaws. He was a very religious and pious man. He was well aware of his failings and shortcomings. He and his society suffered tragic disasters attempting to meet the sins of his time. Each time, he strove to confront defeat with commitment and hard work. For this he was admired even by naysayers amid the deserved criticism. In the end Lynch was a man of his times, with all the flaws and accomplishments of his era.

Epilogue

Lynch's station in the annals of the American Catholic Church is complicated and perhaps too controversial to make him famous. Even in the chronicles of South Carolina Catholicism, Bishop John England cast a shadow over his successors—and this is just, in all likelihood. Yet the distinguished character and achievements of the third bishop of the Diocese of Charleston deserve recognition. He took the leadership of an ecclesiastical jurisdiction that lacked geographical definition. England founded the see, and Reynolds built upon those foundations. When Lynch took controls, the Church and the state of South Carolina were poised on the edge of an historical abyss. A conflagration in Charleston destroyed much of the physical presence of the diocese. The Civil War and social revolution laid waste to the state and region he loved. The end of African American slavery, an institution to which he lent his support, left Lynch and his diocese in economic and social chaos. In spite of legitimate questions about his loyalty at the end of the war, when he was allowed to return home, he immediately began to rehabilitate the churches and to assimilate the liberated former slaves into a revived, transformed diocese. By modern standards many of his values and acts must be called into question. Nevertheless, he sought to do good within the fractured milieu of nineteenth-century Charleston and the South. His contributions to the Church he loved and the city he cherished cannot be challenged. His loyalty to the Union, his support of secession and his devotion to the Southern Confederacy, and, finally, his efforts to reconcile the reconstituted United States of American reveal his characteristic determination to make the best of circumstances that confronted him. A biographer has noted: "So magnificently did Bishop Lynch comport himself that when he returned from the courts of Europe where he worked in the interest of the Confederacy he could not only immediately address the Catholics of the great Cathedral of New York, but also solicit help for his ruined diocese. And while for a moment there was a press flare-up, it was quickly extinguished as soon as his calm and charitable reply caught the eye of the public. Whatever may be said of Bishop Lynch, he was always a man of the highest and noblest sense that word connotes. Patriotism, devotion to public service, and a high type of personal and official qualities were the endowments of Bishop Lynch. He was the Archbishop Hughes of the Southland."[1]

Despite his intellect and erudition, Lynch's greatest virtue was his "all-embracing charity and kindness." He reportedly never said or allowed to be said in his presence an unkind word about another person. When confronted with such behavior he demonstrated feelings of genuine pain. His standard response when someone spoke ill of a priest was, "But he is God's anointed." He was pious and reverent to all whom he met. Generous to a fault, he promised and delivered full financial restitution to all who had lost money from their investments in the diocese shattered by war.[2]

Lynch's education and judgment made him a compelling leader of the American Catholic Church. At war's end he took a prominent role in the Second Plenary Council in Baltimore, which restored Church unity more effectively than was the case for any other Christian denomination that had been sundered by slavery and secession. He demonstrated to his ecclesiastical colleagues his abilities in the First Vatican Ecumenical Council in Rome. Upon the death of his friend Pope Pius IX he gave voice to the Church's loss in solemn services in New York, Boston, Philadelphia, Richmond, and at home in Charleston. His name appeared on several short lists for appointment to the highest positions within the American Catholic hierarchy. But, his humility and commitment to the restoration of his diocese moved him to reject advancement.

After the Civil War Lynch dedicated his life to rebuilding the cathedral and the diocesan infrastructure. To that end he availed himself of every opportunity to promote his cause throughout the eastern United States. He traveled for seventeen years, giving academic lectures and parochial sermons to solicit funds needed to rebuild his diocese. His eloquence allowed him to serve his fellow bishops by delivering sermons at ecclesiastical services from Boston to Savannah and from Baltimore to Chicago. He consecrated bishops, dedicated cathedrals, delivered scientific discourses, and lectured with authority on history and the arts. One biographer wrote, "as an eloquent public orator, a learned lecturer, a profound scientist, a cogent dogmatic controversialist, an exhaustive reviewer and essayist, Bishop Lynch had few equals."[3]

Lynch faced criticism, particularly by diocesan clergy, for his frequent absences from his city and state. Yet, had he neglected to travel extensively throughout the United States and Europe, resources for his parishes and priests would have been scarce. Travels brought him acclaim, but he refused ecclesiastical promotions that would have taken him from his diocesan commitments.

Lynch's sense of secular public service was commensurate with his church dedication. He belonged to numerous social, cultural, and academic associations. He gave public lectures on a wide variety of subjects. He applied his geological knowledge to searching out artesian water for the City of Charleston. He even took time from his activities at the First Vatican Council to consult with the officials of the town of Cisterna in west-central Italy, famed for its deep flowing waters. Everywhere he went, Lynch showed his generosity and established good will for his diocese, enabling him to ask for assistance to rebuild his broken homeland.

Lynch restored the diocese to a degree of soundness not seen since the destructive fire of 1861 and the four years of devastation of the Civil War. When he assumed the bishopric, in 1858, South and North Carolina possessed nineteen churches, forty mission stations, fifteen clergy, one college, two academies for girls, and one orphan asylum. At the time of his death, the Diocese of Charleston had been reduced in geographical range to just the state of South Carolina but had actually grown in population and resources despite war and massive casualties. There were eighteen churches, six chapels, twenty clergy, three academies, two asylums, and four parochial schools.[4] Property had been acquired and funds raised for the construction of three additional churches, as well. Lynch had taken steps to incorporate the increasing numbers of African American Catholics with the building of two black Catholic churches in Charleston. To have accomplished this degree of recovery in the face of a financial debt approaching $400,000 was a remarkable achievement. When Lynch died, in 1882, he had reduced that debt to about $10,000. These extraordinary feats should cause those who assailed his absences to consider a new perspective.

The one-year-old boy who was taken from his native Ireland in 1819 became a distinguished bishop and citizen dedicated to contributing to his city, state, and nation and, indeed, to his beloved Catholic world. His parents' dreams as they fled their homeland were fulfilled in succeeding generations by their own work and the labors of their illustrious offspring. His life is part of the broader Irish contribution to the making of America.

ABBREVIATIONS

(AAAS)	American Association for the Advancement of Science Proceedings
(AAB)	Archives of the Archdiocese of Baltimore
(AAM)	Archives of the Archdiocese of Mobile
(AANY)	Archives of the Archdiocese of New York
(ACHSPR)	American Catholic Historical Society of Philadelphia Records
(ADJ)	Archives of the Diocese of Jackson
(ADStA)	Archives of the Diocese of St. Augustine
(AESC)	Archives of Edgefield, S.C.
(AICR)	Archives of the Irish College, Rome, Letters of Tobias Kirby
(AJA)	Archives of the Josephite Fathers
(APF)	Archives of the Propaganda Fide
(AUND)	Archives of the University of Notre Dame
(AUS)	Archives of the Ursuline Sisters, Louisville, Ky.
(CCDR)	Charleston County Death Rolls
(CDA Cathedral Vestry)	Records of Vestry, St. Finbar's Cathedral, 1855–1891
(CDA)	Charleston Diocesan Archives
(CHS)	Clogher Historical Society
(CLS)	Charleston Library Society
(CofCSC)	College of Charleston Library, Special Collections Department
(CUA)	Collegio Urbano, Archivio
(HC)	Historic Cheraw. Catherine Richardson.
(LC)	Library of Congress
(LC)	Pickett Papers in Confederate States of America Papers in Library of Congress
(NARA)	National Archives and Records Administration
(NCC)	Collection of Nancy L. Crockett, Lancaster, S.C.
(NFA)	Northrop Family Archives
(PFA)	Paulist Fathers Archives. Hecker Papers
(PRF)	Congregation de Propaganda Fide Records
(PUC)	Pontifical Urban College, Registro
(PUU)	Pontifical Urban University, Rome
(RCRD)	Richland County, S.C., Register of Deeds

(SCDAH)	South Carolina Department of Archives and History
(SCL-USC)	South Caroliniana Library, University of South Carolina
(SMPE)	St. Mary's Parish Edgefield, S.C.
(US CENSUS)	Slave Schedules, 1850, 1860
(USDS)	U.S. Dept. of State, Dispatches from United Sates Ministers to France, 1789–1906
(USWDCR)	United States War Department, Confederate Records
(VM)	Valentine Museum Richmond

NOTES

PROLOGUE

1. Washington Light Infantry Scrapbook, 1807–1873, Charleston Library Society, 166.

CHAPTER 1: BEGINNINGS

1. Wolfe, "Patrick Neison Lynch," 165. This was Monsignor Wolfe's M.A. thesis at Mount St. Mary's Seminary, Emmitsburg, Maryland.
2. Copeland, comp., "Lynch Family,"1.
3. The parish of Clones historically straddled the border between counties Monaghan and Fermanagh with about equal portions on either side. The parish churches in Clones were at Clones and Clontask in the Monaghan end and at Drumsword in Fermanagh. In the parish of Roslea (all in Fermanagh there are churches at Roslea and Templetate. Some sources state that Conlaw Peter Lynch was born in Magheraveely(?) (Magheraveely is not an actual townland but more of an area that straddles the border between Clones and Newtonbutler). Correspondence from Padrig Clerkin, Monaghan County Museum.
4. James Hardiman, *History of the Town and County of Galway* (Galway, Ireland, 1820), ch. 1, cited in Wolfe, "Patrick Neison Lynch," 3.
5. Wolfe, "Patrick Neison Lynch," 4–5; "The family coat of arms is an azure shield with silver chevrons (crosses), the trefoil (clover) gold, the lynx representing vigilance.—the trefoil or clover which they were forced to eat, and 'simper fidelis' (faithful to the end)."
6. Robert A. Lynch, "A History of the Lynch Family," unpublished notes, Waltham, Mass., 1891.
7. Copeland, "Lynch Family," 2.
8. Mrs. James M. Googe Jr., "Lynch Family Genealogy," 2. Nina Googe was a descendant of Dr. John Lynch, the brother of Patrick Neison Lynch
9. Francis to Patrick Neison Lynch (hereafter PNL), Charleston Diocesan Archives (hereafter CDA) 15P6. In this letter, dated 1 April 1866, he referred to their parents' upcoming fiftieth wedding anniversary.
10. Copeland, "Lynch Family," 3.
11. Hugh P. McElrone, "Bishop Lynch," *Catholic World* 35 (1882): 160.
12. Ibid., 160–61; O'Connell, *Catholicity*, 128; Wolfe, "Patrick Neison Lynch," 10.
13. Livingstone, *Monaghan Story*, 177.
14. Wolfe, "Patrick Neison Lynch," 5–6.
15. "John Lyde Wilson," BDSC Senate, 1757–59.
16. Gregg, *History of the Old Cheraws*, 464.

17. Ibid., 464.
18. Spruill, "Cheraw," 60–161.
19. Taylor, *South Carolina Naturalists,* 3.
20. Ibid., 464.
21. Catherine Richardson, "*Historic Cheraw.*"
22. Ibid., 282.
23. O'Connell, *Catholicity,* 128–29; James Alexander Thomas, *History of Marlboro County,* 60–61.
24. O'Connell, *Catholicity,* 129; McElrone, "Bishop Lynch," 161. Henry Copeland says that Conlaw was "a builder by trade": Copeland, "Lynch Family," 1; *Historic and Architectural Inventory, Cheraw Historical District* (Catawba, S.C.), 11.
25. Census, 1850, Chesterfield District, S.C.; Sarah Cain Spruill, "Bank Follows Trade," *Cheraw Chronicle,* bicentennial edition, July 1, 1972, 10B; communications from Sarah Cain Spruill, February 18 and March 1, 2004.
26. Wolfe, "Patrick Neison Lynch," 11.
27. Robert A. Lynch compiled from notes at Malden, Mass., June 18, 1891; in unpublished family history written by Mrs. James M. Googe Jr., a descendant of Robert, Amelia Island, Fla., 2004–2005.
28. Wolfe, "Patrick Neison Lynch," 10–15.
29. Copeland, "Lynch Family," 1–2.
30. Gregg, *History of the Old Cheraws.*
31. Wolfe, "Patrick Neison Lynch," 19–20.
32. *Miscellany,* June 26, 1822, CDA box 724, item 19.
33. O'Brien, *John England,* 28.
34. Rogers, *Charleston in the Age of the Pinckneys,* 150.
35. See Guilday, *Life and Times of John England;* see O'Brien, *John England.* See also records of the Catholic Diocese of Charleston.
36. Various city directories of Charleston, S.C.
37. Fraser, *Charleston! Charleston!,* 206.
38. Freehling, *Prelude to Civil War.*
39. Lowman, "James Andrew Corcoran," 1–30.
40. Ibid., p. 1, 83; England to Paul Cullen, December 16, 1833, "Papers Relating to the Church in America," 468.
41. McSuidhne, *Paul Cullen,* 1:8.
42. England to Cullen, December 17, 1833, 472; England to Cullen, January 3, 1834, 474; both in "Papers Relating to the Church in America," 472.
43. Guilday, *Life and Times of John England,* 293–95.
44. Kowalsky, *Pontificio Collegio Urbano,* 7–8, 12–13; Hoffman, "Propagation of the Faith," 840-41.
45. Spalding, *Spalding,* 11; Hoffman, "Propagation of the Faith," 840 41.
46. Heuser, "Monsignor Corcoran," 323; *Catalogus Alumnorum Collegii Urbani qui ab anno MDCCCXIX ad MDCCCXXXVIII ad Fidem Propagandam veljam Pridierunt vel adhuc instiuntur,* fol. 173 verso.
47. Handwritten signed oath, Pontificio Collegio Urbano de Propaganda Fide, Archivio, vol. 8, no. 3, 145–46; Pontificio Collegio de Propaganda Fide, *Registro,* 1834, s.v. "Lynch, Neison) Patritius."

48. Kowalsky, *Pontificio Collegio Urbano*, 7–8, 12–13. On winter conditions see John Henry Newman to David Lewis, November 15, 1846, in Dessain et al., eds., *Letters of John Henry Newman*, 11:276 (hereafter Newman, *Letters*); Newman to F. S. Bowles, November 26, 1846, in ibid., 11:285; Newman to Mrs. John Mozley, January 26, 1847, in ibid., 12:23; Spalding, *Spalding*, 12.
49. Spalding, *Spalding*, 18; "La Congrégation de la Propagande," 124–26.
50. PNL to Gregory Duggan, June 1834, CDA, 3M7. The letter was addressed to "My dear Duggan." Duggan was ordained for the Diocese of Charleston in 1837. He later served in the Diocese of Savannah and was pastor in Augusta, Ga., from the 1830s to the 1860s. He died in 1870.
51. Spalding, *Spalding*, 12–13; *Regole*, 7–8.
52. Spalding, *Spalding*, 17–18; Kowalski, *Pontificio Collegio Urbano*, 28–29.
53. Lynch, "Dissertatione philosophica ex physica mathematica &c &c," ms. in Lynch's hand, CDA, Patrick N. Lynch Transfer File, folder IL4.
54. Jezernik, "Il Pontificio Collegio Urbano de Propaganda Fide," in *Sacrae Congregationis de Propaganda Fide, Memoria Rerum: 350 anni a servizio delle missioni . . . 1622–1972*, vol. 3, pt. 1, 100–01; Garhammer, *Seminaridee und Klerusbildung bei Karl August Graf von Reisach*, 59–63.
55. John Joseph Weidenfeller to PNL, October 11, 1881, CDA, 73S4.
56. Weidenfeller to PNL, November 15, 1879, CDA, 69H5.
57. "Diary of Bishop Lynch's Vacation at Tusculum While he was a Student in Rome, September and October 1837," manuscript and typescript copy, CDA, Lynch Transfer File, folder L8; Jezernik, "Pontifio Collegio Urbano," 161.
58. Newman to Mrs. J. W. Bowden, November 15, 1846, in Newman, *Letters*, 11:272–73; *Regole*, no. 25, 12.
59. Lynch, "Rules and Regulations for Acquiring a Correct & Elegant English Style, February 11, 1837 [with later additions]," manuscript, CDA, Patrick N. Lynch Transfer File, folder IL7.
60. Collegio Urbano de Propaganda Fide, *Registro*, May 8, 1840. Sincere thanks for obtaining a copy of the list of professors are expressed to Father Willi Henkel, Librarian Emeritus, Pontifical Urban University, Rome.
61. McSuidhne, *Paul Cullen*, 10.
62. See for example, Palma, *Praelectiones historiae ecclesiasticae quas in Collegio Urbano Sacrae Congregationis de Propaganda Fide et in Pontificio Seminario Romano habuit Joannes Palma*, vol. I, pt. 1, iv–vi; vol. 4, pt. 2, 7 ff.
63. Piccolanti, "Graziosi (Giuseppe Maria)," 1331–32; Sorti, "Datary, Apostolic," *New Catholic Encyclopedia*, 4:651–52.
64. Cossa, *Necrologia di Filippo Cossa*, 6–7.
65. Caraman, *University of the Nations*, 87–88; Hocédez, *Histoire de la théologie au XIXe siècle*, 2:353–55; Perrone, *Praelectiones theologicae quas in Collegio Romano S.J. habebat Joannes Perrone . . . , passim;* Spalding, *Spalding*, 25.
66. Newman to John D. Dalgairn, December 22, 1846, in Newman, *Letters*, 11:279; McNally, "Corcoran," 52. The superbly educated Newman tended to fall asleep during lectures.
67. Gervasoni, *Angelo Mai*, 31–43; Lowman, "James Andrew Corcoran," 185; McNally, "Corcoran," 52.

68. Russell, *Life of Cardinal Mezzofanti,* 321–25; de Camillis, *Il Cardinale G. Mezzofanti,* 6–9; Gasnault, "La Réglementation des universités pontificales au XIXe siècle," 1107–9.
69. Frank, *Vincenzo Pallotti,* 368–71; Weber, *Vincent Pallotti,* 144–46; Amoroso, *San Vincenzo Pallotti,* 57–60.
70. Lynch, "Notes on Eight Days Retreat in the Urban College of Propaganda Fide under Father Massa, S.J.," handwritten ms., CDA, Patrick N. Lynch Transfer File, folder IL9.
71. *Regole,* no. 19, 10–11; Lowman, "James Andrew Corcoran," 86; Heuser, "Monsignor Corcoran," 324–25; England to Cullen, January 3, 1834, in "Papers Relating to the Church in America," 474. On the condition of Roman streets see Newman to F. S. Bowles, November 26, 1846, and Newman to J. Walker, December 18, 1846, in Newman, *Letters,* 11:285, 301.
72. Newman to Antonio Bressciani, June 1847, in Newman, *Letters,* 12:88–90.
73. *Solemnis praemium distributio apud Collegium Urbanum de Propaganda Fide pridei kal. D.C. A. A. P. V. MDCCCXXXVII,* 406; *Solemnis praeemiorum distributio apud Collegium Urbanum de Propaganda Fide VII. Idus Sept. An. A. P. V. MDCCCXXXIX,* 3–6; Lowman, "James Andrew Corcoran," 32; Wolfe, "Patrick Neison Lynch," 22.
74. Lynch's diploma was preserved by his family in Columbia, S.C., where it was seen by Father Wilfrid Foley in 1929 or 1930: Foley, "Patrick N. Lynch," 5. The author does not know the current whereabouts of the diploma. Lynch received the S.T.D. (*sacrae theologiae doctor*) degree, but he always used D.D. (doctor of divinity) after his name, since this was the customary American doctoral degree in theology.
75. Pontifical Urban College, *Registro,* 1834, s.v. Lynch (Nisen) [*sic*] Patritius (author's translation).
76. Propaganda Fide to England, June 5, 1840, APF, Lettere, vol. 332, fol. 516 rv, AUND, MPRF, Reel 116, IV, 490; note by Giovanni Battista Palma, June 6, 1840, APF, Udienze di N.S. 1840. P. I., vol. 92, fol. 515r, AUND, MPRF, Reel 97, VII, 456.
77. Solemnis Praemorum distributo apud Collegium Urbanum De Propaganda Fide, Pridie Kal Dec. An. MDCCXXXVII.
78. ACH SPR cited in Lowman, "James Andrew Corcoran," 1–30.
79. CDA, March 31, 1938 4W6.
80. Kenrick, *Diary and Visitation Record,* 193.
81. Clarke, *Lives of Deceased Bishops,* 3:70; Wolfe, "Patrick Neison Lynch," 25.
82. Conlaw Peter Lynch to PNL, September 2, 1840, CDA, Patrick N. Lynch Correspondence.

Chapter 2: Priest in Charleston

1. "Diocese of Charleston: Address," *Miscellany,* November 14, 1840, 145. In the November 21, 1840, *Miscellany* (vol. 20, 158) there is a notice from Propaganda Fide that PNL had received his DD on September 4, 1840. It did confirm that PNL was at the Second Annual Diocesan Convention on November 8, 1840, as per published minutes. So we can report that PNL returned to Charleston sometime between the two dates (September 4–November 8). It is probable that he

arrived closer to November 8. He likely provided the Propaganda Fide notice to the *Miscellany,* and it's fair to assume that if the publication had gotten it sooner (that is, if PNL had arrived sooner), it would have been printed sooner than November 21. The safe bet is that PNL was a last-minute arrival at the conference.

2. *Miscellany,* November 21, 1840.
3. Foley, "Patrick N. Lynch," 5. As of 1930 England's letter of appointment was preserved by Lynch's family in Columbia; present whereabouts unknown.
4. Letter from John England to Paul Cardinal Cullen, February 23, 1836, cited in Guilday, *Life and Times of John England,* 151–52 ff.
5. Guilday, *Life and Times of John England,* 270 ff.
6. A good statement of England's arguments is found in John England to John Forsyth, September 28, 1840, in England, *The Works of the Right Rev. John England, First Bishop of Charleston,* 3:114–16; also in John England, *Letters of the Late Bishop England to the Hon. John Forsyth, on the Subject of Domestic Slavery . . . .,* ix–xi.
7. Madden, "Catholics of South Carolina" (unpublished), ms. #1, 68.
8. England to Whitfield, March 25, 1842, quoted in Guilday, *Life and Times of John England,* 2:537.
9. Madden, "Catholics of South Carolina" (unpublished), ms. #1, 3, 114; *Miscellany,* February 11, March 11, and 18, April 9, May 27, 1843.
10. "Provincial Councils of Baltimore," in Herbermann, ed., *Catholic Encyclopedia.* This article incorporates text from a publication now in the public domain.
11. Francis Patrick Kenrick to Peter Richard Kenrick, July 20, 1842, in F. E. Toursher, ed., *The Kenrick-Frenaye Correspondence,* 149. A terna is a list of three candidates that seem most appropriate for consideration for the office of bishop. It is used in the episcopal selection process of the Roman Catholic Church. The terna is sent to the Holy See, together with all the information that has been gathered on them and accompanying the information with the conclusions that he himself draws from the evidence.
12. Wolfe, "Patrick Neison Lynch,"19–20; Palmer, *Life and Letters,* 41–45. On the Cheraw Academy see Laney, "Matheson Library," February 27, 1985, 1–2. Another academy pupil was Alexander Gregg (1819–1893), later the first Episcopal bishop of Texas and author of a history of the early Cheraw area.
13. Wolfe, "Patrick Neison Lynch,"19–20; Palmer, *Life and Letters,* 43–44.
14. Farmer, *Metaphysical Confederacy,* 65–66, 189. On Thornwell see also Kelly, *Preachers with Power,* 61–83.
15. Catholics considered many writings to be apocryphal but recognized as part of the canon several works that had been included in the Septuagint Bible used by Jews centered in Alexandria. These they termed Deuterocanonical, or books of the second canon. The English translators of the King James Bible had translated these but put them in a separate volume.
16. James Henley Thornwell, "The Apocryphal Books," *Miscellany,* March 18, 1843, 290 ff.; Palmer, *Life and Letters,* 226–27.
17. Thornwell, "Letter I," in Thornwell, *The Collected Writings of James Henley Thornwell,* 419–20.

18. Ibid.
19. Thornwell, "Letter VII," in ibid., 518, 522.
20. PNL, "Letter I," *Miscellany,* March 18, 1843, 292–95. See also PNL, "Letter II," *Miscellany,* March 25, 1843, 299–300; PNL, "Letter III," *Miscellany,* April 1, 1843, 308–10; PNL, "Letter IV," *Miscellany,* April 8, 1843, 316–18.
21. Thornwell to R. J. Breckenridge, March 28, 1843, in Palmer, *Life and Letters,* 245.
22. Farmer, *Metaphysical Confederacy,* 190.
23. Ibid.
24. Thornwell to Nancy Witherspoon Thornwell, May 19, 1845, in Palmer, *Life and Letters,* 286.
25. Farmer, *Metaphysical Confederacy,* 190.
26. Thornwell to R. J. Breckenridge, February 17, 1846, in ibid., 289.
27. Thornwell, *Sacramental Sorcery,* esp. 27, 37 ff., 45.
28. PNL, "The Chagrin of Catholics at the Late Presbyterian Decision Regarding Baptism," *Miscellany,* July 19, 1845, 11.
29. Farmer, *Metaphysical Confederacy,* 192.
30. See for example John Lynch to PNL, January 23, 1854, CDA, 8A4; John Lynch to PNL, January 31, 1854, CDA, 8A5.
31. See for example "Knight's Problem in Chess" and "Problem to Find the length of the circumference of a given circle on a strai[gh]t line or the Quadration of a circle," in CDA, Patrick Lynch Transfer File, folder JJ; Francis G. Cart to PNL, July 3, 1876, CDA, 60N7; Cart to PNL, July 18, 1876, CDA, 60R3; Cart to PNL, August 4, 1876, CDA, 60T6; PNL to Francis G. Cart, August 7, 1876, CDA, 60T7; PNL to Francis G. Cart, August 17, 1876, CDA, 60W3.
32. Gannon, *Rebel Bishop,* 7–10.
33. Holifield, *Gentlemen Theologians,* 80–85.
34. Pease and Pease, "Intellectual Life in the1830s," 237.
35. Moltke-Hansen, "The Expansion of Intellectual Life," 21.
36. England, *Oration,* 36.
37. Ibid., 44–45.
38. Sanders and Anderson, *Natural History Investigations,* 19, 27; Mazÿck, "The Charleston Museum," p. 15-16.
39. Shecut, *Medical and Philosophical Essays,* 41, 49; Sanders and Anderson, *Natural History Investigations,* 27–38; Charleston Library Society, Minute Book, 1815–1841, June 21, 1815; various dates 1815–1829 and 1842–1867; Charleston Library Society, Membership Records; "The Museum of South-Carolina," *Charleston Courier,* November 27, 1827, 2.
40. PNL to Robert Seton, August 13, 1879, AUND, CSET, II-1-a; Benoit, "Diary of a Trip to America, 140.
41. *Proceedings of the Elliott Society of Natural History of Charleston, South Carolina,* meeting of January 18, 1854; Stephens, "Scientific Societies in the Old South," 58 ff.; Sanders and Anderson, *Natural History Investigations,* 69–70; Hughes, "The Elliott Society," 25–31.
42. PNL, "Rules for the Government of the Museum," CDA, Bishop Patrick N. Lynch Papers, misc. mss., "Elliott Society."

43. Stoney, ed., "Memoirs of Frederick Adolphus Porcher," 214–27; Edgar, "South Carolina Historical Society Sesquicentennial Address," 103–4, 110.
44. Mimis, "Paul Hamilton Hayne," 2278–83; Stern, "John Russell: 'Lord John' of Charleston," 285–99.
45. Oscar M. Lieber to Francis Lieber, March 17, 1859, Francis Lieber Papers, SCL, USC; Loftis, "A Study of *Russell's Magazine*," 451–53; Cohen, "Three Notable Ante-bellum Magazines," 38.
46. Ryan, "The Opinions of Editor William Gilmore Simms," 25.
47. Ryan, "The Southern Quarterly Review," 8–10.
48. William Gilmore Simms to PNL, June 1, 1849, CDA, 6K6; Simms to Nathaniel Beverley Tucker, July 14, 1849, in William Gilmore Simms, *The Letters of William Gilmore Simms*, 2:539. PNL, "Review of Austen Henry Layard, *Nineveh and Its Remains*," 1–3.
49. Simms to Tucker, July 27, 1849, in Simms, *Letters*, 2:542.
50. Simms to Marius Claudius Marcellus Hammond, October 11, 1851, in ibid., 3:143.
51. Simms to William John Grayson, ca. November 20, 1852, in ibid., 3:209.
52. American Association for the Advancement of Science, *Proceedings* (*AAAS* 1849), xiv; Kohlstedt, *The Formation of the American Scientific Community*, 100–04. Lynch was the second Catholic bishop to be a member. Bishop John Baptist Purcell of Cincinnati was elected to membership in 1851: *AAAS Proceedings*, Fifth Meeting, Cincinnati, Ohio, 1851, iii, xvii.
53. PNL to American Association for the Advancement of Science, July 31, 1868, CDA, 44N5; *AAAS Proceedings*, Eleventh Meeting, Montreal, 1857, viii; ibid., Twelfth Meeting, Baltimore, 1858, xi; *Miscellany*, August 22, 1857, 47.
54. Swallow, "Grape Culture in Missouri," *AAAS Proceedings*, 268–82; "American Association," *Charleston Courier*, May 3, 1858, 2. Lynch was acquainted with the Catholic Santo Domingo French family of De Caradeuc. These people worked vineyards near Aiken, S.C., which produced wine commercially. Notably they provided sacramental wine for the Catholic Church during the Civil War: bills for altar wine for Cathedral of St. John and St. Finbar, July 31, 1863, CDA, 29H5; March 2, 1864, CDA, 30H7; March 16, 1864, CDA, 30K6; James Achille de Caradeuc to PNL, January 18, 1869, CDA, 45Y7; Moore, "From Vine to Keg," 52–53. James Achille de Caradeuc (1816–1895) was buried in Charleston's St. Lawrence Cemetery in 1895.
55. This account of Charleston's wells is based in large part on Lynch, Shepard, and Geddings, "Artesian Wells, 1823–1879," 257–315.
56. See for example "Artesian Wells," *The Penny Magazine*, 131–32; "Artesien [*sic*] Wells," *American Quarterly Review*, 336–49; "Professor Buckland on Artesian Wells," *Littall's Living Age*, 68–72.
57. PNL et al., "Artesian Wells," 259–65.
58. "The Lecture This Evening," *Charleston Mercury*, March 3, 1848, 2; "Dr. Lynch's Lecture Before the Lyceum," *Charleston Mercury*, March 6, 1848, 2.
59. Tuomey, *Report on Artesian Wells*, 5 and *passim*. On Tuomey see Michael Tuomey, *The Papers of Michael Tuomey*, xvii–xxviii.

60. Tuomey to Franklin H. Elmore, April 12, 1848, in Tuomey, *Papers of Michael Tuomey*, 169–71.
61. For brief descriptions of artesian wells see Freeze and Cherry, *Groundwater*, 47–49; Schwalbaum, *Understanding Groundwater*, 19–24. The stratigraphy below Charleston is diagrammed in *Surface and Subsurface Stratigraphy, Structure, and Aquifers of the South Carolina Coastal Plain* (Columbia: University of South Carolina, Department of Geology, 1983). The author is greatly indebted to Dr. Francis H. Chapelle, a hydrologist at the U.S. Geological Survey, for guidance and generous assistance with this topic.
62. PNL, Synopsis of strata, CDA, 6M5.
63. Patrick N. Lynch, "The Artesian Well. No. I," *Charleston Evening News*, February 20, 1849, 2.
64. PNL, "The Artesian Well. No. II," *Charleston Evening News*, February 22, 1849, 2; "Artesian Wells. No. III," *Charleston Evening News*, February 24, 1849, 3; "Artesian Wells. No. IV," *Charleston Evening News*, February 28, 1849, 4; "Artesian Wells. No. V," *Charleston Evening News*, March 2, 1849, 2; Benoit Diary, CB6–135, 141–42.
65. "Public Improvements of Charleston—Part 2," *DeBow's Review*, 340–45.
66. Lynch et al., "Artesian Wells," 258, 270, 283–84. PNL, "Artesian Well Calculations, January 15, 1878," CDA, Patrick N. Lynch Papers, Transfer File, folder I. Lynch's calculations of water flow through different pipe diameters were skillful and accurate. The author is indebted to Dr. Francis H. Chapelle for reviewing the calculations. In 2009 only one of the wells was still flowing at the surface. The amount of water pumped from the aquifer for local needs reduced the pressure, and the other wells stopped flowing in the late 1980s: Jones, "Drilling Might Help Replenish Water Supply," *Post and Courier*, January 26, 1995, 1; Robert Behre, "Fountain Plans Are Bubbling Up," *Post and Courier*, April 30, 1997, 1.
67. Raymond Thomassy to PNL, February 13, 1858, CDA, 10T6 (in French, author's translation). Thomassy was the author of *Géologie pratique de la Louisiane* (New Orleans, 1860; repr., New York: Arno Press, 1978).
68. On Geddings see "Necrology. J. F. M. Geddings," 145; Waring, *A History of Medicine in South Carolina*, 2:238–39. On Shepard see Waring, *A History of Medicine in South Carolina*, 2:291–92.
69. Courtenay to PNL, May 5, 1881, CDA, 72W4; J. F. M. Geddings to PNL, August 2, 1878, CDA, 66E1; Geddings to PNL, August 5, 1878, CDA, 66E6; Lynch et al., "Artesian Wells," 276–78; "The Sad Death of Mr. J. D. Budds from the Effects of Sunstroke," *News and Courier*, July 18, 1887, 8.
70. James Hall to PNL, March 24, 1877, CDA, 6N6; Hall to PNL, June 21, 1880, in Lynch et al., "Artesian Wells," 275–76; Clarke, *James Hall of Albany*, 462–66.
71. George H. Cook to Professor C. U. Shepard Jr., December 7, 1880, CDA, 72A6; Cook to PNL, January 8, 1881, CDA, 72D7; Geological Survey of New Jersey, *Annual Report of the State Geologist for the Year 1880*, 168–70. Lynch was asked by Charleston's city engineer in 1875 to encourage public support for continuing the wells project: Louis J. Barbot to PNL, July 30, 1875, CDA, 58S1.

72. Benoit Diary, CB6–135, 141; James Cardinal Gibbons, Episcopal Diary (Acta Episcopalia), second part: October 19, 1877–April 28, 1917, entry for February 26, 1882, Archives of the Archdiocese of Baltimore.
73. Oscar Lieber to PNL, January 17, 1857, CDA, 10B4; Lieber to PNL, February 11, 1857, CDA, 10C1; Lieber to PNL, June 19, 1857, CDA, 10H6; Lieber to PNL, July 22, 1857, CDA, 10K4; Lieber to PNL, December 5, 1857, CDA, 10P1; Lieber to PNL, December 29, 1857, CDA, 10P7; Lieber to PNL, June 4, 1858, CDA, 23C2; South Carolina Mineralogical, Geological and Agricultural Survey, *Report on the Survey of South Carolina*; Millbrooke, "South Carolina State Geological Surveys," 32–36; Taylor, "Oscar Montgomery Lieber," 191–95. Oscar Lieber was a strong Southern nationalist who volunteered for the Confederate Army, served in Wade Hampton's Legion, and was killed in 1862 near Williamsburg, Va.: Freidel, *Francis Lieber*, 300–01, 306, 325–26; Roys, "Francis Lieber," 123. Oscar Lieber published an article titled "The Vocabulary of the Catawba Language."
74. Lieber to his parents, May 7, 1858, Francis Lieber Papers, SCL, USC.

CHAPTER 3: ADVANCEMENT IN THE 1850S

1. Fisher, *Community of Immigrants*, 46–47.
2. Bachman, *A Defence of Luther*, 1.
3. *Charleston Daily Courier*, March 13, 1852, 2.
4. John Bellinger to Orestes Bronson, January 16, 1845; and Bellinger to Brownson, August 22, 1845: AUND, CARO, I-3-h; *Miscellany*, August 18, 1860, 46–47. On Bellinger see Waring, *A History of Medicine in South Carolina*, 2:205–6; Krebsbach, "Black Catholics," 155.
5. Bellinger's remarks in "Leahey's Lectures—Discussion in the City Council," *Charleston Courier*, March 26, 1852, 2; "Leahey's Lectures, &c," *Miscellany*, March 27, 185, 294–95. The controversial speaker was referred to in the press as E. Leahey or Leahy.
6. John Bachman, "To the Public. No. I," *Charleston Evening News*, April 29, 1852, 2; "By Request—From the U.S. Catholic Miscellany," *Charleston Evening News*, May 3, 1852, 2; Bachman, "To the Public. No. II," *Charleston Evening News*, May 5, 1852, 2; "To the Editor of the Catholic Miscellany [by] a Protestant though No Lutheran," *Charleston Evening News*, May 6, 1852, 2; "From the Richmond Watchman and Observer to John Bellinger," *Charleston Evening News*, May 8, 1852, 2; "Letter of John Bellinger to the News," *Charleston Evening News*, April 22, 1852, 2; Stephens, *Science, Race and Religion*, 213–14; Lowman, "James Andrew Corcoran," 120–35.
7. Stephens, *Science, Race, and Religion*, 211–13; Bost, "The Reverend John Bachman," 298–304; Bachman, Haskell, and Audubon, *John Bachman*, 318–24.
8. Billington, *Protestant Crusade*, 290–91. The complete text of Hughes's lecture is in Hughes, *Complete Works*, 2:87–102.
9. "The Nuncio's Report," in Connelly, *The Visit of Archbishop Bedini*, 237–58.
10. Ibid. There were numerous articles in the *Miscellany*: *Miscellany*, July 23, 1853, 3; "Particulars of the Plot to Assassinate Mgr. Bedini," November 19, 1853, 137;

"Letter from the Nuncio," November 26, 1853, 148; "An Attempt at Riot" and "Foreign Relations," January 7, 1854, 264–65; "The Cincinnati Riots," January 2, 1854, 12–13; "Domestic, Ecclesiastical," February 11, 1854, 233–34; "The Pope's Nuncio Insulted by Rowdies at Pittsburg,—Great Excitement," December 24, 1853, 179. On the Bedini visit see D'Agostino, *Rome in America,* 33–35; Connelly, *Visit of Archbishop Bedini;* McGreevy, *Catholicism and American Freedom,* 25; Endres, "Know-Nothings," 179–200; Franco, *Parallel Empires,* 6–19.

11. Quoted in Madden, "Catholics of South Carolina" (unpublished), ms. #1, vol. 5, ch. 9, 39.
12. *Charleston Mercury,* February 15, 1854, 2.
13. The hospital controversy discussed in Campbell, "Bishop England's Sisterhood," 68–72.
14. John Lynch to PNL, September 26, 1852, CDA, 7H1.
15. William B. Ryan to PNL, October 8, 1852, CDA, 7H6; PNL to Gallagher, Huger, Fitch, Smith, April 22, 1853, CDA, 7P5; Edward Gallagher to PNL, April 25, 1853, CDA, 7P6; Dr. Whitford Smith to PNL, May 2, 1853, CDA, 7R2; PNL to Dr. Whitford Smith, May 9, 1853, CDA, 7R3; Madden, "Catholics of South Carolina"; Campbell, "Bishop England's Sisterhood," 68–72. Details on the operation of the hospital, the religious denominations of patients, and the names of Protestant ministers who attended non-Catholics are in PNL to Hon. T. L. Hutchinson, Mayor of Charleston, October 1852; PNL to C. D. Carr, Chairman of Select Committee, October 1852; and other related items among "Papers of St. Mary's Relief Hospital," CDA, box 12, folder C.
16. Bachman, *Defence of Luther,* 416 ff.
17. PNL to *Charleston Evening News,* August 17, 1852, 4; and PNL to John Bachman, August 3, 1852; in Bachman, *Defence of Luther,* 314–20, 328.
18. "Dr. Bachman and His Book," *Miscellany,* July 9, 1853, 401; Lowman, "James Andrew Corcoran," 131–32.
19. Mulligan, "Dr. James Donnelly," 367.
20. "The New Cathedral," *Charleston Daily Courier,* April 6, 1854, 1.
21. Overdyke, *Know-Nothing Party,* 70, 95–96, 98–101, 298–99.
22. Bailey, Morgan, and Taylor, eds., *Biographical Directory of the South Carolina Senate,* 1:275–76; Communication from William Kanapaux, August 9, 2004; communication from William Kanapaux, August 9, 2004. Carew later served in both the state House of Representatives and the state Senate.
23. "To the Voters of Charleston District" and "Newly-Made Citizens," *Charleston Courier,* July 3, 1855, 1; "Why Is Charles E. Kanapaux Persecuted?" *Charleston Courier,* July 4, 1855, 1; "Sheriff's Election," *Charleston Courier,* July 12, 1855, 2; Madden, *Catholics in South Carolina,* 71.
24. "The Late Election," *Miscellany,* July 14, 1855, 415.
25. Madden, *Catholics in South Carolina,* 64.
26. O'Connell, *Catholicity,* 65, 245.
27. Ibid., 241–46.
28. Ibid., 247–48.
29. Jeremiah J. O'Connell (hereafter JJO) to PNL, April 1, 1855, CDA, 9A6; JJO to PNL, May 21, 1855, CDA, 9B7.

30. McNally, "A Peculiar Institution," 1:156. As late as 1980, estimates were that Catholics made up only 0.8 percent of the population of North Carolina and 1.3 percent of the population of South Carolina, CDA records.
31. Quoted in Guilday, *Life and Times of John England,* 2:38.
32. Frémont was a troublesome student at the college, which expelled him in 1831, although he received his baccalaureate degree in 1836: Easterby, *History of the College of Charleston,* 82.
33. Billington, *Protestant Crusade,* 427–28.
34. "'Our' Candidate," *Miscellany,* September 6, 1856, 63.
35. Kenrick, *The Kenrick-Frenaye Correspondence,* 386–87.
36. Francis Patrick Kenrick (hereafter FPK) to Propaganda, May 2, 1855, APF, Scritt. orig. rif. Nelle cong. gen. 1856, vol. 981, fols. 1022r–1027v, AUND, MPRF, reels 17–18, VI, 630.
37. FPK to Peter Richard Kenrick (hereafter PRK), November 20, 855, *Kenrick-Frenaye Correspondence,* 393.
38. John McCloskey (hereafter JMcC) to John McCaffrey, April 11, 1857, quoted in Meline and McSweeny, *Story of the Mountain,* 1:513–14.
39. Bishop Andrew Byrne of Little Rock to Archbishop Anthony Blanc of New Orleans, July 25, 1856, AUND, CANO, VI-1-k-1.
40. Hughes to McCaffrey, quoted in Madden, "Catholics of South Carolina" (unpublished), ms. #1, vol. 5, ch. 9, 20.
41. FPK to PNL, April 3, 1857, CDA, 10E1.
42. PNL to FPK, April 7, 1857, AAB, 30M1.
43. FPK to PNL, July 20, 1857, CDA, 10K2.
44. APF, Acta, Anno 1857, Ristratto con sommario sulla scelta del Vescovo di Charleston e del Vicario Apostoloato della Florida nell'America settenrionale, 7a settembre, 1857, fol. 293 ff.
45. *Charleston Daily Courier,* February 4, 1858, 2.
46. "The See of Charleston," *Charleston Daily Courier,* February 8, 1858, 2.
47. "The Chamber of Commerce—Thirty-Fifth Anniversary," *Charleston Daily Courier,* February 9, 1858, 2.
48. Madden, *Catholics in South Carolina,* 72–73.
49. "Bishop Lynch's Consecration," *Charleston Daily Courier,* March 15, 1858, 2.
50. Catholic Church, Province of Baltimore, 9th Provincial Council (1858). *Pastoral Letter* (Baltimore, 1858), 11–13. The signers were Archbishop Kenrick; the bishops of Pittsburgh, Richmond, Philadelphia, Savannah, and Charleston; and the vicar apostolic of Florida. Philadelphia Coadjutor James Wood and David Whelan, procurator of the bishop of Wheeling, also signed.
51. Guilday, *Councils of Baltimore,* 182; Ellis, *American Catholicism,* 94; McGreevy, *Catholicism and American Freedom,* 59 ff.; Caravaglios, *American Catholic Church,* 118–19; Lynch, "Duty of Priesthood to negroes after the war" (ms. draft) [1867], CDA, Patrick N. Lynch Transfer file, case I folder W.
52. Fogarty, *American Catholic Biblical Scholarship,* 14–21.
53. PNL to Cardinal Wiseman, October 1, 1858 (draft), CDA, 23E1.
54. Newman to PNL, December 7, 1858, in Dessain et al., eds., *The Letters and Diaries of John Henry Newman,* 18:531–34.

55. Fogarty, *American Catholic Biblical Scholarship*, 20–21; Ward, *Life of John Henry Cardinal Newman*, 1:425–29.
56. PNL to Diocesan Consultors, July 23, 1858, CDA, 23C9; Campbell, "Bishop England's Sisterhood," 86.
57. PNL to Diocesan Consultors, July 23, 1858, CDA, 23C9; Purcell to PNL, March 12, 1857, CDA, 10D3; PNL to Purcell, March 18, 1857, AUND, CACI, II-4-n.
58. Campbell, "Bishop England's Sisterhood," 86–87.
59. Madden, *Catholics in South Carolina*, 74.
60. Sister M. Ignatia, OSU, to James F. Edwards, July 31, 1887, AUND, CEDW, XI-1-e; Mother St. Charles Weid, OSU, to James F. Edwards, July 31, 18887, AUND, CEDW, XI-1-e.
61. PNL to Dr. J. Boatwright, October 17, 1859, CDA, 24G1; Madden, *Catholics in South Carolina*, 74.
62. Madden, *Catholics in South Carolina*, 74.O'Connell, *Catholicity*, 278–79.
63. O'Connell, *Catholicity*, 231–32; *Miscellany*, July 25, 1829, 30.
64. "Early Conversions in South Carolina (typescript of newspaper clippings)," 1920; "In Memoriam (Dr. John Harwood Burt)"; both in Burt Family File, Archives of Edgefield, S.C.; Chapman, *History of Edgefield*, 350; O'Connell, *Catholicity*, 233.
65. Bryan, *Creating the South Carolina State House*, 18–19, 32–36; Madden, *Catholics in South Carolina*, 73–75.
66. O'Connell, *Catholicity*, 233–35; CDA, file "Edgefield,"; Fahey, *Catholic Diocese of Charleston; A History*, 130–31; Madden, *Catholics in South Carolina*, 75.
67. "City Intelligence: Consecration of St. Joseph's Church," *Charleston Daily News*, May 6, 1860, 2.
68. "City Intelligence: Dedication of St. Paul's Church. Society street," *Charleston Daily News*, May 13, 1860, 2.
69. Ibid.
70. Madden, "Catholics of South Carolina" (unpublished), ms. #1, 19.
71. Corcoran took over as editor of the *U.S. Catholic Miscellany* in 1850 and remained in that position until its demise in the Great Charleston Fire of 1861. Madden, *Catholics in South Carolina*, 67.
72. "A Discovery," *Miscellany*, September 13, 1856, 71.
73. Madden, "Catholics of South Carolina" (unpublished), ms. #1, 19.
74. On the Catholic press and the abolitionists see Rice, *American Catholic Opinion in the Slavery Controversy*, esp. ch. 5; McGreevy, *Catholicism and American Freedom*, 51–53.
75. Osthaus, *Partisans of the Southern Press*, 69–70.

Chapter 4: Slaveholdings

1. A great part of this chapter was previously published as David C. R. Heisser, "Bishop Lynch's People: Slaveholding by a South Carolina Prelate," *South Carolina Historical Magazine* 102, no. 4 (July 2001): 238–62 (hereafter Heisser, "Bishop Lynch's People").
2. Key passages of the apostolic constitution are in Zanca, *Catholics and Slavery*, 27–28. On the preparation of the apostolic constitution of 1839 see McGreevy,

Catholicism and American Freedom, 50, 52; Renault, "Aux origines de la lettre apostolique de Grégoire XVI *In supremo* (1839)," 143–49; Prudhomme, "La Papauté face à l'esclavage: quelle condamnation?," 135–60.

3. For history of Catholic theological views on slavery see Capizzi, "Development of Doctrine," *passim;* Panzer, *The Popes and Slavery, passim;* Maxwell, *Slavery and Catholic Church, passim;* Rice, *American Catholic Opinion,* chs. 1–3.
4. John England, to John Forsyth, September 28, 1840, in England, *The Works of the Right Rev. John England, First Bishop of Charleston,* 3:114–16. England expressed the desire that the institution not continue, but he saw no way to end it in the near term. For his views on slavery see Clarke, *A Free Church,* 396–406; Clarke and Underwood, "Bishop John England."
5. Ellis, *American Catholicism,* 90; Brokhage, *Kenrick's Opinion on Slavery,* 123–31.
6. Miller, "Slaves and Southern Catholicism"; Wakelyn, "Catholic Elites in the Slaveholding South"; Hennesey, *American Catholics,* 143–47; Davis, *History of Black Catholics,* 40–41.
7. Gleeson, *Irish in the South,* 122–24. On Jewish slaveholders, see Rosen, *The Jewish Confederates,* 35 ff., 61–63.
8. Davis, *History of Black Catholics,* 40–41; Curran, "'Splendid Poverty': Jesuit Slaveholding in Maryland, 1805–1838"; Duncan, "Catholics and the Church in the Upper South."
9. Fitz, "Religious and Slavery," 347–49.
10. Ochs, *Black Patriot,* 21–22.
11. Golla, "Father Badin's Slaves," 1–24.
12. Rice, *American Catholic Opinion,* 46; Spalding, *Spalding,* 129–30; Lemarié, *A Biography of Msgr. Benedict Joseph Flaget,* 2:105–10; Poole and Slawson, *Church and State,* 148–50, 158–60, 185; Ochs, *Black Patriot,* 108; Meline and McSweeny, *Story of the Mountain,* 1:244.
13. Slave Schedules, 1860, New Orleans, La., 041, 252, 1860 census.
14. Patrick Neison Lynch (hereafter PNL), "Responsiones R. D. Episcopi Carolopolitani ad Quaestiones pro relatione status dioeceseos, ad Sacram Congregationem de Propaganda Fide, Oct. 15, 1864," APF, Scritture riferite nei Congressi-America Centrale (hereafter Scritt. rif.), vol. 20, fols. 1056r–1056v, AUND), MPRF, reel 66, III, 417.
15. Census 1830, Charleston District, S.C., 102; *Miscellany,* May 14, 1831, 366, and May 21, 1831, 374; Thigpen, "Aristocracy of the Heart," 621.
16. Bill of sale, Antonio della Torre to John England in Trust for the Ursuline Nuns, October 21, 1835 (recorded October 23, 1835), South Carolina Department of Archives and History, Secretary of State Miscell. Records (Bills of Sale), vol. 50, 776; Clarke and Underwood, "Bishop John England," 199.
17. Quoted in Clarke, *A Free Church,* 394.
18. O'Connell, *Catholicity,* 117, 226, 333–34; Madden, *Catholics in South Carolina,* 69; CDA, Cathedral of St. John the Baptist, Marriage Records, 1845–1886, entry for July 14, 1850. In 1850 Wallace owned four slaves, a forty-eight-year-old woman and three young men: Moore, *Columbia and Richland County,* 132–33.
19. Census 1830, Chesterfield District, S.C., 250; Census, 1840, Chesterfield District, S.C., 355; Slave Schedules, 1850, Chesterfield District, S.C., 7; Slave

Schedules, 1860, Chesterfield District, S.C., 95–96, and Richland District, S.C., 92; John Lynch (hereafter JL) to PNL, November 20, 1862, CDA, 14N6; Francis Lynch to PNL, August 19, 1863, CDA, 14W9.

20. Catherine Lynch to Mary Lynch Spann, August 10, 1847, CDA, 5R3; Mother Baptista Lynch (hereafter BL) to PNL, December 19, 1860, CDA, 13T7; Henrietta B. Lynch (hereafter HBL) to PNL, January 29, 1861, CDA, 13W5; JL to Louisa Blain, July 16, 1861, CDA, 14A10; Hugh Lynch to PNL, November 24, 1863, CDA, 14N7.

21. JL to PNL, August 8, 1850, CDA, 6W4; JL to PNL, October 22, 1856, CDA, 9Y6; JL to PNL, October 26, 1857, CDA, 10N3; JL to PNL, January 5, 1858, CDA, 10R4.

22. Contract between Françoise Antoinette Césarine Barbot and Patrick N. Lynch, December 18, 1857, CDA, 12R2; communication from Dr. Clyde N. Wilson, ed., *The Papers of John C. Calhoun,* University of South Carolina, January 31, 1996. The family was of Santo Domingan French origin; the widow Barbot was a member of St. Mary's Parish, Charleston: South Carolina Historical Society, "Family Record (typescript)," Barbot Family Papers, MS 11/67/25; U.S. WPA, Cemetery Index for Charleston County (S.C.), St. Mary's Catholic Church, 25, 61.

23. Will of Martin Dowd, CDA, Patrick N. Lynch Transfer File, folder "Martin Dowd."

24. "Christenthum und Sklaverei," *Historisch-politische Blätter* 62 (1868): 195 (author's translation).

25. *List of the Taxpayers of the City of Charleston for 1858,* 33; *List of the Taxpayers of the City of Charleston for 1859,* 241; *List of the Taxpayers of the City of Charleston for 1860,* 171; Charleston City Tax Books, 1860, Lower Wards, CLS.

26. Cf. Patrick N. Lynch, "A Few Words on the Domestic Slavery in the Confederate States of America," pt. 1, 89.

27. Wade, *Slavery in the Cities,* 55–58; Powers, *Black Charlestonians,* 58, 62.

28. Bailey, Morgan, and Taylor, *Biographical Directory of SC Senate,* 2:1003–4; Davidson, *The Last Foray,* 106.

29. O'Connell, *Catholicity,* 297.

30. Ibid.; will of William McKenna (printed copy), CDA, 23R8; Madden, *Catholics in South Carolina,* 79.

31. Daniel J. Quigley (hereafter DJQ) to PNL, October 17, 1859, CDA, 24H7; Pettus and Bishop, *Lancaster County,* 55; Louise Pettus, "McKenna Will Case" (typescript), collection of Ms. Nancy L. Crockett, Lancaster, S.C.

32. Indenture between PNL et al. in resettlement of McKenna Estate, November 2, 1860, Lancaster County, S.C., Deed Book S, 182–96, South Carolina Department of Archives and History, County Deeds, microfilm roll C8207; indenture between PNL et al., in resettlement of McKenna Estate, August 14, 1861, CDA, 26H8; DJQ to PNL, June 14, 1860, CDA, 25K8; BL to PNL, July 31, 1860, CDA, 13S2; John F. G. Mittag to Jeremiah J. O'Connell, July 1, 1861, CDA, 26G1; Henry A. DeSaussure to DJQ, March 20, 1894, CDA, 81H2; Madden, *Catholics in South Carolina,* 79; O'Connell, *Catholicity,* 297–98.

33. Will of William McKenna; "Estate Sale, Estate of William McKenna Deceased . . . ," *Lancaster Ledger* (S.C.), January 2, 1861, 3; Tadman, *Speculators and Slaves,* 59, 258, 281; Bancroft, *Slave Trading,* 170–71, 176n, 191; "Cathedral Fund" (record

of contributions), CDA, Patrick N. Lynch Transfer File, folder "Finance." The building that held Ryan's Mart is now Charleston's Old Slave Mart Museum.

34. Charles B. Northrop (CBN) to PNL, June 24, 1861, CDA, 26E9; CBN to PNL, July 19, 1861, CDA, 26H1; BL to PNL, January 28, 1863, CDA, 14R7; DJQ, "List of Negroes, 14 November 1860," along with a list of families and prices, CDA, Lynch Unclassified Papers, Box 309L; *Catalogue of Negroes*, CDA, 25Y8.
35. Russell, "Sale Day in Antebellum South Carolina," 219–20, 225. After the sale the bishop paid Thomas Ryan a fee of $3,047.25: Cash Book, South-Western Rail-Road Bank in Account with P. N. Lynch, D.D., entry for March 11, 1861, CDA, Patrick N. Lynch Transfer File, folder "Finance."
36. This figure is derived by adding the number of McKenna slaves to the ten or so already in Charleston.
37. Barrett, *Councils of Baltimore and Code of Canon Law*, 187, 194; Fanning, "Property, Ecclesiastical, in the United States," *Catholic Encyclopedia* vol. 12: 472–73.
38. Dolan, *American Catholic Experience*, 171–72.
39. Sisters of Our Lady of Mercy, Council Meeting Book, vol. 4, Council Minutes (March 6, 1856–March 29, 1862), meeting of January 15, 1861, Archives of the Sisters of Charity of Our Lady of Mercy, Charleston, S.C.
40. Patrick N. Lynch, "A Few Words," pt. 1; Patrick N. Lynch, "A Few Words," pt. 2.
41. O'Connell, *Catholicity*, 220–25; PNL to Rev. Augustine Hewit, April 10, 1858, CDA, 23A5; communication from Horace E. Harmon, director, Lexington County Museum, January 23, 1996. The site of the Wallace plantation became part of the suburban sprawl near the junction of two interstate highways. Wallace also had owned a strip of land in Columbia along the Broad River. This, too, was controlled by Bishop Lynch: communication from Dr. Colin Bennett, Department of Mathematics, University of South Carolina, March 1, 2002; Lexington County, S.C., Deed book AA, 116, 259–60; Lexington County, S.C., Deed book Z, 543–45, 556. The author expresses thanks to Dr. Colin Bennett for information about the Wallace properties.
42. John Lynch later served as the state surgeon-general and professor at the University of South Carolina's School of Medicine: Waring, *History of Medicine in South Carolina*, 2:251; Hillis, *University of South Carolina*, 2:51, 69, 355, 359. On Mother Baptista see Madden, "Lynch, Baptista, Mother," *New Catholic Encyclopedia*, 8:1110; "Annals of the Ursuline Convent, Columbia, S.C.," and "St. Peter's Parochial School, 1872–1947," Archives of the Ursuline Sisters, Louisville, Ky.; "Ursulines Begin Celebration of 100th Anniversary in Columbia," *Catholic Banner* 46, no. 33 (December 15, 1951): 1A, 4A.
43. JL to PNL, May 14, 1861, CDA, 14A4; JL to PNL, May 24, 1861, CDDA, 14A6; JL to PNL, June 8, 1861, CDA, 14A7; A. Buff to PNL, November 28, 1862, CDA, 28D5; Census, 1850, Lexington District, S.C., 348.
44. DJQ to PNL, June 14, 1860, CDA, 25K8; Claudian Bird Northrop (hereafter CBN) to Harrry P. Northrop (hereafter HPN), October 27, 1860, CDA, 25W1; HPN to PNL, June 24, 1861, CDA, 26E9; Claudian B. Northrop Jr. (hereafter CBN Jr.) to HPN, March 7, 1864, CDA, 30K2; Moore, *Confederate Commissary General*, 5, 7, 28, 37–43; Moore, "Northrop Pedigree" (unpublished); Sims, *My*

Life, 104–5; Stoney, ed., "Memoirs of Frederick Adolphus Porcher," 201–2; Smith, "The Passing of Bishop Northrop," *Sunday News* (Charleston, S.C.), August 8 and 15, 1920 (clippings in scrapbook), Charleston Library Society; Tax Returns, Lancaster District, 1861, box 27, folder 4, South Carolina Department of Archives and History; Gray, *History of Agriculture,* 2:923; Northrop, *Southern Odes, by the Outcast, passim;* Northrop, *Political Remarks,* 14.

45. Of the approximately eighty-five slaves whom the bishop purchased in January 1861, he paid taxes on fifty-six in Lancaster District in the fall of that year: South Carolina, Comptroller General, Tax Return Books, Lancaster District, 1861, box 27, folder 34, South Carolina Department of Archives and History; CBN to PNL, June 24, 1861, CDA, 26E9. Northrop gave the number of Lynch's Lancaster slaves as fifty-four in July: CBN to PNL, July 19, 1861, CDA, 25H1.
46. CBN to PNL, March 7, 1864, CDA, 30K2.
47. JL to PNL, June 8, 1861, CDA, 14A7; DJQ to PNL, May 19, 1861, CDA, 26E8; CBN to PNL, December 2, 1861, CA, 26P7. The 1860 Census listed Patrick McKennaa as a fifty-year-old hotel "watchman"—in Lancaster. He resented the bishop and Northrop as interlopers: Census, 1860, Lancaster District, S.C., 218; communication from Nancy L. Crockett, Lancaster, S.C., July 7, 1996.
48. CBN to PNL, June 24, 1861, CDA, 26E9.
49. Nichols, *Story of Great March,* 184.
50. DJQ to PNL, June 14, 1860, CDA, 25K8.
51. JL to PNL, March 9, 1861, CDA, 13W9; Helen M. Burt to PNL, December 15, 1861, CDA, 26T7; JL to PNL, January 6, 1862, CDA, 14E1; CBN to PNL, January 7, 1862, CDA, 26W3; JL to PNL, May 29, 1862, CDA, 14H9; BL to PNL, June 1, 1862, CDA, 14H10; BL to PNL, June 4, 1862, CDA, 14H11; Ellison S. Keitt to PNL, June 1, 1862, CDA, 27H2; BL to PNL, July 22, 1862, CDA, 14K9; JL to PNL, January 18, 1864, CDA, 15D7; JL to PNL, January 21, 1864, CDA, 15D8; JL to PNL, [undated] 1864, CDA, 15G8; "Early Conversions in South Carolina (typescript of newspaper clippings)," 1920, and "In Memoriam (Dr. John Harwood Burt)," both in Burt Family File, Archives of Edgefield, S.C.; Madden, *Catholics in South Carolina,* 74–75; deed, Ellison S. Keitt to Patrick N. Lynch, October 2, 1862 (recorded February 18, 1890), Richland County, S.C., Register of Deeds, Deed Book U, 220, and Plat A/103.
52. Charleston City Tax Books, 1862, 1863, 1864, Charleston Library Society; Madden, *Catholics in South Carolina,* 69; auctioneer's receipt, February 2, 1863, CDA, 28M7; Edward Dennis Lofton, "Reverend Doctor James Andrew Corcoran," 80–81 (including a facsimile of the receipt).
53. Lynch, "A Few Words," pt. 1, 70.
54. Ibid., 87–88; Capizzi, "Development of Doctrine," 189, 213–14.
55. CBN to PNL, December 2, 1861, CDA, 26P7; Hartman, "Civil War Experience," 21–22; Weiner, *Mistresses and Slaves,* 157 ff.
56. Lynch, "A Few Words," pt. 1, 91–92. On the labor systems see Edgar, *South Carolina,* 313–15.
57. Lynch, "A Few Words," pt. 1, 91–93; JL to PNL, December 13, 1863, CDA, 15C2.
58. Lynch, "A Few Words," pt. 2, 94.

59. Ibid., 95–96.
60. History and Baptismal Record, St. Mary's Parish [Edgefield, S.C.], 1850–1871, entry for August 12, 1861, CDA, box 304E.
61. BL to PNL, February 14, 1863, CDA, 14R10.
62. CBN to PNL, October 30, 1861, CDA, 26N3; CBN to PNL, September 1, 1862, CDA, 27R2; BL to PNL, January 28, 1863, CDA, 14R7; CBN Jr. to HPN, March 7, 1864, CDA, 30K2.
63. Lynch, "A Few Words," pt. 1, 92.
64. Ibid., 92–94.
65. JL to PNL, January 22, 1862, CDA, 14E6; JL to PNL, February 2, 1863, CDA, 14R8; JL to PNL, August 19, 1863, CDA, 14W8.
66. Cf. Savitt, "Slave Health and Southern Distinctiveness," 142–43.
67. CBN to PNL, January 8, 1862, CDA, 26W4; CBN to PNL, September 1, 1862, CDA, 27R2; CBN to PNL, January 20, 1863, CDA, 28K7.
68. CBN to PNL, January 8, 1862, CDA, 26W4; CBN to PNL, July 25, 1862, CDA, 27K6; CBN to PNL, January 20, 1863, CDA, 28K7; CBN to PNL, June 5, 1863, CDA, 29C2; Helfand, "James Morison and His Pills," 101–6.
69. CBN to PNL, October 18, 1862, CDA, 28A6; CBN to PNL, December 1, 1863, CDA, 28E3; CBN to PNL, January 20, 1863, CDA, 28K7; CBN to PNL, June 15, 1863, CDA, 29C2; BN to PNL, June 25, 1863, CDA, 29C5; CBN to PNL, August 17, 1863, CDA, 29K7; CBN to PNL, August 26, 1863, CDA, 29M4; CBN to PNL, September 22, 1863, CDA, 29P1; Wiley, *Southern Negroes,* 28–32; Hartman, "Civil War Experience," 25–27.
70. Lynch, "A Few Words," pt. 2, 103. On the effort of Southern clergy to promote legal guarantees for slaves' marriages and families see Genovese, A *Consuming Fire,* 17–23, 51–52.
71. Lynch, "A Few Words," pt. 2, 99; Kolchin, *American Slavery,* 122–23; Hudson, *To Have and to Hold,* 141 ff.; Ochs, *Black Patriot,* 22–23.
72. Lynch, "A Few Words," pt. 2, 100; CBN to PNL, June 13, 1862, CDA, 27G3.
73. Lynch, "A Few Words," pt. 2, 100.
74. CBN to PNL, December 2, 1861, CDA, 26P7; CBN to PNL, December 1, 1862, CDA, 28E3; CBN to PNL, January 20, 1863, with a postscript, January 21, 1863, CDA, 28K7.
75. CBN to PNL, December 2, 1861, CDA, 26P7; CBN to PNL, June 13, 1862, CDA, 27G3; CBN to PNL, January 20, 1863, CDA, 28K7. In the latter part of the war both Ned and Mahaly were owned by Patrick McKenna—so perhaps the lovers got their way even before emancipation.
76. Lynch, "A Few Words," pt. 1, 95–98.
77. CBN to PNL, December 2, 19861, CDA, 26P7; CBN to PNL, January 7, 1862, CDA, 26W3. Cf. Wiley, *Southern Negroes,* 67–68, 72–84; Mohr, *On the Threshold,* 222–32.
78. JL to PNL, August 27, 1861, CDA, 14B7.
79. Lynch, "A Few Words," pt.1, 98.
80. CBN to PNL, December 2, 1861, CDA, 26P7; CBN to PNL, December 27, 1861, CDA, 26T9. Cf. Mohr, *On the Threshold,* 213–35.

81. JL to PNL, November 13, 1861, CDA, 14C7; JL to PNL, January 6, 1862, CDA, 14E1; JL to PNL, January 22, 1862, CDA, 14E6.
82. JL to PNL, March 17, 1862, CDA, 14G6; Jones, "'My Mother Was Much of a Woman," 204.
83. Brewer, *The Confederate Negro,* 6 ff., 152–54; Wiley, *Southern Negroes,* 53, 115 ff.; Hartman, "Civil War Experience," 23.
84. CBN to PNL, March 22, 1864, CDA, 20M7.
85. CBN to PNL, September 1, 1862, CDA, 27R2; CBN to PNL, September 13, 1862, CDA, 27S3; CBN to PNL, September 23, 1862, CDA, 27W4; CBN to PNL, November 20, 1862, CDA, 28D4; CBN to PNL, June 25, 1863, CDA, 29C5; CBN to PNL, August 26, 1863, CDA, 29M4; BL to PNL, September 9, 1863, CDA, 14Y6 JL to PNL, September 18, 1863, CDA, 15A2; CBN to PNL, March 22, 1864, CDA, 30M7; NARA, RG 109, Slave Payroll #5236 (Kinloch's Landing, S.C., 1st Quarter 1864), War Department, Confederate Records; Burton, *Siege of Charleston,* 133.
86. O'Connell, *Catholicity,* 298.
87. Charleston City Tax Books, 1864, Charleston Library Society; Charleston, S.C., *Ordinances of the City of Charleston, 1783–1844,*.278; Jenkins, *Seizing the New Day,* 31.
88. Corcoran to PNL, August 6, 1865, CDD, 2R6; Lucius C. Northrop (hereafter LCN) to HCN, October 9, 2865, CDA, 33C5; "The Enemy in Lancaster," *York Enquirer* (S.C.), March 16, 1865, 2; Sims, *My Life,* 105–6; communication from Dr. Jerrold Northrop Moore, December 6, 1995. Dr. Moore is Claudian Northrop's great-grandson. Jeremiah O'Connell believed that Northrop had died of apoplexy: O'Connell, *Catholicity,* 302. After the war the black man who had helped Northrop bury his will and other papers assisted Bishop Lynch in their recovery: George Pannell Northrop to Eldridge Cutts, April 1, 1903, Northrop Family Archives. In later years Bishop Northrop had his father reburied in St. Lawrence Cemetery, Charleston.
89. Cf. Sherman's comments on the foragers' role: Miers, *William Tecumseh Sherman,* 229–30.
90. Davis, *Sherman's March,* 39–41, 192–96; Barrett, *Sherman's March through the Carolinas,* 100–01; Foster, "When Sherman Passed through Lancaster," 1:344–51.
91. *Historic and Architectural Inventory, Cheraw Historic District,* 15–16.
92. Anna Lynch to Sister Antonia of the Purification, June 15, 1865, CDA, 15H5.
93. BL to PNL, July 17, 1865, CDA, 15H7.
94. Merrill, *William Tecumseh Sherman,* 284–85; Powers, *Tar Heel Catholics,* 171.
95. BL to PNL, July 17, 1865, CDA, 15H7; BL to PNL, December 27, 1865, CDA, Unprocessed Letters of Mother Baptista Lynch; PNL to General Ralph Ely, December 27, 1865, CDA, 33S3; BL to PNL, January 8, 1866, CDA, 15M4.
96. LCN to HPN, October 9, 1865, CDA, 33C5; William M. Connors (hereafter WMC) to PNL, October 14, 1865, CDA, 33C7; Mary M. Northrop (hereafter MMN) to PNL, April 1, 1866, CDA, 33C6; MMN to PNL, August 21, 1866, CDA, 37A5; GPN to EC, April 13, 1903, Northrop Family Archives.
97. Will of William McKenna, section 9; MMN to PNL, June 8, 1866, CDA, 35Y1; T. M. Belk to PNL, July 3, 1866, CDA, 36F6; T. M. Belk to PNL, October 31, 1866, CDA, 37S3; William A. Moore to PNL, November 20, 1867, CDA, 41P7;

PNL to Messrs. Kershaw and Connors, May 1, 1871 (typescript copy), Collection of Nancy L. Crockett, Lancaster, S.C.; WMC to DJQ, June 12, 1873, CDA, 55G5; WMC to DJQ, May 1, 1875 (photocopy), Collection of Nancy L. Crockett; Thomas H. Clyburn, as administrator of John McKenna, decd., vs. D. A. Williams, as administrator of . . . William McKenna, decd. Lancaster County, S.C., Court of Common Pleas, October 3, 1879. On the statute see Powers, *Black Charlestonians,* 39–40.

98. Census, 1870, Lancaster County, S.C., 307, 319, 368, 373, 374, 377; Census, 1870, York County, S.C., 407; Census, 1880, Soundex, S.C., Lancaster County; *Lancaster County Black History,* 32–33; Madden, *Catholics in South Carolina,* 204–5.
99. BL to PNL, January 28, 1863, CDA, 14R7; JL to PNL, February 2, 1863, CDA, 14R8.
100. CBM to PNL, January 7, 1862, CDA, 26W3; CBN to PNL, October 5, 1862, CDA, 27Y7; CBN to PNL, January 14, 1864, CDA, 30D5; mortgage contract between Patrick McKenna and Patrick N. Lynch, April 24, 1862, Lancaster County, S.C., Deed Book S, 323–24, SCDAG, S.C. County Deeds, microfilm roll C8207. Patrick McKenna subsequently reclaimed Mahaly and her offspring upon payment of his debt.

Chapter 5: The War

1. Mitchell, *Hibernian Society,* 64.
2. Ibid., 64–65; Fraser, *Charleston! Charleston!,* 241–42.
3. "It Has Come at Last," *Miscellany,* November 10, 1860, 142–43.
4. Edgar, *South Carolina,* 350–51.
5. Osthaus, *Partisans of the Southern Press,* 92–93; Morrill, *The Civil War in the Carolinas,* 16–17.
6. "The Present Crisis," *Miscellany,* December 8, 1860, 174; discussed in Rice, *American Catholic Opinion,* 145.
7. Fraser, *Charleston! Charleston!,* 244. On the signing ceremony and the application of the pendent great seal see Lesser, *Relic of the Lost Cause,* 8.
8. "South Carolina," *Miscellany,* December 22, 1860, 190.
9. *Miscellany,* December 29, 1860, 198; Madden, *Catholics in South Carolina,* 77; Lowman, "James Andrew Corcoran," 196; Blied, *Catholics and the Civil War,* 701.
10. Compare Gleeson, *Irish in the South,* 142.
11. PNL to Hughes (draft), January 6, 1861, CDA, 25Y2; Lowman, "James Andrew Corcoran," 197; Wight, ed., "Some Wartime Letters of Bishop Lynch," 21–25. Wight wrote that the letter was addressed to John McNally, editor of the *Metropolitan Record* of New York, which Archbishop Hughes had founded in 1859. However, it seems evident from the salutation to "Most Rev. Dear Sir" that it was actually addressed to Hughes.
12. PNL to William H. Seward, June 24, 1865, NARA, RG 94, Records of the Adjutant General's Office, 1780s-1914, Amnesty Files.
13. JL to PNL, November 16, 1860, CDA, 13T4.
14. FL to PNL, December 27, 1860, CDA, 13T9; Mrs. Henry W. Conner to General James Conner, August 13, 1861, in Mary Conner Moffett, ed., *Letters of General James Conner, C.S.A.,* 46–47.

15. Sitterson, *Secession Movement*, 180 ff., 196 ff.; Crafts, *Reluctant Confederates*, 222 ff.
16. PNL to FPK, February 7, 1861, AAB, 30M17.
17. "The Crisis," *Miscellany*, November 24, 1860, 158; "The Present Crisis," *Miscellany*, December 8, 1860, 174; Madden, "Catholics of South Carolina" (unpublished), ms. #1, vol. 6, ch. 10, 2, 11–114; Madden, *Catholics in South Carolina*, 80–81; D'Agostino, *Rome in America*, 40–43.
18. Bermingham, Diary, entry for March 1, 1861 (hereafter Bermingham, Diary); Timothy Bermingham (hereafter TB) to PNL, April 1861, CDA, 26C7.
19. "Castle Pinckney," *Miscellany*, January 6, 1861, 206; Morrill, *Civil War*, 37; Fraser, *Charleston! Charleston!*, 246. The text of Lynch's sermon has not been found. After Thomas Francis Meagher joined the Union army, the Meagher Guards changed its name to the Emerald Light Infantry: Madden, *Catholics in South Carolina*, 370.
20. Marschall, "Francis Patrick Kenrick," 348.
21. PNL to FPK, February 9, 1861, AAB, 30M17. The Latin phrase may be translated as "It would be better for the man." Thanks to Professor Frederick J. Booth, Chairman, Classical Studies Department, Seton Hall University, for assistance with the translation.
22. Ibid.
23. FPK to Archbishop Peter Richard Kenrick, February 28, 1861, in *Kenrick-Frenaye Correspondence*, 457–58.
24. TB to PNL, February 27, 1861, CDA, 25A2.
25. Bishop James Wood to PNL, January 25, 1861, CDA, 25Y3.
26. Detzer, *Allegiance*, 131–35; Baker, *Cadets in Gray*, 15–25.
27. PNL to Major Robert Anderson, January 10, 1861, Robert Anderson Papers, Library of Congress; Detzer, *Allegiance*, 174.
28. *Charleston Mercury*, April 15, 1861, 2; PNL to Horace Greeley, March 3, 1866 (copy), CDA, 34W3. See Greeley's criticism of Lynch: *New York Daily Tribune*, March 3, 1866, 6.
29. "Our Victory," *Miscellany*, April 20, 1861, 325.
30. JL to PNL, April 12, 1861, CDA, 13Y4.
31. Ibid.
32. Madden, *Catholics in South Carolina*, 81.
33. "Blessing of a Banner," *Miscellany*, September 14, 1861, 71; "The New Standard of the Irish Volunteers," *Miscellany*, September 21, 1861, 74; Campbell, "Bishop England's Sisterhood," 92–93; Madden, *Catholics in South Carolina*, 81–82
34. On the blessing of flags by Catholic clergy in Alabama and Louisiana see Lipscomb, "John Quinlan," 78, nos. 1–4 (March–December 1967): 42; Baudier, *Catholic Church in Louisiana*, 426–28. Flags of many South Carolina Confederate units are illustrated in Dedmondt, *Flags*.
35. Marschall, "Francis Patrick Kenrick," 355.
36. Quinlan to PNL, May 15, 1861, CDA, 25D5;PNL to FPK, June 12, 1861, AAB, 30M18.
37. PNL to FPK, September 27, 1861, AAB, 30M19; Marschall, "Francis Patrick Kenrick," 355–56; Gannon, *Rebel Bishop: Life and Era of Augustin Verot*, 63–64.

38. PNL to John Hughes (hereafter JH), August 4, 1861, printed in *Miscellany,* September 14, 1861, 66–67; reprinted in Ellis, ed., *Documents of American Catholic History,* 348–56.
39. JH to PNL, August 23, 1861, in Kehoe, ed., *Complete Works of the Most Rev. John Hughes,* 513–20; "Archbishop Hughes on the War, *New York Times,* September 4, 1861, 8.
40. *Miscellany,* September 21, 1861, 78.
41. *Miscellany,* September 28, 1861, 86.
42. PNL to Martin John Spalding (hereafter MJS), May 1865, AAB, 34U3.
43. Ibid.
44. "Report of the Board for the Relief of Families of Soldiers in the Parishes of St. Philip and St. Michael," *Charleston Daily Courier,* January 2, 1863, 4.
45. Edgar, *South Carolina,* 360–61; Morrill, *Civil War,* 151.
46. Madden, *Catholics in South Caroline,* 87; *Sadlier's Catholic Almanac and Guide,* 1864, 61.
47. Campbell, "Bishop England's Sisterhood," 98–100.
48. Ibid., 99–100.
49. Fraser, *Charleston! Charleston!,* 253–55; Burton, *Siege of Charleston,* 82–83; Ferrara, "Moses Henry Nathan and the Great Charleston Fire of 1861," 259, 272–75; PNL to Propaganda Fide, August 15, 1864, APF, Scritt. rif., vol. 20, fols. 1001r–1008v, AUND, MPRF, reel 67, III, 396; JAC to Bishop John Quinlan of Mobile, April 30, 1863, AAM; Lipscomb, "John Quinlan," 42–43.
50. "Dreadful Conflagration," *Miscellany,* December 12, 1861, 174–75.
51. O'Connell, *Catholicity,* 125. Another reference is a diocesan statement in South Carolina Inter-State and West Indian Exposition, *Charleston To-day and Yesterday,* 50. It is often said that the policy had lapsed one week before the fire, but this cannot be confirmed from extant diocesan records. Cf. Burton, *Siege of Charleston,* 83.
52. Ferrara, "Moses Henry Nathan," 259, 275; Fraser, *Charleston! Charleston!,* 253.
53. "A Proclamation," and related announcements, *Charleston Courier,* December 12, 1861, 2. The Reverend Dr. Anthony Toomer Porter (1828–1902), vicar of the Episcopal Church of the Holy Communion, was, like Lynch, an ardent Confederate. On Porter see "Rev. Dr. Anthony Toomer Porter," *Cyclopedia of Eminent and Representative Men of the Carolinas of the Nineteenth Century,* 1:493–95.
54. PNL to the Mayor and City Council (draft), CDA, Patrick N. Lynch Transfer File, folder "Fire Relief."
55. Charleston Fire Relief Committee, Report of Special Committee on Pecuniary Compensation (printed), CDA, Patrick N. Lynch Transfer File, folder "Fire Relief."
56. "Free Market of Charleston," *Charleston Daily Courier,* January 27, 1864, 2; TB to Conseil de la Société de la Propagation de la Foi, Paris, May 8, 1863, AUND, MPRF, reel M10, doc. 2135.
57. Morrill, *Civil War in the Carolinas,* 276–81; Worsley, "Catholicism in Antebellum North Carolina," 415, 417–18; Power, *Tar Heel Catholics,* 110–11, 194.
58. Burton, *Siege of Charleston,* 99; on the Battle of Secessionville see 98–114.

59. JAC to PNL, May 29, 1862, CDA, 27E3.
60. Sister M. Agatha McNamara to Sister DeSales Brennan, May 29, 1862, CDA, 27E4.
61. John Moore (hereafter JM) to PNL, June 6, 1862, CDA, 27G1.
62. Phelps, *Charlestonians in War,* 91.
63. Morrill, *Civil War in the Carolinas,* 320–24; Edgar, *South Carolina,* 365; Burton, *Siege of Charleston,* 183–89.
64. PNL to John McGill (hereafter JMcG), July 26, 1863 (copy), CDA, 29H1.
65. Lowman, "James Andrew Corcoran," 215.
66. For details of the bombardment see Phelps, *The Bombardment of Charleston, passim.* Locations of the guns and areas shelled are shown on map facing p. 27.
67. Records of Vestry, St. Finbar's Cathedral, 1855–1891, entries for January 17, 1862, and January 8, 1863, CDA, Box 305C.
68. Hopkins, "St. Mary's Church, Charleston, S.C.," *City of Charleston Yearbook,* 1897, 487–88; Madden, *Catholics in South Carolina,* 86.
69. Campbell, "Bishop England's Sisterhood," 128–31.
70. PNL to Conseils Centraux de la Société de la Propagation de la Foi, Lyon, June 17, 1864, AUND, MPFL, F31, reel M10 (French; author's translation).
71. Madden, *Catholics in South Carolina,* 86.
72. Sheeran, *Confederate Chaplain: A War Journal of Rev. James B. Sheeran,* 70.
73. Madden, "History of St. Joseph's Parish" (typescript), CDA, Parish Records, folder "St. Joseph's, Charleston," 4–5; "Exciting Scene in a Church," *News and Courier,* June 6, 1884, 1; reprinted in Madden, *Catholics in South Carolina,* 90.
74. Campbell, "Bishop England's Sisterhood," 131–34.
75. Emilio, *A Brave Black Regiment,* 405; Rosen, *Confederate Charleston,* 114.
76. PNL to William H. Seward, June 24, 1865, NARA, RG 94, Records of the Adjutant General's Office, 1780s–1914, Amnesty Files; Campbell, "Bishop England's Sisterhood," 134; JM to Martin John Spalding, July 12, 1865, AAB, 35J8; Westwood, *Black Troops, White Commanders,* 86–105; Wise, *Gate of Hell,* 124–27. On the Florence Stockade see King, "Death Camp at Florence," 34–41. Nelson Mitchell's funeral was held in St. Paul's Church. He was buried in Charleston's Magnolia Cemetery.
77. Campbell, "Bishop England's Sisterhood," 131.
78. Communications from Clark T. Donlin, September 4, 2004, and June 23, 2005. Mr. Donlin kindly made a portion of Sawyer's manuscript available to the author.
79. PNL to JMcG., July 26, 1863 (copy), CDA, 29H1; Madden, *Catholics in South Carolina,* 90; "Flag of Truce. Exchange of Prisoners," *Charleston Courier,* July 25, 1863, 1.
80. Craven, *Prison Life of Jefferson Davis,* 289–90; "The President's Movements," *Charleston Mercury,* November 5, 1863, 2.
81. Verot, *Tract for the Times;* Verot to PNL, May 7, 1861, CDA, 22D1; reproduced in Wight, ed., "Letters of the Bishop of Savannah," 95–96. The sermon and its publication are discussed in Gannon, *Rebel Bishop,* 31 ff.
82. Verot, *Tract for the Times,* 7.

83. Ibid., 10.
84. Verot to PNL, May 7, 1861, CDA, 22D1; Gannon, *Rebel Bishop,* 50–51.
85. Martin, *Lettre pastorale,* 6–8; Caravaglios, "A Roman Critique of the Pro-Slavery Views," 67–81; Zanca, *American Catholics and Slavery,* 219–25.
86. Marschall, "Francis Patrick Kenrick," 369–70.
87. JMcG to PNL, July 23, 1863, CDA, 29G6; JMcG to PNL, July 24, 1863, CDA, 29G7; both published in Wight, "War Letters of the Bishop of Richmond," 264–66.
88. PNL to JMcG, July 26, 1863, CDA, 29H1; quoted in part in Madden, *Catholics in South Carolina,* 88–89.
89. JMcG to PNL, September 3, 1863, CDA, 29N1; JMcG to PNL, October 22, 1863, CDA, 29S6; both in Wight, "War Letters of the Bishop of Richmond," 266–68; Verot to PNL, October 5, 1863, CDA, 29R2; printed in Wight, "Letters of the Bishop of Savannah," 102. Regarding the U.S. government's earlier refusal to permit McGill to travel north and thence to Europe, see FPK to PNL, August 24, 1862, CDA, 27P4.
90. This account of Spalding's election is based on Spalding, *Spalding,* 148–50.
91. JMcG to PNL, September 3, 1863, CDA, 29N1; Wight, "War Letters of the Bishop of Richmond," 266.
92. Spalding, *Spalding,* 150, 156.
93. BL to PNL, March 7, 1864, CDA, 14S5.
94. Blanton, *Medicine in Virginia in the Nineteenth Century,* 298.
95. Campbell, "Bishop England's Sisterhood," 96.
96. Ibid., 97.
97. Ibid., 97–98.
98. The removal to Montgomery White Sulphur Springs is described in Campbell, "Bishop England's Sisterhood," 107–9; Madden, *Catholics in South Carolina,* 83–84; McKinney, *The Civil War in Greenbrier County, West Virginia,* 135–36; Bodell, *Montgomery White Sulphur Springs,* 28–36.
99. McKinney, *Civil War,* 136, 266.
100. PNL to Gen. P. G. T. Beauregard (draft), September 15, 1862, CDA, 27S7; Hugh Lynch to PNL, October 14, 1862, CDA, 14N4; Hugh Lynch to PNL, November 18, 1862, CDA, 14N7; Francis Lynch to PNL, April 9, 1863, CDA, 14T1; Copeland, "Lynch Family," 2.

Chapter 6: Rome Mission

1. Substantial portions of this chapter were published as Heisser, "Bishop Lynch's Civil War Pamphlet on Slavery." The author has relied significantly on Schmidt, *Patrick N. Lynch,* and on the complete unpublished text of the dissertation (hereafter Schmidt, "Patrick N. Lynch" [unpublished]). The author is indebted to Monsignor Liam Bergin, Rector of the Irish College, Rome, and to the Secretariat of the Pontifical Gregorian University for making this text available to him.
2. On Confederate diplomacy generally see Owsley, *King Cotton Diplomacy*; Hyman, ed., *Heard Round the World;* Hubbard, *Burden;* Crook, *North, South.*

3. On the Holy See in the diplomacy of the Civil War see Alvarez, "Papacy," 227–48; Stock, "United States at the Court of Pius IX," 103–22; Stock, "Catholic Participation," 1–18; Stock, *United States Ministers;* Hastings, "United States-Vatican Relations," 24–55, esp. 26–28; Feiertag, *American Public Opinion.*
4. Franco, *Parallel Empires,* 28–30. The United States did not name any representatives with the title of ambassador before 1893, when ambassadors were accredited to France, Germany, Italy, and the Court of St. James's: Mayer, *The Diplomats,* 33–34.
5. Hughes's European mission is discussed in Alvarez, "Papacy," 231–33; Andrews, "Archbishop Hughes, 6–10.
6. Andrews, 10.
7. Lalli and O'Connor, "Roman Views, 25–35.
8. De Rosa, *La Civiltà Cattolica,* 29–31.
9. Lalli and O'Connor, "Roman Views," 25–35.
10. William J. Silliman to Seward, September 16, 1862, in Stock, *Consular Relations,* 252–53; Alvarez, "Papacy," 237.
11. Pope Pius IX to Hughes, October 18, 1862, in *Official Records of the Union and Confederate Navies in the War of Rebellion* (hereafter *O.R.N.*), ser. II, 3:559–60; *New York Times,* August 3, 1863, 6, "War Items"; Spalding, *Spalding,* 143, note 82; Feiertag, *American Public Opinion,* 112–14; "Some Civil War Documents," 264–66.
12. Patrick N. Lynch, *Pastoral Prayers for Peace* [printed], November 26, 1863, CDA, 29Y7.
13. Craven, *Prison Life of Jefferson Davis,* 290.
14. Spalding, *Spalding,* 145.
15. Owsley, *King Cotton Diplomacy,* 497.
16. On the agents generally see Ryan, "Confederate Agents in Ireland," 51 ff.
17. Ibid.; Faherty, *Exile in Erin,* esp. 130–37; Faherty, *The Fourth Career of John B. Bannon,* esp. 71–78; Tucker, *The Confederacy's Fighting Chaplain,* chs. 8 and 9. Regarding Tucker's account see important corrections in Jeremiah Hackett, review of *The Confederacy's Fighting Chaplain* in *SCHM* 95, no. 3 (1994): 267–72.
18. Tucker, *Confederacy's Fighting Chaplain,* 161; Owsley, *King Cotton Diplomacy,* 500–01; Faherty, *Exile in Erin,* 132; Hackett, "Review of *Confederacy's Fighting Chaplain,*" 271; Benjamin to Mann, September 23, 1863; Davis to Mann, September 4, 1864; both in Richardson, *Messages and Papers of the Confederacy,* 2: 570.
19. Davis to Pius IX, September 3, 1863, in Richardson, *Messages and Papers of the Confederacy,* 2:571; "Some Civil War Documents," 268–69.
20. Mann to Benjamin, November 14, 1863 (received at Richmond December 22, 1863), in Richardson, *Messages and Papers of the Confederacy,* 2:591–95.
21. Pius IX to Davis, December 3, 1863, in ibid., 2:603–4.
22. Mann to Benjamin, December 9, 1863, in ibid., 2:602. The texts of letters exchanged by Davis and the pope were printed in translation in the *Charleston Daily Courier,* January 25, 1864, 1.
23. Alvarez, "Papacy," 242–43; Ryan, "Confederate Agents," 73–74.
24. Benjamin to Mann, February 1, 1864, in Richardson, *Messages and Papers of the Confederacy,* 2:622–23.

25. King to Seward, March 19, 1864, in Stock, *United States Ministers,* 288–89; Stock, "United States at the Court of Pius IX," 118–19; Alvarez, "Papacy," 243.
26. Mann to Davis, February 2, 1864, in Baylen and White, eds., "A. Dudley Mann's Mission in Europe," 326–28.
27. Mann to Davis, October 13, 1883 in Moore, ed., *"My Ever Dearest Friend,"* 84–86.
28. Essig and Moore, "U.S.-Holy See Diplomacy," 743.
29. Patrick N. Lynch, Memorandum on Roman Mission, July 13, 1864, CDA, Lynch Collection, box "CSA-Vatican" (hereafter Lynch, Memorandum on Roman Mission).
30. Barnabò's life and career are discussed in "Barnabò (Alessandro)," 858; *Histoire universelle des missions catholiques,* 3:84–85; Metzler, "Präfekten und Sekretäre der Kongregation im Zeitalter der neueren Missionsäre," 3:1, 40–48. Barnabò headed the Propaganda from 1856 until his death, in 1874.
31. Lynch, Memorandum on Roman Mission; PNL to Benjamin, March 3, 1864, in "Reports of Bishop Lynch of Charleston, South Carolina, Commissioner of the Confederate States to the Holy See," 248.
32. Ibid.
33. Ibid.
34. On Benjamin's boyhood in Charleston see Evans, *Judah P. Benjamin,* 4–22.
35. Verot to PNL, March 22, 1864, CDA, 30N2; PNL to Benjamin, March 25, 1864, in "Reports of Bishop Lynch," 249–50.
36. PNL to Benjamin, March 25, 1864, in "Reports of Bishop Lynch," 249.
37. Verot to PNL, March 22, 1864, CDA, 30N2.
38. PNL to William H. Seward, June 24, 1865, NARA, RG 94, Records of the Adjutant General's Office, Amnesty Files, no. 1476.
39. Timothy J. Sullivan to PNL, March 22, 1864, CDA, 30N1; Madden, "Catholics of South Carolina" (unpublished), ms. #1, vol. 6, ch. 10, 82–83.
40. PNL to "Rev. Dear Sir," March 1864, CDA, 30R4 (manuscript in Lynch's hand).
41. Leon Fillion to PNL (in French), April 6, 1964, CDA, 30T4.
42. PNL to John Moore (hereafter JM), April 10, 1864, Archives of the Diocese of St. Augustine (hereafter ADStA), 2A13; Madden, *Catholics in South Carolina,* 91.
43. Jefferson Davis, commission to Patrick N. Lynch, March 4, 1864, original document, CDA; text in Madden, "Catholics of South Carolina" (unpublished), ms. #1, vol. 6, ch. 10, 85–86.
44. Benjamin to PNL, April 4, 1864, in Richardson, *Messages and Papers of the Confederacy,* 2:470–73; Confederate States of America (Pickett) Papers (hereafter Pickett Papers), Library of Congress, vol. 17, reel 10.
45. List of Papers Delivered with These Instructions, Miscellaneous Agents File, Pickett Papers, Box 60, reel 33; copy of Benjamin's letter of introduction to Cardinal Antonelli, April 4, 1864, CDA, Lynch Collection, box "CSA-Vatican Documents."
46. Benjamin to PNL, April 4, 1864, Pickett Papers, vol. 17, reel 10.
47. Benjamin, two letters of credit for Bishop Lynch to Fraser, Trenholm and Company, April 4, 1864; Benjamin to PNL, April 4, 1864; both in Pickett Papers, vol. 17, reel 10. On Fraser, Trenholm's role in supporting Confederate commissioners in Europe see Nepveux, *George Alfred Trenholm,* 24–30.

48. After the war Lynch had £1,000 on deposit: Fraser, Trenholm and Company to PNL, August 18, 1865, CDA, 32S7.
49. Benjamin to Hotze, April 4, 1864, Pickett Papers, vol. 17, reel 10.
50. Gen. P. G. T. Beauregard to PNL, March 30, 1864, CDA, 30P7.
51. Bassham, *Conrad Wise Chapman,* esp. 160 ff. Chapman's magnificent oil paintings of fortifications are in museums including the Museum of the Confederacy, The Valentine Richmond Museum, the Chicago Historical Society and the Gibbes Museum, Charleston.
52. "Monsignore D. J. Quigley," *News and Courier,* November 28, 1903, 8.
53. PNL to Benjamin, March 25, 1864 (draft in Lynch's hand), CDA, 30N5; "Reports of Bishop Lynch," 249–50; LC, Pickett Papers, vol. 4, reel 4.
54. S. R. Mallory to PNL, March 31, 1864, CDA, 30R2.
55. Maj. Gen. Whiting, permit to sail from Wilmington, April 9, 1864, CD, 30T5; Schmidt, "Patrick N. Lynch" (unpublished), 66–69; Madden, "Catholics of South Carolina" (unpublished), ms. #1, vol. 6, ch. 10, 87; Chapman to "My dear comrade" (probably John S. Wise), March 3, 1910, copy in Valentine Museum Richmond (original in Museum of the Confederacy); Price, "Ships That Tested the Blockade," 35.
56. PNL to Baptista Lynch, April 15, 1864 in Wight, ed., "Some Wartime Letters of Bishop Lynch," 32–33; John Tracy Bourne to B. W. Hart, Esq, April 16, 1864, in Vandiver, ed., *Confederate Blockade Running through Bermuda.* 60. Bourne, a Bermudian, was a Confederate commercial agent in St. George's.
57. Bassham, *Conrad Wise Chapman,* 169–70. Some of the sketches done aboard all three ships are reproduced on pp. 170–71. No portrait of Bishop Lynch by Chapman has been found.
58. PNL to Baptista, April 15, 1864, in Wight, ed., "Some Wartime Letters of Bishop Lynch," 32.
59. Robert A. Lynch to Yates Snowden, December 28, 1916, South Caroliniana Library, John Bannon Papers; PNL to Mother Baptista, April 16, 1864, in Wight, ed., "Some Wartime Letters of Bishop Lynch," 35. Robert Lynch later moved to Massachusetts, made a career in law, and became a leading and respected Catholic layman: "Robert A. Lynch Dies at Hospital," *Malden [Mass.] Evening News,* November 1, 1928, 1. Writing in old age, Robert mistakenly remembered that he had encountered his uncle on St. Croix in the Danish West Indies.
60. PNL to Benjamin, June 20, 1864, in "Reports of Bishop Lynch," 250–51; "Bishop Lynch's Arrival in Halifax, Nova Scotia," *Charleston Mercury,* May 18, 1864, 2; "Bishop Lynch's Arrival in Halifax, Nova Scotia," *Charleston Daily Courier,* May 19, 1864, 1. Both newspaper accounts were based on an article in the Halifax *Reporter* of April 28.
61. PNL to Conseil de la Société de la Propagation de la Foi, Paris, May 7, 1864, AUND, MPFL, reel 10, doc. 2134.
62. The portrait is preserved at the Valentine Museum, Richmond, Va. Quigley's portrait is accession no. 59–107.18. Quigley was later to be a monsignor and vicar general of the diocese.
63. "The Roman Catholic Church," *Impartial Reporter* (Enniskillen, Ireland), May 26, 1864.

64. PNL to Benjamin, June 20, 1864, in "Reports of Bishop Lynch," 251–54; Quigley to PNL, May 13, 1864, CDA, 30Y4; Cullen to PNL, May 16, 1864, CDA, 30Y6; Bishop William Delaney of Cork to PNL, CDA, 31C7; Robert Lynch to Bannon, May 19, 1864, CDA, 31A2; Robert Lynch to Yates Snowden, December 28, 1916, South Caroliniana Library, Bannon Papers; PNL's Notes from the Lynch Family Register, Rosslea, Ireland, May 18, 1864, CDA, 31A1; Bannon to Benjamin, April 9, 1864, and May 28, 1864, in Pickett Papers, vol. 61, reel 33; Hotze to Benjamin, June 10, 1864, in *O.R.N.*, ser. II, 3:1146–1147; Meehan, "Confederate Agents in Ireland," 60 ff., 84–85.
65. Lynch to Benjamin, June 20, 1864, in "Reports of Bishop Lynch," 254; Hotze to Benjamin, May 28, 1864, Pickett Papers, vol. 54, reel 29.
66. PNL to Benjamin, June 10, 1864, in "Reports of Bishop Lynch," 254–56. Cf. Owsley, *King Cotton Diplomacy*, esp. 337 ff.
67. Case and Spencer, *The United States and France: Civil War Diplomacy*, 347–53, 600, and *passim.*
68. PNL to Benjamin, June 10, 1864, in "Reports of Bishop Lynch," 257–59; Slidell to Benjamin, June 20, 1864, in *O.R.N.*, ser. II, 3:1162; Slidell to Benjamin, June 20, 1864, Pickett Papers, vol. 552, reel 30; Slidell to Benjamin, June 30, 1864, in Richardson, *Messages and Papers of the Confederacy*, 2:659. Although Lynch reported that Chigi was writing to Cardinal Antonelli to apprise him of his imminent arrival in Rome, no mention of this appears in the nuncio's official report to the Vatican: Schmidt, "Patrick N. Lynch" (unpublished), 77, note 44. On Edwin De Leon see Rosen, *Jewish Confederates*, 155–58; "De Leon, Edwin," in Wakelyn, *Biographical Dictionary*, 169. On Chigi see Lipari, "Chigi, Flavio," 24:751–54.
69. Bermingham to Barnabò, March 18, 1864, Archives of the Propaganda Fide (hereafter APF), Scritt. rif., America Centrale, vol. 20, fols. 731r–732r; Bermingham to Barnabò, March 20, 1864, in ibid., fols. 733r–734r; Barnabò to Conseil de la Société de la Propagation de la Foi, Paris, July 9, 1862, AUND, MPFR, reel 10, doc. 2131; PNL to Conseil de la Société de la Propagation de la Foi, Paris, August 10, 1863, AUND, MPRF, reel 10, doc. 2139.
70. DJQ to PNL, July 21, 1864, CDA, 31E8; Schmidt, "Patrick N. Lynch" (unpublished), 81–82; Rev. S. Cuttoli, Chancellor of the Archdiocese of Paris, to PNL, June 16, 1864, CDA, 31C5.
71. William W. McCl.oskey to PNL, May 31, 1864, CDA, 31B1; McCloskey to PNL, July 1, 1864, CDA, 31D6; CBN Jr. to HPN, July 1, 1864, CDA, 31D4; McCloskey to Archbishop J. B. Purcell, July 16, 1864, AUND, CACI, II-5-b; Schmidt, "Patrick N. Lynch" (unpublished), 17–18.
72. W. G. Meriwether to PNL, May 24, 1863, CDA, 29A7; McNamara, *The American College in Rome*, 128–29.
73. There is some confusion in the sources as to whether this was no. 8 or no. 18 Via Condotti, to the southwest of the Piazza di Spagna. Dr. Paul Schmidt concluded that no. 18 was more likely and indeed that building seems most appropriate today: Schmidt, *Patrick N. Lynch*, 18; William McCloskey to PNL, July 1, 1864, CDA, 31D6; PNL to Fraser, Trenholm and Company, August 26, 1864 (copy in Lynch's hand), CDA, 31H6; Rufus King to William H. Seward, June 26, 1865, in Stock, *United States Ministers*, 344.

74. PNL to Benjamin, July 5, 1864 (copy in Lynch's hand), CDA, Patrick N. Lynch Collection, box "CSA-Vatican Documents" (hereafter PNL to Benjamin, July 5, 1864). This document may not have reached the Confederate government. No copy is found in the Pickett Papers. On this see Schmidt, "*Patrick N. Lynch,*" 20.
75. PNL to Benjamin, July 5, 1864.
76. Ibid.
77. Ibid.
78. Ibid.
79. Coppa, *Cardinal Giacomo Antonelli,* 125 ff.
80. PNL to Benjamin, July 5, 1864; Robert A. Lynch to Yates Snowden, December 28, 1916.
81. PNL to Benjamin, July 5, 1864; King to Seward, June 22, 1864, in Stock, *United States Ministers,* 307; *L'Unità Cattolica* (Turin), July 20, 1865, 955; scripture verses from the Douay Bible; Schmidt, *Patrick N. Lynch,* 21.
82. PNL to Benjamin, July 5, 1864.
83. Robert A. Lynch to Yates Snowden, December 28, 1916; Schmidt, *Patrick N. Lynch,* 23.
84. PNL to Isaac Hecker, December 21, 1879, Hecker Papers, Paulist Fathers Archives. This was written in response to Hecker's inquiry: Isaac Hecker to PNL, December 1879, CDA, 69N8.
85. PNL to John McCloskey (hereafter JMcC), July 1, 1865, Archives of the Archdiocese of New York (hereafter AANY), A-31.
86. Odo Russell to Earl Russell, British Foreign Secretary, July 30, 1864, in Blakiston, ed., *The Roman Question,* 288.
87. Schmidt, *Patrick N. Lynch,* 24–25.
88. King to Seward, July 30, 1864, and August 16, 1864, in Stock, *United States Ministers,* 313–14; Alvarez, "Papacy," 244–47.

Chapter 7: Slavery Treatise

1. PNL to Benjamin, July 5, 1864; Bermingham, Diary of a Trip to Europe and Palestine, 1861 (manuscript). This chapter is based in large part on the author's earlier article: Heisser, "Lynch's Pamphlet," It also relies on Schmidt, *Patrick N. Lynch.*
2. May, ed., *Union, Confederacy, and Atlantic Rim,* 17; Cullop, *Confederate Propaganda,* 56 ff., 70–83; Pinckney, "France and the Civil War," 100; De Leon, *Thirty Years,* 2:47, 62, 68–69; De Leon, *La Vérité,* esp. 23–27; Owsley, *King Cotton Diplomacy,* 155, 160–68; Gavronsky, *French Liberal Opposition,* 73–75.
3. Hudson, *Der Zweite Unabhängigskeits-Krieg in Amerika;* Hudson, *Second War of Independence,* title page., v–x, 140–42; communication from Prof. Dr. Michael Löffler, Humboldt-Universität Berlin, February 25, 1996.
4. Ibid; Williams, *The South Vindicated,* 36; Williams, *Die Rechtfertigung,* iv–vi; Owsley, *King Cotton Diplomacy,* 158–61; Cullop, *Confederate Propaganda,* 117–23.
5. Lalli and O'Connor, "Roman Views," 25–35.
6. Hubbard, *Burden of Confederate Diplomacy,* 171; Crook, *The North and the South,* 356–57.

7. Hubbard, *Burden of Confederate Diplomacy*, 165–66.
8. Mansi to PNL, August 13, 1864, CDA, 31H1; Mansi to PNL, August 26, 1864, CDA, 31H6; Mansi to PNL, September 17, 1864, CDA, 31K6; Mansi to PNL, December 9, 1864, 31T6; Schmidt, *Patrick N. Lynch*, 25; Lynch, *Lettera di un missionario*.
9. Copy in Vatican Library, call no. Chigiana opuscoli CXCV 19. Author's translation of Italian inscription.
10. De Leon to PNL, August 1, 1864, CDA, 31G5; Wight, "Lynch, Confederate Propagandist," 10–11.
11. On De Leon's contretemps with Slidell and dismissal from service see Owsley, *King Cotton Diplomacy*, 164–68. But his continued work for the Confederacy is witnessed by his correspondence with Lynch, now in the Charleston Diocesan Archives.
12. Shadler to Robert Lynch, June 13, 1864, CDA, 31C3. Information about the German edition comes from letters Shadler wrote to Bishop Lynch from Aschaffenburg, Bavaria, December 26, 1864, CDA, 31Y3; December 26, 1864, CDA, 31Y4; December 29, 1864, CDA, 31Y7; and Schmidt, *Patrick N. Lynch*, 34–35. On Shadler see Madden, *Catholics in South Carolina*, 105–6, 139, 141, 148.
13. Princess Wittgenstein to PNL, [undated] 1864, CDA, 31P5 (in French); Princess Wittgenstein, *Almanach de Gotha, 1863*, 206–7.
14. Seton, *Memories of Many Years*, 157–58.
15. King to Seward, October 25 and November 12, 1864, in Stock, *U.S. Ministers*, 321–22.
16. Limberti to PNL, October 4, 1864, CDA, 31R5; Limberti to PNL, November 7, 1864, CDA, 31S2.
17. *L'Unità Cattolica*, November 15, 1864, 1354; W. McCloskey to PNL, November 22, 1864, CDA, 31S7.
18. Cardinal DeLuca to PNL, October 29, 1864, CDA, 31P1; Princess Wittgenstein to Countess von Schlitz, October 29, 1864, CDA, 31P4.
19. Letters from Shadler to PNL cited in note 13. On Moufang see Anton Brück, "Moufang, Christoph"; Götten, *Christoph Moufang, Theologe und Politiker, 1817–1890*, 33–53 and *passim*. On Ketteler see Iserloh, *Wilhelm Emmanuel von Ketteler—sein Kampf für Freiheit und soziale Gerechtigkeit*, *passim*.
20. The author expresses thanks for assistance in obtaining a copy of the German edition to Prof. Dr. Peter Landau and Prof. Dr. Andreas Thier, Leopold-Wenger-Institut für Rechtsgeschichte, Universität München.
21. E. Dentu to PNL, November 1864, CDA, 31T5; communication from Professor Jean-Claude Caron, Université de Besançon, January 6, 1996.
22. Jouaust to (probably) James Hamilton, December 23, 1864, CDA, 31W7; Hamilton to De Leon, December 23, 1864, CDA, 31Y1; Hamilton to PNL, December 26, 1864, CDA, 31Y5; Wight, "Lynch, Confederate Propagandist," 50; Lynch, *Esclavage*, 137–43.
23. Drafts 1, A, and B are in CDA, Lynch Transfer File, folder GG; Draft C is in CDA, folder "Confederate States." For the English-language text see Lynch, "A Few Words on the Domestic Slavery in the Confederate States of America," pt. 1

(hereafter Lynch, "A Few Words," pt. 1); Lynch, "A Few Words on the Domestic Slavery in the Confederate States of America," pt. II, (hereafter Lynch, "A Few Words," pt. 2).

24. Davis, *History of Black Catholics in the United States,* 68–69; Holifield *The Gentlemen Theologians,* 30–31; Tise, *Proslavery,* 124 ff.; Thigpen, "Aristocracy of the Heart," 619 ff.; Madden, *Catholics in South Carolina,* 68–69.
25. Genovese and Fox-Genovese, "The Religious Ideals of Southern Slave Society," 9–10.
26. Rice, *American Catholic Opinion,* 72 ff.; Lofton, "Reverend Doctor James A. Corcoran," 86–97; Davis, *History of Black Catholics,* 58–59. For writings of bishops and other Catholics see Zanca, *American Catholics and Slavery.*
27. Lynch, "A Few Words," pt. 1, 78–82. Cf. John England to John Forsyth, September 28, 1840, in England, *The Works of the Right Rev. John England,* 3:114–16; Brokhage, *Kenrick's Opinion on Slavery,* 123–31.
28. Verot, *Tract for the Times,* 11–12; Gannon, *Rebel Bishop,* 49–50. Bishop McGill thought that failure to respect slaves' marriages brought down God's wrath upon the South: Wimmer, "American Catholic Interpretations of the Civil War," 266.
29. Spalding, ed., "Martin John Spalding's Dissertation," 81; Spalding, *Spalding,* 141. Bishop William Henry Elder of Natchez warned of chaos if the slaves were freed en masse; Misch, "American Bishops" (unpublished) 109–15.
30. Sharrow, "Northern Catholic Intellectuals," 36; Sharrow, "John Hughes and Slavery," 236–52; Andrews, "Archbishop Hughes and the Civil War," 50–52, 62–65; O'Connor, "The Northern Catholic Position," 37.
31. Summaries are in Wight, "Lynch, Confederate Propagandist," 12–14; Schmidt, *Patrick N. Lynch,*" 37 ff.; Wolfe, "The Life and Times of Patrick N. Lynch," 66 ff; Misch, "American Bishops," 109–15.
32. Lynch, *Sclaverei,* 3–4; Lynch, "A Few Words," pt. 1, 70. Cf. Hughes's characterization of slavery as a sickness: Sharrow, "John Hughes and Slavery," 259.
33. Lynch, "A Few Words," pt. 1, 74. Draft 1, 3, has "two in a thousand."
34. Lynch, "A Few Words," pt. 1, 76.
35. Reference is to the funeral of King Gezo, staged in 1860 with much human sacrifice by his son, King Glele: Cornevin, *Histoire du Dahomey,* 126–27.
36. This view had been espoused by Lynch's friend and fellow Charlestonian Wiliam Gilmore Simms and other important Southern writers: Fredrickson, *Black Image in White Mind,* 49–52.
37. On Southern whites' belief in "Negroes'" laziness see Genovese, *Roll, Jordan, Roll,* 295–301. Lynch was no doubt familiar with the biblical verses "Fodder, and a wand, and a burden, are for an ass; bread, and correction, and work for a slave. . . . The yoke and the thong bend a stiff neck, and continual labors bow a slave. . . . For idleness hath taught much evil. Set him to work, for so it is fit for him.": Ecclesiasticus (Sirach) 33:25–30 (Douay Bible). On Charleston blacks' Sabbath finery see Powers, *Black Charlestonians,* 21–22.
38. Lynch, "A Few Words," pt. 1, 89.
39. Ibid., 90–94. On the relatively good food and health enjoyed by American slaves see Kolchin, *American Slavery, 1619–1877,* 113.

40. Lynch, "A Few Words," pt. 1, 95.
41. Ibid., 97–98. Cf. the justification of flogging by Lynch's fellow South Carolinian William Henry Hammond: "Letter to an English Abolitionist."
42. Lynch, "A Few Words," pt. 1, 99–100. On South Carolina's strict laws, see Cornelius, *"When I Can Read My Title Clear,"* esp. ch. 2.
43. Madden, *Catholics in South Carolina,* 26; Terry, "A Study of the Impact of the French Revolution and the Insurrections in Saint-Domingue upon South Carolina, 1790–1805," 174–78. On Southern clerics' concern for slaves' religious instruction see Tise, *Proslavery,* 293–98; Kolchin, *American Slavery,* 128–29.
44. Lynch, "A Few Words," pt. 2, 94–95. Lynch was not alone in disparaging black worship. Cf. Raboteau, *Slave Religion,* 220–22; Myers, ed., *The Children of Pride,* 482–83. Antinomianism: "If good works . . . do not help to salvation, so evil ones do not hinder it and therefore Christians are not bound to observe the law": *New Catholic Dictionary,* 52.
45. This story had appeared in Olmsted, *A Journey in the Seaboard Slave States,* 123–24; discussed in Genovese, *Roll, Jordan, Roll,* 245.
46. Lynch, "A Few Words," pt. 2, 95–96. Cf. Archbishop Hughes's belief that "Catholic leadership was needed to improve the Negroes: Sharrow, "John Hughes," 265.
47. Lynch, "A Few Words," pt. 2, 97. Lynch shared Southern whites' generally low opinion of free blacks: Genovese, *Roll, Jordan, Roll,* 398–400.
48. Lynch, "A Few Words," pt. 2, 97. Cf. Mary Boykin Chesnut's remark, "We live surrounded by prostitutes": C. Vann Woodward, ed., *Mary Chesnut's Civil War,* 29.
49. Lynch, "A Few Words," pt. 2, 97–98. Cf. South Carolina chancellor William Harper's view "that the intercourse which takes place with enslaved females, is less depraving in its effects, than when it is carried on with females of their own caste." "Slavery in the Light of Social Ethics," in Elliott, *Cotton Is King,* 583.
50. Lynch, "A Few Words," pt. 2, 103. Owners usually did promote and respect slave marriages, and slave families were often strong: Gutman, *The Black Family in Slavery and Freedom,* xxii, 14, 17; Kolchin, *American Slavery,* 122–23.
51. Lynch, "A Few Words," pt. 2, 103–4. Cf. Tadman, *Speculators and Slaves,* 121–29.
52. Lynch, "A Few Words," pt. 2,105–6. Cf. Marina Wikramanayake, *A World in Shadow,* 39–43.
53. Lynch, "A Few Words," pt. 2, 106–7. Reference is to the Waikato War of 1863–1864: Belich, *The New Zealand Wars,* 200, 299–300; and remarks of Earl Grey, May 30, 1864, *Parliamentary Debates, Lords,* 3rd ser., vol. 175 (1864), col. 794.
54. Lynch, "A Few Words" pt. 2, 109. This figure represented slightly more than $1.7 billion at the then-current rate of exchange in Paris.
55. Ibid., 109–10.
56. Ibid., 117–20; *Index* (London), August 25, 1864, 538; reports by U.S. Treasury Agent W. H. Wilder to S. W. Cozzens, Superintendent of Plantations, Bureau of Plantations, U.S. Treasury Department, especially reports dated September 17 and 27, 1863, 97–103 and 118–21, in "Reports of Inspectors to the Superintendent of Plantations," NARA, RG 366, item 479. On the system of federally

administered Louisiana plantations see Gerteis, *From Contraband to Freedman,* 65 ff.

57. Lynch, "A Few Words," pt. 2, 120. Reference is to William Aiken (1806–1887), governor of South Carolina and U.S. representative, whose Jehossee Plantation slaves were stricken with cholera in 1853: Waring, *A History of Medicine in South Carolina,* 2:47–48; Clifton, "Jehossee Island," 56–59, 64–65; *Congressional Globe,* 32nd Congress, 2nd sess., 545 (February 10, 1853).

58. Lynch "A Few Words," draft 1, 56. Reference is to the nineteenth-century Haitian monarchies. Cf. Fitzhugh, "Free Negroes in Hayti," 526–49.

59. Lynch, "A Few Words," pt. 2, 117.

60. Martin, *Lettre pastorale,* 6–8; Caravaglios, "A Roman Critique," 67–81; Zanca, *American Catholics and Slavery,* 219–25. Francis Patrick Kenrick and Augustin Verot quoted scripture in defense of Negro servitude: Brokhage, *Kenrick's Opinion on Slavery,* 110–12; Verot, *Tract for the Times,* 5–7. On the Kenner mission see Bauer, *A Leader among Peers.*

61. Congress of the Confederate States, Joint Resolution; Young, *Senator James Murray Mason,* 177–78.

62. Benjamin to Mason [circular], August 25, 1864, in *O.R.N.*, ser. II, 3:1190–94; and in Richardson, *Messages and Papers of the Confederacy,* 2:664–70; Mann to Benjamin, October 15, 1864, in *O.R.N.*, ser II, 3:1223–24; Mason to Benjamin, November 10, 1864, in Richardson, *Messages and Papers of the Confederacy,* 2:678–83; Mann to Benjamin, November 5, 1864, in *O.R.N.*, ser. II, 3:1230; Slidell, Mason, and Mann to Drouyn de Lhys, November 11, 1864, in Richardson, *Messages and Papers of the Confederacy,* 2:685–86; Antonelli to Mann, Mason and Slidell, December 2, 1864, in Richardson, *Messages and Papers of the Confederacy,* 2:690–91; J. T. Soutter to Slidell, December 5, 1864, in Richardson, *Messages and Papers of the Confederacy,* 2:691–92.

63. Lord John Russell to Slidell, Mason, and Mann, November 25, 1864, in Richardson, *Messages and Papers of the Confederacy,* 2:687; Soutter to Antonelli, November 18, 1864, in *O.R.N.*, ser. II, 3:1247; Slidell to Benjamin, November 17, 1864, in *O.R.N.*, ser. II, 3:1241–1243; Soutter to Slidell, December 5, 1864, in Richardson, *Messages and Papers of the Confederacy,* 2:691–92; Young, *Senator James Murray Mason,* 178; Schmidt, *Patrick N. Lynch,* 31–34.

64. Bannon to PNL, November 15, 1864, CDA, 31S6; Tucker, *Confederacy's Fighting Chaplain,* 180–81.

65. Bannon to PNL, January 8, 1865, CDA, 32B4; Bannon to PNL, October 18, 1865, CDA, 33D6; PNL to Bannon, February 8, 1866, South Caroliniana Library, John Bannon Papers.

66. PNL to John G. Chapmen, August 22, 1864, collection of Robert Mayo, Gloucester, Va.; PNL, statement extending C. W. Chapman's furlough, September 3, 1864 (copy), CDA, Patrick N. Lynch collection, box "CSA-Vatican Documents"; Bassham, *Conrad Wise Chapman,* 177–83; C. W. Chapmen to PNL, November 12, 1864, CDA, 31S3. According to Paul Schmidt, Lynch's authorization of Chapman's furlough was probably his only official act as commissioner: Schmidt, *Patrick N. Lynch,* 31.

67. *La Civiiltà Cattolica* (Rome), anno decimoquinto, ser. V, vol. XII (1864), 2127 (author's translation); "The Confederate Cause in France," *Index* (London), February 16, 1865, 105; *Army and Navy Gazette* (London), February 25, 1865, 122; *L'Unità Cattolica* (Turin), December 25, 1864, 1517; Schmidt, *Patrick N. Lynch,* 53; De Leon to PNL, February 28, 1865, CDA, 32E2; Mansi to PNL, December 9 1864, CDA, 31T6; Mansi to PNL, March 26, 1865, CDA, 32G1; "Christenthum und Sklaverei," 195–97.
68. Montalembert, "La Victoire du Nord auxEtats-Unis," 9–10 (author's translation); Lecanuet, *Montalembert,* III:402–3.
69. Cochin to PNL, May 28, 1865, CDA, 32M2 (author's translation).
70. Gannon, *Rebel Bishop,* 87.
71. PNL to Propaganda Fide, December 24, 1863, APF, Scritt. rif., America Centrale, vol. 20, fols. 1192 rv–1193v, AUND, MPRF, reel 66, 468. The author has found no evidence that his letter of resignation reached the Confederate government.
72. PNL to Martin John Spalding, May 1865, AAB, 34U3; Shadler to PNL, June 29, 1865, CDA, 32N5; Hamilton to PNL September 15, 1865, CDA, 33A5; Hamilton to PNL, October 15, 1865, CDA, 33D3.

Chapter 8: War's End and Return Home

1. Edgar, *South Carolina,* 375.
2. O'Connell, *Catholicity,* 274.
3. This account is based on Edgar, *South Carolina,* 372–73; Lucas, *Sherman and the Burning of Columbia,* 78–120; Madden, "Catholics of South Carolina" (unpublished), ms. #1, vol. 6, ch. 10, 95–104.
4. Sherman, *Memoirs,* 2:279–70.
5. "A Truthful Account of the Burning of the Ursuline Convent and Academy (May 1865)" (unsigned manuscript), CDA, 32M4. The author claimed to have been an eyewitness.
6. Woodward, ed., *Mary Chesnut's Civil War,* 744, 750. Cf. statement in a 1966 work: "For a Catholic, William Tecumseh Sherman did something quite amazing. He celebrated the Lenten season in Columbia by having his men burn a Catholic convent": Trindel, *Mary Surratt,* 100.
7. Kennett, *Sherman,* 35; Merrill, *William Tecumseh Sherman,* 21, 62, 369–72.
8. "Annals of Ursuline Convent, Columbia, S.C.," 33–37, 42, 49–50.
9. Sherman, *Memoirs,* 2:287.
10. Mother Baptista Lynch, Statement to Citizen's Committee of Columbia, May 1866, in "Destruction of Property in Columbia, S.C., by Sherman's Army." See also Madden, "Catholics of South Carolina" (unpublished), ms. #1, vol. 6, ch. 10, 98–100; O'Connell, *Catholicity,* 275–76.
11. Baptista Lynch to "most reverend bishop," May 1865, CDA, 32M4.
12. Baptista Lynch to PNL, October 28, 1865, CDA, 15K1; Madden, "Ursuline Convent," 14A; Heisser, "Bishop Lynch's People," 260.
13. Baptista Lynch to Mrs. M. C. Barry, July 14, 1872, CDA, 53D7.
14. Sister M. Ignatia, OSU, to James F. Edwards, July 31, 1887; Mother St. Charles Weid, OSU, to James F. Edwards; both in AUND, CEDW, xi-1–3 3/06.

15. The figure $150,000 is given in Madden, "Ursuline Convent," 14A, and Madden, "Catholics of South Carolina" (unpublished), ms. #1, vol. 6, ch. 10, 103. A claim was later presented to the U.S. government for the sum of $100,000: Madden, "Catholics of South Carolina" (unpublished), ms. #1, vol. 6, ch. 10, 103. A final effort to obtain reparations for both the Ursuline Convent and Academy and the Washington Street Methodist Church was made in 1929 and 1930 by Senator Coleman L. Blease of South Carolina. At that time Blease estimated the Ursulines' losses at $112,538: *Destruction of Property,* 32–33. On the controversy see Lucas, *Sherman and the Burning of Columbia,* 128–62.
16. Davis, *Sherman's March,* 39–41, 192–95; Barrett, *Sherman's March,*100–01; Foster, "When Sherman Passed through Lancaster," 1:344–51.
17. *Historic and Architectural Inventory, Cheraw Historical District,* 15–16.
18. Merrill, *William Tecumseh Sherman,* 284–85; Powers, *Tar Heel Catholics,* 171.
19. Edgar, *South Carolina,* 373–74; Fraser, *Charleston! Charleston!,* 268–72.
20. McNally, "Reconstruction," 150–51. This section is based on primary sources, Father McNally's article, and Brother Thomas Spalding's biography of Martin John Spalding.
21. John Moore (hereafter JM) to Martin John Spalding (hereafter MJS), February 21, 1865, AAB, 35J1; *Daily Courier,* February 22, 1865, 2; John Prime to MJS, October 1 and October 2, 1864, AAB, 35P5; Spalding, *Spalding,* 163–64; MJS to JAC, May 27, 1865, Spalding Letterbook, 113.
22. JM to MJS, February 23, 1865, AAB, 35J1; same to same, March 30, 1865, AAB, 35J2; same to same, April 21, 1865, AAB, 35J3.
23. John Prime to MJS, October 1 and October 2, 1864, AAB, 35P5; Spalding, *Spalding,* 163–64; MJS to JAC, May 27, 1865, AAB, Spalding Letterbook, I-113.
24. MJS to JM, April 12, 1865, AAB, Spalding Letterbook, I-95; MJS to JM, May 29, 1865, Archives of the Diocese of St. Augustine (hereafter ADStA), 2A15.
25. JAC to MJS, May 22, 1865, AAB, 33M7; MJS to JAC, May 27, 1865, Spalding Letterbook, 113.
26. JM to MJS, April 21, 1865, AAB, 35J3; same to same, May 20, 1865, AAB, 35J5.
27. JM to MJS, May 20, 1865, AAB, 35J5; Madden, *Catholics in South Carolina,* 98; MJS to JM, June 9, 1865, ADStA, 2A16; JM to MJS, June 23, 1865, AAB, 35J7; MJS to JM, June 29, 1865, ADStA, 2A17.
28. JM to MJS, July 12, 1865, AAB, 35J8.
29. JM to MJS, June 23, 1865, AAB, 35J7.
30. JM to MJS, August 26, 1865, AAB, 35J12.
31. Williams, *Shamrocks and Pluff Mud,* 25, 51–52; St. Patrick's Benevolent Society, Minutes May 12, 1857–June 13, 1878, CDA, entry for March 17, 1865.
32. Moore to MJS, September 16, 1865, AAB, 35J13; quoted in part in Madden, "Catholics of South Carolina" (unpublished), ms. #1, vol. 6, ch. 10, 132.
33. MJS to JM, September 2, 1865, ADStA, 2A19.
34. JM to MJS, July 28, 1865, AAB, 35J9. Aiken had received Lynch's letter on June 18: William Aiken to PNL, June 29, 1865, CDA, 32Q7.
35. JM to MJS, July 28, 1865, AAB, 35J9; BL to PNL, September 25, 1865 (typescript copy), and BL to PNL, October 28, 1865 (typescript copy), both in CDA,

Madden Collection, box "Ellen (Baptista) Lynch, Letters to Patrick N. Lynch, 1841–1880)," 258, 262–63. Spalding explained to Moore that the Bishop Lynch who had visited New York City was in fact Bishop John Joseph Lynch of Toronto, Ontario: MJS to JM, August 16, 1865, ADStA, 2A20. Bishop Lynch of Toronto had been born in 1816 in Clones, County Monaghan. Lynch of Toronto raised the question whether the two were related, and despite some doubts they decided that they were cousins: John Joseph Lynch to PNL, April 6, 1867, CDA, 39T5; same to PNL, November 23, 1868, CDA, 45P5; same to PNL, December 5, 1881, CDA, 74A3.

36. PNL to JM, August 21, 1865, ADStA, 2A18.
37. Ibid.; PNL to Harry P. Northrop, August 15, 1865, CDA, 32S4. Charles Croghan and the Sisters of Our Lady of Mercy in fact returned to Charleston from Montgomery White Sulphur Springs on July 9, following a difficult odyssey via New York City: JM to MJS, July 12, 1865, AAB, 35J8; Campbell, "Bishop England's Sisterhood," 154–55.
38. MJS to JM, September 2, 1865, ADStA, 2A19; same to same, October 2, 1865, ADStA, 2A21.
39. J. J. O'Connell to MJS, October 20, 1865, AAB, 39B-G14.
40. "Distribution of the Fund Collected in the Archdiocese of Baltimore," AAB, 39B-G1; JM to MJS, October 14, 1865, AAB, 39B-G11; J. J. O'Connell to MJS, October 20, 1865, AAB, 39B-G14; JAC to MJS, February 19, 1866, 39B-G8.
41. On the fall of Wilmington and its significance see Barrett, *Civil War in North Carolina,* 284.
42. JAC to MJS, May 22, 1865, AAB, 33M7.
43. Heuser, "Monsignor Corcoran," 334.
44. King to Seward, March 11, 1865, in Stock, *U.S. Ministers,* 332.
45. King to Seward, March 4, 1865, in ibid., 336.
46. King to Seward, March 4, 1865, in ibid., 331.
47. William McCloskey to Bishop Francis Patrick McFarland of Hartford, May 5, 1865, UNDA, CHAR, I-1-b. In fact, Conlaw Peter Lynch lived until 1870.
48. PNL to Spalding, May (20?), 1865, AAB, 34U3.
49. David T. Gleeson, "'No Disruption of Union,'" 174–75.
50. PNL to Archbishop John McCloskey (hereafter JMcC), May 20, 1865, AANY, A-22.
51. William McCloskey to JMcC, May 20, 19865, AANY, A-31.
52. King to Seward, June 26, 1865, in Stock, *U.S. Ministers,* 344; PNL to John Moore, August 21, 1865, ADStA, 2A18; Fraser, Trenholm and Company, to PNL, August 18, 1865, CDA, 32T2.
53. MJS to PNL, June 27, 1865, AAB, Spalding Letterbook, 514.
54. The efforts of Spalding and the other American hierarchy are discussed in Spalding, *Spalding,* 167–71; Schmidt, "Patrick N. Lynch" (unpublished), 148–78; Madden, "Catholics of South Carolina" (unpublished), ms. #1, vol. 6, ch. 10, 109–35. The present author has greatly benefited from the work of these researchers.
55. JM to PNL, April 28, 1865, CDA, 32K2. Lynch received this missive, but it is unclear on what date. Moore's statement about the bishop's communication from

Halifax is confirmed by Baptista: Baptista to PNL, July 17, 1865 (typescript copy), CDA, Madden Collection, "Ellen (Baptista) Lynch, Letters to Patrick N. Lynch, 1841–1880," box 1.

56. JMcC to MJS, May 21, 1865, AAB, 35E3.
57. James F. Wood to MJS, June 8, 1865, AAB, 36S19.
58. MJS to James Speed, June 8, 1865, AAB, Spalding Letterbook, A-122; MJS to R. J. A. Walter, June 8, 1865, AAB, Spalding Letterbook, 124; Walter to MJS, June 9, 1865, AAB, 36K5.
59. MJS to Maj. Gen Quincy A. Gilmore, June 8, 1865, AAB, Spalding Letter Press Book, A-114.
60. Schmidt, "Patrick N. Lynch" (unpublished), 161; MJS to Seward, June 13, 1865, AAB, Spalding Letter Book, A-128; original, NARA, RG94 Records of the Adjutant General's Office, 1780s-1914, Amnesty Files, no. 1476, Patrick N. Lynch (hereafter Lynch Amnesty File; Timon to Seward, June 10, 1865, in Lynch Amnesty File; MJS to JMcC, June 15, 1865, AAB, Spalding Letter Book, A-130; original in AAN Y, A-32.
61. MJS to J. B. Purcell, June 221, 1865, UNDA, CACI, II-5-c; J. B. Purcell to MJS, June 23, 1865, AAB, 35R14; "Philadelphia Correspondence," 212; Fortin, *Faith and Action,* 140–44; Joseph, "'Long Live the Republic!,'" 26–27, 34–39.
62. Spalding, *Spalding,* 171; MJS to JMcC, August 30, 1865, AAB Spalding Letter Press Book, I-154.
63. Walter to MJS, June 26, 1865, AAB, 36K7; W. McCloskey to JMcC, May 20, 1865, AANY, A-31; U.S. President, Proclamation, May 29, 1865, in *Compilation of Messages and Papers of the Presidents,* 1:33508–510; King to Seward, June 24, 1865, in Stock, *U.S. Ministers,* 342–43; W. J. Stillman, *Autobiography*, 1:308. Stillman was U.S. consul in Rome in 1865.
64. King to William Hunter (Seward's secretary), June 2, 1865; King to Seward, June 24, 1865; both in Stock, *U.S. Minister,* 341–43.
65. PNL to Seward, June 24, 1865, NARA, Lynch Amnesty File; copy sent to Spalding in AAB, 34U4; Gleeson, "'No Disruption of Union,'" 174–75.
66. Spalding, "Martin John Spalding," in Fogarty, ed., *Patterns of Episcopal Leadership*, 110.
67. Timon to MJS, June 28, 1865, AAB, 36F11; Wood to Monsignor Tobias Kirby, July 17, 1865, Irish College, Rome, Letters of Tobias Kirby, vol. III, 159; MJS to Timon, July 21, 1865, AAB, Spalding Letter Book, I-141; MJS to Walter, July 21, 1865, Spalding Letterbook, I-124; Spalding, *Spalding*, 169–70; Zanca, "Civil War Era Catholic Press," 5–11; Trindel, *Mary Surratt,* 173, 206–8, 215–21.
68. PNL to JMcC, May 20, 1865, AANY, A-22; same to same, August 21, 1865, AANY, A-22; PNL to B. F. Perry, August 8, 1865 (copy), CDA, 32Q11; PNL to W. W. Boyce, August 11, 1865 (copy), CDA, 32Q13; PNL to MJS, October 7, 1865, AAB, 34U7; PNL to JM, August 21, 1865, ADStA, 2A18; Baptista Lynch to PNL, July 17, 1865 (typescript copy), CDA, Richard C. Madden Papers; Edgar, *South Carolina,* 383.
69. PNL to JMcC, July 1, 1865, AANY, A-31; and copy in Hogan Papers, Archives of the Josephite Fathers. Robert Meade had been captured and imprisoned in

South Carolina. General Meade's family had contacted Bishop Lynch during the war, seeking his solicitation about the young man's welfare. Robert was freed in a prisoner exchange in October 1864: General Meade to Mrs. George C. Meade, October 19, 1864, in Meade, *Life and Letters*, 2:235. It is not certain whether Lynch actually contacted the Meade family. Monsignor (later Archbishop) Kirby (1803–1895) was rector of the Irish College.

70. MJS to PNL, June 27, 1865, AAB, Spalding Letter Book, I-514; JMcC to PNL, June 19, 1865, CDA, 32Q4; same to same, July 18, 1865, CDA, 32Q10; Schmidt, "Patrick N. Lynch" (unpublished), 172; Van Deusen, *Thurlow Weed*, 319–25; Field, "Weed, Thurlow," 882–83.

71. MJS to Andrew Johnson, July 31, 1865, AAB, Spalding Letter Press Book, I-146.; Spalding, "Martin John Spalding,."110.

72. MJS to PNL, June 27, 1865, AAB, Spalding Letter Press Book, I-514; "The Diary of Bishop Verot, Third Bishop of Savannah and Administrator and Bishop of St. Augustine (1858–1876)"; Verot to PNL, August 10, 1865, CDA, 32S1; and copy in Wight, ed., "Letters of the Bishop of Savannah," 106.

73. Augustin Cochin, *L'Abolition de l'esclavage*. A translation of vol. 2 was published as *The Results of Slavery* (Boston: Walker, Wise, 1863. On Cochin: Prevost, "Cochin (Famille)" and "Cochin, Pierre-Suzanne, dit *Augustin*," vol. 9, cols. 75–76.

74. Cochin to PNL, May 28, 1865, CDA, 32M2; Gavronsky, *French Liberal Opposition*, 73–75.

75. JMcC to PNL, June 19, 1865, CDA, 32Q4; Cochin to Bigelow, September 2, 865; Bigelow to Cochin, September 5, 1865, and Bigelow to Seward, September 5, 1865 (English translations by U.S. Foreign Service), all in U.S. Department of State, *Dispatches from United Sates Ministers to France, 1789–1906*, NARA, microfilm M34, reel 61 ; Cochin to PNL, September 7, 1865, CDA, 32Y3.

76. MJS to Barnabò, August 11, 1865, APF, Scrit. rif., America Centrale, vol. 20, fols. 1545r–1546, UNDA, MPRF, III, 604; MJS to Archbishop Odin, August 11, 1865, UNDA, CANO, vi-2-j-3.

77. Joseph R. Chandler to Tobias Kirby, August 17, 1865, Archives of the Irish College, Rome, Tobias Kirby's letters, 181. The author is indebted to Monsignor Liam Bergin, rector of the Irish College, for making these resources available to him.

78. Andrew Johnson, pardon of Patrick N. Lynch, August 4, 1865, original document, CDA, 32R4; W. A. Browning to MJS, August 7, 1865, CDA, 32R5; PNL to MJS, October 7, 1865, AAB, 34U7; Schmidt, "Patrick N. Lynch" (unpublished), 176.

79. APF, Udienze del Emo. Prefetto, August 24, 1865, vol. 151 (anno 1865), fol. 17887; and August 24, 1865, ibid., fols. 1757r–1758rv; Propaganda to PNL, August 26, 1865, CDA, 32T4.

80. PNL to Lyons Council, Society of the Propagation of the Faith, October 10, 1865, UNDA, MPFL, reel 10; PNL to MJS, October 7, 1865, AAB, 34U7; PNL to Barnabò, October 19, 1865, APF, Scrit. Rif., America Centrale, vol. 20, fols. 1645rv, UNDA, MPFR, III, 637. Lynch's original signed loyalty oath, October 14, 1865, CDA, 33D1.

81. PNL to Bannon, February 8, 1866, South Caroliniana Library, Bannon Papers; quoted in Madden, *Catholics in South Carolina,* 373, note 28.
82. PNL to JMcC, January 12, 1866, AANY, A-34; PNL to Barnabò, May 4, 1866, APF, Scritt. rif., America Centrale, vol. 20, fol. 1704, UNDA, MPRF, VIII, 83; "Bishop Lynch of Charleston," *New York Freeman's Journal and Catholic Reporter,* November 18, 1865, 5; "Bishop Lynch's Sermon," ibid., November 25, 1865, 1; "Rt. Rev. Bishop P. N. Lynch," *Charleston Daily Courier,* December 5, 1865, 2. The author has not found sources to confirm that Lynch saw President Davis at this time. He did visit Davis at Fortress Monroe in 1866.
83. *New York Daily Tribune,* March 3, 1866, 6; PNL to Horace Greeley (partial copy in Lynch's hand), March 3, 1866, CDA, 34W3; "A Card from Bishop Lynch of Charleston," *New York Freeman's Journal and Catholic Register,* March 24, 1866, 8; PNL to Isaac Hecker, December 21, 1879, Hecker Papers, Paulist Fathers Archives; copy in CDA, 69M6; Gurn, "Bishop Lynch's Vindication," 18–19, 40.
84. PNL to John Bannon, February 8, 1866, South Caroliniana Library, Bannon Papers. "Endless money forms the sinews of war": Cicero, *Philippics V,* 2:5.
85. PNL to Bishop Elder, January 10, 1865 [1866], Archives of the Diocese of Jackson, file "Elder-L."
86. PNL to JMcC, January 12, 1866, NYAA, A-34; quoted in Madden, *Catholics in South Carolina,* 101.
87. Edgar, *South Carolina,* 396–97; Fraser, *Charleston! Charleston!,* 275. Examples of appeals to the bishop: John Quinlan to PNL, December 20, 1867, CDA, 416; Mrs. C. A. Sabel to PNL, January 4, 1868, CDA, 42B2; Mrs. G. M. Lelane to PNL, January 5, 1868, CDA, 42B5; Mrs. Mary Callahan to PNL, February 19, 1866, CDA, 34S1; Mrs. Mary Fleming to PNL, May 15, 1867, CDA, 40H2; Agnes Walsh to PNL, February 17, 1867, CDA, 39D7; Hugh Greelish to PNL, April 24, 1868, CDA, 43E7; L. H. Glover to PNL, January 2, 1866, CDA, 33W2;Mrs. S. J. Magwood to PNL, May 18, 1867, CDA, 40K3; Sarah Miles to PNL, February 13, 1867, CDA, 39C7.
88. Frederick Fanning to PNL, May 17, 1867, CDA, 40K3; Rev. James Hasson to PNL, August 2, 1866, CDA, 36R6; Lowman, "James Andrew Corcoran," 60–264; JAC to PNL, June 21, 1868, CDA, 44B5.
89. Catherine Agnes Doyle to PNL, January 10, 1866, CDA, 33Y6; same to same, January 12, 1866, CDA, 34A2.
90. J. A. Davis to PNL, April 9, 1866, CDA, 35D1.
91. Edward Lonergan, May 6, 1866, CDA, 35P3; Edward Lonergan et al. to PNL, July 23, 1866, CDA, 36P2. Other requests came from New Bern, N.C. (S. F. Stanley to PNL, February 8, 1866, CDA, 34M3); and Barnwell, S.C. (Mary Ryan to PNL, February 10, 1866, CDA, 34N4).
92. Sister Mary Joseph, O.L.M., to PNL, December 28, 1865, CDA, 33S5.
93. MJS to PNL, January 25, 1866, CDA, 34E2.
94. For an excellent summary of their needs see Gleeson, "'No Disruption of Union,'" 172–74.
95. PNL to Conseil Central de la Société de la Propagation de la Foi, Lyon, September 7, 1865 (copy), CDA, 32W2; PNL to George Schwarz, Leopoldinen-Stiftung,

Vienna (copy), September 1865, CDA, 33C3; Madden, "Catholics of South Carolina" (unpublished), ms. #1, 80. Here Madden refers to the Austrian as Charles G. Schwatz.

96. Between 1828 and 1922 Charleston received a total of $220,360, placing it behind Galveston and Indianapolis (Vincennes) in receipts from the French missionary society: Hickey, *The Society of the Propagation of the Faith,* 188–89; Roemer, *Ten Decades of Alms,* 247.
97. Blied, *Austrian Aid to American Catholics,* 26–27; Georges Schwarz to PPNL, October 14, 1865, CDA, 33D2.
98. Roemer, *The Ludwig-Missionsverein,* 104.
99. List of contributions of Union prisoners of war, June 25, 1866, CDA, 36D4.
100. Mrs. Algernon Sydney Sullivan to PNL, January 20, 1867, CDA, 38Y7; same to same, February 22, 1867, CDA, 39G4; same to same, March 1, 1867, CDA, 39K2; same to same, March 9, 1867, CDA, 39M6; same to same, March 22, 1867, CDA. 39R7; same to same, March 30, 1867, CDA, 39S3; same to same, April 5, 1867, CDA, 39T1; Rosine della Torre to PNL, April 9, 1867, CDA, 29W1; Algernon Sydney Sullivan Foundation, *Algernon Sydney Sullivan,* 20–29 and *passim.*
101. Andrew Parker to PNL, April 6, 1867, CDA, 39T3; same to same, April 13, 1867, CDA, 39W5.

Chapter 9: Baltimore Second Plenary

1. Valuable for study of the Second Plenary are Guilday, *Councils of Baltimore;* Spalding, *Spalding,* especially ch. 7; Hennesey, "Baltimore Council"; Hennesey, *American Catholics;* Misch, "American Bishops"; Misch, "Catholic Church"; Davis, *History of Black Catholics,* especially ch. 5; Ochs, *Desegregating the Altar.*
2. Spalding, *Spalding,* 194–95; Guilday, *Councils of Baltimore,* 193–94.
3. Spalding, *Spalding,* 202; MJS to PNL, 19 January 1866, CDA, 34B7.
4. Spalding, *Spalding,* 202–3.
5. JAC to PNL, June 21, 1866, CDA, 36C1; Lowman, "James Andrew Corcoran," 252–55.
6. Spalding, *Spalding,* 211; Hennesey, *American Catholics,* 159; Guilday, *Councils of Baltimore,* 196–200; Guilday, ed., *Sermons Delivered during the Second Plenary Council of Baltimore, October 1866,* 16–28.
7. Hennesey, *American Catholics,* 159–60; Shaughnessy, *Immigrant,* 153.
8. Powers, *Tar Heel Catholics,* 177–79.
9. MJS to Propaganda Fide, July 7, 1867; Ellis, *Life of Gibbons,* 1:62–63.
10. Hennesey, "Baltimore Council," 166–67.
11. Misch, *American Bishops,* 15; "The Catholic Congress of Malines and Bishop Lynch," *Gazette,* October 3, 1867, 3; Gillard, *Colored Catholics,* 86–87.
12. Misch, *American Bishops,* 17.
13. "The Catholics and the Freedmen," *Charleston Daily Courier,* October 23, 1866, 2.
14. Spalding, *Spalding,* 220.
15. Ibid., 215.
16. Misch, "Catholic Church," 37; Davis, *History of Black Catholics,* 118–19; Spalding, *Spalding,* 220.

17. Misch, *American Bishops,* 39.
18. Ibid., 40.
19. Ibid., 43.
20. Ibid., 78. Peter Claver (1584–1654) ministered to Negro slaves in Colombia. He was beatified by Pius IX in 1850 and canonized by Leo XIII in 1888. Benedict the Moor (1529–1589) and Martin de Porres (1579–1639) were black. Martin de Porres was canonized by Pope John XXIII in 1962.
21. Ibid., 26.
22. Ibid., 45; Davis, *History of Black Catholics,* 119–20.
23. Misch, *American Bishops,* 151.
24. Ibid., 46–47.
25. Davis, *History of Black Catholics,* 120–21; Misch, *American Bishops,* 48; Spalding, *Spalding,* 222; Guilday, *Councils of Baltimore,* 213.
26. On the decrees see Guilday, *Councils of Baltimore,* 202–14; Hennesey, "Baltimore Council," 166–67.
27. Gannon, *Rebel Bishop,* 125.
28. Gleeson, "'No Disruption of Union,'" 177.
29. Guilday, *National Pastorals,* 20–221; Misch, *American Bishops,* 49–50; Davis, *History of Black Catholics,* 121–22.
30. Lowman, "James Andrew Corcoran," 257–59.
31. Spalding, *Spalding,* 227–326.
32. Misch, *American Bishops,* 57–62.
33. HPN to PNL, November 19, 1866, CDA, 34Y6; Lowman, "James Andrew Corcoran," 259–60.
34. PNL to Barnabò, October 20, 1866, PRF, UNDA, reel 22, vol. 994, fols. 908–11; Father William McCloskey to PNL, November 9, 1866, CDA, 37W1; "Bishop Lynch Visits Jefferson Davis," *New York Times,* October 20, 1866, 1; Major (Bvt. Brig. Gen.) William Hays, pass for Bishop Lynch, Fort Monroe, October 23, 1866, CDA, 37R5; Eaton, *Jefferson Davis,* 4–5; Jefferson Davis to the Editor of *The Catholic Universe,* March 1878, in Davis, *Private Letters,* 473–74; Craven, *Prison Life,* 288–90.
35. PNL, Lenten Pastoral, February 24, 1867, AJF.
36. Spalding, *Spalding,* 231.
37. Ochs, *Desegregating the Altar,* 40–42; Misch, *American Bishops,* 54–56; Davis, *History of Black Catholics,* 120–22, 136; Gleeson, "'No Disruption of Union,'" 180–81.
38. O'Connell, *Catholicity,* 45. By "foreign" priests O'Connell referred to the Mill Hill Fathers.

Chapter 10: Reconstruction

1. TB to PNL, June 28, 1866, CDA, 36D6; Moore's remarks quoted in McNally, Reconstruction," 54.
2. Wolfe, "Patrick Neison Lynch," 125.
3. Madden, *Catholics in South Carolina,* 112.
4. Wolfe, "Patrick Neison Lynch," 126; Madden, *Catholics in South Carolina,* 105; *Sholes's Charleston City Directory,* 1882, 30.

5. Wolfe, "Patrick Neison Lynch," 124–25, 127.
6. Madden, *Catholics in South Carolina,* 129, 143; CDA Box 601, Item 6; *Charleston City Directory,* 1877–1886.
7. Heisser, "Bishop Lynch's Civil War Pamphlet," 693–94 ; Lynch, "A Few Words," Pt. II, 116–17.
8. PNL to Société de la Propagation de la Foi, September 1865.
9. Communication from Aaron Pope, Zoning Administrator, City of Folly Beach, S.C., December 2, 2008.
10. MJS to PNL, Januray 19, 1866, CDA, 34B7.
11. Boniface Wimmer to PNL, April 23, 1866, CDA, 35G7. Wimmer later changed his mind and assigned priests and monks to work in the South, especially out of pity for "those entirely neglected Negroes." In 1877 the Benedictines started a project to work among blacks on Skidaway Island, Ga., at the request of Bishop William Gross of Savannah. David Gleeson points to the failure of the Skidaway project as an indicator that Lynch's island plan would likely also likely to have failed: Gleeson, "'No Disruption of Union,'" 179; Oetgen, *American Abbot: Boniface Wimmer,* 89; Oetgen, "Origins of the Benedictine," 168 ff.
12. Sorin to PNL, January 18, 1866, CDA, 36B4; Sorin to Propaganda Fide, January 18, 1866, APF, Scrit. Rif., America Centrale, vol. 21, fols. 84v–87, AU ND, MPRF, reel 69, VIII, 22; Luers to Propaganda Fide, June 2, 1866, APF, Lettere . . . 1866, vol. 357, fols. 570 rv–571, AUND, MPRF, reel 123, VIII, 847; Propaganda Fide to Sorin, June 27, 1866, APF, Lettere . . . 1866, vol. 357, fols. 571–572v., MPR, reel 123, VIII, 848.
13. On the White House see Poston, *Buildings of Charleston,* 598–99.
14. Pynchon, *Dan Sickles*, esp. ch. 28, 215 ff.; Swanberg, *Sickles,* 275 ff.; BL to PNL, February 2, 1866; same to same, April 21, 1866; both in CDA, Reverend Monsignor Richard C. Madden Personal Papers, 1938–1982, Letters of Ellen Baptista Lynch, 1865–1866, 1007.004; Campbell, "Bishop England's Sisterhood," 161.
15. In later years Sickles converted to Catholicism.
16. Sickles to PNL, August 20, 1866, CDA, 37A3; same to same, October 7, 1866, CDA, 37M6; Bl to PNL, September 8, 1866, CDA, 15T3; C. J. Croghan to PNL, May 4, 1866, CDA, 35N4; Campbell, "Bishop England's Sisterhood," 159–63.
17. PNL to O. O. Howard, February 1, 1866 (draft), CDA, 34H2. General Oliver Otis Howard (1830–1909) was commissioner of the Bureau of Refugees, Freedmen and Abandoned Lands.
18. Gleeson, "'No Disruption of Union,'" 178–79; Madden, "Catholics of South Carolina" (unpublished), ms. #1, vol. 7, ch. 11, 49–50; communication from Dr. Michael Musick, National Archives and Records Administration, April 1, 1999.
19. On federal efforts for black farmfolk on the Sea Islands see Rose, *Rehearsal for Reconstruction,* 21ff., 32ff. 212ff.; Ochiai, *Harvesting Freedom,* esp. 2–82, 135–76; McFeely, *Yankee Stepfather,* esp. 45–64, 84–106; Williamson, *After Slavery,* 59–63, 79–86.
20. PNL to Société de la Propagation de la Foi, June 17, 1867, *Annales de la propagation de la foi* 40 (1868): 88–89.
21. "The Catholic Congress of Malines and Bishop Lynch," *Gazette* (Charleston, S.C.), October 3, 1867, 3.

22. Quoted in Madden, "Catholics of South Carolina" (unpublished), ms. #1, vol. 7, ch. 11, 56.
23. PNL to MJS, January 12, 1866, AAB, 34U8. Lynch's island colony project is discussed in Gleeson, "'No Disruption of Union,'" 178–79; Madden, "Catholics of South Carolina," ms. #1, vol. 7, ch. 11, 48 ff.; Madden, *Catholics in South Carolina,* 103.
24. Caulfield and Ford to Bishop Lynch, February 20, 1867, in DCA 39E6. Patrick Ford and Martin Caulfield operated a press at 307 East Bay Street, where they published the *Gazette*. Ford had earlier made an offer to Bishop Lynch to establish another paper, the *Leader*, as the diocesan organ. The bishop never responded to that proposal.
25. "Prospectus," *Gazette,* May 4, 1867, 4.
26. Bill of sale, Caulfield and Ford to Bishop Lynch, February 20, 1867, CDA 44 D5.
27. Charleston *Courier Tri-Weekly,* July 2, 1868, 1.
28. "Advertisement," *Gazette,* July 4, 1868, 4.
29. Caulfield, "Editorial," *Gazette,* July 4, 1868, 4.
30. Budds, "Editorial," *Gazette,* July 11, 1868, 4.
31. Budds to Lynch, CDA 44 E5. Thomas O'Keefe was a machinist who lived at 29 Hasell Street. Mr. Roberts, a printer, resided at 24 Church Street. T. Tupper and Sons are listed as commercial merchants on Prioleau Street. W. H. Shaffer was a dentist who owned the building at 307 King Street, where the newspaper offices were located. *Charleston City Directory,* 1867–1868, 129, 139.
32. Budds to Lynch, CDA 44 K3.
33. Budds to Lynch, CDA 44 T4.
34. Bermingham to Lynch, October 25, 1868, CDA 45 K6.
35. Budds to Lynch, CDA 46 K3. W. C. Dolan, a printer, lived at 73 Broad. *Charleston City Directory,* 1869–70, 116.
36. Budds to Lynch, CDA 46 K3. Budds was at the time listed in the *City Directory* as living at 11 St. Philips Street. The following year his address was 8 Short Street, where he had previously resided in the late 1850s and early 1860s, just prior to the war.
37. Madden, *Catholics in South Carolina,* 109.
38. Bill of sale for the *Gazette* from Bishop Lynch to Lucius C. Northrop, June 8, 1869, CDA 72W9.
39. *Charleston City Directory,* 1869, 112.
40. Lucius Northrop to Bishop Lynch, October 30, 1869, CDA 47C7.
41. Ibid.

Chapter 11: 1870s to His Death

1. "Rt. Rev. Bishop P.N. Lynch," *Charleston Daily Courier*, December 5, 1865, 2.
2. "Bishop Lynch at the Cooper Institute," *New York Times,* May 1, 1866, 8.
3. "Speech of the Pope to the Italian Deputation," *Chicago Tribune,* July 23, 1867, 3.
4. "Bishop Lynch's Lecture," *Charleston Daily Courier,* January 11, 1868, 2. This was followed by an account of the event in the same paper on January 13, 1868, 2.
5. "Bishop Lynch in Boston," *Charleston Daily Courier,* February 29, 1868, 1.

6. Madden, *Catholics in South Carolina,* 110; "The Apostolic Briefs," *Charleston Daily Courier,* August 13, 1868, 1; "Consecration of Catholic Bishops," *Charleston Daily Courier,* August 17, 1868, 2. This account contains excerpts from an article that appeared in the *Baltimore Sun* on August 15, 1868.
7. "Consecration in Baltimore of Bishop Becker of the New See of Wilmington, and of Rev. James Gibbons, Vicar Apostolic of North Carolina—Interesting Ceremonies," *New York Times,* August 17, 1867, 1.
8. "Personal—Right Rev. Bishop Lynch," *Charleston Daily Courier,* April 6, 1868, 2.
9. "St. John's Day," *Charleston Daily Courier,* June 25, 1968, 2.
10. "Ordination at the Paulist Church, Fifty-ninth Street," *New York Times,* September 22, 1869, 2.
11. Madden, *Catholics in South Carolina,* 110–11; Hennessey, *The First Council of the Vatican,* 134.
12. Madden, *Catholics in South Carolina,* 110.
13. Hennessey, "Bishops at the First Vatican Council" (unpublished dissertation), ch. 1.
14. Lynch, "The First Oecuminical Council of the Vatican"; Lynch, "The Vatican Council—Number Two"; Lynch, "The First Oecuminical Council of the Vatican —Number Three"; Lynch, "The Vatican Council—Number Four"; Lynch, "The First Oecuminical Council of the Vatican—Number Five"; "The First Oecuminical Council of the Vatican—Number Six"; Lynch, "The First Oecuminical Council of the Vatican—Number Seven"; Lynch, "The First Oecuminical Council of the Vatican—Number Eight."
15. Lynch, "The First Oecuminical Council of the Vatican—Number Eight," 842.
16. "Bishop Lynch's Lecture," *Banner of the South* 3, no. 17 (July 9, 1870), 8.
17. "Bishop Lynch on the Council," *Chicago Tribune,* June 25, 1870, 2.
18. "The Warren-Street Home for Boys Lecture by Bishop Lynch at Cooper Institute," *New York Times,* October 21, 1870, 8.
19. "Our Sumter Correspondent," *Charleston Daily Courier,* July 4, 1970, 2.
20. "Bishop Lynch in Greenville," *Charleston Daily Courier,* December 26, 1870, 1.
21. "Ceremonies of Imposing the Scarlet Baretta on Cardinal McCloskey at the Cathedral," *New York Times,* April 27, 1875, 1
22. "The Boston Cathedral: Dedication of the Great Church of the Holy Cross," *Chicago Daily Tribune,* December 12, 1875, 2. Also see Cathedral of the Holy Cross history at http://www.boston catholicdirectory.com/Parishes-And-People/Mini-Site.aspx?id=4320.
23. Madden, *Catholics in South Carolina,* 123; "A New Church in Greenville," *News and Courier,* October 20, 1876, 1.
24. "Invested with the Pallium," *Washington Post,* February 11, 1878, 1.
25. "In Honor of Pope Pius," *Washington Post,* February 12, 1878, 1. Also, "Prayers for Pope Pius—The Grand and Impressive Ceremonies of the Solemn Mass of Requiem," *Washington Post,* February 14, 1878, 1.
26. "Mass for the Repose of Pius IX," *New York Times,* February 22, 1878, 1.
27. "An Imposing Catholic Ceremony—Vicar-General Quinn Lays the Cornerstone of the New Church of St. Francis Xavier," *New York Times,* May 6, 1878, 1

28. "A Welcome to Cardinal McCloskey," *Washington Post,* May 14, 1878, 1.
29. "The Bishop's Mitre—A Grand Excursion Arranged for a Trip to Richmond," *Washington Post,* August 23, 1878, 1.
30. "Cardinal McCloskey Officiating," *New York Times,* March 3, 1879, 8.
31. "An Imposing Ceremonial: Blessing of the New Roman Catholic Cathedral," *New York Times,* May 26, 1879, 1.
32. "The New Catholic Church," *News and Courier,* April 10, 1880, 1; "The New Catholic Church," *News and Courier,* April 12, 1880, 4.
33. PNL to Cardinal Barnabò, 1872, 6 May 1872,CDA Item 52W5.
34. "Bishop Lynch of South Carolina," *New York Times,* July 6, 1877, 5.
35. "Pulpit and Preacher—Notes of Current Interest to Religious Minded Readers," *New York Times,* September 19, 1880, 3.
36. "Rome and the Cardinal," *New York Times,* October 8, 1880, 8.
37. Mother Baptista to PNL, March and April 1870, in Monsignor Richard C. Madden Papers, CDA 2007–04, Box 2, Folder 24.
38. Mother Baptista to PNL, May 27, 1 870, in Monsignor Richard Madden Collection, CDA 2007–04, Box 2, Folder 24.
39. "In Memoriam," *Banner of the South* 3, no. 16, June 18, 1870, 6.
40. Mother Baptista to PNL, May 27, 1870, in Monsignor Richard C. Madden Papers, CDA 2007–04, Box 2, Folder 24.
41. Mother Baptista to PNL, June 27, 1877, in Monsignor Richard C. Madden Papers, CDA 2007–04, Box 3, Folder 3.
42. *Columbia Register* announcement as printed in "Death of Bishop Lynch's Mother," *News and Courier,* June 28, 1877, 4.
43. PNL to D. J. Quigley, September 4, 1877, 1, CDA 63S4.
44. William Turner, M.D, on staff at Medical University of South Carolina. A friend, William Scott McDougal, M.D., at Massachusetts General Hospital, in August 2003, through personal e-mail correspondence. Dr. McDougal had access to the archival records of Massachusetts General Hospital. Vesical calculus is more simply bladder stones or hard buildups of minerals that form in the urinary bladder.
45. The lithotrite was used to performed transurethral lithotripsy, the first known minimally invasive surgery, to crush stones inside the bladder without having to open the abdomen (lithotomy). To remove a calculus, the instrument was inserted through the urethra and holes bored in the stone. Afterward, the stone was crushed with the same instrument and the resulting fragments aspirated or allowed to flow normally with urine.
46. PNL to D. J. Quigley, September 4, 1877, 2–3, CDA 63S4.
47. Madden, *Catholics in South Carolina,* 133.
48. Ibid., 135.
49. Details of the last hours of his life have been taken from the obituaries in the local newspapers. His profession of faith as recounted by eyewitnesses appeared in "Death of Bishop Lynch," *News and Courier*, February 27, 1882, 1.
50. Ibid.
51. Charleston County Death Rolls, 1821–1926, vol. 43–176.

52. Editorial, "The Death of Bishop Lynch," *News and Courier*, February 27, 1882, 4.
53. "The Late Bishop Lynch," *News and Courier*, February 28, 1882, 1.
54. "The Late Bishop Lynch," *News and Courier*, March 1, 1882, 1.
55. Ibid.
56. "Bishop Lynch's Funeral—The Ceremonies at the Cathedral Yesterday," *News and Courier*, March 2, 1882, 1.
57. "Bishop Lynch's Funeral," *New York Times*, March 2, 1882, 4.
58. "St. Patrick's Day," *News and Courier*, March 17, 1882, 2.
59. "Erin's Patron Saint: The Hibernian Society," *News and Courier*, March 18, 1882, 1.
60. Daniel J. Quigley to PNL, October 16, 1877, CDA, 64D2; College of Charleston Library, Special Collections Department, College of Charleston, Trustee Minutes, 4:1865–1887, meetings of October 15, 1877, April 6, 1878, October 14, 1878, November 22, 1880; Easterby, *A History of the College of Charleston*, 107–9, 124–25, 185–86.
61. Lynch, "The Divinity of Christ. Part I"; Lynch, "The Divinity of Christ. Part II"; McElrone, "Bishop Lynch," 167.
62. "The Rt. Rev. P. N. Lynch, D.D.," *City of Charleston Year Book*, 1882, 326.
63. Lynch, "Charleston Harbor" (handwritten manuscript), CDA Patrick N. Lynch Transfer File, folder EE; Bonds, "Opening the Bar: First Dredging at Charleston," 230–50.
64. PNL to MJS, January 12, 1866, AAB, 34U8; "Bishop Lynch's Lecture," *Charleston Mercury*, February 11, 1867, 4; Coulter, *George Walton Williams*, 226–27 ; Lynch, "America before Columbus," 105–27. For theories in circulation about pre-Columbian visits from overseas see for example Davis, *Antiquities of Central America, passim*; Gaffard, *Etude sur les rapports de l'Amérique et de l'ancien continent avant Christophe Colomb*, 105–34.
65. Lynch, "The Coming Transit of Venus," 145–61; Chapman, "The Transits of Venus," 148–51.
66. Charles Brady to PNL, January 15, 1873, CDA, 54G4; Lynch, "What to Read & How to Read—notes of lecture," CDA, Patrick N. Lynch Transfer File, folder BB. Lynch apparently also gave this lecture in Columbia, S.C.
67. Lynch, "Tunneling the Alps," ms. text of lecture, CDA, Lynch Transfer File, folder CC; McElrone, "Bishop Lynch," 167; "The Rt. Rev. P. N., Lynch, D.D.," *City of Charleston Year Book*, 1882, 325.
68. "The Rt. Rev. P. N., Lynch, D.D.," *City of Charleston Year Book*, 1882, 325.
69. Lynch, "Chaldean Accounts of the Creation," 490–512.
70. Lynch, "Liquefaction of the Blood of St. Januarius. Part I," 772–84; Part II, 33–49; Part III, 14, 201–12; Part IV, 391–400; Part V, 526–49; Lynch, *The Liquefaction of the Blood of St. Januarius, at Naples; An Historical and Critical Examination of the Miracle;* Lynch's original handwritten draft of "The Liquefaction," CDA, Patrick N. Lynch Transfer File, folder Z. For contemporary supportive discussion of Lynch's essay see Binsse, "The Liquefaction of the Blood of St. Januarius," 835 ff.
71. Lynch, "Galileo Galilei and the Copernican System," 85–114.

72. "Apprentices Library Society," *Charleston Daily Courier,* December 3, 1844, 2; "The Lecture This Evening," *Charleston Mercury,* March 3, 1848, 2; "Dr. Lynch's Lecture before the Lyceum,"*Charleston Mercury,* March 6, 1848, 2.
73. George Dening Wolff to PNL, October 19, 1877, CDA, 64D5; McElrone, "Bishop Lynch," 167–68.
74. CDA, Patrick N. Lynch Transfer File, folder FF. The statements that follow in the text are based on this manuscript.
75. Cf. Michael Tuomey, "Report on the Geology of South Carolina (1848)," excerpted in Taylor, *South Carolina Naturalists,* 146–48.
76. Betts, "Darwinism, Evolution, and American Catholic Thought," 161–163 and *passim.*
77. On Vatican concerns about Darwin see Artigas, Glick, and Martínez, *Negotiating Darwin,* 52ff.

Epilogue

1. Wolfe, "Patrick N. Lynch," 166–67.
2. Ibid.
3. Clarke, *Lives of Deceased Bishops,* 97.
4. *Catholic Directory of 1859; Catholic Directory of 1882;* both cited in Wolfe, 46–48, 149–52. This was most likely *Sadlier's Catholic Directory, Almanac and Ordo,* which John G. Shea compiled and edited for the Church.

BIBLIOGRAPHY

Articles and Sections of Books

Alvarez, David J. "The Papacy in the Diplomacy of the American Civil War." *Catholic Historical Review* 69, no. 2 (1983): 227–48.

"American Association." *Charleston Courier,* May 3, 1858.

"Artesien [*sic*] Wells." *American Quarterly Review* 22 (December 1837): 336–49.

"Artesian Wells." *Penny Magazine* 4, no. 193 (April 4, 1835): 131–32.

"An Attempt at Riot" and "Foreign Relations." *U.S. Catholic Miscellany,* January 7, 1854.

"Archbishop Hughes on the War." *New York Times,* September 4, 1861.

Bachman, John. "By Request—From the *U.S. Catholic Miscellany.*" *Charleston Evening News,* May 3, 1852.

____________. "From the Richmond Watchman and Observer to John Bellinger." *Charleston Evening News,* May 8, 1852.

____________. "To the Editor of the Catholic Miscellany [by] A Protestant Though No Lutheran." *U.S. Catholic Miscellany,* May 6, 1852.

____________. "To the Public No. I." *Charleston Evening News,* April 29, 1852.

____________. "To the Public No. II." *Charleston Evening News,* May 5, 1852.

"Barnabò (Alessandro)." (1912) Dictionnaire d'histoire et de géographie ecclésiastiques, vol. 2, Paris: LeTouzey et Ané.

Baylen, Joseph O., and William W. White, eds. "A. Dudley Mann's Mission in Europe, 1863–1864: An Unpublished Letter to Jefferson Davis." *Virginia Magazine of History and Biography* 69 (July 1961): 324–28.

Behre, Robert. "Fountain Plans Are Bubbling Up." *Post and Courier,* April 30, 1997.

Betts, John Richards. "Darwinism, Evolution, and American Catholic Thought, 1860–1900." *Catholic Historical Review* 45, no. 2 (1959): 161–85.

"Bishop Lynch's Arrival in Halifax, Nova Scotia." *Charleston Mercury,* May 18, 1864.

"Bishop Lynch's Arrival in Halifax, Nova Scotia." *Charleston Daily Courier,* May 19, 1864.

"Bishop Lynch of Charleston." *New York Freeman's Journal and Catholic Reporter,* November 18, 1865.

"Bishop Lynch's Sermon." New York Freeman's Journal and Catholic Reporter, November 25, 1865.

"Blessing of a Banner." *U.S. Catholic Miscellany,* September 14, 1861.

Bonds, John B. "Opening the Bar: First Dredging at Charleston, 1853–1859." *South Carolina Historical Magazine* 98, no. 3 (July 1997): 230–50.

Brück, Anton. "Moufang, Christoph." In Erwin Gatz, ed., *Die Bischöfe der deutschsprachigen Länder,* 1785/1803 bis 1945.

Capizzi, Joseph Edward. "A Development of Doctrine: The Challenge of Slavery to Moral Theology." Doctoral dissertation, University of Notre Dame, 1998.

Caravaglios, Maria Genoino. "A Roman Critique of the Pro-Slavery Views of Bishop Martin of Natchitoches, Louisiana." *Records of the American Catholic Historical Society of Philadelphia* 83 (1972): 67–81.

____________. (1974) Unterkoefler, Ernest L. ed. *The American Catholic Church and the Negro Problem in the XVIII-XX Centuries.* Charleston, S.C: Caravaglios.

"A Card from Bishop Lynch of Charleston." *New York Freeman's Journal and Catholic Register,* March 24, 1866.

"Castle Pinckney." *U.S. Catholic Miscellany,* January 6, 1861.

"The Catholic Congress of Malines and Bishop Lynch." *Gazette* (Charleston, S.C.), October 3, 1867.

Chapman, Allan. "The Transits of Venus." *Endeavour* 22, no. 4 (1998): 144–51.

"Christenthum und Sklaverei." *Historisch-politische Blätter* 62 (1868): 195.

"The Cincinnati Riots." *U.S. Catholic Miscellany,* January 2, 1854.

"City Intelligence: Consecration of St. Joseph's Church." *Charleston Daily News,* May 6, 1860.

"City Intelligence: Dedication of St. Paul's Church. Society street." *Charleston Daily News,* May 13, 1860.

Clarke, Peter, and James Lowell Underwood. "Bishop John England and the Compatibility of the Catholic Church and American Democracy." In James Lowell Underwood and W. Lewis Burke, eds., *The Dawn of Religious Freedom in South Carolina.* Columbia: University of South Carolina Press, 2006, 184–210.

Clifton, James M. "Jehossee Island: The Antebellum South's Largest Rice Plantation." *Agriculture History* 59 (1985): 56–65.

Cohen, Sidney Jacobi. "Three Notable Ante-bellum Magazines of South Carolina." *Bulletin of the University of South Carolina,* no. 42, pt. 2 (1915): 38 ff.

"The Confederate Cause in France." *Index* (London), February 16, 1865.

"The Crisis." *U.S. Catholic Miscellany,* November 24, 1860.

Curran, R. Emmet. "'Splendid Poverty': Jesuit Slaveholding in Maryland, 1805–1838." In Randall M. Miller and Jon L. Wakelyn, eds., *Catholics in the Old South: Essays on Church and Culture.* Macon: Mercer University Press, 1983, 125–46.

"De Leon, Edwin." In Jon L. Wakelyn, *Biographical Dictionary of the Confederacy.* Westport, Conn.: Greenwood Press, 1977, 169.

De Rosa, Giuseppe. La Civiltà Cattolica: 150 anni al servizio della chiesa, 1850–1993. Rome: La Civiltà Cattolica, 1999.

"A Discovery." *U.S. Catholic Miscellany,* September 13, 1856.

"Dr. Bachman and His Book." *U.S. Catholic Miscellany,* July 9, 1853.

"Dr. Lynch's Lecture before the Lyceum." *Charleston Mercury,* March 6, 1846.

"Domestic, Ecclesiastical." *U.S. Catholic Miscellany,* February 11, 1854.

"Dreadful Conflagration." *U.S. Catholic Miscellany,* December 12, 1861.

Duncan, Richard R. "Catholics and the Church in the Antebellum Upper South." In Randall M. Miller and Jon L. Wakelyn, eds., *Catholics in the Old South: Essays on Church and Culture.* Macon: Mercer University Press, 1983, 77–98.

Edgar, Walter B. "South Carolina Historical Society Sesquicentennial Address," *South Carolina Historical Magazine* 106, nos. 2–3 (April–July 2005): 102–17.

"Edgefield." In Brian P. Fahey, *The Catholic Diocese of Charleston: A History*. Charleston: Diocese of Charleston, 2008, 130–31.

"The Enemy in Lancaster." *York Enquirer* (South Carolina), March 16, 1865.

Endres, David J. "Know-Nothings, Nationhood, and the Nuncio: Reassessing the Visit of Archbishop Bedini." *U.S. Catholic Historian* 21, no. 4 (Fall 2003): 1–16.

Essig, Andrew M., and Jennifer L. Moore. "U.S.-Holy See Diplomacy: The Establishment of Formal Relations, 1984." *Catholic Historical Review* 95, no. 4 (October 2009): 741–64.

"Exciting Scene in a Church." *News and Courier*, June 6, 1884.

Fanning, William H. W. "Property, Ecclesiastical, in the United States." *Catholic Encyclopedia* 12, New York: Robert Appleton Company, 1912.

Ferrara, Marie. "Moses Henry Nathan and the Great Charleston Fire of 1861." *SCHM* 104, no. 4 (October 2003): 258–80.

Field, Phyllis F. "Weed, Thurlow." *American National Biography*, vol. 22., New York: University of Oxford Press, 1999.

Fitz, James. "U.S. Catholic Religious and Slavery: A Seldom Told Story." *Review for Religious* 58, no. 4 (1999): 335–51.

Fitzhugh, George. "Free Negroes in Hayti." *De Bow's Review*, November 27, 1859, 526–49.

"Flag of Truce. Exchange of Prisoners." *Charleston Courier*, July 25, 1863.

Foster, Mrs. J. H. "When Sherman Passed through Lancaster." In *United Daughters of the Confederacy, South Carolina Division, South Carolina Women in the Confederacy*. 2 vols. Columbia, S.C.: The State Company, 1902–1907, vol. II: 344–51.

"Free Market of Charleston." *Charleston Daily Courier*, January 27, 1864.

Gasnaul, François. "La Réglementation des universités pontificales au XIXe siècle." *Mélanges de l'Ecole Française de Rome, Moyen Âge–temps modernes* 76, no. 2 (1984).

Genovese, Eugene D., and Elizabeth Fox-Genovese. "The Religious Ideals of Southern Slave Society." *Georgia Historical Quarterly* 70 (1986): 1–16.

Gleeson, David T. "'No Disruption of Union': The Catholic Church in the South and Reconstruction." In Edward J. Blum and W. Scott Poole, eds., *Vale of Tears: New Essays on Religion and Reconstruction.* Macon, Ga.: Mercer University Press, 2005, 164–86.

Golla, C. Walker. "The Role of Father Badin's Slaves in Frontier Kentucky." *American Catholic Studies* 115, no. 1 (Spring 2004): 1–24.

Gurn, Joseph. "Bishop Lynch's Vindication." *Columbia* 7, no. 5 (December 1927): 1.

Hackett, Jeremiah. "Review of The Confederacy's Fighting Chaplain." *South Carolina Historical Magazine* 95, no. 3 (1994): 267–72.

Hammond, William Henry. "Letter to an English Abolitionist." In Drew Gilpin Faust, ed., *The Ideology of Slavery: Proslavery Thought in the Antebellum South, 1830–1860.* Baton Rouge: Louisiana State University Press, 1981, 168–205.

Harper, Chancelor. "Slavery in the Light of Social Ethics." In E. N. Elliott, *Cotton Is King and Pro-Slavery Arguments.* Augusta, Ga.: Pritchard, Abbott and Loomis, 1860, 577–85 (microfiche LAC 10262).

Hastings, Martin. "United States-Vatican Relations." *Records of the American Catholic Historical Society of Philadelphia* 69 (March–June 1958): 24–55.

Heisser, David C. R. "Bishop Lynch's Civil War Pamphlet on Slavery." *Catholic Historical Review* 84, no. 4 (October 1998): 682–96.

————. "Bishop Lynch's People: Slaveholding by a South Carolina Prelate." *South Carolina Historical Magazine* 102, no. 4 (July 2001): 238–62.

Helfand, William H. "James Morison and His Pills: A Study in the Nineteenth-Century Pharmaceutical Market." *British Society for the History of Pharmacy: Transactions* 1 (1974): 101–6.

Hennesey, James. "The Baltimore Council of 1866: An American Syllabus." *Records of the American Catholic Historical Society of Philadelphia* 76 (1965): 157–73.

Heuser, Herman J. "Monsignor Corcoran." *American Ecclesiastical Review* 1, no. 9 (September 1899): 321–38.

Historic and Architectural Inventory, Cheraw Historic District. Columbia, S.C.: Gettys Associates, 1990.

Hopkins, Thomas F. "St. Mary's Church, Charleston, S.C." *City of Charleston Yearbook,* 1897.

Hughes, Horatio. "The Elliott Society." Proceedings of the South Carolina Historical Association (1938): 25–31.

"It Has Come at Last." *U.S. Catholic Miscellany,* November 10, 1860.

Jezernik, Maksimilijan. "Il Pontificio Collegio Urbano de Propaganda Fide." In *Sacrae Congregationis de Propaganda Fide, Memoria Rerum: 350 anni a servizio delle mission 1622–1972.* 3 vols. Rome: Herder, 1975.

Jones, Jacqueline. "'My Mother Was Much of a Woman': Black Women, Work, and the Family Under Slavery." In Paul Finkelman, ed., *Women and the Slave Family in a Slave Society.* New York and London: Garland, 1989, 195–229.

Jones, Patricia B. "Drilling Might Help Replenish Water Supply." *Post and Courier,* January 26, 1995.

Joseph, Satish. "'Long Live the Republic!' Father Edward Purcell and the Slavery Controversy: 1861–1865." *American Catholic Studies* 116, no. 4 (Winter 2005): 25–54.

Kenrick, Archbishop Frederick Patrick et al. Catholic Church. Province of Baltimore. 9th Provincial Council (1858). *Pastoral Letter* (Baltimore, Md., 1858).

King, G. Wayne. "Death Camp at Florence." *Civil War Times Illustrated* 12, no. 9 (January 1974): 34–42.

Krebsbach, Suzanne. "Black Catholics in Antebellum Charleston." *SCHM* 108, no. 2 (April 2007): 143–59.

"La Congrégation de la Propagande." *Annales de la Propagation de la Foi* 60 (1888).

Lalli, Anthony B., and Thomas H. O'Connor. "Roman Views on the American Civil War." *Catholic Historical Review* 57, no. 1 (April 1971): 21–41.

Lancaster County Black History; A Photographic and Literary Document, 1785 to 1991. Lancaster: Lancaster County Black Heritage Committee, 1991.

Laney, Lynn Ingram. "Matheson Library." *Chesterfield County Shopper* (Cheraw, S.C.), February 27, 1985.

"Leahey's Lectures—Discussion in the City Council." *Charleston Courier,* March 26, 1852.

"Leahey's Lectures, &c." *U.S. Catholic Miscellany,* March 27, 1852.

"The Lecture This Evening." *Charleston Mercury,* March 3, 1848.

"Letter from the Nuncio." *U.S. Catholic Miscellany,* November 26, 1853.

Lipari, C. M. "Chigi, Flavio." *Dizionario biografico degli Italiani,* vol. 24, Rome: Treccani Pulbishers, 1960-2013.

Lipscomb, Oscar Hugh Lipscomb. "The Administration of John Quinlan, Second Bishop of Mobile, 1859–1883." *Records of the American Catholic Historical Society of Philadelphia* 78, nos. 1–4 (March–December 1967): 30–48.

"List of the Taxpayers of the City of Charleston for 1859." Charleston: Steam-Power Press of Walker, Evans and Cogswell, 1860.

"List of the Taxpayers of the City of Charleston for 1858." Charleston: Steam Press of Walker, Evans and Company, 1859.

"List of the Taxpayers of the City of Charleston for 1860." Charleston: Steam-Presses of Walker, Evans and Cogswell, 1861.

Lofton, Edward Dennis. "Reverend Doctor James Andrew Corcoran and the 'United States Catholic Miscellany,' Concerning Questions of Slavery and the Confederacy." *Records of the American Catholic Historical Society of Philadelphia* 93 (1982): 77–101.

Lynch, Patrick N. "America before Columbus." In Ambrose Manahan, *Manahan's American Catholic Museum.* New York: Printed for Manahan's American Catholic Museum, 1867, 1:105–27.

____________. "The Artesian Well. No. I." *Charleston Evening News,* February 20, 1849.

____________. "Artesian Wells. No. II." *Charleston Evening News,* February 22, 1849, 2.

____________. "Artesian Wells. No. III." *Charleston Evening News,* February 24, 1849, 3.

____________. "Artesian Wells. No IV." *Charleston Evening News,* February 28, 1849, 4.

____________. "Artesian Wells. No. V." *Charleston Evening News,* March 2, 1849. P. 2.

____________. "The Chagrin of Catholics at the Late Presbyterian Decision Regarding Baptism." *U.S. Catholic Miscellany,* July 19, 1845.

____________. "Chaldean Accounts of the Creation." *Catholic World* 24, no. 142 (January 1877): 490–512.

____________. "The Coming Transit of Venus." *Catholic World* 19, no. 110 (May 1874): 145–61.

____________. "The Divinity of Christ. Part I." *American Catholic Quarterly Review* 1, no. l (January 1876): 101–23.

____________. "The Divinity of Christ. Part II." *American Catholic Quarterly Review* 1, no. 3 (July 1876): 475–503.

____________. "A Few Words on the Domestic Slavery in the Confederate States of America." Part 1. Edited by David C. R. Heisser. *Avery Review* 2 no. 1 (Spring 1999): 64–103.

____________. "A Few Words on the Domestic Slavery in the Confederate States of America." Part 2. Edited by David C. R. Heisser. *Avery Review* 3, no. 1 (Spring 2000): 93–103.

____________. "Liquefaction of the Blood of St. Januarius. Part I." *Catholic World* 13, no. 78 (September 1871): 772–84.

____________. "Liquefaction of the Blood of St. Januarius. Part II." *Catholic World* 14, no. 79 (October 1971): 33–49.

____________. "Liquefaction of the Blood of St. Januarius. Part III." *Catholic World* 14, no. 80 (November 1871): 201–12.

____________. "Liquefaction of the Blood of St. Januarius. Part IV." *Catholic World* 14, no. 81 (December 1871): 391–400.

____________. "Liquefaction of the Blood of St. Januarius. Part V." *Catholic World* 14, no. 82 (January 1872): 526–49.

____________. *Pastoral Prayers for Peace* [printed], November 26, 1863.

____________. "Review of Austen Henry Layard, *Nineveh and Its Remains*." *Southern Quarterly Review* 16, no. 31 (October 1849): 1–3.

____________, Charles Upham Shepard Jr., and John Frederic Meckel Geddings. "Artesian Wells, 1823–1879, with Analysis of Artesian, Cistern and Well Waters in and near the City of Charleston, S.C.; Report to the Mayor and City Council." *Charleston City Year Book*, 1881, 257–315.

McElrone, Hugh P. "Bishop Lynch." *Catholic World* 35 (1882): 167.

McNally, Michael J. "A Peculiar Institution: A History of the Catholic Parish Life in the Southeast (1850– 1980)." In Jay Dolan, ed., *The American Catholic Parish*, 2 vols. Mahwah, N.J.: Paulist Press, 1987, 1:156–72.

____________. "James A. Corcoran and St. Charles Borromeo Seminary–Overbrook, 1871–1907." *American Catholic Studies* 110 (Spring–Winter 1999): 49–71.

____________. "Reconstruction and Parish Life in Charleston, South Carolina, 1865–1877: A Pastor's Perspective." *American Catholic Studies* 117, no. 1 (Spring 2006): 45–68.

____________. "Lynch, Baptista, Mother." *New Catholic Encyclopedia*. Vol. 8, New York: McGraw Hill Press, 2002.

____________. "Ursuline Convent, Columbia, Burned." *Catholic Banner* 49, no. 32 (December 4, 1960), Washington, D.C.: Catholic University of America, p. 14a.

Mazÿck, William P. "The Charleston Museum, Its Genesis and Development." *City of Charleston Year Book*, 1907, appendix 15–16.

Metzler, Josef. "Präfekten und Sekretäre der Kongregation im Zeitalter der neueren Missionsäre (1818–1918)." In Josef Metzler, ed., *Sacrae Congregationis de Propaganda Fide: Memoriam Rerum, 1622–1972*. 3 vols. Rome: Herder, 1971–1975.

Millbrooke, Anne. "South Carolina State Geological Surveys of the Nineteenth Century." In James X. Corgan, ed., *The Geological Sciences in the Antebellum South*. University: University of Alabama Press, 1982, 26–38.

Miller, Randall M. "Slaves and Southern Catholicism." In John B. Boles, ed., *Masters and Slaves in the House of the Lord: Race and Religion in the American South, 1740–1870*. Lexington: University of Kentucky Press, 1988, 127–52.

Mimis, Edwin. "Paul Hamilton Hayne, 1830–1886." *Library of Southern Literature*. Atlanta: Martin and Hoyt, 1907, 5:2278–83.

Misch, Edward J. "The Catholic Church and the Negro, 1865–1884." *IntegratEDucation* 12, no. 4 (1974), p. 36-40.

Moltke-Hansen, David. "The Expansion of Intellectual Life: A Prospectus." In Michael O'Brien and David Moltke-Hansen, eds., *Intellectual Life in Antebellum Charleston*. Knoxville: University of Tennessee Press, 1986, 3–44.

"Monsignore D. J. Quigley." *News and Courier*, November 28, 1903.

Montalembert, Charles de. "La Victoire du Nord aux Etats-Unis." *Le Correspondant* 65 (May 15, 1865), p. 6-160.

Moore, John Hammon. "From Vine to Keg: A History of Winemaking in South Carolina." *Sandlapper* 13, no. 1 (Spring 2002), p. 51-55.

Mulligan, Patrick. "Dr. James Donnelly: The Early Years." *Clogher Record* 11, no. 3 (1984), p. 364.

"The Museum of South-Carolina." *Charleston Courier,* November 27, 1827.

"Necrology. J. F. M. Geddings." Transactions of the South Carolina Medical Association (1887).

"Newly-Made Citizens." *Charleston Courier,* July 3, 1855.

"The New Standard of the Irish Volunteers." *U.S. Catholic Miscellany,* September 21, 1861.

O'Connor, Charles P. "The Northern Catholic Position on Slavery and the Civil War: Archbishop Hughes as a Test Case." *Records of the American Catholic Historical Society of Philadelphia* 96 (1986): 35–48.

Oetgen, Jerome. "The Origins of the Benedictine Order in Georgia." *Georgia Historical Quarterly* 53 (1969): 165–83.

"Our Victory." *U.S. Catholic Miscellany,* April 20, 1861.

"'Our' Candidate." *U.S. Catholic Miscellany,* September 6, 1856.

"Papers Relating to the Church in America . . . Second Series." *Records of the American Catholic Historical Society of Philadelphia* 7 (1896).

"Particulars of the Plot to Assassinate Mgr. Bedini." *U.S. Catholic Miscellany,* November 19, 1853.

Pease, Jane H., and William H. Pease. "Intellectual Life in the1830s: The Institutional Framework and the Charleston Style." In Michael O'Brien and David Moltke-Hansen, eds., *Intellectual Life in Antebellum Charleston.* Knoxville: University of Tennessee Press, 1986, 233–54.

"Philadelphia Correspondence." *Catholic Telegraph,* June 28, 1865.

Piccolanti, A. "Graziosi (Giuseppe Maria)." *Dictionnaire d'histoire et de géographie ecclésiastiques,* vol. 21, LeTouzey et Ané, Paris: 1918.

Pinckney, David H. "France and the Civil War." In Harold Hyman, ed., *Heard Round the World: The Impact Abroad of the Civil War*. New York: Knopf, 1969, 97–144.

"The Pope's Nuncio Insulted by Rowdies at Pittsburg,—Great Excitement." *U.S. Catholic Miscellany,* December 24, 1853.

Powers, William F. *Tar Heel Catholics: A History of Catholicism in North Carolina.* Lanham, Md.: University Press of America, 2003.

"The Present Crisis." *U.S. Catholic Miscellany,* December 8, 1860.

"The President's Movements." *Charleston Mercury,* November 5, 1863.

Prevost, Michel. "Cochin (Famille)" and "Cochin, Pierre-Suzanne, dit *Augustin.*" In *Dictionnaire de biographie française,* vol. 9, LeTouzey et Ané, Paris: 1933.

Price, Marcus W. "Ships That Tested the Blockade of the Carolina Ports, 1861–1865." *American Neptune* 8 (1948): 29–36.

"A Proclamation" [and related announcements]. *Charleston Courier,* December 12, 1861.

"Professor Buckland on Artesian Wells." *Littall's Living Age* 3, no. 26 (November 9, 1844): 68–72.

"Prospectus." *Gazette*, Charleston, SC: May 4, 1867.

Prudhomme, Claude. "La Papauté face à l'esclavage: quelle condamnation?" *Mémoire Spiritaine*, no. 9 (1er semestre 1999).

"Public Improvements of Charleston—Part 2." *DeBow's Review* 1, no. 14 (October 1849): 340–45.

Renault, François. "Aux origines de la lettre apostolique de Grégoire XVI *In supremo* (1839)." *Mémoire Spiritaine*, no. 2 (November 1995).

"Report of the Board for the Relief of Families of Soldiers in the Parishes of St. Philip and St. Michael." *Charleston Daily Courier*, January 2, 1863.

"Reports of Bishop Lynch of Charleston, South Carolina, Commissioner of the Confederate States to the Holy See." *American Catholic Historical Researches*, new ser., 22, no. 1 (1905): 245–61.

"Rev. Dr. Anthony Toomer Porter." *Cyclopedia of Eminent and Representative Men of the Carolinas of the Nineteenth Century*. Madison, Wis.: Brant and Fuller, 1902, 493–95.

"Rt. Rev. Bishop P. N. Lynch." *Charleston Daily Courier*, December 5, 1865.

"Robert A. Lynch Dies at Hospital." *Malden [Mass.] Evening News*, November 1, 1928.

"The Roman Catholic Church." *Impartial Reporter* (Enniskillen, Ireland), May 26, 1864.

Roys, Gerald R. "Francis Lieber at South Carolina College, 1835–1856; A Clash of Values." *Proceedings of the South Carolina Historical Association* (1998): 116–27.

Ryan, Frank W., Jr. "The Opinions of Editor William Gilmore Simms of the *Southern Quarterly Review*, 1849–1854." *Proceedings of the South Carolina Historical Association* (1959): 23–35.

Ryan, Ignatius L. "Confederate Agents in Ireland." *Historical Records and Studies* 26 (1936): 39–59.

"The Sad Death of Mr. J. D. Budds from the Effects of Sunstroke." *News and Courier*, July 18, 1887.

Savitt, Todd L. "Slave Health and Southern Distinctiveness." In Todd L. Savitt and James Harvey Young, eds., *Disease and Distinctiveness in the American South*. Knoxville: University of Tennessee Press, 1991, 120–53.

Sharrow, Walter G. "John Hughes and a Catholic Response to Slavery in Antebellum America." *Journal of Negro History* 57 (July 1972): 254–69.

____________. "Northern Catholic Intellectuals and the Coming of the Civil War." *New-York Historical Society Quarterly* 58 (1974): 35–56.

"Sheriffs Election." *Charleston Courier*, July 12, 1855.

"Some Civil War Documents, A.D. 1862–1864." *Records of the American Catholic Historical* Society of Philadelphia 14 (1903): 250–71.

Sorti, N. "Datary, Apostolic." *New Catholic Encyclopedia*, vol. 4, McGraw Hill Press, New York: 2002.

"South Carolina." *U.S. Catholic Miscellany*, December 22, 1860.

Spalding, David, ed. "Martin John Spalding's Dissertation on the American Civil War." *Catholic Historical Review* 52 (April 1966): 66–85.

Spalding, Thomas. "Martin John Spalding." In Gerald P. Fogarty, ed., *Patterns of Episcopal Leadership*. New York: Macmillan, 1989, 227–36.

Spruill, Sarah Cain. "Bank Follows Trade," *Cheraw Chronicle*, bicentennial edition, July 1, 1972, 10b

____________. "Cheraw." In Walter Edgar, ed., *South Carolina Encyclopedia*. Columbia: University of South Carolina Press, 2006.

Stephens, Lester D. "Scientific Societies in the Old South: The Elliott Society and the New Orleans Academy of Sciences." In Ronald L. Numbers and Todd L. Savitt, eds., *Science and Medicine in the Old South*. Baton Rouge: Louisiana State University Press, 1989, 59–78.

Stern, Madeleine B. "John Russell: 'Lord John' of Charleston." *North Carolina Historical Review* 26, no. 3 (July 1949): 285–99.

Stock, Leo Francis. "Catholic Participation in the Diplomacy of the Southern Confederacy." *Catholic Historical Review* 161, no. 1 (April 1930): 1–18.

____________. "The United States at the Court of Pius IX." *Catholic Historical Review* 9 (April 1923): 103–22.

Stoney, Samuel Gaillard, ed. "The Memoirs of Frederick Adolphus Porcher." *SCHM* 46, no.3 (December 1945): 25–39, 78–92, 140–58, 198–208.

____________. "Memoirs of Frederick Adolphus Porcher, chapter XIII—Continued," *SCHM* 47, no. 4 (October 1946): 32–52, 83–108, 150–62, 214–27.

Taylor, David, ed. "Oscar Montgomery Lieber." In David Taylor, ed., *South Carolina Naturalists: An Anthology, 1700–1860*. Columbia: University of South Carolina Press, 1998, 191–95.

Taylor, John, Jr., and James Coit. Agents for the Chatham Town Company, "Cheraw, South Carolina," *Carolina Observer and Fayetteville Gazette*. February 6, 1823, Cheraw Historical Society.

Thornwell, James Henley. "From the Spirit of the XIX Century. The Apocryphal Books." *U.S. Catholic Miscellany*, March 18, 1843.

"To the Voters of Charleston District." *Charleston Courier*, July 3, 1855.

Tuomey, Michael. "Report on the Geology of South Carolina (1848)." Excerpted in David Taylor, ed., *South Carolina Naturalists: An Anthology, 1700–1860*. Columbia: University of South Carolina Press, 1998, 144–56.

"Ursulines Begin Celebration of 100th Anniversary in Columbia." *Catholic Banner* 46, no. 33 (December 15, 1951).

Verot, Augustin. "The Diary of Bishop Verot, Third Bishop of Savannah and Administrator and Bishop of St. Augustine (1858–1876)." Edited by the Reverend Father Bernard. *Bulletin of the Catholic Layman* (August 8, 1925): 3–7.

Wakelyn, Jon L. "Catholic Elites in the Slaveholding South." In Randall M. Miller and Jon L. Wakelyn, eds., *Catholics in the Old South: Essays on Church and Culture*. Macon, Ga.: Mercer University Press, 1983, 211–40.

"Why Is Charles E. Kanapaux Persecuted?" *Charleston Courier*, July 4, 1855.

Wight, Willard E., ed., "Letters of the Bishop of Savannah, 1861–1865." *Georgia Historical Quarterly* 42, no. 1 (1958): 93–106.

____________. "Some Wartime Letters of Bishop Lynch." *Catholic Historical Review* 43, no. 1 (April 1957): 20–27.

____________. "War Letters of the Bishop of Richmond." *Virginia Magazine of History and Biography* 67, no. 3 (July 1959): 359–70.

Will of William McKenna. "Estate Sale, Estate of William McKenna Deceased. . . ." *Lancaster Ledger* (S.C.), January 2, 1861.

Worsley, Stephen C. "Catholicism in Antebellum North Carolina." *North Carolina Historical Review* 60, no. 4 (October 1983): 409–23.

Zanca, Kenneth J. "The Civil War Era Catholic Press on the Trial and Execution of Mary Surratt." *American Catholic Studies* 116, no. 1 (Spring 2005): 1–28.

Theses, Dissertations, and Papers

Andrews, Rena Mazyck. "Archbishop Hughes and the Civil War." Ph.D. dissertation, University of Chicago, 1935.

"Annals of the Ursuline Convent, Columbia, S.C.," and "St. Peter's Parochial School, 1872–1947." Archives of the Ursuline Sisters, Louisville, Ky.

Barrett, John. "Councils of Baltimore and the Code of Canon Law." Doct. dissertation. Washington, D.C., Catholic University of America, 1932.

Benoit, Canon Peter L. "Diary of a Trip to America, January 6, 1875, to June 8, 1875." Typescript. CB6–134, p. 140, Baltimore: Mill Hill Fathers Archives, copy in Archives of the Josephite Fathers.

Bermingham, Timothy. Diary of a Trip to Europe and the Holy Land. CDA, Priests Files, Box "Father Timothy Bermingham," entry for March 1, 1861.

Bill of sale, Antonio della Torre to John England in Trust for the Ursuline Nuns, October 21, 1835 (recorded October 23, 1835). South Carolina Department of Archives and History, Secretary of State Miscell. Records (Bills of Sale), vol. 50.

Bost, Raymond Morrris. "The Reverend John Bachman an the Development of Southern Lutheranism." Ph.D. dissertation, Yale University, 1963.

Campbell, Sister M. Anne Francis. "Bishop England's Sisterhood, 1829–1929." Ph.D. dissertation, St. Louis University, 1968.

"Catalogue of Negro Slaves of the Estate of the Hon. William McKenna, Deceased . . . To Be Sold by Thomas Ryan and Son, Auctioneers, at Lancaster Court House on January 21, 1861." CDA, folder 25Y8.

"Cathedral Fund" (record of contributions). CDA, Patrick N. Lynch Transfer File, folder "Finance."

Charleston City Tax Books, 1862, 1863, 1864. Charleston Library Society.

Charleston Fire Relief Committee. "Report of Special Committee on Pecuniary Compensation" (printed). CDA, Patrick N. Lynch Transfer File, folder "Fire Relief."

Congress of the Confederate States. Joint Resolution Declaring the Dispositions, Principles and Purposes of the Confederate States in Relation to the Existing War with the United States. (Senate No. 13-secret). Richmond: s.n., 1864. *Confederate Imprints* (microfilm), reel 5, no. 164–1.

Contract between Françoise Antoinette Césarine Barbot and Patrick N. Lynch, December 18, 1857, CDA, 12R2.

Copeland, Henry deSaussure, comp. "Lynch Family (2nd–8th Generations) Descendants of Conlaw Peter Lynch and Eleanor (McMahon) Neison of Clones, County Monaghan, Ireland, and Cheraw, South Carolina." Typescript, 1993, rev. 2002, CDA, "Lynch Files."

"Destruction of Property in Columbia, S.C., by Sherman's Army." Speech of Hon. Cole L. Bleas Delivered in the Senate, May 15, 1930, U.S. Congress. Senate, 71st Cong., 2nd sess., Senate Document No. 149.

"Distribution of the Fund Collected in the Archdiocese of Baltimore." Archives of the Archdiocese of Baltimore, Md.

"Early Conversions in South Carolina." Burt Family File, Archives of Edgefield, S.C.

Foley, Wilfrid. "Patrick N. Lynch, Catholic Bishop and Confederate Statesman." Master's thesis, University of Notre Dame, 1930.

Gibbons, James Cardinal, Episcopal Diary (Acta Episcopalia), second part: October 19, 1877–April 28, 1917, entry for February 26, 1882. Archives of the Archdiocese of Baltimore, Md.

Googe, Mrs. James M., Jr. "Lynch Family Genealogy," CDA, "Lynch Files."

Hartman, Robert. "The Civil War Experience in Lancaster County, 1861–1865." Senior thesis, University of South Carolina, 1991. South Caroliniana Library, Walter B. Edgar Papers.

Hennessey, James John, Rev., S.J. "The Bishops of the United States at the First Vatican Council." Ph.D. dissertation, Catholic University of America, 1963.

Hickey, Edward John. *The Society of the Propagation of the Faith, Its Foundation, Organization and Success (1822–1922)*. Ph.D. dissertation, Catholic University of America, 1922; repr., New York: AMS Press, 1974.

"In Memoriam (Dr. John Harwood Burt)." Burt Family File, Archives of Edgefield, S.C.

"List of Negroes, 14 November 1860," along with a list of families and prices. CDA, Lynch Unclassified Papers, Box 309L.

Loftis, Alton Taylor. "A Study of *Russell's Magazine*, Ante-bellum Charleston's Last Literary Periodical." Ph.D. dissertation, Duke University, 1973.

Lowman, Sister Mary Margian, O.S.U. "James Andrew Corcoran: Editor, Theologian, Scholar 1820–1889." Ph.D. dissertation, St. Louis University, 1958.

Lynch, Patrick N. "Artesian Well Calculations, January 15, 1878." CDA, Patrick N. Lynch Papers, Transfer File, folder 1.

____________. "Diary of Bishop Lynch's Vacation at Tusculum While he was a Student in Rome, September and October 1837." Manuscript and typescript copy. CDA, Lynch Transfer File, folder L8.

____________. "Dissertatione philosophica ex physica mathematica &c &c." CDA, Patrick N. Lynch Transfer File, folder IL4.

____________. "Duty of Priesthood to negroes after the war." Ms. draft, 1867. CDA, Patrick N. Lynch Transfer file, folder, "Lynch Files."

____________. "McKenna Will Case." Typescript. Collection of Ms. Nancy L. Crockett, Lancaster, S.C.

____________. "Memorandum on Roman Mission, July 13, 1864." CDA, Lynch Collection, box "CSA-Vatican." Charleston Diocesan Archives.

____________. "Notes on Eight Days Retreat in the Urban College of Propaganda Fide Under Father Massa, S.J." Handwritten ms. CDA, Patrick N. Lynch Transfer File, folder IL9.

____________. "Responsiones R. D. Episcopi Carolopolitani ad Quaestiones pro relatione status dioeceseos, ad Sacram Congregationem de Propaganda Fide, Oct. 15, 1864." Archives of the Propaganda Fide, Scritture riferite nei Congressi-America Centrale, vol. 20, fols. 1056r–1056v.

_____________. "Rules and Regulations for Acquiring a Correct & Elegant English Style, February 11, 1837 [with later additions]." Manuscript. CDA, Patrick N. Lynch Transfer File, folder IL7.

_____________. "Rules for the Government of the Museum." CDA, Bishop Patrick N. Lynch Papers, misc. mss., "Elliott Society."

_____________. Signed loyalty oath, October 14, 1865, CDA, "Lynch Files."

_____________. "Tunneling the Alps." Ms. text of lecture. CDA, Lynch Transfer File, folder CC.

_____________. "What to Read & How to Read—Notes of Lecture." CDA, Patrick N. Lynch Transfer File, folder BB.

Lynch, Robert A. "A History of the Lynch Family." Unpublished notes, Waltham, Mass., 1891.

Madden, Richard. "Catholics of South Carolina." Unpublished. Manuscript #1.

_____________. "History of St. Joseph's Parish." Typescript. CDA, Parish Records, folder "St. Joseph's, Charleston."

Marschall, John Peter. "Francis Patrick Kenrick, 1852–1863: The Baltimore Years." Ph.D. dissertation, Catholic University of America, 1962.

Misch, Edward J. "The American Bishops and the Negro from the Civil War to the Third Plenary Council of Baltimore (1865–1884)." Ph.D. dissertation, Pontifical Gregorian University, 1968.

Moore, Jerrold Northrop. "Northrop Pedigree." Unpublished manuscript in Moore family possession.

Russell, Thomas David. "Sale Day in Antebellum South Carolina: Slavery, Law, Economy and Court-Supervised Sales." Ph.D. dissertation, Stanford University, 1993.

Ryan, Frank W., Jr. "The Southern Quarterly Review, 1842–1857: A Study in Thought and Opinion in the Old South." Ph.D. dissertation, University of North Carolina, 1956.

St. Patrick's Benevolent Society. Minutes, May 12, 1857–June 13, 1878. CDA.

Schmidt, Paul J. "Patrick N. Lynch, Bishop of Charleston, South Carolina, Commissioner of the Confederate States of America to the States of the Church (1864–1865)" Excerpta of Ph.D. dissertation, Pontifical Gregorian University, Rome, 1967.

Smith, John Gilmore. "The Passing of Bishop Northrop." *Sunday News* (Charleston, S.C.), August 8 and 15, 1920. (Clippings in scrapbook). Charleston Library Society.

South Carolina Comptroller General. Tax Returns, Lancaster District, 1861. Box 27, folder 4, South Carolina Department of Archives and History.

Swallow, G. C. "Grape Culture in Missouri." *AAAS Proceedings.* Twelfth Meeting, Baltimore, Md., 1858, 268–82.

Terry, George D. "A Study of the Impact of the French Revolution and the Insurrections in Saint-Domingue upon South Carolina, 1790–1805." Master's thesis, University of South Carolina, 1975.

Thigpen, Thomas Paul. "Aristocracy of the Heart: Catholic Lay Leadership in Savannah, 1820–1870." Ph.D. dissertation, Emory University, 1995.

"A Truthful Account of the Burning of the Ursuline Convent and Academy (May 1865)." Unsigned manuscript. CDA, 32M4.

United States Naval War Records Office, *Official Records of the Union and Confederate Navies in the War of Rebellion*, ser. II, vol. 3, Washington: United States Naval War Records Office, 2002.

Wight, Willard E. "Bishop Patrick N. Lynch, Confederate Propagandist." Unpublished paper given at the Forty-Fourth Annual Meeting of the American Catholic Historical Association, Washington, D.C., December, 1963. Heisser collection, CDA.

Wimmer, Judith Conrad. "American Catholic Interpretations of the Civil War." Ph.D. dissertation, Drew University, 1979.

Wolfe, Henry Francis. "The Life and Times of Patrick Neison Lynch (1817–1882)." Unpublished master's thesis, Mount St. Mary's Seminary, Emmitsburg, Md., 1929.

Books

Algernon Sydney Sullivan Foundation. *Algernon Sydney Sullivan.* Morristown, N.J.: Algernon Sydney Sullivan Foundation, 1956.

American Association for the Advancement of Sciences. *Proceedings of the American Association for the Advancement of Sciences*, repri., Ulan Press, 2012

Amoroso, Francesco. *San Vincenzo Pallotti.* Rome: Società dell'Apostolato Cattolico, 1962.

Artigas, Mariano, Thomas E. Glick, and Rafael A. Martínez. *Negotiating Darwin: The Vatican Confronts Evolution, 1877–1902.* Baltimore, Md.: Johns Hopkins University Press, 2006.

Bachman, C. L., John Bachman Haskell, and John James Audubon. *John Bachman, The Pastor of St. John's Lutheran Church, Charleston.* Charleston: Walker, Evans and Cogswell, 1888.

Bachman, John. *A Defence of Luther and the Reformation: Against the Charge of John Bellinger, M.D., and Others.* Charleston: William Paxton, 1853.

Bailey, Louise, Mary L. Morgan, and Carolyn R. Taylor, eds. *Biographical Directory of the South Carolina Senate, 1776–1985.* 3 vols. Columbia: University of South Carolina Press, 1986.

Baker, Gary R. *Cadets in Gray: The Story of the Cadets of the South Carolina Military Academy and the Cadet Rangers in the Civil War.* Columbia, S.C.: Palmetto Bookworks, 1989.

Bancroft, Frederic. *Slave Trading in the Old South,* repr., Columbia: University of South Carolina Press, 1996.

Barrett, John G. *The Civil War in North Carolina.* Chapel Hill: University of North Carolina Press, 1963.

____________. *Sherman's March through the Carolinas.* Chapel Hill: University of North Carolina Press, 1956.

Bassham, Ben L. *Conrad Wise Chapman, Artist and Soldier of the Confederacy.* Kent, Ohio: Kent State University Press, 1998.

Baudier, Roger. *The Catholic Church in Louisiana.* New Orleans: A. W. Hyatt Stationery Mfg. Company, 1939.

Bauer, Craig A. *A Leader among Peers: The Life and Times of Duncan Farrer Kenner.* Lafayette: Center for Louisiana Sudies, University of Southwestern Louisiana.

Belich, James. *The New Zealand Wars and the Victorian Interpretation of Racial Conflict.* Auckland: Auckland University Press, 1986.

Billington, Ray Allen. *The Protestant Crusade, 1800–1860: A Study of the Origin of American Nativism.* New York: Macmillan, 1938.

Biographical Directory of the South Carolina Senate. Columbia: University of South Carolina Press, 1986.

Blakiston, Noel, ed. *The Roman Question: Extracts from the Despatches of Odo Russell from Rome, 1858–1870.* London: Chapman and Hall, 1962.

Blanton, Wyndham B. *Medicine in Virginia in the Nineteenth Century.* Richmond: Garrett and Massie, 1933.

Blied, Benjamin J. *Austrian Aid to American Catholics, 1830–1860.* Milwaukee: Author, 1944.

____________. *Catholics and the Civil War.* Milwaukee: Author, 1945.

Bodell, Dorothy H. Montgomery *White Sulphur Springs: A History of the Resort, Hospital, Cemeteries, Markers, and Monuments.* Blacksburg, Va.: Pocahontas Press, 1993.

Brewer, James H. *The Confederate Negro: Virginia's Craftsmen and Military Laborers 1861-1865,* Tuscaloosa: University of Alabama Press, 1970.

Brokhage, Joseph D. *Francis Patrick Kenrick's Opinion on Slavery.* Washington, D.C.: Catholic University of America Press, 1955.

Bryan, John M. *Creating the South Carolina State House.* Columbia: University of South Carolina Press, 1999.

Burton, E. Milby *The Siege of Charleston, 1861–1865.* Columbia: University of South Carolina Press, 1970.

Camillis, Marie de. Il *Cardinale G. Mezzofanti, principe dei poliglotti.* Rome: Lucci Tip., 1937.

Caraman, Philip. *University of the Nations: The Story of the Gregorian University with Its Associated Institutes, the Biblical and Oriental, 1551–1962.* New York: Paulist Press, 1981.

Caravaglios, Maria Genoino. The American Catholic Church and the Negro Problem in the XVIII–XIX Centuries. Rome: Tipografia delle Mantellate, 1974.

Case, Lynn M., and Warren F. Spencer. *The United States and France: Civil War Diplomacy.* Philadelphia: University of Pennsylvania Press, 1970.

Catalogus Alumnorum Collegii Urbani qui ab anno MDCCCXIX ad MDCCCXXXVIII ad Fidem Propagandam veljam Pridierunt vel adhuc instiuntur. Rome: Ex Typographico Collegii Urbani, [1837]), Collegio Urbano, Archivio, vol. 17 (1836–1842), fol. 173 verso.

Chapman, John A. *History of Edgefield County From the Earliest Settlements to 1897.* Newberry, S.C.: A. H. Aull, 1897; repr., Spartanburg, S.C.: The Reprint Company, 1980.

Charleston City Directory. Charleston: Jno. Orrin Lea & Co. Publishers, 1869.

Charleston City Directories. Charleston: A.E. Sholes Charleston Directory, 1877–1886.

City of Charleston Year Book. The News and Courier Book Presses, No.19, Broad Street, Charleston, SC, 1882.

Clarke, John Mason. *James Hall of Albany, Geologist and Palaeontologist, 1811–1898.* Albany, N.Y., 1921.

Clarke, Richard Henry. *Lives of Deceased Bishops of the Catholic Church in the United States.* 3 vols. New York: R. H. Clarke, 1888.

Courtney, William Ashemead. *Scrapbook.* Charleston Library Society, Courtney Colleciton.

Cochin, Augustin. *L'Abolition de l'esclavage.* 2 vols. Paris: J. Lecoffre, 1861.

____________. *The Results of Slavery.* Boston: Walker, Wise, 1863.

A Compilation of the Messages and Papers of the Presidents, 1789–1897, with Additions, vol. 1. New York: Bureau of National Literature, 1900.

Connelly, James F. *The Visit of Archbishop Bedini to the United States of America (June 1853–February 1854).* Rome: Libreria Editrice dell'Università Gregoriana, 1960.

Coppa, Frank J. *Cardinal Giacomo Antonelli and Papal Politics in European Affairs.* Albany: State University of New York Press, 1990.

Cornelius, Janet Duitsman. "When I Can Read My Title Clear": *Literacy, Slavery, and Religion in the Antebellum South.* Columbia: University of South Carolina Press, 1991.

Cornevin, Robert. *Histoire du Dahomey.* Paris: Berger-Levrault, 1962.

Cossa, Pietro. *Necrologia di Filippo Cossa.* Rome: Tip. Salviucci, 1868.

Coulter, E. Merton, and George Walton Williams. *The Life of a Southern Merchant and Banker, 1820–1903.* Athens, Ga.: Hibriten Press, 1976.

Crafts, Daniel W. *Reluctant Confederates: Upper South Unionists in the Secession Crisis.* Chapel Hill: University of North Carolina Press, 1989.

Craven John J. *Prison Life of Jefferson Davis.* New York: Carleton Publisher, 1866.

Crook, David Paul. *The North, the South, and the Powers, 1861–1865.* New York: Wiley, 1974.

Cullop, Charles P. *Confederate Propaganda in Europe, 1861–1865.* Coral Gables, Fla.: University of Miami Press, 1969.

D'Agostino, Peter R. *Rome in America: Transnational Catholic Ideology from the Risorgimento to Fascism.* Chapel Hill: University of North Carolina Press, 2004.

Davidson, Chalmer Gaston. *The Last Foray: South Carolina Planters of 1860, A Sociological Study.* Columbia: University of South Carolina Press, 1987.

Davis. A. *Antiquities of Central America and the Discovery of New England by the Northmen, Five Hundred Years before Columbus.* 4th ed. New York: Samuel Colman, 1839.

Davis, Burke. *Sherman's March.* New York: Random House, 1980.

Davis, Cyprian. *The History of Black Catholics in the United States.* New York: Crossroad, 1990.

Dedmondt, Glenn. *The Flags of Civil War South Carolina.* Gretna, La.: Pelican Publishing Company, 2000.

De Leon, Edwin. *La Vérité sur les Etats Confédérés d'Amérique.* Paris: E. Dentu, 1862.

____________. *Thirty Years of My Life on Three Continents.* 2 vols. London: Ward and Downey, 1890.

Detzer, David. *Allegiance: Fort Sumter, Charleston, and the Beginning of the Civil War.* New York: Harcourt, 2001.

Dolan, Jay P. *The American Catholic Experience: A History from Colonial Times to the Present.* Garden City, N.Y.: Doubleday, 1985.

Easterby, J. Harold. *A History of the College of Charleston.* Charleston: Trustees of the College of Charleston, 1935.

Eaton, Clement. *Jefferson Davis*. New York: The Free Press, 1977.

Edgar, Walter B. *South Carolina: A History*. Columbia: University of South Carolina Press, 1998.

Ellis, John Tracy. *American Catholicism*. 2nd rev. ed. Chicago: University of Chicago Press, 1969.

____________, ed. *Documents of American Catholic History*. Milwaukee: Bruce Publishing Company, 1961.

Emilio, Luis Fenollosa. *A Brave Black Regiment: History of the Fifty-Fourth Regiment of Masssachusetts Volunteeer Infantry*. 1894; repr., New York: Arno Press, 1969.

England, John. *Letters of the Late Bishop England to the Hon. John Forsyth, on the Subject of Domestic Slavery*. Baltimore, Md.: John Murphy, 1844.

____________. *Oration, Delivered on the Anniversary of the Literary and Philosophical Society of South Carolina, on Wednesday, the 9th of May, 1832, in the Cathedral Church of St. Finbar, in the City of Charleston*. Baltimore, Md.: J. Myres, 1832.

____________. The Works of the Right Rev. John England, First Bishop of Charleston. 5 vols. Baltimore, Md.: John Murphy, 1849.

Evans, Eli N. *Judah P. Benjamin, the Jewish Confederate*. New York: Free Press, 1988.

Faherty, William Barnaby. *Exile in Erin: A Confederate Chaplain's Story: The Life of Father John Bannon*. St. Louis: Missouri Historical Society Press, 2002.

____________. *The Fourth Career of John B. Bannon*. Portland, Ore.: C and D Publishing, 1994.

Farmer, James Oscar, Jr. *The Metaphysical Confederacy: James Henley Thornwell and the Synthesis of Southern Values*. Macon, Ga.: Mercer University Press, 1986.

Feiertag, Sister Loretta Clare. *American Public Opinion on the Diplomatic Relations Between the United States and the Papal States (1847–1867)*. Washington, D.C.: Catholic University of America Press, 1933.

Fisher, James T. *Community of Immigrants: A History of Catholics in America*. New York: Oxford University Press, 2002.

Fogarty, Gerald P. American *Catholic Biblical Scholarship: A History from the Early Republic to Vatican II*. San Francisco: Harper and Row, 1989.

Fortin, Roger. *Faith and Action: A History of the Archdiocese of Cincinnati, 1821–1966*. Columbus: Ohio State University Press, 2002.

Franco, Massimo. *Parallel Empires: The Vatican and the United States—Two Centuries of Alliance and Conflict*. New York: Doubleday, 2008.

Frank, Josef. *Vincenzo Pallotti, Gründer des Werkes vom katholischen Apostolat*. 2 vols. Frankfurt am Main: Verlag für Kunst und Wissenschaft (O. Hamacher), 1865.

Fraser, Walter J., Jr. *Charleston! Charleston! The History of a Southern City*. Columbia: University of South Carolina Press, 1989.

Fredrickson, George M. *The Black Image in the White Mind: The Debate on Afro-American Character and Destiny, 1817–1914*. New York: Harper and Row, 1971.

Freehling, William W. *Prelude to Civil War: The Nullifcation Controversy in South Carolina, 1816–1836*. New York: Oxford University Press, 1965.

Freeze, R. Allan, and John A. Cherry. *Groundwater*. Englewood Cliffs, N.J.: Prentice Hall, 1979.

Freidel, Frank. *Francis Lieber, Nineteenth Century Liberal*. Baton Rouge: Louisiana State University Press, 1947.

Gaffard Paul. *Etude sur les rapports de l'Amérique et de l'ancien continent avant Christophe Colomb.* Paris: Ernest Thorin, 1869.

Gannon, Michael V. *Rebel Bishop: The Life and Era of Augustin Verot.* Milwaukee: Bruce Publishing Company, 1964.

Garhammer, Erich. *Seminaridee und Klerusbildung bei Karl August Graf von Reisach.* Stuttgart: Verlag W. Kohlhammer, 1990.

Gavronsky, Serge. *The French Liberal Opposition and the American Civil War.* New York Humanities Press, 1968.

Genovese, Eugene D. *A Consuming Fire: The Fall of the Confederacy in the Mind of the White Christian South.* Athens: University of Georgia Press, 1998.

Genovese, Eugene D. *Roll, Jordan, Roll: The World the Slaves Made.* New York: Pantheon Books, 1974.

Geological Survey of New Jersey, Annual Report of the State Geologist for the Year 1880. Trenton: John L. Murphy, Book and Job Printer, 1880.

Gerteis, Louis S. *From Contraband to Freedman: Federal Policy toward Southern Blacks, 1861–1865.* Westport, Conn.: Greenwood Press, 1973.

Gervasoni, Giovanni. *Angelo Mai.* Bergamo: Edizioni Orobiche, 1954.

Gleeson, David T. *The Irish in the South, 1815–1877.* Chapel Hill: University of North Carolina Press, 2000.

Götten, Josef. *Christoph Moufang, Theologe und Politiker, 1817–1890.* Mainz: Hase and Koehler Verlag, 1969.

Gray, Lewis Cecil. *History of Agriculture in the Southern United States to 1860.* 2 vols. Repr., New York: Peter Smith, 1941.

Gregg, Rt. Rev. Alexander. *History of the Old Cheraws.* Baltimore, Md.: Genealogical Publishing Company, 1967.

Guilday, Peter. *A History of the Councils of Baltimore, 1791–1884.* Repr., New York: Arno Press and the New York Times, 1969.

____________. *The Life and Times of John England, First Bishop of Charleston (1786–1842).* Vol. 2. New York: The America Press, 1927.

____________. *National Pastorals of the American Hierarchy (1792–1916).* Westminster: The Newman Press, 1954.

Gutman, Herbert G. *The Black Family in Slavery and Freedom, 1750–1925.* New York: Pantheon, 1976.

Hennesey, James. *American Catholics: A History of the Roman Catholic Community in the United States.* New York: Oxford University Press, 1981.

Hennessey, James, S.J. *The First Council of the Vatican: The American Experience.* New York: Herder and Herder, 1963.

Herbermann, Charles, ed. "Provincial Councils of Baltimore." *Catholic Encyclopedia.* New York: Robert Appleton Company, 1913.

Hillis, David Wallace. *University of South Carolina.* 2 vols. Columbia: University of South Carolina Press, 1951–1956.

Histoire universelle des missions catholiques. 4 vols. Paris: Librairie Grund, 1956–1959.

Historic and Architectural Inventory, Cheraw Historical District. Catawba, S.C.: Gettys Associates, 1960.

Hocédez, Edgar. *Histoire de la théologie au XIXe siècle.* Vol. 2. Brussels: Edition Universelle, 1947–1952.

Holifield, E. Brooks. *The Gentlemen Theologians: American Theology in Southern Culture, 1795–1860.* Durham, N.C.: Duke University Press, 1978.

Hubbard, Charles M. *The Burden of Confederate Diplomacy.* Knoxville: University of Tennessee Press, 1998.

Hudson, Eduard Maco. *Der Zweite Unabhängigskeits-Krieg in Amerika,* 2nd rev. ed. Berlin: Verlag von A. Charisius, 1862.

__________. *The Second War of Independence in America.* Translated by the author. London: Longman, Green, Longman, Roberts and Green, 1863.

Hudson, Larry E., Jr. *To Have and to Hold: Slave Work and Family Life in Antebellum South Carolina.* Athens: University of Georgia Press, 1997.

Hyman, Harold, ed. *Heard Round the World: The Impact Abroad of the Civil War.* New York: Knopf, 1969.

Iserloh, Erwin. *Wilhelm Emmanuel von Ketteler—sein Kampf für Freiheit und soziale Gerechtigkeit. Akademie der Wissenschaften und der Literatur. Abhandlungen der Geistes- und Sozialwissenschaftlichen Klasse,* Jahrgang 1987, no. 8.

Jenkins, Wilbert L. *Seizing the New Day: African Americans in Post–Civil War Charleston.* Bloomington and Indianapolis: Indiana University Press, 1998.

Kehoe, Lawrence, ed. *Complete Works of the Most Rev. John Hughes, D.D., Archbishop of New York.* 2 vols. New York: Lawrence Kehoe, 1865.

Kelly, Douglas F. *Preachers with Power: Four Stalwarts of the South.* Edinburgh: The Banner of Truth Trust, 1992.

Kennett, Lee. *Sherman, A Soldier's Life.* New York: HarperCollins, 2001.

Kenrick, Francis Patrick. *Diary and Visitation Record of the Rt. Rev. Francis Patrick Kenrick, Administrator and Bishop of Philadelphia, 1830–1851: Later Archbishop of Baltimore.* Lancaster, Pa.: Wickersham Printing Company, 1916.

__________. *The Kenrick-Frenaye Corresondence.* Translated and edited by Frederick Edward Tourscher. Philadelphia: Wickersham Printing Company, 1920.

Kohlstedt, Sally Gregory. *The Formation of the American Scientific Community: The American Association for the Advancement of Science, 1848–60.* Urbana: University of Illinois Press, 1976.

Kolchin, Peter. *American Slavery, 1619–1877.* New York: Hill and Wang, 1992.

Kowalsky, Nicola Kowalsky. *Pontificio Collegio Urbano de Propaganda Fide.* Rome: The College, 1956.

Lecanuet, Edouard. *Montalembert.* 3 vols. Paris: C. Poussielgue, 1899–1902.

Lemarié, Charles. *A Biography of Msgr. Benedict Joseph Flaget, b. 1763–d. 1850, First Bishop of the Diocese of Bardstown-Louisville, Kentucky, 1811–1850.* Translated by Mary Wedding, in collaboration with Rachel Willett. 3 vols. Bardstown: Flaget-Lemarié Group in conjunction with St. Joseph Proto-Cathedral Archives, 1992.

Lesser, Charles H. *Relic of the Lost Cause: The Story of South Carolina's Ordinance of Secession.* Columbia: South Carolina Department of Archives and History, 1990.

Livingstone, Peadar. *The Monaghan Story: A Documented History of the County Monaghan from the Earliest Times to 1976. Enniskillen, Ireland:* Clogher Historical Society, 1980.

Lucas, Marian Brunson. *Sherman and the Burning of Columbia.* College Station: Texas A & M University Press, 1976.

Lynch, Patrick N. *L'Esclavage dans les Etats Confédérés, par un missionnaire.* Paris: E. Dentu, 1865.

_____________. *Lettera di un missionario sulla schiavitù domestica degli Stati Confederati di America.* Rome: Tipografia di Giovanni Cesaretti, 1864.

_____________. *The Liquefaction of the Blood of St. Januarius, at Naples: An Historical and Critical Examination of the Miracle.* New York: Catholic Publication Society, 1872.

_____________. *Die Sclaverei in den Südstaaten Nord-Amerika's, dargestellt von einem katholischen Missionär.* Frankfurt a Main: Verlag für Kunst und Wissenschaft (O. Hamacher), 1865.

Madden, Richard. *Catholics in South Carolina.* Lanham, Md.: University Press of America, 1968.

Martin, August-Marie. *Lettre pastorale de Mgr l'Evêque de Natchitoches à l'occasion de la guerre du Sud pour son indépendance.* Natchitoches, La., 1861.

Maxwell, John Francis. *Slavery and the Catholic Church: The History of Catholic Teaching Concerning the Moral Legitimacy of the Institution of Slavery.* Chichester and London: Barry Rose, 1975.

May, Robert, ed. *The Union, the Confederacy, and the Atlantic Rim.* West Lafayette, Ind.: Purdue University Press, 1955.

Mayer, Martin. *The Diplomats.* New York: Doubleday, 1983.

McFeely, William S. *Yankee Stepfather: General O. O. Howard and the Freedmen.* New Haven and London: Yale University Press, 1968..

McGreevy, John T. *Catholicism and American Freedom: A History.* New York: Norton, 2003.

McKinney, Tim. *The Civil War in Greenbrier County, West Virginia.* Charleston, W.Va.: Quarrier Press, 2004.

McNamara, Robert F. *The American College in Rome, 1855–1955.* Rochester, N.Y.: Christopher Press, 1956.

McSuidhne, Peadar. *Paul Cullen and His Contemporaries, with Their Letters from 1820–1902.* Vol 1. Naas, County Kildare: Leinster Leader, 1961.

Meade, George. *Life and Letters of George Gordon Meade, Major-General United States Army.* 2 vols. New York: Charles Scribner's Sons, 1913.

Meline, Mary M., and Edward F. X. McSweeny. *The Story of the Mountain: Mount St. Mary's College and Seminary, Emmitsburg, Maryland.* 2 vols. Emmitsburg, Md.: Weekly Chronicle, 1911.

Merrill, James M. *William Tecumseh Sherman.* Chicago: Rand McNally, 1971.

Miers, Earl Schenck. *William Tecumseh Sherman and His March to Fame and Infamy.* New York: Knopf, 1951.

Miller, Randall M.. and Jon L. Wakelyn, eds. *Catholics in the Old South: Essays on Church and Culture.* Macon, Ga.: Mercer University Press, 1983.

Mitchell, Arthur. *The History of the Hibernian Society of Charleston, South Carolina, 1799–1981.* Charleston: Hibernian Society, 1981.

Moffett, Mary Conner, ed. *Letters of General James Conner, C.S.A.* Columbia, S.C.: R. L. Bryan, 1950.

Mohr, Clarence L. *On the Threshold of Freedom: Masters and Slaves in Civil War Georgia.* Athens: University of Georgia Press, 1986.

Moore, Jerrold Northrop. *Confederate Commissary General: Lucius Bellinger Northrop and the Subsistence Bureau of the Southern Army.* Shippensburg, Pa.: White Maine Publishing Company, 1996.

Moore, John Hammond. *Columbia and Richland County: A South Carolina Community, 1740–1990*. Columbia: University of South Carolina Press, 1993.

Moore, John Preston, ed. *"My Ever Dearest Friend": The Letters of A. Dudley Mann to Jefferson Davis 1869–1889*. Tuscaloosa, Ala.: Confederate Publishing Company, 1960.

Morrill, Dan L. *The Civil War in the Carolinas.* Charleston: Nautical and Aviation Pubishing Company, 2002.

Myers, Robert Manson, ed. *The Children of Pride: A True Story of Georgia in the Civil War* New Haven: Yale University Press, 1972.

New Catholic Dictionary. New York: Universal Knowledge Foundation, 1929.

Newman, John Henry. *The Letters and Diaries of John Henry Newman.* Edited by Charles Stephen Dessain et al. 32 vols. London: Thomas Nelson and Sons, 1961– .

Nichols, George Ward. *The Story of the Great March from the Diary of a Staff Officer.* New York: Harper and Brothers, 1865.

Northrop, Claudian B. *Political Remarks by "N," Numbers IX, X, XI.* Charleston: Steampower Presses of Evans and Cogswell, 1861.

____________. *Southern Odes, by the Outcast.* Charleston: Harper and Calvo, 1861.

Norton, Herman. *Rebel Religion: The Story of Confederate Chaplains.* St. Louis: Bethany Press, 1961.

Nepveux, Ethel Trenholm Seabrook. *George Alfred Trenholm and the Company that Went to War, 1861–1865.* Anderson, S.C.: Electric City Printing Company, 1994.

O'Brien, Joseph L. *John England—Bishop of Charleston: The Apostle of Democracy.* New York: Edward O'Toole, 1914.

O'Brien, Michael, and David Moltke-Hansen, eds. *Intellectual Life in Antebellum Charleston.* Knoxville: University of Tennessee Press, 1986.

Ochiai, Akiko. *Harvesting Freedom: African American Agrarianism in Civil War Era South Carolina.* Westport, Conn.: Praeger, 2004.

Ochs, Stephen J. *A Black Patriot and a White Priest: André Cailloux and Claude Paschal Maistre in Civil War New Orleans.* Baton Rouge: Louisiana Sate University Press, 2000.

____________. *Desegregating the Altar: the Josephites and the Struggle for Black Priests, 1871–1960.* Baton Rouge and London: Louisiana State University Press, 1990.

O'Connell Jeremiah J. *Catholicity in the Carolinas and Georgia: Leaves of Its History.* New York: D. and J. Sadler, 1879.

Oetgen, Jerome. *An American Abbot: Boniface Wimmer, O.S.B., 1809–1887.* Rev. ed. Washington, D.C.: Catholic University of America Press, 1997.

Olmsted, Frederick Law. *A Journey in the Seaboard Slave States, with Remarks on Their Economy.* New York: Dix and Edwards, 1856.

Ordinances of the City of Charleston, 1783–1844. Charleston: Walker and Burke, 1844.

Osthaus, Carl R. *Partisans of the Southern Press: Editorial Spokesmen of the Nineteenth Century.* Lexington: University Press of Kentucky, 1994.

Overdyke, W. Darrell, *The Know-Nothing Party in the South.* Baton Rouge: Louisiana State University Press, 1950.

Owsley, Frank Lawrence. *King Cotton Diplomacy: Foreign Relations of the Confederate States of America.* 2nd rev. ed. Chicago: University of Chicago Press 1959.

Palma, Giovanni Battista. *Praelectiones historiae ecclesiasticae quas in Collegio Urbano Sacrae Congregationis de Propaganda Fide et in Pontificio Seminario Romano habuit Joannes Palma.* Vol. 1, pt. 1. Rome: In Collegio Urbano de Propaganda Fide, 1838–1846.

Palmer, Benjamin Morgan. *The Life and Letters of James Henley Thornwell.* Richmond: Whittet and Shepperson, 1875; repr., New York: Arno Press and the New York Times, 1969.

Panzer, Joel S. *The Popes and Slavery.* Parliamentary Debates, Lords, 3rd series, vol. 175 (1864).

Perrone, Giovanni. *Praelectiones theologicae quas in Collegio Romano S.J. habebat Joannes Perrone.* . . . 2nd rev. ed. Rome: Typis Collegii Urbani, 1843.

Pettus, Louise, and Martha Bishop. *Lancaster County: A Pictorial History.* Norfolk and Virginia Beach: The Donning Company, 1984.

Phelps, W. Chris. *The Bombardment of Charleston, 1863–1865.* Gretna, La.: Pelican Publishing Company, 2002.

———. *Charlestonians in War.* Gretna, La.: Pelican Publishing Company, 2004.

Poole, Stafford, and Douglas J. Slawson. *Church and State in Perry County, Missouri, 1818–1865.* Lewiston, N.Y., and Queenstown, Ont.: Edward Mellen Press, 1986.

Poston, Jonathan. *Buildings of Charleston.* Historic Charleston Foundation. Columbia: University of South Carolina Press, 1997.

Power, William F. *Tar Heel Catholics.* Lanham, Md.: University Press of America, 2003.

Powers, Bernard E., Jr., *Black Charlestonians: A Social History, 1822–1885.* Fayetteville: University of Arkansas Press, 1994.

Pynchon, Edgcumb. *Dan Sickles, Hero of Gettysburg and "Yankee King of Spain."* Garden City, N.Y.: Doubleday, Doran, 1945.

Raboteau, Albert J. *Slave Religion: The "Invisible Institution" in the Antebellum South.* New York: Oxford University Press, 1978.

Ravenel, Beatrice St. Julien. *Architects of Charleston.* 2nd rev. ed. Charleston: Carolina Art Association, 1964.

Rice, Madeleine Hooke. *American Catholic Opinion in the Slavery Controversy.* New York: Columbia University Press, 1944.

Richardson, Catherine. *Historic Cheraw.* N.p.: Cheraw Historic Comission, 2010.

Richardson, James D. *A Compilation of the Messages and Papers of the Confederacy.* 2 vols. Nashville, Tenn.: United States Publishing Company, 1906.

Roemer, Theodore. The *Ludwig-Missionsverein and the Church in the United States (1838–1918).* Washington, D.C.: Catholic University of America, 1933.

———. *Ten Decades of Alms.* St. Louis and London: B. Herder, 1942.

Rogers, George. *Charleston in the Age of the Pinckneys.* Columbia: University of South Carolina Press, 1980.

Rose, Willie Lee. *Rehearsal for Reconstruction: The Port Royal Experiment.* Indianapolis: Bobbs-Merrill, 1964.

Rosen, Robert N. *Confederate Charleston: An Illustrated History of the City and the People during the Civil War.* Columbia: University of South Carolina Press, 1994.

———. *The Jewish Confederates.* Columbia: University of South Carolina Press, 2000.

Russell, C. W. *The Life of Cardinal Mezzofanti.* London: Longman, Brown, 1858.

Sadlier's Catholic Almanac and Guide, 1864. New York: D&J Sadler & Co., 1864.

Sanders, Albert E., and William D. Anderson Jr. *Natural History Investigations in South Carolina from Colonial Times to the Present.* Columbia: University of South Carolina Press, 1999.

Schwalbaum, W. Jesse. *Understanding Groundwater*. Commack, N.Y.: Nova Science Publishing, 1997.

Seton, Robert. *Memories of Many Years (1839–1922)*. London: John Long, 1923.

Shecut, John L. E. W. *Medical and Philosophical Essays*. Charleston: A. E. Miller, 1819.

Sheeran, James B. *Confederate Chaplain: A War Journal of Rev. James B. Sheeran, C.SS.R., 14th Louisiana, C.S.A.* Edited by Joseph T. Durkin. Milwaukee: Bruce Publishing Company, 1960.

Sherman, William Tecumseh. *Memoirs of General W. T. Sherman by Himself.* 2 vols. New York: D. Appleton, 1875.

Sholes's Charleston City Directory, 1882, Compiled by Albert Elliot Sholes, Printed by Evans & Cogswell Press.

Sims, Marion. *The Story of My Life.* New York: D. Appleton, 1884.

Simms, William Gilmore. *The Letters of William Gilmore Simms.* Collected and edited by Mary C. Simms Oliphant, Alfred Taylor Odell, and T. C. Duncan Evans. 6 vols. Columbia: University of South Carolina Press, 1952–1982.

Sitterson, Joseph Carlyle. *The Secession Movement in North Carolina.* Chapel Hill: University of North Carolina Press, 1939.

Solemnis praemorum distributo apud Collegium Urbanum De Propaganda Fide, Pridie Kal Dec. An. MDCCXXXVII. Rome: Ex Typographia Collegii Urbani.

Solemnis praemium distributio apud Collegium Urbanum de Propaganda Fide, pridei kal. D.C. A. A. P. V. MDCCCXXXVII. Rome: Ex Typographia Collegii Urbani, 1837.

Solemnis praemiorum distributio apud Collegium Urbanum de Propaganda Fide VII. Idus Sept. An. A. P. V. MDCCCXXXIX. Rome: Ex Typographia Collegii Urbani, 1839.

South Carolina Inter-State and West Indian Exposition. *Charleston To-day and Yesterday* Charleston: T. J. Neville, 1901.

South Carolina Mineralogical, Geological and Agricultural Survey. *Report on the Survey of South Carolina,* 1st–4th. by Oscar M. Lieber. Columbia, S.C.: R. W. Gibbes, State Printer, 1853–60.

Spalding, Thomas W. *Martin John Spalding, American Churchman.* Washington, D.C.: Catholic University of America Press, 1973.

Stephens, Lester D. *Science, Race and Religion in the American South: John Bachman and the Charleston Circle of Naturalists, 1815–1895.* Chapel Hill: University of North Carolina Press, 2000.

Stillman, W. J. *The Autobiography of a Journalist.* 2 vols. London: Grant Richards, 1901.

Stock, Leo Francis. *Consular Relations between the United States and the Papal States: Instructions and Despatches.* Washington, D.C.: American Catholic Historical Association, 1945.

____________. *United States Ministers to the Papal States: Instructions and Despatches, 1848–1868.* Washington, D.C.: Catholic University of America Press, 1933.

Surface and Subsurface Stratigraphy, Structure, and Aquifers of the South Carolina Coastal Plain. Columbia: University of South Carolina, Department of Geology, 1983.

Swanberg, W. A. *Sickles the Incredible.* New York: Charles Scribner's Sons, 1956.

Tadman, Michael. *Speculators and Slaves: Masters, Traders and Slaves in the Old South.* Madison: University of Wisconsin Press, 1989.

Taylor, David, ed. *South Carolina Naturalists: An Anthology, 1700–1860.* Columbia: University of South Carolina Press, 1998.

Thomas, James Alexander. *A History of Marlboro County, with Traditions and Sketches of Numerous Families.* Atlanta: Foote and Davies, 1897.

Thornwell, James Henley. *Arguments of Romanists from the Infallibility of the Church and the Testimony of the Fathers in Behalf of the Apocrypha, Discussed and Refuted.* New York: Leavitt, Trow, 1845.

____________. *The Collected Writings of James Henley Thornwell.* Vol. 3. Richmond, Va.: Presbyterian Committee of Publication, 1871–1873; repr., Edinburgh: The Banner of Truth Trust, 1974.

____________. *Sacramental Sorcery: The Invalidity of Roman Catholic Baptism.* 1845; repr., Unicoi, Tenn.: Trinity Foundation, 2006.

Tise, Larry E. *Proslavery: A History of the Defense of Slavery in America, 1701–1840.* Athens: University of Georgia Press, 1987.

Trindel, Elizabeth Stieger. *Mary Surratt, An American Tragedy.* Gretna, La.: Pelican Publishing Company, 1996.

Tucker, Philip Thomas. *The Confederacy's Fighting Chaplain: Father John B. Bannon.* Tuscaloosa: University of Alabama Press, 1992.

Tuomey, Michael. *The Papers of Michael Tuomey.* Edited by Lewis S. Dean. Spartanburg: The Reprint Company, 2001.

____________. *Report on Artesian Wells.* Charleston: Miller and Browne, City Job Printers, 1847.

Toursher, F. E., ed. *The Kenrick-Frenaye Correspondence, 1830–1862.* Philadelphia: Wickersham Printing Company, 1920.

Udienze del Emo. *Prefetto, August 24, 1865,* vol. 151 (1865).

Underwood, James Lowell. and W. Lewis Burke, eds. *The Dawn of Religious Freedom in South Carolina.* Columbia: University of South Carolina Press, 2006.

Van Deusen, Glendon G. *Thurlow Weed, Wizard of the Lobby.* Boston: Little, Brown, 1947.

Vandiver, Frank E., ed. *Confederate Blockade Running through Bermuda, 1861–1865: Letters and Cargo Manifests.* Austin: University of Texas Press, 1947.

Verot, Augustin. *A Tract for the Times: Slavery and Abolitionism.* Baltimore, Md.: John Murphy, 1861.

Wade, Richard C. *Slavery in the Cities.* New York: Oxford University Press, 1964.

Ward, Wilfrid. *The Life of John Henry Cardinal Newman.* 2 vols. New York: Longmans, Green, 1912.

Waring, Joseph Ioor. *A History of Medicine in South Carolina.* Vol. 2. Charleston: South Carolina Medical Association, 1964–1971).

Weber, Eugene. *Vincent Pallotti, An Apostle and Mystic.* Staten Island, N.Y.: Alba House, 1964.

Weiner, Marli F. *Mistresses and Slaves: Plantation Women in South Carolina, 1830–80.* Urbana and Chicago: University of Illinois Press, 1998.

Westwood, Howard C. *Black Troops, White Commanders, and Freedmen during the Civil War.* Carbondale: Southern Illinois University Press, 1992.

Wikramanayake, Marina. *A World in Shadow: The Free Black in Antebellum South Carolina.* Columbia: University of South Carolina Press, 1973.

Wiley, Bell Irvin. *Southern Negroes, 1861–1865.* Baton Rouge: Louisiana State University Press, 1974, (1938).

Williams, Donald M. *Shamrocks and Pluff Mud: A Glimpse of the Irish in the Southern City of Charleston, South Carolina.* Charleston: published by the author, 2005.

Williams, James. *Die Rechtfertigung der Südstaaten Nordamerika's.* Berlin: Verlag von A. Charisius, 1863.

___________. *The South Vindicated: Being a Series of Letter Writeen by the American Press During the Canvas for the Presidency in 1860.* London: Longman, Green, Longman, Roberts and Green, 1862.

Williamson, Joel. *After Slavery: The Negro in South Carolina during Reconstruction, 1861–1877.* Chapel Hill: University of North Carolina Press, 1965.

Wittgenstein, Princess *Almanach de Gotha, 1863. Almanac Which Tracked Royal and Titled Familes of Germanic States From 1763 to Present.* N.p.: Justus Perthes Publishing, 1863.

Wise, Stephen R. *Gate of Hell.: Campaign for Charleston Harbor, 1863.* Columbia: University of South Carolina Press, 1994.

Woodward, C. Vann, ed. *Mary Chesnut's Civil War.* New Haven: Yale University Press, 1981.

Young, Robert W. *Senator James Murray Mason, Defender of the Old South.* Knoxville: University of Tennessee Press, 1998.

Zanca, Kenneth J., comp. and ed. *Catholics and Slavery: 1789–1866: An Anthology of Primary Documents.* Lanham, Md.: University Press of America, 1994.

INDEX

ABOUT THE AUTHORS

DAVID C. R. HEISSER (1942–2010) was an associate professor and reference/documents librarian of the Daniel Library at the Citadel in Charleston, South Carolina.

STEPHEN JENNINGS WHITE, SR., is executive director of the Karpeles Manuscript Museum and the founder and director of the Charleston Historical Society.